Masculine and Feminine

Sex Roles Over The Life Cycle

Marie Richmond-Abbott
Eastern Michigan University

Random House New York

For Hank, Charlie, and Kim

Library of Congress Cataloging in Publication Data

Richmond-Abbott, Marie.
   Masculine and feminine.

   1. Sex role.   2. Life cycle, Human.   I. Title.
HQ1075.R53 1983   305.3   82-11400
ISBN 0-394-34848-6

First Edition
98765

Preface

When I wrote this book, I wanted to do three things that I believed were not being done in present sex-role textbooks. The first was to attempt an equal balance between discussions of the masculine- and the feminine-stereotyped roles in this society. The second was to present a life-cycle perspective of sex roles and to show how sex-role socialization continues while sex-role prescriptions change in the adult years. The third objective was to include material on certain groups whose sex roles seem to deviate somewhat from the American cultural norm. I believed that these groups, such as single-parent families, remarried families, and black families, could tell us a great deal about changing roles and the possibilities and probabilities for different kinds of behavior in the future.

I found it difficult to meet my first objective and strike a balance between discussions on men's and on women's roles in the culture. Although history and social science are written for the most part by and about men, the recent literature dealing with socialization into sex roles has concentrated largely on women. The original literature dealing with men's roles is largely anecdotal, and while research is now emerging, it does not match either in quantity or in quality the material gathered on women's roles. I found that I had to search in many areas for information about men. Research on sports and health yielded some data, and research on occupations and even on organizational development yielded other information. The relatively recent literature on the mid-life crisis and aging was another useful source of data. The difficulty in using this information was that it was localized and sparse; it did not cover all areas, and the studies were not comparable to those done on women. In addition, it was difficult to discuss the male role in some areas because it is the dominant or normative role. When I discussed change, I wanted to discuss possible variations from the dominant norm rather than to restate what most people knew about the cultural stereotype.

The pursuit of the second objective was less difficult. There is a growing fund of information about adult socialization into sex roles and the changes in personality traits and sex-role behavior in the older years.

I am indebted to the work of Neugarten, Guttman, Levinson, and others who deal with middle age and aging. In addition, the family literature, particularly the literature on marital power and marital satisfaction, provides needed information about adult roles.

Including information about various groups that might be the vanguard of changing sex roles was more difficult than I had imagined. Here it was a matter of sorting through mountains of data on a subject like the black family to find what was relevant and up to date. There was always the temptation to wait for the latest article that was to be published or the next book that was coming out to add more complete and specific information. Finally, however, deadlines had to be met, and I can only say that there will be a wealth of forthcoming new material to add to the information in this text.

Writing a book that attempts to present a balanced account of roles for males and females in our culture has other problems. As a woman it is tempting to emphasize the problems of stereotypical women's roles over those of men's and to push for change that will aid women and perhaps not necessarily help men. I have tried to be evenhanded, but I am well aware that I have not succeeded. My apology is only half-hearted, however, because while men have had responsibilities and restrictions, they have also, historically, had power.

The other problem in writing a book that is not avowedly feminist in its orientation is the risk that in trying to be evenhanded, I may have actually done an injustice to the data on women. Jessie Bernard has pointed out succinctly that the research on sex differences has been done on the variables that are valued in our society, that interest men, and that, not coincidently, are possessed by men.[1] Because the research on sex differences has these characteristics, to discuss this research and emphasize the differences may ignore important characteristics or variables that belong to women.

There has also been a feminist backlash against discussing sex differences, because some of these differences have been used in an attempt to show that the lower status of women is inherently justified. Some feminists have attempted to deny that sex differences exist or they have said that, at least, these differences do not in any way determine social roles. For many feminists, it is not a question of whether a particular feminine role *is* different; it is a question of whether that role *has to be* different from a similar masculine role. Thus, feminists are not particularly concerned that women *are* the childraisers (because that role could be changed), but they object strongly when they are told that they *must be* the childraisers for biologically determined reasons. It is my position in this text that physical predispositions toward certain kinds of behavior may exist, but that *they do not in any way* predetermine social roles. Human behavior is infinitely malleable, as has been shown by comparing different cultures or by comparing different periods in the same culture.

Another difficulty in discussing sex roles and sex-role socialization is that the emphasis on socialization may detract from a perspective that shows us that societies initiate and perpetuate the kind of socialization that they want. While sex-role socialization is important, it is only a reflection of the larger society. What would it serve women, for example, to be socialized to be achievement-oriented and competitive if they are kept out of sports, academia, and rewarding occupations? Would it help men a great deal to learn to express their emotions and to be nurturant if the corporate world continues to punish that kind of behavior? I want to emphasize that societal values and institutions give us the kind of sex-role socialization that we have, and the institutions of the society must change if we are truly to socialize our children in a different fashion. The various kinds of changes must come simultaneously to be effective.

Finally, I need to say a word about the terminology used throughout the book. There has been concern among many researchers about the use of the word *gender* or the term *sex,* as in *gender roles* or *sex roles.* Some scholars have preferred the use of the word *gender* so that sex-role behavior is not confused with sexuality. However, contemporary usage usually defines *gender* as referring to biological sex, and *sex role* as including the culturally prescribed traits and behaviors that are usually attributed to that gender. Barrie Thorne and Helena Lopata have also stressed that gender role, or sex role, is different from other roles in that it has no institutional location (the way the role of "plumber" is located in the economy) and that it is an ascribed, underlying status that influences all other roles.[2] They believe (and I strongly concur) that many of the differences between the sexes are better explained by differences in power and status rather than by gender itself. Thus, when I use the term *gender role* or *sex ??,* I am implying a status ranking, with the feminine sex role being ??ked lower than the masculine sex role.

Thorne and Lopata have also decried the term *sex role* as unnecessary vague because it can refer to personality traits, attitudes, behavior, ??ral values. While I agree in principle, it is hard to find a practical ??ve. I have compromised by using the term *sex role* and attempting ?? in most places the element to which it refers. I do distinguish ??x-role behavior and sex role, however. I have tried to use the *?? behavior* as the behavior that is traditionally linked to gender ?? and to use *sex role* to refer to a combination or sum of sex-??nd social role. Thus, the *feminine sex role* would include a ??ch as "mother" or "wife," as well as behaviors like in-??occupations.

??hare with the reader my definition of *androgyny.* An-??ed as a "condition under which the characteristics ??an impulses expressed by men and women are ??this sense it is based on values and norms held ??'a full range of experience open to individuals, who may, as women, be aggressive; as men, be tender; it suggests a spectrum upon which human beings choose their places without regard to propriety or custom."[4] The individual is freed from sex-role limitations and can call upon "masculine" or "feminine" behaviors across a variety of situations. A number of studies have shown that individuals who are rigidly sex typed show numerous deficiencies. Sex-typed women, in particular, are portrayed as having less self-confidence and self-esteem than non-sex-typed women, as well as having a narrower range of behavioral responses to situations. While the male role is more valued in our society than the female role and does not seem to have the same limitations, it also has a limited repetoire of behavior and may result in health problems induced by stress. Thus, androgyny, with its larger set of possibilities for response to situations, seems to lead to greater social competence as well as better mental and physical health for both sexes.[5]

One of the major tasks of this book is to try to document the assertions of the preceding paragraph: that traditional sex roles are limiting to human potential and that androgyny or some other form of moving beyond those rigid sex roles is a healthier and more productive state for the individual and for the culture. To that end I have tried to trace the process and reasons why we are socialized into traditional roles so that we can see the sources of our own oppression. We must keep in mind, also, that the kind of socialization we have is the result of the types of institutions that dominate the society.

Chapter 1 discusses the historical and cross-cultural roots of the different status accorded each gender. I have attempted to show that traditional roles are deeply embedded in our cultural history and reinforced by societal institutions. Chapter 2 examines the controversial question about physical differences between the genders, with an emphasis on the paucity of differences and the extent of similarity in the physical makeup and behavioral traits of the sexes. Chapters 3 and 4 trace the mechanism by which children are socialized into these traditional roles: parental expectations, toys and play, books, television, and school. Chapters 5 and 6 describe the adolescent years, with their emphasis on establishing a mature individual identity and the convenient, but terribly limiting definition of such an identity that traditional roles give the adolescent. I have tried to point out in these chapters the extreme difficulty young people have in deviating from traditional roles; it is difficult enough to establish an identity approved of by parents, peers, and the culture, much less to risk charting the unknown territory of self-knowledge and different behavior.

Chapter 7 continues the emphasis on the cultural definition of traditional roles with a discussion of the "ideal family," of the American dream. This ideal family was and continues to be a myth, but its supposed existence and desirability pushes many people to conform to family stereotypes, such as provider and childraiser. Chapter 8 discusses variations on the white, middle-class "ideal-family" norm. As we look at childless couples, dual-career families, single-parent families, black families, and other variations of the American family, we see that families that differ from the "ideal" may actually produce more androgynous behavior. Marginal people in any society have usually been the sources of change, as they are not blinded by slavish loyalty to a cultural tradition. Perhaps these families that do not, and perhaps *can* not, reflect the cultural norm of the "ideal family" are the vanguard of a movement toward more androgynous sex roles. Chapters 9 and 10 discuss how the economic and political institutions of our country have reinforced traditional sex roles, the rise of the women's movement, and the possibilities for change within the present institutional structure. Finally, chapter 11 examines the limits of traditional sex roles and the possibilities and probabilities for moving beyond them in the future.

As I wrote this manuscript, I became more and more aware of the interconnection between individual socialization and behavior, the constraints of societal institutions, and the pervasive power of cultural values. I am convinced that initiating change in one area without initiating changes in all three is of little use. At the same time, I am even more convinced of the need to initiate such change, to move beyond stereotyped sex roles as we have known them. If we can free ourselves from the behavior and social roles assigned to each of us because of our biological sex, we have greatly increased the possibility that each person can realize his or her individual human potential.

Acknowledgments

I gratefully acknowledge the help of all those who have aided me in preparing this manuscript. I am particularly indebted to my editorial review board: to Robert Stein of the Sociology Department of the University of Northern Colorado, Barrie Thorne of the Sociology Department at the Michigan State University, and Beth Van Fossen of the Sociology Department at the State University of New York at Brockport, who patiently read drafts of the manuscript, made comprehensive and constructive suggestions for improvement, and shared many resources with me. I also wish to thank Linda Green of Normandale Community College in Bloomington, Minnesota, Katherine Jensen of the Department of Sociology at the University of Wyoming, Jane Prather of the School of Social and Behavioral Research at California State University at Northridge, and William Simon of the Department of Sociology at the University of Houston for reading parts of the manuscript and making additional helpful suggestions for improvement. I also especially thank Anne Fausto-Sterling of the Department of Biology and Medicine at Brown University for sharing with me important information about physiology that she had gathered for her forthcoming manuscript and Neal Cazenave of Brown University for sharing with me his research about black men and black families. I am also indebted to my editor, Ron Hill, who saw the promise of this book and spurred me on to its completion, and I owe a special debt of thanks to my copy editor, Jacqueline Dormitzer, for her insightful reworking of the text.

My graduate assistants, Rachel Shaw and Peggy Wiechek, were of tremendous help in locating and reviewing sources, helping me sort through ideas, and aiding me with the countless details of manuscript preparation. Our department secretary, Ruth Hall, was invaluable in typing drafts and providing many other kinds of aid that helped the process of writing. My thanks, too, to my typists, Linda Greig, Carole Bell, and Jane Baldwin, for their patience, persistence, and professionalism.

Finally, my special gratitude to my husband, Hank Abbott, who aided me with his editorial skill and his encouragement, and to my children, Charlie and Kim, who put up with my preoccupation and diminished time for family affairs while this manuscript was being prepared.

Ann Arbor, Michigan   M. R. A.
September 1982

Notes

1. Jessie Bernard, "Sex Differences: An Overview," in Andrea Kaplan and Joan Bean, eds., *Beyond Sex Role Stereotypes: Readings toward a Psychology of Androgyny* (Boston: Little, Brown, 1976).
2. Helena Z. Lopata and Barrie Thorne, "On the Term, Sex Roles," *Signs* 3, no. 3 (1978):718–21; Barrie Thorne, "Gender . . . How Is It Best Conceptualized?" in Laurel Richardson and Verta Taylor, eds., *Readings in Sex and Gender* (Lexington, Mass.: Heath, 1981).
3. Carolyn Heilbrun, *Toward a Recognition of Androgyny* (New York: Knopf, 1973), p. x.
4. *Ibid.*
5. Judith Long Laws, *The Second X: Sex Role and Social Role* (New York: Elsevier, 1979).

Contents

Chapter Three

Chapter Four

Chapter Five

Chapter Six

Adolescence: Friendship, Dating, and Sexuality   *183*

Chapter Seven

The "Ideal Family" of the American Dream   *213*

Chapter Eight

The "Ideal Family" of the American Dream: Variations   *261*

Chapter Nine

The Marketplace: Men's and Women's Roles at Work   313

Chapter Ten

The Polling Place: Law, Politics, and the Women's Movement   359

Chapter Eleven

Chapter One

Why Status Differences Exist Between the Sexes

> . . . but this is fixt
> As are the roots of earth and base of all;
> Man for the field and woman for the hearth;
> Man for the sword and for the needle she;
> Man with the head and woman with the heart;
> Man to command and women to obey:
> All else confusion . . . .
>
> —Tennyson, "The Princess"

When we look at women and men in the American culture today, we can see vast differences in power and prestige between the sexes. Women still make fifty-nine cents for every dollar a man makes, and few women are top corporation executives or wield political power. Such differences in power and prestige seem to have existed since the beginning of recorded history in all human societies about which we have information. Where and why did these differences begin? The obvious bodily differences between the genders are certainly not enough to account for the tremendous differences in power, prestige, and opportunity that have developed between men and women. Although men on the average have larger and more muscular bodies than women, this difference should not necessarily mean that men should gain power, especially in societies that do not depend heavily on physical strength. Nor should having and caring for young children be a handicap that pushes women into the inferior status that is theirs in many, if not all, cultures. Indeed, what is defined as appropriate for men and women in terms of labor or behavioral characteristics varies from culture to culture. Yet in almost every society, it is

1

men who make the rules, control the economic system, and define the rituals and the ideology.

Many authors have been tempted to say that because this kind of stratification has existed for so long and is so widespread, it must be "natural" and therefore is the way that things should be. Yet biological and social evidence as well as information from more recent history tells us that this power difference is not at all "natural." Nor is it a difference that would be fruitful to continue in the future. While men have had prestige and power, they have also had crippling stress and high death rates; women have had unfulfilled opportunities and depression. Cultures need healthy, creative people of both sexes contributing to the building of society. We need to examine the history and nature of the power differences between women and men so that we can understand our past and plan toward a better future.

What Determines Differences in Power? Stratification by Sex and Social Role

Although by themselves physical differences between the sexes are not enough to create the vast differences in power that seem to exist between the genders in most cultures, each sex is linked to different sex-specific *social positions*. A social position could be that of husband or wife, for example, or of nurse, secretary, soldier, or football player. We almost always think of a female when we think of the social position of wife and usually when we think of secretary or nurse. In contrast, we think of a male whenever we think of the social position of husband and almost always when we think of soldier or football player. However, gender is attached to social position in different ways according to time and culture. In our earlier history, secretaries and nurses were almost always male. Among the Dahomeans of Africa, wealthy women may fulfill the position of "husband" supporting a wife and (with the help of a male acquaintance) having and raising children by this wife.[1]

In addition to the social positions often associated with a particular gender, being born male or female means that you are expected to perform a general *social role* in the sense of a "man's role" or a "woman's role." This is more easily seen in less highly specialized societies than ours. In such societies, men may defend the group, do the trading, and carry on certain rituals, while women may provide most of the food and do any child-rearing and homemaking chores. Social-role expectations also vary according to time and culture. Social role may involve certain *personality characteristics* that are expected of each gender. Sometimes these personality characteristics seem to be needed to fulfill the social positions held by a gender, as in the case of all women being expected to have nurturing and supportive personality characteristics because mothers need to be warm and nurturing. Sometimes the expected personality characteristics seem to have developed indirectly or by chance and may even be dysfunctional in fulfilling social roles, as in the case of the supposed passivity and dependence of women.

A great deal of overlap between the sexes exists in personality characteristics, in social roles, and more and more in social positions. However, when differentiation in these areas does occur, it seems to lead to *stratification*. That is, some social positions and social roles are ranked higher or lower than others. In almost every culture about which we have information, the social role played by men and the social positions held by men seem to be ranked higher than those of women.[2]

We can measure this stratification by sex in a variety of ways. Nielsen suggests that rewards associated with social positions fall into four general categories. First are *material rewards* such as money and material possessions, which indicate one's position in the economic structure. Another kind of reward is *prestige*, or the respect one gets for holding a particular social position. *Formal or informal power* is a third kind of reward. And various kinds of *psychological gratification*, such as personal satisfaction and feelings of doing something worthwhile, are the fourth category.[3]

All four areas may be high in measuring overall status associated with a position, or some areas may be higher and some lower. In almost all cases, material rewards, prestige, and formal power are higher in the social positions associated with men; women's status sources are more informal and indirect. Women's access to social positions and roles that are high in status has been limited, because in almost every culture it is men who make the rules, control the economic system, and define the rituals and the ideology.

Thus, when we ask about differences in power and prestige between the sexes, we are really asking about differences in the ranking of social positions and social role. Why are some social positions valued more highly than others? (A great deal of consensus exists in our own culture, at least, on which positions are valued the most highly in terms of prestige.)[4] We are also asking why certain social positions have historically been associated with one or the other gender. We must therefore begin our quest for the reasons behind sex-linked power and prestige differences by looking at how social positions came to be divided between the sexes and how some kinds of labor gained more rewards than others. We will see that ideology, ritual, and socialization practices developed to justify and perpetuate the original division of labor.

How It All Began

Many kinds of theories have been developed to account for the original division of labor between the sexes. *Biological theories* usually stress the physical characteristics of each sex that may have influenced how labor in primitive societies was divided. Biologists and anthropologists who have studied primates and early humankind agree on the general facts of evolution and the division of labor but disagree in their emphasis on and interpretation of these facts.

Biological Roots of Differences in Social Roles

It is generally believed that one of the primary events in the evolution of human social bonds was the loss of estrous, or seasonal sexuality, in the female. Many anthropologists believe that as female humans became receptive all year round, males were more likely to stay in the vicinity of the female and her children and thus form a bond with them.[5] The fact that humans developed bipedal locomotion and walked upright is also considered important. This upright posture not only freed hands for tool development and use but may also have led to increasing interaction among early hominids. In primates, the seasonal sexuality of females is usually announced by a pink swelling in the genital region, which alerts males to the fact that the female will be sexually receptive. With upright posture, no physical sign of sexual receptivity could be seen, so females may have had to develop social signs to show their interest in mating. There were, however, probably no *long-term* pair associations other than mother and child among the very early hominids, although the reproductive unit was the fundamental core of short-term social association.[6] Anthropologists hypothesize that as climate changes brought on droughts and protective forests receded, small family-like units may have joined forces into hunting bands so that they could protect one another and share food. Gradually there was a dividing of labor in this food finding, whereby males did more of the far-ranging hunting and females—who were literally held down by clinging infants—did more of the close-to-home gathering.[7]

Emphasis on the roles of female and male diverges at this point. Zuckerman stresses the importance of "man the hunter." She suggests that as early human beings lost some of their original physical advantages, such as strong teeth and jaws, protective fur coats, and a tail that enabled them to swing up into the branches away from harm, they needed an enlarged brain to survive. However, it would have been quite difficult for a larger infant head to pass in childbirth through a woman's narrow pelvic area. Therefore, the human brain remained small in infants, with the potential of growing about four times as large in the adult. Human infants were helpless and dependent for a long time after birth.

Frequent pregnancies may have made it difficult for mothers to provide enough food for themselves and several children. Therefore, Zuckerman suggests, the female may have needed a companion to provide food for herself and her children. This providing of food by a companion conveniently coincided with (or perhaps resulted from) the year-round sexuality that encouraged males to stay nearby. Thus, in Zuckerman's view, the males sustained the species. She believes they also developed cooperation during their periods of hunting, which helped reverse the dominance hierarchies related to sexual competition for females. Thus, male-female pairs could develop instead of a dominant male monopolizing many females.[8]

Tanner, Zhilman, and others emphasize the role of "woman the gatherer" and point out that females must have provided 50 to 90 percent of the food. They also stress the importance of the female in developing human culture and suggest that she not only originated significant social signs but also developed tools to gather and carry food and a "sling" to carry her baby when she no longer had fur to which the baby could cling. They suggest that the female chose the more social, cooperative males with whom to mate and therefore by her choice determined which genes would be passed on.[9]

Haraway points out that the same facts are given different interpretations by Zuckerman and by Tanner and Zhilman.[10] What Zuckerman calls female receptivity is called female choice by Tanner and Zhilman, who also emphasize the role of the female in developing culture. In addition, Tanner and Zhilman suggest that small canine teeth developed as males fought less (and sociably mated) rather than resulted from the different diet caused by a changing environment. Tanner and Zhilman's perspective is believed by many feminists to correct an original male bias in the description of early human history. Whatever perspective one chooses to emphasize, however, all anthropologists seem to agree that labor probably divided so that females did the child care while males were more likely to roam and hunt.[11]

Another well-known anthropologist, Judith Brown, specifies that this division of labor was a functional one. She points out that while women are capable of doing the physically taxing hunting and herding (for example, there are women seal hunters among the Copper Eskimos and women reindeer herders among the Tungus)[12] these activities are usually incompatible with simultaneous child watching. Such work is potentially dangerous; it requires that the participant roam far from home, it requires intense concentration, and it is not easily interrupted to care for a child's needs. Another anthropologist, Ernestine Friedl, who also has developed theories about the early division of labor, agrees that it made sense to train as hunters the group that was likely to be the most mobile and able to hunt. She stresses, however, that there is nothing inevitable in this original division of labor, pointing out that when needed (as in the Ojibwa tribe, where women have had to take care of families when male hunters are killed), women are also trained as hunters.[13]

Social and Environmental Roots of Differences in Social Roles

Assuming that males were the hunters for the reasons given above, various anthropologists and other writers have developed other biologically based theories about how this original division of labor was elaborated into social roles to give males more power and prestige.

Friedl postulates that as males brought home and distributed meat, they gained power and dominance. She argues that in the hunting and gathering societies where men and women gather for themselves and their families and where there is very little hunting of meat, women usually have power relatively equal to that of men. She believes one can see this equality in the fact that women and men are equally free to choose spouses, to take on lovers, and to separate when they wish. In an intermediate form of society where the men may hunt and provide 30 to 40 percent of the food, women have less power. The men have power derived from their skill as good hunters and can, in a sense, exchange meat for women; women have less chance to choose their own mates. In the hunting and gathering societies where men provide almost all the food, as in the Eskimo culture, women have the least power. They have little control over their destinies; they may be treated as sex objects and literally passed from man to man. Female infanticide may exist, as parents want male sons to provide for them in their old age.[14]

One of the interesting parts of Friedl's theory is that it is not the amount of food itself that seems to be the major differentiating factor in developing power for one sex; rather, it is the control over distribution of a valued product. In the intermediate style of society, women provide over 60 percent of the food from gathering, but men still have much more power. Even in societies where women provide virtually all the food, men may still have greater power. Friedl points out that the hunt results in large quantities of food that must be distributed beyond the family unit, and in its distribution men develop systems of bonds and alliances that women do not have the chance to form. Later these bonds may lead to economic power.[15]

While this dominance based on distribution of the valued result of the hunt exists only among hunting and gathering societies, Friedl believes that the same basic dominance also results among shifting agriculturalists because the men have a monopoly on the clearing of land.* Men

---

*Schlegel and Michaelson and Goldschmidt disagree; they believe that women have more power in horticultural or simple agrarian societies because they have more control over the land and economic processes than do men in such cultures. (See note 16.)

clear the land not only because they are physically stronger but because new land often borders on territories of other people, so warfare is possible. She says that men, by virtue of their control over warfare and land, "are more deeply involved than women in economic and political alliances which are extradomestic and which require for their maintenance the distribution and exchange of goods and services. Thus by monopolizing the resources by which they can establish extra-familial bonds, men develop power."[16]

Friedl, however, has been criticized because her theory does not apply to all societies. Male dominance is not characteristic of foragers who rely mainly on gathering; where the sexes share gathering chores, there is little differentiation of social position by sex and little stratification. It is also not clear why meat should have greater value and its distribution lead to more power than does the continual providing of the basic subsistence diet. Friedl has also been criticized because she does not deal in depth with the informal ways in which women may exercise power and modify the stratification system.[17]

At this point, we need to digress from the mainstream of anthropological theory to discuss the theory of a writer who believes that men's power developed from their hunting tasks. Lionel Tiger, in *Men in Groups,* proposes that men who did the hunting developed a complex series of rituals and signs that constituted their early "bonds." He believes that these early bonds carried over into other kinds of male enterprises, such as politics, and that men are thus better suited to these fields because they recognize certain signs from one another. According to Tiger, one of the signs is sexual activity and the rituals surrounding it. Thus, sexual relationships with females and dominance over them become an important part of the whole culture. If women need protection from predators, then they must submit and be lower in the dominance scale, he says.[18]

As you might guess, Tiger's theory has been thoroughly discredited by scholars. While most anthropologists admit that male dominance hierarchies existed that protected females and also established sexual relationships with them, the whole concept of "male bonding" has found little support. It is difficult to believe that men, more so than women or any other group, have a particular series of rituals, signs, and signals or that these supposed ancient signs and signals would carry over into modern activities and make males better suited to dominate prestigious areas. Yet Tiger's book must be discussed because it remains popular, although controversial. Many people still seek a justification for contemporary stratification by sex.

While we are discussing popular writers, we might also show how sociobiology can be used to paint an entirely different picture of evolution. Elaine Morgan postulates an even more controversial theory of human origin in her book *The Descent of Woman*. Morgan does not believe that hunting activities or sexual needs developed human differences. She raises the question of whether humans were even around—at least on land—during the period usually associated with hominids. She points out that few fossils have been found for that period, and she also asks why we developed only two-legged motor abilities when four legs were usually faster. Her belief is that humankind took an entirely different evolutionary trend. She postulates that during the long drought when there were no trees to offer protection from predators, humankind took to the water and became aquatic mammals. Thus, she suggests we developed a layer of fat not found in our ape relatives, and our fur disappeared, but hair remained on our heads to which infants could cling. She points out that we are much more similar in many ways to swimming mammals than to apes. In terms of sexual differentiation of labor, she believes that it was the need to spend hours gathering, planting, and cultivating to take care of infants that kept women close to home when they emerged from their aquatic state.[19]

While Morgan's book has been suspected of being written tongue in cheek, it still shows us that one can interpret biological facts in many ways. However, neither Tiger nor Morgan has evidence to support their basic contentions. We must return to the mainstream of anthropological thought to gain further knowledge about why the power difference developed between the sexes.

In a version that is similar to Friedl's, Sanday postulates that society's energy was split among the functional tasks of reproduction, defense, and food production. Women had to take care of reproduction, which left defense for men, and men and women shared food production. She states that as men did more warmaking and cooperative hunting, they developed political organization and bonds, while women were isolated from each other.

Her theory does not explain why women did not develop the same bonds or why value was attached to defense and hunting but not to gathering and reproduction. However, she does try to answer the question of why, when women do *all* the providing of food, they still have lower status. She suggests that possibly in that kind of situation, men are busy with defense and thus women are dependent on men in a dangerous environment, or that if women provide the daily food, men are freed to accumulate surpluses and gain monetary rewards. Thus, she suggests that control over surplus goods or the need for defense may give the group that provides it more power. In addition, the ability to form alliances and bonds adds to that power.

Sanday goes on to point out that there is a relationship among subsistence, the harshness of the environment, whether the sexes do segregated or integrated tasks, and ideology. Sanday suggests that in a harsh or dangerous environment separate roles develop, with men taking care of defense and women doing food production. When separation occurs, a "separate but equal" situation may develop, but the likelihood is that stratification, or ranking of tasks, will begin. Separation of work means different social roles and *sexual scripts* for men and women, and it is often accompanied by ways to keep women separate and to curtail their power, she believes.[20] She believes that the sexual scripts and the ideology of the culture are closely related. If the environment is harsh and promotes migratory and animal-hunting behavior, an "outer" orientation becomes prominent. If the environment is more serene, an "inner" orientation results. In "inner" societies, females get power as a natural part of the ideology of the culture. In "outer" societies, females get power only as they have access to "male" sources of power. Sanday points out that women are most likely to gain power when they themselves are able to produce a surplus product that is demanded and when they form organizations and groups that consolidate their power and give them access to power sources.[21]

Interaction of Biology and Stages of Development

Sanday, as Friedl before her, believes that with the coming of more technologically advanced societies, the power of women markedly declined. While one might expect women to gain more nearly equal power where physical strength was not needed as much, in fact the development of technology usually favored men. It was men rather than women who gained access to technological advances or were called upon to do the heavy work connected with technological society, such as mining and steel work. This was particularly true when traditional societies were colonized by more developed nations. For example, when the Dutch opened gold mines in South Africa, African men got the jobs that gave them cash and power. In other cases the role of women in planting and raising crops was ignored, and new seed, plows, and fertilizer were given to the men, who then raised surpluses that gave them power. Thus, men worked for cash or controlled the production of exchange crops, and women were left with raising food for the family and with household chores. Men increased their share of the "public sphere" of trade and exchange, and women were relegated to the "private sphere" of the household, although they may have previously been cultivators and traders. In the process, leadership roles changed as well. In the village or tribe, women could inherit rank or property and wield a great deal of influence. In the new urban centers, men consolidated their "public" power to take over leadership roles.[22]

In another theory that describes the interaction of biology and stages of development, Collins stresses the size and strength of males and suggests that they will dominate unless their force is curtailed in some way. When their use of physical strength is curtailed, he says, their power positions will be curtailed as well, and he suggests that the curtailment of male force takes place in conjunction with particular types of economies.

In the hunting and gathering economy, all must work to survive, and a restriction on male force is needed if women are to work and to mate. However, in the agrarian economy, men produce more food and provide valuable defense and land-clearing services. As women are dependent on men, men do not need to curtail their force in the same way, and women become subject to sexual restrictions. In advanced technological societies, he believes that men are restrained by law from using force, but women are still at a disadvantage economically as they seldom have access to the market to produce and sell a surplus on their own.[23]

Engels carried one step further the idea that men would gain power in technological society. He stated that with the development of technological skill, men could produce surpluses, and this surplus became established as individual private property. Men wished to pass this surplus on to their heirs and to be sure that only their own blood relatives did inherit. Thus restrictions on women increased as men wished to limit sexual access to their wives so that they could be sure the child their wife bore was their own. Thus, according to Engels, private property was the root cause of sexual discrimination.[24]

Private versus Public Social Roles

We still do not have a complete answer to the question of why men's roles became more elaborated and men's activities were usually found to be more valued. Rosaldo has suggested that while there seem to be certain universals of females caring for children and of male dominance, we must be careful in our interpretation of the record. She suggests that it is possible that the many histories written by men overstate male power. She points out that there is an infinite variation in the kinds and degrees of power recorded and that women often had great informal power. She believes that we also must not ignore the role of chance in selecting and elaborating certain cultural activities.[25]

Finally, Rosaldo postulates that male activities were probably more elaborated and more rewarded because they were public and showy. She believes that as women were confined to domestic roles, they were not able to develop obvious sources of prestige and authority. Thus, according to Rosaldo, while the domestic/public division as it appeared was not a *necessary* division, it was an "intelligible" (or understandable) product of mutual accommodation of human history and human biology.[26] As men dissociated themselves from the grubby, intimate details of life, they stood apart and developed their own identities in terms of artificial hierarchies and roles; women developed their identities in interpersonal relationships in the interactions of daily life.[27] Finally, men's "public sphere" became elaborated and ritualized. Men themselves became identified with the "public," with legitimate power or authority, even when women developed some power or economic competency of their own. She points out that in African societies like the Yoruba, women may control a good part of the food and trade in distant markets and accumulate wealth; yet when they approach their husbands, the wives must pretend to be dumb and obedient and kneel to serve the men.[28]

In a complement to the idea of public and private, Ortner suggests that men are associated with "culture," or "civilization," while women are associated with nature. Ortner points out that women are seen as closer to nature for several reasons. Women's bodies are involved more of the time with natural functions like reproduction, and the domestic role of women is seen as noncultural or nonpublic.[29] As humankind moves toward a mastery of nature, admiration of the natural declines. Men who manipulate nature by doing such things as irrigating or fertilizing see themselves as dominating nature, and the cultural is seen as superior to the natural. Thus, women become identified with the natural, the domestic, the private or family side of life; men become identified with the cultural, the technological, the public sphere. The value placed on the cultural and public part of life is greater, and ideology develops that gives authority and value to the roles and activities of men.[30]

We can see relationships among the ideas of the anthropologists. Although each emphasizes different points, they all assert the relationship among biology, the production of food, the separation of tasks, the kind of environment, and human control over the environment in the development of male power. Collins and Friedl assert that labor is divided between the sexes according to what was biologically functional for early humankind. Men come to control more surplus production and even subsistence production in most stages of societal development. Distribution and control of surplus goods help men establish bonds, and so they gain political power. As labor is divided, it becomes stratified or ranked, with men's activities being valued more highly than women's. Sanday, Ortner, and Rosaldo believe that the stratification of sex-linked social positions is encouraged by a distinction between the private/natural realm of women and the public/cultural realm of men. As societies dominate nature, they are more likely to degrade natural functions and to glorify the male, cultural realm. In the developed, "outer" societies, women gain access to power only as they enter the public realm or the activities of the sexes become more alike by men entering the domestic realm.

We still do not have a complete answer to the question of why males developed more formal power than females. We still are not quite sure why public, male activities gained more respect than what to early humans must have seemed the almost miraculous event of bringing new life into the world. We have also not yet really considered the extent of informal female power that countered formal male sources of authority.

A Word about Formal and Informal Power

We have seen that formal authority or legitimate power lies with men in almost every society. However, women may have a large degree of informal power. Indeed in their own realm or through manipulation of various sorts, they can exert a great deal of influence; but legitimate public power is reserved for men.

As societies developed and changed, women seemed able to use *formal power* only if they inherited it or if they moved into the male realm of activity. The difference between a woman getting power through inheritance and a man achieving it on his own is important and interesting and is related to public and private spheres. When a woman inherits power, she does so through the private sphere, her family. As the private sphere or family is indeed considered woman's place, this power is considered legitimate (she got her power in the right way; she did not achieve it and threaten the roles of men and women). In a present-day example, widows of deceased congressmen in our society are elected to Congress, although they would be unlikely to achieve that position on their own. We also have examples like Indira Ghandi, the prime minister of India. She is prime minister in a nation where women have notoriously low status, but she inherited her political standing from the position of her famous father. In the business world of the United States, women who sit on corporate boards have almost always inherited their positions. In these situations, a woman's power is understood as derived from the power of a man in her family.

While men can also inherit power, the great majority of them attempt to achieve it. In most societies, achievement (competition, aggression, wheeling and dealing, dominance) is part of the "public realm." Thus, achieved power comes to be associated with the public sphere and with men. Because achievement is not as easy to define and specify as inheritance, it is often surrounded by rituals and ranks, which become symbols of authority.

Belief Systems Perpetuating Status Differences
Primitive Fear and Envy of Women's Sexuality

The view of women as "nature" was traditionally connected with a view of women's nature as fearful. Joseph Campbell says, "There can be no doubt that in the very earliest ages of human history, the magical force and wonder of the female were no less a marvel than the universe itself, and this gave to women a prodigious power. It has been one of the chief concerns of the masculine part of the population to break, control, and employ [this power] to its own ends."[31]

Why indeed were women feared in this way in early human societies and perhaps even today? A general fear of the power of women was associated with childbirth. As the whole process of conception was not very well understood among primitive humans and its relationship to sexual intercourse was not always perceived, in many cases it was believed that women themselves brought forth children when they wished to do so. This was certainly evidence of power and seen as magic to some degree.

Fear of the blood connected with childbirth and with menstruation also existed in early human societies. To early humans blood was connected with injury and even with the possibility of death. Yet, women bled monthly without injury and did not seem to suffer from the bloody flow. Fear of menstrual blood, in particular, and taboos about it were extremely widespread. Such blood was seen as having magical powers, and menstruating women could make people sicken and die, sometimes even by merely casting their shadow upon them.[32]

Finally, there was a fear of sexual union with women. Perhaps this fear stemmed from the fact that intercourse with women could leave men weakened. Many primitive tribes forbade intercourse to their hunters before the hunt. Hays also suggests that another aspect of this fear of sexual union with women was the fear that perhaps women were able to perform limitlessly in sex and could not be controlled or kept at home.[33]

Men could control or manage these fears by several means. One of the ways they could control the fear of childbearing was to participate vicariously in the childbirth process. In the "couvade," a set of customs developed in which a husband participated ritually in the birth of his child by adopting some of the behavior and taboos of his wife. Sometimes he actually seemed to experience labor pains and postpartum fatigue; but at the minimum, he kept to the house after the birth so he could recover. He often received more attention than his wife.[34] Male initiation ceremonies also seemed frequently to be designed as an imitation of the childbirth ritual, with the drinking of the blood of animals simulating the blood of childbirth.

However, the male initiation ritual was also a way of separating from women, while at the same time identifying with the power women possessed. Chodorow has pointed out that "maleness" is not a thing that a boy can simply grow into as a young girl can grow into the female role. To the extent that women raise both boys and girls and male models are not present for boys to emulate, the boys may adopt stereotyped and rigid notions of the masculine role. They may also need to separate themselves strongly and definitely from the feminine world with some ritual like a male initiation rite. Unfortunately, as Chodorow makes us aware, such separation may force the boys to reject and denounce the women's world and to adopt a masculine role that excludes and deprecates women's activities.[35]

Another way that men could control their fear of childbirth and menstruation on a daily basis was by separating themselves from women or at least from women seen as threatening. Women in many societies were and are still isolated in menstrual huts during their menses, and they are similarly contained after childbirth.[36] It is interesting that this separation of women may have actually served to increase their power, as they had the chance to establish bonds between themselves while so isolated.[37]

A final kind of control was that over women's sexuality itself. Clitoridectomy, or the cutting out of the clitoris, the nerve center that is the seat of a woman's center of sexual pleasure, was adopted in some groups. Taboos about sexual activity were also widespread; in particular, married women who engaged in illicit sexual activity could be severely punished.[38]

Religious Ideology and Status Differences

Primitive Religions and Female-Dominated Society.   Some primitive attitudes toward sexuality were perpetuated in religious myth and ideology. Early religious ideology, however, did not reflect a dominance by either sex. Fisher says, "It seems likely that before the concept of a queen or king of heaven appeared, some few thousand years ago, the universe was viewed as a pantheistic collection of forces inherent in nature, forces that were female and male, animal and human, and combinations of both."[39] The early Mesopotamian pantheon of the fourth millennium had nature gods like the mountain range, the sky, and the divine cow.

Reuter reports an early image of woman as a nature goddess in the myths of Babylonia and Canaan. These myths picture the cosmos as a world egg or womb that differentiates into sky and earth, which are male and female divinities. The earth mother and her daughter, the fertility goddess, are seen as powerful and autonomous figures.[40] The king is the son of the earth mother, who grows up to be her consort and produces a young king, who takes his place. Reuter points out, however, that it is a son, not a daughter, whom the Great Mother puts on the throne. As time passes, sky and earth, which were once on the same level, become ranked in a status hierarchy. Maleness (the sky) is identified with intellectuality and spirituality, and femaleness is identified with lower material nature.[41] Enki, the male God, takes center stage from about 2000 B.C. on. Myths have him ejaculating and filling the Tigris River with water; he becomes important in dominating the pantheon of other gods. Nannu, "she who gave birth to heaven and earth," becomes a housekeeper. Her daughter, the fertility goddess Inanna, remains; but judging from the change in ritual mating poses between the fourth millennium and 700 B.C., Inanna comes to be dominated by her consort. Another indication that male gods are predominant is the fact that the last king to use a female goddess's name did so around 2000 B.C. During the second and first millennia, both kings and male commoners used only the names of gods.[42]

One evolutionary anthropologist, Bachofen, believes that ancient myths, surviving customs, and language all point to a pattern in which matriarchy was the original form of society. He proposes that matriarchal inheritance of property and residence with the woman's family developed during the time of the Great Mother–goddess ideologies, somewhere in the fourth millennium B.C.[43]

Others believe that matriarchies did not necessarily come first in human history, but that there have been various periods in history when women were dominant. In their book *The Dominant Sex: A Study on the Sociology of Sex Differentiation,* Mathilde and Mathias Vaerting believe that one can identify the states in which women ruled by the marriage practices of the people in those states. In states ruled by women, they believe that the man contributed a dowry and had to be faithful over the period of the marriage. Women were entitled to divorce their partners if they were no longer pleased by them, and they could also dispose of any common possessions. They believe that the husband adopted the name and nationality of his wife, adorned himself in fancy clothes, and was considered as somewhat less intelligent but more sociable than the female. The Vaertings classify ancient Egypt and several other societies as ones in which females were dominant, although many historians today would reject that claim.[44]

How accurate are these theories of early matriarchy? We do know that mother-goddess myths existed in the early societies of human civilization and that women in many of these societies had relatively high status. Murdock, in his study of 250 societies, also identifies some matrilineal tribes and even some all-female tribes that existed in Africa and South America. For the most part, however, he found no early or later societies of both men and women where the women were actually dominant. Men frequently had the political titles even when women controlled some power. Although Murdock found matriarchy appearing at all levels of economic and technical development, in no case did it mean that women were really the dominant force in the society.[45]

While the presence of mother-goddess myths does not mean that matriarchies necessarily existed, these myths probably do indicate certain respect for women and their position in society. The development of ideologies and religions dominated by male deities is synonymous with a markedly inferior position for women in most of the cultures studied.

Judeo-Christian Religion and Male-Dominated Society.   Sometime in the thousand years preceding the birth of Christ, men attempted to free themselves from their dependency on nature. They raised domestic animals and bred them, they tried irrigation, and in other ways they attempted to assert the mastery of humans over nature. At the same time, they began to believe that there is a principle beyond the body, that there is a higher being, a soul. In the developing religious thought of this period, mostly early Judaism, women remained linked to the subordinate and inferior natural world of the body, the body's desires, and the earth that man was dominating. Maleness became identified with intellectuality and spirituality. Older feelings about women's sexuality and its dangers became incorporated into the new ideologies.

The developing religious thought of this time believed that one would achieve divinity and spirituality by purging the evil of the earthly body and looking for the divine soul. As women were associated with the earthly body and its desires, they also became associated with impurity and with evil. We begin to find Greek tales such as that of Pandora's box, where a woman loosed all manner of evil upon the world. Later, in Christianity, Eve was the evil woman who tempted Adam out of the Garden of Eden, with the result that all humankind is supposedly cursed with original sin.[46] Intensified attempts were made to control women's sexuality and to protect men from its base influence. Early menstrual taboos were carried over into the major religions as they developed. In Judeo-Christian tradition, a menstruating woman was held to be unclean, and a man who lay with her would also be unclean.[47] There is an implication that if the couple had sexual relations during the menstrual period, they could be cut off from their people if discovered, although this was obviously difficult to enforce. In a like fashion, the woman who gave birth was considered unclean, although not as much for a male child as for a female. Leviticus 12:2–5 tells us, "If a woman conceives and bears a male child, then she shall be unclean for seven days . . . but if she bears a female child then she shall be unclean for two weeks." And Job 4:4 asks, "How can he be clean that was born of a woman?"

Women were also seen as being obsessed by sex and using their sexual nature to tempt men and weaken them so that they could not complete their important work in life. This image of women as sexual temptresses who beguile and seduce men is seen in the Bible in the stories of Samson and Delilah, Bathsheba and David, and Jezebel and Ahab. The name Jezebel today has become synonymous with one who deceives.

It was believed that women were so obsessed with sex that they had to be protected from their own base interests, and men had to be protected from them. Various manners of control over female sexuality show up in written ideology or in the laws and customs of the time. Talmudic writers went so far as to prohibit a widow from keeping slaves or pet dogs for fear the widow would use them to commit sexual indecencies.[48] Another way to control female sexuality was to be sure that women could not indulge in sex outside of marriage without great penalty. Virgins had to protect their honor at all costs. It was preferable to die than to be dishonored. A bride who was found not to be a virgin on her wedding night was sent home in disgrace and the bride price refunded. Adulteresses could be stoned to death and frequently were. In contrast, the man who strayed was ignored, unless he damaged someone else's property. To keep women from enjoying sex—and thus, theoretically, from straying— the process of clitoridectomy continued to be widespread. It was reasoned that if you removed the site of a woman's pleasure, she would have no reason to want to participate in sex.[49] Thus we see in Biblical statements, in religious practices, and in civil law and custom various attempts to control women's sexuality.

While abstinence and virginity were preferable, realistically marriage was considered the saving grace that directed sex to procreation and saved man from his lustful nature. Women were thus married early and kept literally under wraps before marriage. This meant that they had little opportunity for education or participation in any but household affairs. It is small wonder that one daily Jewish orthodox prayer for men says, "I thank thee, O Lord, that thou hast not made me a woman."[50]

Much of the doctrine that developed about women in early Christianity seemed to be based on the Old Testament and earlier Jewish tradition as well as on interpretation by church leaders rather than on the teachings of Jesus himself.[51] Paul, in particular, regarded sexual intercourse and marriage only as concessions to the human condition and stated, "Now concerning the things whereof ye wrote unto me. It is good for a man not to touch a woman. . . . Nevertheless, to avoid fornication, let every man have his own wife, and let every woman have her own husband" (I Corinthians 7:1–2).

Religious doctrine also underlined the idea of women as secondary and inferior beings who were to submit themselves to men. Ephesians 5:21–23 states, "Wives, submit yourselves unto your husbands . . . for the husband is the head of the church," and Paul added, "Let the women learn in silence with all subjection . . . I suffer not a woman to usurp authority over men, but to be in the silence" (I Corinthians 14: 34–35). The last phrase has often been used to justify keeping women out of church positions of authority.

Ironically, the mother-goddess tradition lingered in the Judeo-Christian religion. As the people of the Old Testament try to drive Baal, the symbolic king of the nature religions, out of the conquered land, Yahweh, the new God, becomes the consort of the goddess-mother. Myth says further that Israel becomes the bride of Yahweh. Later in Christian thought, the Church is seen as feminine and allied with God, as the mediator between God and his children.[52] In the words of the old hymn:

The Church's one foundation is Jesus Christ the Lord,
She is his new creation by water and the word,
From heaven he came and sought *her,* to be his holy *bride,*
And with his blood he bought *her,* and for *her* sins he died.

The other obvious female symbol in the new religion is the figure of Mary, the mother of God. She becomes the maternal mediator between God and the faithful of the Church. It is interesting that there was little interest in Mary until around the fourth century A.D., when strong prohibitions about a sexual life were at their height. With the puritanical beliefs of this period, Mary became a symbol of the ideal of virginity. The virgin birth was stressed, and traditions about the natural earlier children of Mary and Joseph were suppressed.

The devotion to Mary developed rapidly in the fourth century, and in Egypt the idea that she ascended into heaven with Jesus developed and spread outward. Devotion to her, though, centered around the perception that she is the merciful and forgiving mother who can understand human inadequacies and intercede with her son so that sins can be forgiven.[53] We see then in the ideology of Judeo-Christianity the development and elaboration of images of women that have remained with us since: women having dual natures—virginal and pure or sexual and evil—and women as subordinate and inferior to men.

Eastern Religions and Status Differences. In other religions, we also see the status differentiation between men and women. Islam rose about the seventh century A.D. with the birth of Mohammed in A.D. 570. Before this time, the Arabs were a male-centered tribal group who practiced polygyny. While Christianity regarded celibacy as the best state one could maintain, under Islam marriage was seen as extremely important. All who could marry were urged to do so, and Mohammed suggested that men "marry of the women who seem good to you, two or three or four and if ye fear that ye cannot do justice to so many, then one . . . ."[54]

As Bullough points out, a positive attitude toward sex in Islam was not enough to encourage a positive attitude toward women. Women were seen as little more than the property of men, to be used for their enjoyment. While there were some laws protecting women, little way existed for them to gain an education or any kind of opportunity in the public sphere.

We see in Islam the isolation of the woman, which kept her subjected. The ideal woman was to be virtuous and entirely devoted to her husband and family. "She speaks and laughs rarely and never without a reason. She never leaves the house, even to see neighbors of her acquaintance. She has no women friends, gives her confidence to nobody, and her husband is her sole reliance. . . . She does not surrender herself to anybody but her husband, even if abstinence would kill her. If her husband shows his intention of performing the conjugal rite, she is agreeable to his desires and occasionally even provokes him."[55]

Interestingly enough, the seclusion and protection of women did lead to some opportunity for professional women in Islamic countries in later years. As women were not supposed to be taught by male teachers or (heaven forbid) examined by male doctors, a group of professional women who devoted themselves exclusively to the service of women was allowed to develop.

Buddhism, like Islam, also kept women in their place. Early Buddhism, however, had the most positive view of women and stated that Nirvana could be open to all. The opening of a religious life for women gave them opportunities beyond marriage and motherhood and even more independence within marriage. But eventually more traditional views developed. In beliefs similar to those of the early Christians, later Buddhism stated that the way to attain Nirvana was to give up worldly sexual desires. Women were viewed as "sexually ravenous, greedy, envious, stupid and generally repulsive." They were sexually insatiable and set traps for men. "It was by withstanding their seduction that the Perfect One (The Buddha) entered into Nirvana and gained saving truth—by triumphing over the world of allure and senses in the world of women."[56]

In Hindu belief, the duality of women's nature was also stressed. For example, Mother Earth was seen as the twin goddesses Nirrti and Prthvi. As Nirrti, she was decay, death, and destruction; as Prthvi, she mothered. These great goddesses—and mortal women—were seen as ineffective or dangerous if they did not have a male to control them. It was believed that "the male principle is necessary if the female principle is to be fertile and good. Alone the female principle tends to be evil and dangerous."[57]

Hinduism further defined the position of women in the belief about reincarnation. Hindu philosophy stressed that we are constantly reborn until we realize our oneness with the divine. The level of one's rebirth is determined by the quality of his or her previous life, or *Karma*. It was commonly believed that no woman could possibly gain salvation except in a future life when she was reborn as a man. Being born female was in itself indicative of having had a bad karma in a past life.

Woman could advance their karma only by being good wives and exhalting their husbands. The Laws of Mana instructed women to be loyal even if their husbands were deformed, unfaithful, drunk, offensive, or debauched. To ritualize this attitude, orthodox religion suggested that the wife adore the big toe of her husband's right foot morning and evening, bathing it, offering it incense, waving lights before it. Because of women's lowered state, wifely duties were the only ones whereby a woman could gain good karma. Women were excluded from other prestigious forms of obtaining good karma, such as the study of the Vedas (religious works) and meditation.[58]

Thus, ideology that justified a lower position for women was developed and enforced by religions that worshiped male deities. They developed philosophies that defined women as inferior or evil and justified their isolation from the everyday affairs of education, trade, politics, and even social contact. In practice, this meant that women were put in a world apart. They had no access to public-power positions or to means of gaining power, such as through trade or education. While some women exercised power informally at home or through women's groups, their isolation and seclusion made even this difficult in some areas. As the religions changed and developed, beliefs about women fluctuated in accordance with economic situations and the philosophy that justified the economy.

European Religious Ideology, Economic Development, and Status Differences

As Christianity spread across Europe, the words of Saint Paul justified the curtailment of women's legal rights and set a pattern for women's subordinate position throughout the following periods. Women's rights were severely limited in the law codes of the Middle Ages, although some noblewomen managed to exert control of land and to gain limited political power, especially when their husbands were off at war or on crusades. Women were also able to practice a chaste, holy life as nuns, and they could become saints. Before A.D. 800 they even had a significant role in church administration. However, when Emperor Charlemagne reorganized the church after A.D. 800 and had clerics function in government, women lost important functions, as they were considered unsuited for political life.[59]

During the Renaissance of the fourteenth through the sixteenth centuries, a renewed interest in Greek and Roman antiquity revived the idea that women were sinful, sexual creatures and that abstinence and sexual chastity were the way to salvation. Although during these Renaissance years wealthy women were allowed greater education, aristocratic women who had run large estates and exercised political influence lost a great deal of their power as state power consolidated. The fourteenth century onward also saw the declining status of working women. Skilled tradeswomen who had acquired their own workshops throughout the Middle Ages were gradually expelled from participation in the guilds that controlled commerce. It was expected, however, that women would continue their important contribution to the family economy. Wives were expected to contribute to the family income by spinning, lace making, farming, and even hiring themselves out as day workers. Popular literature warned workingmen not to marry wives without trades.[60] By the sixteenth and seventeenth centuries, the home was the focus of religious, educational, and commercial activities. Although the husband was dominant over wife and children, women's contributions were recognized.

The Protestant Reformation of the sixteenth century also gave women some access to sources of power that they had not had before. If, as Protestantism said, each person communicated personally with God and negotiated his or her own salvation according to faith, then women were on an equal footing with men and could be equally saved. This did not mean that they would get any position in the hierarchy of the church, but they could ascend equally into heaven. Protestantism also meant a church of all believers, and women were supposed to read scripture and sing with the men. In fact, the Protestants insisted that everyone should be able to read the scriptures and thus encouraged literacy among women.[61]

Protestantism also established the precedent that it was correct, even preferable, to have romance in marriage and to be in love with one's spouse. This meant that women became viewed as something more than property and could even exercise some power through their romantic attachments to their spouses. In addition, the new faith aided women as it sought to consolidate marriage by attacking wife beating and the double standard of sexual norms. The sexual nature of men and women was deemed to be more alike, and women were no longer viewed as wanton, unable to control their desires, and likely to lead men into sin.

A darker side of this whole period was the difficulty of proving one's faith when ritual and hierarchy did not establish it for you. Any sign of rebellion or talking back in women could be construed as the work of the devil, and the women could be considered "witches." Indeed, the very word *fe-minus* was construed as meaning "lacking in faith." Thousands of women died in witch hunts in both Europe and America.[62] We see again the continuation of the theme that women are connected to evil and the devil's work, and the way to prove one's "faith," if a woman, was to be good and obedient.

In some ways, women had more freedom in the sixteenth and seventeenth centuries than before, as they did not have the direct care of many young children. Many children were wet nursed and later apprenticed outside the home. As fathers worked in and near the home, they took on a large part of child rearing and job training for their children. The father was supposed to take over basic child training once the child reached an educable age. However, seventeenth-century women worked hard: they tended animals, produced and marketed food, made clothes, and participated in their artisan husbands' work. Widowed women also had opportunities to run their own businesses, and many women took over the family business when husbands were away at war. Bloch says of this era, "Women were measured against essentially the same standard as men and were judged worthy of a position on the ladder, although one rung beneath men."[63] However, in the eighteenth and nineteenth centuries, the pendulum swung back, and the work of women was devalued again. In the 1800s the industrial revolution was a major development that affected human work and gender roles. As surplus production for cash was taken out of the home and centered in factories, it was also taken out of women's control, and women lost power. Domestic work other than surplus production for cash was seen as having little value, and while many women and children worked in mines and factories during the early days of the industrial revolution, they gained no power by doing so. They had little real say about the long hours, terrible working conditions, and low pay they received; their wages were so minimal that they had nothing left with which to trade or build up reserves.[64]

With growing industrialization, many middle-class women withdrew entirely from the paid labor force. By the middle of the 1800s, most middle-class women did not work outside the home. The focus of their domestic work changed from economic production to child rearing. As fathers left the home for business enterprises outside, as wet nurses and servants went out of fashion, and as children were seldom apprenticed outside the family, mothers became the principal childraisers.[65]

At the same time, the ideal of romantic love developed and the new "leisure class" of women was idealized as pure and asexual. In the middle class it was reasoned that if women were not producers, then they must be frail and delicate. The idealized body was sought by lacing women into tight corsets and having them wear high-heeled shoes. The image of women as frail and fainting easily was probably reasonably accurate, with the tightly laced "stays" cutting off breath. This new, fragile image was not connected to the earth-mother image of past women, but represented a new image of an asexual Madonna figure. Her counterpart, the temptress Eve, was found in the numerous prostitutes who flourished during these Victorian days.

In a total reversal of viewpoint, the wanton woman of the past was now seen as a force for good who would control the base impulses of men. Women were seen as the enforcers of moral and religious standards. As they could participate in public life through churches and the arts (although women were seen as supporters of art and not as creative artists), they turned their attention to these areas while men moved into the secular, competitive economic realm.[66] The spheres of men and women were now seen as separate and distinct, as were the sexual nature and personality traits attributed to each sex. This perception of distinct spheres continued into the first part of the twentieth century. It was not until after 1940 that married women moved slowly back into the world of paid employment, and later still that men again began to share family responsibilities so that ideas about the particular nature of each sex were reopened to debate.

Status Differences in Early America

So far we have looked in general at the Western cultural tradition that has influenced our attitudes toward the different positions of men and women. We now need to look specifically at the women in the United States. While many of the European attitudes toward women carried over into the United States, certain elements specific to the colonies and later frontier led to differing attitudes toward both men and women and their interaction.

One of the factors that influenced the position of women in the United States was their scarcity. In the colonies and later on the frontier, women were a valued and desired commodity. They were also able to perform needed economic tasks in the early days of the country. Both in the colonial areas and on the frontier, women's roles were vital. Not only did women spin and weave and cook, but in many cases they had to do such tasks as making soap and candles. They also worked in the fields and, in more isolated areas, they had to be able to pick up a gun and help protect the settlement from Indian attack.

In some instances, the absence of men meant that the women had to take care of the day-to-day business in the settlement. Bullough describes Nantucket Island where the whaling fleets kept men away from home on voyages from two to five years long. The women of the island handled business, and their status was linked to how well they could protect their husbands' money in the men's absence.[67] On the frontier, women might be similarly left to manage alone for long periods.

As we have implied throughout, the contribution to economic resources of the community has meant a great deal in terms of the status and power accorded either sex. One tangible measure of women's higher status on the frontier was the fact that it was the western states that restored the right of women to vote. Women often had the right to vote in the early colonies, but the colonial legislatures gradually withdrew such rights. In the western territories, this vote was often restored before it was elsewhere. Wyoming gave women the vote in 1869, prompted by a desire to double the vote of respectable married people against the gamblers and hustlers, and also in the hope that more women would be attracted to the territory.[68]

Another measure of the status of women is how much they are able to move about in society and to choose their own mates. In early American society women were able to move freely in the public domain, with the exception of such places as bars or gambling houses. Women also had a great deal of freedom in choosing their mates and were able to associate relatively freely with men before marriage. In fact the American custom of casual dating was unique in Western tradition. The purpose of the custom was to let a couple get to know each other well enough to know whether they were suited to marry; but if "keeping company" did not end in marriage, there were no hard feelings. An even more surprising extension of the custom in early America was the practice of "bundling." Young men would come courting and would often have to spend the night, as the distances between farms and houses were long and the roads were not good. The young couple would want to stay up and talk and get to know each other, but firewood was often scarce. Rather than heating the whole house so that they could stay up, they were allowed to get into bed under the covers. They were fully dressed, and an honor system, helped along by the presence of a younger brother or other chaperone in the room, was supposed to operate to prevent any sexual activity. While the practice worked to get couples married, a major aim of their parents, the honor system was not always perfect. If a baby was born early and the young couple wanted it baptized, the couple had to confess to fornication. By these confession records, we can estimate that almost one-fifth of the brides in the early colonies were pregnant when they got married.[69] By the standards of that day, it was remarkable that women had so much freedom in courting and premarital sexual adventures.

This is not to say that women in the early American colonies or on the frontier were considered the equals of men or that, under normal circumstances, they were supposed to do men's work. Indeed, as the American nation became more settled, women's work and place became more limited. If they were not needed to till the fields, then nice women stayed away from such work; if they were not needed to tend to business while husbands were away, then nice women were not to meddle in men's affairs. Women were supposed to be wives and mothers and to take care of domestic affairs. They were supposed to limit their education, and there were even special textbooks for them like *The Lady's Geography*, so that they would not tax their minds. They were to learn enough reading and mathematics to handle simple affairs, but it was believed that excessive mental efforts could make women ill. When the wife of Governor Hopkins of Connecticut became mentally ill, people thought that her insanity was caused by spending so much time reading and writing.[70] Women, on the other hand, were considered basically moral and pure and were the guardians of religion and culture.

Southern white women and black slave women were in an unusual situation that provoked attitudes that varied from those in the rest of the country. In the views toward white and black womanhood, we see the old story of the Virgin Mary and Eve the temptress played out. Southern white women were elevated to a pedestal and put in the position of being unrealistically protected and restricted so that their morality would remain unsullied. In contrast, the black slave woman was considered the sexual property of her master. Bullough maintains that the elevation of the white woman was guilty compensation for the treatment of the black woman during this period.[71]

Thus, women in colonial America and later on the frontier were viewed as intellectually inferior to men but were not regarded with overt hostility. However, they had few legal advantages and apparently still carried some of the taint of the temptress Eve in spite of the looser laws about courting. There was a definite limit as to how much they could get out of their "place" if their work was not actually needed. Women who showed more ability than feminine weaknesses would allow were often accused of being witches, and the witchcraft trials of that time resulted in the death of a number of such women. There were people like Benjamin Franklin and Mary Wollenstonecraft who attempted to modify the inferior view of women, but their efforts seemed to have had little success; formal structures of power remained under the control of men. As industrialization reached America in the nineteenth century, women's power decreased even further. An attempt was made to emphasize women's "finer nature," but this could not make up for her loss of power in the productive and public realm.

As time progressed, this "finer nature" was also defined to include a lack of interest in sex, and so women were again confined to the Madonna role. One of the well-known American doctors of the time, Dr. William Sanger, spelled out the tremendous difficulty too much sexual desire could bring to a woman. He stated, "The full force of sexual desire is seldom known to a virtuous woman, . . . and [evil could only result if] a mutual appetite equally felt by both [occurred]." Once a woman had enjoyed sex, he said, she would enter into a bottomless pit of sexuality from which she was likely to become promiscuous and turn to prostitution.[72] Although feminists resisted this view and even pressed for birth control information, Sanger's were commonly held beliefs.

We thus find transplanted to America the dualistic views of women and their sexuality that had existed with the early mother-goddess religions. On the one hand, women were seen as pure, nurturing, and asexual mothers; on the other hand, the threat from their sexuality was always present, and they could become the source of evil and temptation for men. In the economic, productive areas, women had many of their functions stripped from them, and if they did work or produce outside the home, it was seen as an extension of their basic wife-and-mother role. While to some degree traditional religion and scientific thought modified their views of the woman as inferior morally and physically, women were not considered equal beings by any stretch of the imagination.

Scientific Ideology and Status Differences

Scientific thought that developed in the nineteenth century further supported different statuses for women and men. In this period, "scientific explanations" of the differences between the sexes proliferated. As these "scientific explanations" of sex differences were linked to the rising respect for and mystique surrounding scientific rational thought, many of the explanations were accepted as factual. As most of the scientists proposing such theories were male, the scientific thought of that time has a male bias.

One of the scientists who greatly influenced our view of women, men, and their capabilities was Sigmund Freud. While we will discuss Freud's theories in more detail elsewhere, we need to summarize them here. Freud assumed that women were inferior beings who really wished to be men. He believed that women suffered in life from two main causes: sexual inhibition and discontent with their social conditions. Freud also equated the masculine with the active and the feminine with the passive. In fact, according to Freud, the three most distinguishing traits of the female personality were passivity, masochism, and narcissism.[73] Perhaps the image of women was improved because, rather than causing the sexual problems of men. Freud believed her sexual problems were now her own; but she was still undoubtedly described as a poor second to men. The widespread acceptance of Freud's philosophy meant that this view of women as inferior had a tremendous impact. After all, if "rational scientific" men described women in this way, who could doubt their conclusions?

Other psychologists who follow, such as Erikson and Jung, modified Freud's position to some degree. Jung reiterated the polarities between the sexes and believed that sexual differentiation was important; the denial of this differentiation would keep a person from having an identity. However, he valued both "masculine" and "feminine" elements of consciousness. He defined the feminine as that "which characterizes the early eras of humanity, . . . childhood and moments of psychological crisis (as well as) creative process," and the "masculine" as patriarchal and involving the rational.[74] Jung believed that every person could have both kinds of consciousness. As Freud before him, though, he distrusted the feminine side of nature. He stated that matriarchal or feminine consciousness can act as a "regressive undertow against the development of a rational ego. The danger of the matriarchal quality of consciousness . . . is a constant possibility of a kind of aimless 'mooning' and drifting along with one's streams of intuitions, with one's feelings and images instead of actively relating them and making them concrete. . . ."[75] Jung also described the feminine principle as having two sides. Its positive expression is symbolized in images of the good mother who bears, protects, and releases, leading from darkness to light. Its negative expression is symbolically "ensnaring, fixating, holding fast, with the idea of the spells of witches that change men into animals or things, the devilish temptress. . . ."[76] Again, we have the Madonna and Eve images of woman. Yet while Jung has not described femininity in a particularly positive way, he has taken a major step forward in delineating the feminine as something that does not just describe physical differences from men or cultural roles for women, but describes a behavior or style that could belong to both sexes.

Erikson took Freud even a little further and challenged the idea that women are men with something missing. He emphasized the view of women as positive contributors. Thus, women were not just passive in reaction to man's activity, but they were passive in the sense of initiating peace, calm, and serenity.[77] It should be noted that none of these psychologists questions the masculine principle of activity. While we see a progression from Freud to Erikson in more positive views of women, we still find that the psychoanalytic and scientific view of humankind not only separates the sexes but, for the most part, assigns women's characteristics and psyche a decidedly inferior role.

Science and Sexual Stereotypes

Many other areas of science have stated "findings" over the years about women's different and usually inferior nature. For a while biologists held that women's smaller brain meant that women had poorer intellectual capabilities. Another supposition was that women had only enough energy for reproduction *or* for intellectual activity, not for both. We could cite innumerable examples of such irrational "rational scientific" thought. One example that typifies the male bias that existed and still exists in science and related fields like medicine is the inaccuracy in reports about women's sexual nature.

In a fascinating summary done in the early 1970s of the information in gynecology textbooks for the previous thirty years, Diana Scully and Pauline Bart discovered that most of the books contained incomplete, inaccurate, and male-biased information about female sexuality. In the period prior to the work of Kinsey and Masters and Johnson, they discovered that female sexuality was either omitted totally from the gynecology textbooks they surveyed (and they read almost everything published) or that the books had inaccurate and biased information. They quote one text published in 1943 as stating, "The fundamental biologic factor in women is the urge of motherhood balanced by the fact that sexual pleasure is entirely secondary or even absent." Two books told gynecologists to instruct patients to fake orgasms.[78]

In 1953 Kinsey published his sex study that exposed as false the idea of vaginal orgasm and showed that, in contrast to popular belief, the vagina had few nerve endings and the seat of a woman's sexual pleasure was the clitoris. Yet even after this, gynecology texts discussed the idea of the vaginal orgasm as the mature response and the clitoral orgasm as the immature and childish one. Some texts went so far as to say that women who could not experience a vaginal orgasm were "frigid," and as late as 1965, gynecology texts talked about the vagina as the main source of a woman's pleasure. After the Masters and Johnson studies of the early 1960s, there was some correcting of inaccurate information in the texts; but even then, two-thirds of the books did not discuss the issue of vaginal or clitoral orgasms. Eight continued to assert that the male sex drive was stronger (contrary to Masters and Johnson), two said that most women were frigid, and half protested that procreation was the major function of sex for the female.

The texts also seemed to prefer "traditional" sex roles, with males dominant and females passive. One text is quoted as saying, "An important feature of sex desire in the man is the urge to dominate the woman and subjugate her to his will; in the woman acquiescence to the masterful man takes a high place," and another stated, "The traits that compose the core of the female personality are feminine narcissism, masochism, and passivity."[79]

Thus, obstetricians and gynecologists, who are supposed to be the helpers and advocates of women, were still being instructed with inaccurate myths about women's sexual nature and social role rather than with the more accurate scientific information that was available. We see the continuation of Victorian beliefs about the asexual wife who can only be given limited sexual pleasure and then only by male penetration. In addition, we see the Freudian influence in views about women being interested only in procreation and suffering from penis envy. All of the textbooks were written by men. One can only wonder at the damage that was wrought by passing on such inaccurate information about their "frigidity" and "immaturity" to women who desired sexual pleasure. One can also wonder why the available information about the nature of female and male sexual response was not incorporated into the later books. As late as 1970, one text stated, "The frequency of intercourse depends entirely upon the male sex drive. . . . The bride should be advised to allow her husband's sex drive to set their pace and she should attempt to gear hers satisfactorily to his. If she finds after several months or years that this is not possible, she is advised to consult her physician. . . . " Popularized versions of gynecological information such as David Reuben's *All You Ever Wanted to Know about Sex* contain passages with similar kinds of inaccuracies and bias.[80]

Thus, much of past and recent scientific thought has portrayed women as passive, immature, asexual, and perhaps a little neurotic as well. The "scientific" portrayal of women has lagged far behind changing information about women's psychological and sexual nature, and the male bias in science has perpetuated a negative view of women. At the same time, the scientific community has perpetuated beliefs about the insatiable nature of the male's sexual appetite that have laid a heavy burden of performance upon men. Scientific "fact" has actually become an ideology that is a conservative force perpetuating stereotypes. The inaccurate portrayal also has had great influence because of the respect given the scientific community, particularly in our technologically oriented society. This scientific "ideology" interacts with religion and other sources of norms and with the economic system of society to shape our perceptions of the proper "social role" for each sex.

American Additions to Traditional Sexual Stereotypes

The different status for each sex, which meant an inferior status for women, survived the long passage through history and other cultures to reemerge in contemporary America. But American culture defined male and female sex roles in a way that emphasized the particular historical background of the new nation. Most other cultures had encouraged a certain blending in the traits of the sexes when male and female roles were defined. While this varied by historical period in the past, men were often allowed large measures of cooperation, displays of emotion, participation in art and dance, and participation in the care of young children, as well as being encouraged to be courageous and skilled. They were encouraged to be creative and literary besides being simply practical or rational. As the difficulties of settling a new land, and particularly a frontier, helped shape our value system, other values became more important

... ere incorporated into the American definition of the masculine sex role. For the new country, practicality and rationality took precedence over intellectual endeavor; the intellectual was put to the service of invention and obtaining immediate useful results for any project. In general, the rough and ready new culture celebrated the man who had the physical skills for survival, and it did not think much of the man who took time to be interested in the arts. It was believed that the refinements of dance, literature, painting, and the like, could be left to the care of women, who supposedly did not have the hard work to do. In addition, in a new country where every man theoretically had the opportunity to succeed, competition came to be emphasized. Cooperation was a virtue to be extolled only in those countries where extended kinship ties and group structures were kept together by ascribed status and the cooperative cement. In America, men stood on their own. Nuclear families were the most common, and such families might be separated from friends and neighbors by many miles. It is no wonder that the new country extolled independence, self-reliance, and achievement as prime components of the masculine sex role.

The new culture was also oriented to an extreme degree to change and to the future. One's achievements were measured by the tangible, by what was achieved, and by the measure of its worth, money. It is not surprising that the phrase "as good as gold" is typically American. Thus, in this change-oriented culture, the ideal man was achievement oriented, competitive, practical, successful, and individualistic. There was little room in the stereotype for the man who was sensitive, contemplative, or intellectual.[81]

Values for Women

The French writer de Tocqueville, who visited America in 1831, pointed out the uniqueness of this value system. He also showed that these values did not apply to women. While frontier women were expected to be able to take over men's concerns if absolutely necessary, the ideal woman was valued for a set of characteristics very different from those desired for men. The woman was to be the support system for the man and to be cooperative, oriented toward people, and concerned with nurturance and peacemaking. She was to be sensitive and to uphold moral and religious truths. Her main concerns in life were to be her husband and her family. At the same time she was supposed to be somewhat delicate and frail and was to be very dependent on her family and husband.[82] It is ironic that these more supportive and delicate traits were admired in women as long as other roles were not needed. However, when women were needed for other work on the frontier or later during war, their more practical sides were equally admired. The delicate, supportive female role that confined women to the work of housekeeper and mother was the product of a settled society that could afford more leisure for its women.

Contemporary Good- and Bad-Girl Stereotypes

Another part of the historical stereotype of women that was transferred to the American culture and codified within it was the dichotomy between the good girl (the Madonna) and the bad girl (the temptress Eve). Usually this dichotomy was used to restrict women, as they were expected to be good girls and thus eligible for marriage and the protection of a man. However, a second element has been added in contemporary times by the commercialism of American advertising. Young girls are expected to be attractive and sexy to attract a man, but not overtly sexual. Obviously, this means walking a tightrope between being a good girl and a bad girl.

In the white, middle-class ideal of the stereotype, if young women are to be considered sexual and feminine, they must develop much like a Barbie doll: slim, but big breasted; a sex object who spends her time dressing up. The idealized "playgirl" is desired but is also looked down upon because she is vain, frivolous, and not really a nice girl. Most men would feel that such a playgirl "gets what she asks for" and can be sexually used without much guilt.

The other half of the sexual norm is the good girl who is pure, chaste, and modest but without much sexual desire. This kind of woman is to be married and makes a safe and reliable wife and mother for a man's children. "He can reassure himself about his masculinity in believing that 'he has taught her all she knows,' and happily chase after playgirls knowing that his wife remains faithful at home."[83] Thus, the American woman is put into a double bind about her sexuality. She must be sexy enough to attract a man, but nice enough to marry one. Even in this age of more liberated sexual norms, or perhaps especially in this age, it is difficult to find the right balance.

The especially difficult part about the good-girl/bad-girl dichotomy is that one can never really achieve good-girl status. The nice girl is rewarded with the protection of men and the respectability of marriage, but "the girl who lapses from nice behavior at any time forfeits these rights."[84] There are few external restraints on behavior, such as restrictive clothing or chaperones, so all restraints must come internally—a tremendous and continuing burden for the "good girl."

Values and Success

Unfortunately, the traits associated with this leisured role for women are not traits likely to be associated with success in the culture. While an American man could possibly achieve success by adhering to the traits prescribed for his sex role (achievement, independence, self-reliance, competitiveness), the American woman is unlikely to achieve cultural success by being supportive, cooperative, religious, and nurturant. We again see the split that we saw in early economic societies. The man achieves success by "doing," by acting; the woman achieves success by "being," by bearing children and raising them. She maintains the life-support system while the impatient male pushes onward with practical and scientific advances. She is not in the forefront of action or exploration; rather, she is expected to be the guardian of ethics, religion, and tradition, which may all be conservative forces. She may well be in the position of supporting philosophies that "keep her in her place." While the man is free to achieve political and economic goals, the woman is often the one to care for others and to keep social relationships active.[85]

As in the past, the different values held to be appropriate for women's role still keep women from achieving success in cultural terms. If she is constantly being a support system, she has neither the time nor the approval to take on roles that might give her power. Jessie Bernard likens the American woman's role to that of an underdeveloped nation. A woman funnels natural resources—that is, emotional support and supportive services such as cooking, housecleaning, and childcare—to the developed nation (the male), which is concerned with economic achievement. In return she gets some degree of economic support and protection, such as an underdeveloped nation might get, but she does not have an equal voice in decision making and, contrary to de Tocqueville's impression, is probably viewed as somewhat inferior.[86] Like the underdeveloped nation she also never has the chance to use her resources for her own development.

While the male role implies a heavy responsibility for success and moving ahead, the female role implies the impossibility of changing one's status. Helen Hacker has made the point that women, like minority groups, suffer from *caste status*. If you have caste status, you have a status inherited from birth and you cannot change it. In contrast, if you have *class status* (as do most men), you have a status that you can change by your ability to succeed and move upward. The caste status of women and minorities is particularly easy to enforce because both groups have identifiable physical characteristics by which they can be spotted and made the target of prejudice. Hacker continues that in the economic area, the treatment of women is also similar to that of minority groups. They are given monotonous work under the supervision of white males and are treated unequally with regard to pay, promotion, or responsibility.[87]

• The implication of this difference in status is very important. It means that within American society women are not considered part of the system. Even when they play by male rules and show the ability to move up the ladder and improve their class situation, the idea of the distinct caste (the special characteristics of women that cannot be changed) is often invoked so that they cannot change their place.[88] Just as with minority groups, women's inferior status is justified by reference to their "innate or inherited inferiority." Women are often said to be biologically inferior, weaker, and less intelligent as well as fearful and emotional. They supposedly are not smart enough to handle money well or to be good drivers, and they are too emotional to hold positions of decision-making power.

If, against all odds, they make the leap from the caste system to the class system and succeed in changing their place in American society, they may find that they have paid a heavy price. If a woman exhibits male qualities and achieves success by using them, she may well be shunned. She may be considered a "hard, cold, unemotional bitch." Actually, she has often had to pay the heavy price of giving up success as a "female." It is almost impossible to be nurturing, supporting, and cooperative while achieving success in the masculine public realm.

On the other hand, if she tries to retain "feminine standards" in the masculine world, she is often not taken seriously by her colleagues and may be belittled in terms such as "illogical" or "overemotional." She has some choice as to whether she will achieve success by masculine or feminine standards, but it is very difficult for her to achieve by using both simultaneously. While success and masculinity may go hand in hand, cultural success and femininity are still not allies.

We therefore see that the differences in power and prestige between the sexes that started so long ago have carried over, with changes, into modern America. Women today still have little power in the productive realm; fear and awe of their sexuality still hinder them, and various ideologies and beliefs about their nature handcuff them in their attempts to join men in the public sphere. Changes are taking place, particularly as women leave the home and enter the public sphere of economic production; yet the beliefs about women's proper role and the old ideologies and taboos remain. The American culture has inherited a history of status differences between the sexes and has added some status differentials of its own.

The male sex role is also rigid. While men enjoy power and prestige and are allowed certain kinds of freedom more than women, the practical, rational orientation of American life has not undergone significant change. Men are also constrained more than ever by norms for unemotional behavior and success-oriented achievement. As few can really succeed in the culture's terms, the masculine sex role may require behavior that is not rewarded.

The next few chapters in this book take a closer look at the differences between the sexes and their contemporary physical and environmental roots. We must remember, as we examine the present, the pervasive influence of the past. The norms that tell us the proper behavior for men and women in this culture have had a long history and will not be changed overnight.

Essay Questions

1. Discuss the two main reasons for the division of labor among early human beings as presented in this chapter. How does Lionel Tiger's theory of "male bonding" possibly influence ideas on this division of labor?

2. Why does Friedl believe that being in charge of hunting activities was important to male power among early human beings? What does she tell us about the social arrangements in tribes where men and women provide different percentages of food that justifies her theory of male power?

3. Discuss the arrangements of power between men and women when a society becomes more technological or "developed." In this power situation, what would you naturally expect when physical strength is no longer highly valued?

4. Sherri Ortner has elaborated the view that man is to woman as "culture" (manmade civilization) is to "nature." Discuss why she believes this comparison to be true and how it affects women's power.

5. Many anthropologists have written about male fear and envy of women's sexuality. Discuss at least three ways in which men fear women's sexuality and three or four ways in which they deal with those fears.

6. How do the major religions deal with the status of men and women? How do they perpetuate the two images of women as the temptress Eve and the virginal Madonna?

7. How did women's roles change with the industrial revolution and the later development of the Victorian era? In particular, how did the more affluent economic situation affect women?

8. How has developing scientific thought affected the statuses of men and women? In particular, discuss the ideas of Freud, Jung, and Erikson.

9. The special conditions of the young American nation and its frontier influenced the values we believe to be correct for the behavior of men and women. Discuss those conditions and how they affected the roles of men and (separately) the roles of women.

10. What is meant by "a man achieves success by 'doing' and a woman achieves success by 'being'"? Why can't a woman just "do" and be successful the way a man can?

Exercises

1. Make up a list of qualities and classify them as either male or female and explain why. You can do the same for all manner of things (musical instruments, drinks, and so on).
2. Draw a life line and discuss what you plan to be after school. Will you get married and have children? If so, when? Who will stay home with the children if you have them? Who will do the housework? If one of you has a chance to move for a job, will the other go? What criteria will you use to decide?
3. Make a list of things you consider to be representative of a man's "doing"; make a similar list of things representative of a woman's "being." Discuss your lists and what they mean.
4. Keep a log for one week and notice the roles you see men and women performing:
   a. At the service station, who is working?
   b. At the restaurant, who are the cooks and who are the servers?
   c. At the department store, who are the managers and who are the sales clerks?
   d. At the elementary school (or the university), who are the teachers and who are the principals or administrators?
   e. _____ (Add other places and other roles.)
5. Try to imagine that everything you have ever read in your life uses only female pronouns: she, her—meaning both girls and boys, women and men. Imagine that most of the voices on the radio and most of the faces on TV are women's, and when important events are covered, you see only female faces. Imagine that you will spend your life dealing almost entirely with female professionals: doctors, lawyers, judges, police officers, and the like. You might prefer to deal with men, but they are not available. Imagine that almost all the politicians are female, and there is only one male senator in Washington. Imagine that there is a female president, and people are saying it will be a very, very long time until there is a male one (as there has never been a male one). *You are a male. How do you feel? Discuss.*

Notes

1. Joyce Nielsen, *Sex in Society: Perspectives on Stratification* (Belmont, Calif.: Wadsworth, 1978), p. 5.

Note: These exercises are appropriate for almost any of the chapters and could be used at the beginning of a class and then again at the end of a term. They are meant to be general and thought-provoking about the different statuses of men and women in our society.

2. *Ibid.*, pp. 3–18.

3. *Ibid.*, p. 11.

4. Inge K. Browerman *et al.*, "Sex Role Stereotypes: A Current Appraisal," *Journal of Social Issues* 28, no. 2 (1972):59–78.

5. Sherwood Washburn, quoted in Donna Haraway, "Animal Sociology and a Natural Economy of the Body Politic," *Signs* 4 (1979):37–60, p. 42.

6. *Ibid.*

7. *Ibid.*

8. Sally Zuckerman, quoted Haraway, *op. cit.*, p. 43.

9. Nancy Tanner and Adrienne Zhilman, "Women in Evolution: Innovation and Selection in Human Origins," *Signs* 1, no. 3 (1976):13; Adrienne Zhilman, "Women in Evolution: Subsistence and Social Organization among Early Hominids," *Signs* 1, no. 4 (1976):4–20; Sally Slocum, "Woman the Gatherer: Male Bias in Anthropology," in Rayna Reiter, ed., *Toward an Anthropology of Women* (New York: Monthly Review Press, 1975).

10. Haraway, *op. cit.*

11. Tanner and Zhilman, *op. cit.*

12. Judith K. Brown, "A Note on the Division of Labor by Sex," *American Anthropologist* 72 (1970):1074.

13. Ernestine Friedl, "Society and Sex Roles," *Human Nature*, April, 1978, pp. 63–75.

14. *Ibid.*

15. *Ibid.*

16. Peggy Sanday, *Female Power and Male Dominance* (Cambridge: Cambridge University Press, 1981), p. 175; Alice Schlegel, *Male Dominance and Female Autonomy* (Washington, D.C.: Human Relations Area File Press, 1972); Evelyn Michaelson and Walter Goldschmidt, "Female Roles and Male Dominance among Peasants," *Southwestern Journal of Anthropology* 27 (1971):330–52.

17. Sanday, *op. cit.*

18. Lionel Tiger, *Men in Groups* (New York: Vintage Books, 1969).

19. Elaine Morgan, *The Descent of Woman* (New York: Stein & Day, 1972).

20. Sanday, *op. cit.*; Sanday, "Toward a Theory of the Status of Women," *American Anthropologist* 75 (1973):1682–1700.

21. Sanday, *Female Power*, pp. 58–68.

22. *Ibid.*, pp. 126–32.

23. Randall Collins, "A Conflict Theory of Sexual Stratification," *Social Problems* 19, no. 1 (1971):3–21.

24. Friedrich Engels, *The Origin of the Family, Private Property, and the State* (1884; reprint ed., New York International Publishers, 1942).

25. Michelle Rosaldo, "The Use and Abuse of Anthropology: Reflections on Feminism and Cross-Cultural Understanding," *Signs* 5, no. 3 (1980):389–417.

26. *Ibid.*, p. 397.

27. Michelle Rosaldo, "Women, Culture, and Society: A Theoretical Overview," in Michelle Rosaldo and Louise Lamphere, eds., *Woman, Culture, and Society* (Stanford, Calif.: Stanford University Press, 1974), p. 30.

28. *Ibid.*; see also Robert A. LeVine, "Sex Roles and Economic Change in Africa," *Ethology* 5, no. 2 (1966):186–93.

29. Sherry B. Ortner, "Is Female to Male as Nature Is to Culture?" in Rosaldo and Lamphere, *op. cit.*, pp. 172–73.

30. *Ibid.*

31. Joseph Campbell, *The Masks of God: Primitive Mythology* (New York: Viking, 1959), p. 315, quoted in Vern Bullough, *The Subordinate Sex* (Baltimore, Md.: Penguin Books, 1974), p. 11.

32. Sanday, *Female Power*, pp. 94–95, 105.

33. H. R. Hays, *The Dangerous Sex: The Myth of Feminine Evil* (New York: Putnam's Sons, 1964), p. 281, in Bullough, *op. cit.*, pp. 16–17.

34. Margaret Mead, *Sex and Temperament* (1935; reprint ed., New York: Dell, 1969).

35. Nancy Chodorow, "Family Structure and Feminine Personality," in Rosaldo and Lamphere, *op. cit.*, pp. 43–66.

36. Sanday, *Female Power*, pp. 94–95, 105.

37. Frederick Engels, *op. cit.*, in Bullough, *op. cit.*, p. 8.

38. Geoffrey May, *Social Control of Sex Expression* (New York: Morrow, 1931), in Bullough, *op. cit.*, p. 18.

39. Elizabeth Fisher, *Women's Creation* (New York: McGraw-Hill, 1980), pp. 383–87.

40. Rosemary Reuter, *New Woman, New Earth: Sexist Ideologies and Human Liberation* (New York: Seabury Press, 1975), pp. 196–204.

41. *Ibid.*, pp. 13–14.

42. Fisher, *op. cit.*, pp. 286–297.

43. S. Bachofen, quoted in D'Andrade, "Sex Differences and Cultural Institutions," in Eleanor Maccoby, *The Development of Sex Differences* (Stanford, Calif.: Stanford University Press, 1971), pp. 173–203.

44. Mathilde and Mathias Vaerting, *The Dominant Sex: A Study in the Sociology of Sex Differentiation* (New York: Doran, 1923), in Bullough, *op. cit.*, p. 13.

45. George Murdock, *Social Structure* (New York, Macmillan, 1944).

46. Bullough, *op. cit.*, p. 34.

47. Leviticus 15:2–4.

48. Bullough, *op. cit.*, pp. 18–19.

49. *Ibid.*

50. *Ibid.*, p. 34.

51. Reuter, *op. cit.*

52. *Ibid.*, pp. 40–46.

53. *Ibid.*, pp. 46–59.

54. Bullough, *op. cit.*, p. 138.

55. *Ibid.*, pp. 146–47.
56. Denise Lardner Carmody, *Women and World Religions* (New York: Parthenon Press, 1979), pp. 48–51.
57. *Ibid.*, p. 42.
58. *Ibid.*, pp. 6–7.
59. Daryl Hafter, "An Overview of Women's History," in Marie Richmond-Abbott, ed., *The American Woman* (New York: Holt, Rinehart and Winston, 1979), p. 3.
60. *Ibid.*, pp. 6–7.
61. Ruth H. Bloch, "Untangling the Roots of Modern Sex Roles: A Survey of Four Centuries of Change," *Signs* 4, no. 2 (1978):238.
62. Reuter, *op. cit.*, p. 103.
63. Bloch, *op. cit.*, p. 245.
64. *Ibid.*, pp. 237–52, Reuter, *op. cit.*, pp. 196–204.
65. Bloch, *op. cit.*, p. 251.
66. *Ibid.*, p. 248; Joan Huber, "Toward a Socio-Technological Theory of the Women's Movement," *Social Problems* 23 (1976):371–88.
67. Bullough, *op. cit.*, p. 300.
68. *Ibid.*, p. 302.
69. Ira Reiss, *Family Systems in America*, 3rd ed. (New York: Holt, Rinehart and Winston, 1980), pp. 88–90.
70. Bullough, *op. cit.*, pp. 297–99.
71. *Ibid.*, pp. 300–301.
72. William Sanger, *A History of Prostitution* (New York: Harper, 1958), quoted in Bullough, *op. cit.*, pp. 324–25.
73. Kate Millet, *Sexual Politics* (New York: Avon Books, 1969).
74. Ann Bedford Ulanaie, *The Feminine in the Philosophy of Jung* (Evanston, Ill.: Northwestern University Press, 1971), pp. 168–69.
75. *Ibid.*, pp. 179–80.
76. *Ibid.*, pp. 157–69.
77. Eric Erickson, *Childhood and Society* (New York: Norton, 1963), pp. 247–74.
78. Diana Scully and Pauline Bart, "A Funny Thing Happened on the Way to the Orifice," in Joan Huber, ed., *Changing Women in a Changing Society* (Chicago: University of Chicago Press, 1973), pp. 283–88.
79. *Ibid.*
80. *Ibid.*
81. Alexis de Tocqueville, *Democracy in America*, 2nd ed. (New York, 1953), pp. 191–92.
82. *Ibid.*
83. Greer Litton Fox, "Nice Girl: Social Control of Women Through a Value Construct," *Signs* 2, no. 4 (1977):805–17.
84. *Ibid.*

85. Marie Richmond-Abbott, "Stereotypes of Men and Women in the American Culture," in Richmond-Abbott, ed., *op. cit.*, pp. 75–76.
86. Jessie Bernard, *Women in the Public Interest* (Chicago: Aldine and Atherton, 1971).
87. Helen Hacker, "Women as a Minority Group," *Social Forces* 30 (1951):60–69.
88. *Ibid.*

Chapter Two

Heredity, Environment, or Both? Similarities and Differences Between the Sexes

Here and in the next two chapters, we attempt to analyze the similarities and differences between the sexes in traits, abilities, and behavior. Any such analysis must always deal with questions about how much any trait or behavior is physically determined (if at all) and what role socialization and cultural expectations play in defining and obtaining certain behaviors. We will defer most of our discussion of socialization and cultural influence until chapters 3 and 4. In this chapter, we emphasize the physical nature of similarities and differences between the sexes.

Problems of Discussing Physical Sex Characteristics

Discussing physical similarities and differences between the sexes is fraught with difficulties, as in the past, physical sex differences have often been used to justify discrimination against women. Biological differences were seen as proof that the sexes had different and supposedly unchangeable functions; for example, women bore the children, so they had to raise them. Early research often argued that physical differences revealed that women had great biological limitations and a similarly limited role in life. For example, early research on brain size came to the conclusion that women had smaller brains, so scientists concluded that women must be less intelligent. Claims were made in the early 1900s that women had less variability in their genes and so would be limited in their achievement and creativity. Even such a talent as Herbert Spencer argued in 1879 that because women bore children, they would have little energy left over for intellectual achievement and their education should be restricted so they would not become overly fatigued. In 1968 Broverman and his colleagues argued that hormones affected the cognitive activity of women such that they could easily learn simple, repetitive tasks but would have difficulty with more complex, creative endeavors. As late as 1977, claims were made that women's hormonal functioning affected their emotional stability and made them unfit for high economic positions or governmental office.[1] Supposed differences between the sexes in mathematical and spatial abilities have also been used to justify keeping women out of advanced math and science courses and engineering programs, thus limiting their career choices. The results of such "research" have found their way into popular and scientific literature and popular contemporary thought. Many of the contentions, such as smaller brains meaning less intelligence or wombs wandering and causing hysteria, have been thoroughly disproved; but related beliefs carry over and influence perceptions about women.

With this background, is it any wonder that feminists become concerned about discussions of sex differences? As Jeanne Gullahorn so succinctly put it, "Our conceptions of sex differences are so deeply engrained in the culture that preconceptions are hard to shift . . . particularly because many stereotypes involve implicit assumptions about biological determinants and about the implications of biological factors."[2]

Not only has past research been used to justify discrimination against women (and against minorities), but because the research was done primarily by men, it emphasized differences connected with the male role, such as aggressiveness and competitiveness. These characteristics are also valued by the American culture and, not so coincidentally, possessed by more men than women. As fewer women were seen to possess these societally valued characteristics, woman's nature was portrayed as different and inferior. Few of the positive characteristics connected with women's roles and in which women could be expected to excel were studied. When they were, "female charactertistics," such as nurturance and compassion, were used to justify women's having a separate "sphere" of activity (home and hearth) and being a support group for the primary male society.[3] Thus, it is not surprising that the characteristics psychiatrists describe as belonging to a mentally healthy adult are also the characteristics that society believes to be possessed by men; conversely, characteristics associated with inferior mental health in our culture, such as passivity, fear, and timidity, are often believed to be possessed more by women.[4] Because of the nature of sex-difference research in the past, many women feel they have not been fairly treated and are defensive about any discussion of sex differences.

In addition, there are legitimate problems with the methodology and reporting of sex-difference research. The studies usually concentrate on finding a sex difference; those that find no difference or find a difference that varies from what is usually expected are not as likely to be published or widely circulated. In most of the studies, the differences are highly overstated, and the great overlap in traits and abilities between the sexes is seldom cited. Sometimes the difference in a trait or ability accounted for by sex is quite small (sometimes less than 1 percent). In very few studies is sex a variable that accounts for more than 5 to 10 percent of the difference in a trait.[5] In some studies, samples are very large, so average differences are likely to be statistically significant even when the differences themselves are very small.

Another problem is that many studies dealing with brain development or hormone function have been done on animal populations, and the results have then been *generalized* to humans. But it is not valid to apply results from animal studies to the far more complex biological structure of humans.

Researchers have also overemphasized biological causation and neglected the influence of social events and psychological states on physical functioning, such as the impact of cultural expectations on female biological experiences like menstruation and childbirth. Although the effects of socialization into sex roles have received more recent emphasis, the interaction between biology and cultural expectations has not yet received enough attention.[6]

Thousands of such studies dealing with sex differences are assessed in Eleanor Maccoby and Carol Jacklin's recent and encyclopedic review, *The Psychology of Sex Differences*.[7] The authors did a tremendous service in collecting and systematizing the research on sex differences, but even this book has been criticized for several reasons. Maccoby and Jacklin themselves point out that negative findings, or studies that find no sex difference, are likely to be underrepresented. Block has also criticized the authors' rationale for including studies in the book. All studies dealing with a given area (such as verbal ability) were considered of equal weight, and their results were averaged; but there is a wide variation in the sampling size and methodology of these studies. One-third of the studies compared in assessing sex differences had sample sizes of sixty or less; 20 percent had sample sizes of forty or less—too few people to supply valid results that could be generalized to a larger population.[8] Many of the studies included used measures that did not seem to measure what they were supposed to or could not later be duplicated by other researchers.

There was also an overemphasis on younger age groupings, where measurement of differences may be difficult to achieve: 75 percent of the studies reported in the book were done on children aged twelve or younger.[9]

Interpretation of the results of sex-difference studies has often been biased as well. While Maccoby and Jacklin were usually very careful in their own work, interpretation of results has often been slanted by other researchers. Kimball points out that "girls' greater verbal ability is not usually interpreted as suiting them to high positions in fields such as politics, law, and academics . . . yet their supposed lack of math ability theoretically makes them unfit for careers in engineering or the sciences."[10]

In sum, great difficulties are involved in finding good research about sex similarities and differences and in reporting the results of that research in an accurate and unbiased manner. We must be aware that there is far more similarity than difference between the sexes, and that far more variation exists in traits within one sex than between the sexes. The amount of difference in a trait accounted for by sex alone is often very small (1 to 10 percent), and the great majority of traits and behaviors show no sex difference at all. When differences are found, we must be careful to interpret them as physical only and to remember that biology predisposes but does not predetermine the functions of human beings. People tend to convert description into prescription and to say, "That's the way things *should* be." Yet we know that biological differences could not possibly account for the variation in sex roles across cultures and even at different times in a single culture. It would seem that neither biology nor environment determines by itself the abilities and behaviors that each of us possesses; rather, human traits come from a unique interaction of the physical with the environmental. Yet while we stress the similarities between the sexes and the importance of the cultural environment, we cannot totally ignore physical differences. With the cautions of this discussion in mind, let us now see what we know about the physical makeup of men and women.

Gender and Heredity

We are used to defining sex as masculine or feminine, and we think of ourselves and others as clearly in one of the classifications, male or female. However, the definition of sex is really not so simple. We may be talking about biological sex (the physical characteristics that we inherit), about our definition of self (the inner understanding that we are male or female), about others' definition of us, or about "gender role," the behavior we exhibit, feminine or masculine or some combination of the two. All of these facets of gender may be the same. We may have male body characteristics, think of ourselves as being male, and exhibit what our culture calls masculine behavior. On the other hand, these aspects of gender may vary and cause confusion or difficulty.

Hoyenga and Hoyenga describe eight definitions of gender; five of them deal with physically inherited aspects of gender and three with culturally determined "gender role."[11] Table 1 displays these definitions.

Chromosomal *gender* refers to the kinds of chromosomes a person inherits. In normal males, the sex chromosomes are XY; and in normal females, XX. Gonadal gender refers to the type of internal sex glands, or gonads, a person possesses. Hormonal gender refers to the type of sex hormones (substances secreted by the gonads) present in the body. Usually hormonal gender is the same before and after birth, but sometimes variations from this pattern occur. Hormones produced by the gonads when the fetus is still in the uterus determine the gender of the internal and external sex organs.

Usually the gender of rearing is determined by the external sexual organs. Parents raise their child as the gender they believe it to be, male or female. From this socialization probably comes gender identity, what we believe ourselves to be, male or female. Usually gender identity is determined directly by physical characteristics and/or the sex of rearing. Thus we see that *gender* may have many meanings. The word may denote strictly physical characteristics, or the feelings we have about ourselves, or the perception others have of us. Finally, it may also mean, in a larger

Table 1   *Eight Definitions of Gender*

Type of definition	Males	Females
Chromosomal Gender	XY	XX
Gonadal Gender	Testes	Ovaries
Hormonal Gender	Mostly androgens	Mostly estrogens and progestins
Gender of Internal Sexual Accessory Organs	Prostate glands, ejaculatory ducts, vas deferens, and seminal vesicles	Uterus and Fallopian tubes
Gender of External Genitals	Penis and scrotal sacs	Clitoris, labia, and vagina
Gender of Rearing	"It's a boy!"	"It's a girl!"
Gender Identity	_X_ Male ___Female	___Male _X_ Female
Gender Role	Masculine behavior	Feminine behavior

Source: Katherine B. Hoyenga and Kermit Hoyenga, *The Question of Sex Differences* (Boston: Little, Brown, 1979), table 1a, p.5.

sense, *gender role,* or appropriate cultural behavior. When people say of someone, "He is a real man!" they do not mean that the person is physically a male; they mean that he exhibits culturally appropriate masculine behavior. Let us now look at how gender is determined in average men and women in our culture and at some of the conflicts that may occur between the various parts or definitions of gender. The abnormalities in one part of gender, usually chromosomes or hormones, may cause confusion in the sex of rearing and in sexual identity.

Chromosomal Gender

When an embryo is conceived in the form of a fertilized egg cell, the ovum and the sperm each contribute twenty-three chromosomes, which align in twenty-three pairs in the fertilized egg. One of these pairs of chromosomes determines the sex of the fetus. The ovum always contributes an X chromosome, and the sperm contributes either an X or a Y chromosome. It is the Y that determines the sex of the fetus. No matter how many X chromosomes are present, the fetus will be male if a Y is also present. New research has proposed that one can determine the sex of a fetus by the timing of fertilization. The androsperm, which contains the father's Y chromosome, is faster but does not endure as long as the gynosperm, which contains the father's X chromosome. Therefore, if one wants to have a girl, it is proposed that fertilization should occur slightly before ovulation so that the father's hardier X chromosome will survive to fertilize the ovum and produce an XX (female) combination of chromosomes. If one wants a boy, fertilization should occur when ovulation has already taken place and the egg is ready, as the Y chromosome will get to the ovum faster and be more likely to produce an XY (male) combination of chromosomes.

The X chromosome is larger and contains more genetic material than the Y chromosome. If, in the process of fertilization, nature makes a mistake and some genetic material is lost, the fetus will survive with only an X chromosome (X——, an abnormality known as Turner's syndrome and discussed below). However, the fetus will not survive with only a Y chromosome.

The hardy, dominant X chromosome also seems to carry useful traits. Ashley Montague has reported that women have a greater resistance to illness and disease than men. He lists fifty-nine ailments that occur more frequently in men than in women and only twenty-nine that occur more frequently in women than in men.[12] Others speculate that there are protective factors located on the X chromosome that protect against specific diseases or increase resistance to various kinds of degeneration.[13]

However, certain characteristics such as hemophilia, color blindness, and possibly the ability to handle concepts about three-dimensional spaces seem to result from recessive genes carried on particular X chromosomes (we will call these "recessive X chromosomes"). These traits do not show up in women with two normal X chromosomes (that is, ones without the particular characteristic) or in women with one normal and one recessive chromosome. The normal X chromosome without the recessive trait is dominant and cancels out the recessive characteristic on the recessive X. The traits will show up in men, however, as the Y chromosome is sparse in the genetic material it carries and is not strong enough to have this canceling effect. The traits will also show up in women with two recessive X chromosomes. Thus, women may carry a trait such as color blindness but are not as likely to exhibit it themselves (they would need two recessive X chromosomes to show it); but their sons will demonstrate the trait if they get a recessive X plus the Y from the father.

Although chromosomal abnormalities where genetic material is lost or duplicated are rare, they do exist. People who possess these abnormalities show us the effect that chromosomes and their resulting hormones have on traits like body build, intelligence, and even behavior. One abnormality is Turner's syndrome (X——), in which only one X chromosome is present in the fetus. People with Turner's syndrome look female but have certain problems. They tend to be very short and may have various physical deformities and performance deficits. They are almost always infertile and, without estrogen therapy from adolescence onward, will not exhibit secondary sex characteristics, such as developing breasts. These women do not have the normal amounts of any of the three major types of sex hormone. Thus, they show that the second X is not necessary for having female genitalia, but it is necessary for having children.

People with Klinefelter's syndrome are males born with extra X chromosomes. They are male in appearance because they have the masculinizing Y chromosome (XXY or even XXXY); but the influence of the multiple X's overwhelms the Y chromosome. Although these humans are male in chromosomes, they are somewhat female in appearance, may show some breast enlargement, and have small penises and little body hair. They show low levels of testosterone (the male hormone) and frequently exhibit mental retardation. They may also have difficulties in social adjustment and are more likely to be found in institutions than the typical XY male.[14]

The male who has XYY chromosomes (an extra Y chromosome) is characterized by being unusually tall and having subnormal intelligence. It has been thought that such men also exhibit high levels of impulsive aggression and have criminal tendencies. The belief about criminal tendencies has led to sensational but inaccurate reports. Some studies showed that XYY males were more prevalent in prison populations than could be accounted for by chance. One particular study surveyed thirty-five instances of XYY males in mental and penal institutions and concluded that the incidence of XYY males in these institutions was approximately twenty times that which would be found by chance alone.[15] However, other studies have disputed the belief that these men exhibit more aggressive behavior than is usual. A review of the actual crimes these XYY men committed shows that they did not commit crimes any more violent than those of other inmates. Some researchers suspect that, much as the Klinefelter's male, these men are overrepresented in prison populations because of their lower intelligence and difficulty in adjusting to normal social patterns; they may commit slightly more minor crimes because of their social behavior pattern and may get arrested more often than men with normal intelligence.[16] The great majority of XYY men, however, lead normal lives among the general population.[17]

Hormones and Their Interaction with Chromosomes

Chromosomes determine the sex of the fetus largely through their ability to form the testes or ovaries that produce the sex hormones. These internal sexual organs are usually formed between the sixth and tenth week in fetal development and afterward secrete an enzyme that helps synthesize appropriate hormones. Although both men and women possess some of all the sex hormones, the primary hormones for men are androgens, particularly testosterone; and for women, estrogen and progesterone. The fetus will differentiate as a female unless the Y chromosome and a sufficient amount of androgen are present. Female fetuses produce large quantities of estrogen in the gonads at around eight weeks.

Sex Hormones and Development

Between the third and the eighth month of human fetal development, it is believed that sex hormones can enter the brain and affect areas like the hypothalamus. It is the hypothalamus that later determines the development and connections among the parts of the brain. Most of the evidence for the effect of sex hormones on the brain comes from animal studies, although humans with certain hormonal abnormalities have also contributed information. It is believed that the "critical period" for humans is from the third to the eighth month of fetal development, as studies show a high concentration of hormones in the amniotic fluid of human fetuses during that time.[18]

One of the hormonal abnormalities that may occur during this critical period is androgenital syndrome. Female fetuses with this syndrome produce an abnormally high amount of androgen. This imbalance can even lead to a masculinization of their external genitals, although they have normal-functioning ovaries and internal female sexual organs. If treated with hormones after birth they will go through a normal puberty and menstrual cycles and later can conceive and deliver babies normally.[19] It has been questioned whether the behavior of these girls differs from "typical female behavior" in childhood. In one Buffalo research sample of seventeen girls who had the syndrome and were compared to their normal sisters, 59 percent of the androgenital girls were identified by themselves and others as tomboys all during childhood.[20] These tomboy girls preferred boys' clothes, toys, and play; they had little or no interest in doll play and showed evidence of reduced maternalism and lack of interest in having children. This pattern was not true of their unaffected sisters. However, we must remember that these girls had been treated with continuous doses of cortisone, a potent drug that might well affect behavior. In addition, the surgical correction undergone by the girls for their genital abnormalities might have produced physical or psychological trauma. Then, too, the mothers of the androgenital girls were aware of their problem and may have treated the girls differently. Finally, we must be cautious about the study because it relied on self-reports of the individuals and their families. Thus, we are not certain to what degree physical factors or environment are operating.

Another study showed that girls who are masculinized by artificial progestins (which have similar properties to androgen), given to their mothers to maintain pregnancies, exhibited behavior similar to that of the androgenital girls. They were reported to be more competitive, self-assertive, independent, and self-reliant than average girls their age; they preferred male playmates and male clothes. There is again the question of environment, however. The parents may well have treated the girls differently because their genitals were somewhat masculine. However, one study that compared only females whose genitals were not masculinized found the same kinds of behavior.[21] Males with androgenital syndrome or exposed to artificial progestins as fetuses seem to have accentuated masculine behavior: they show even greater interest in sports and athletics than most boys and are more independent and self-assured than males the same age.

Another abnormality is that of androgen insensitivity. In this case, it is a male (XY) fetus whose body cells are insensitive to androgen. The male internal organs and external genitals do not develop in response to the androgen produced by the testes. There are no internal female organs either; but in the absence of androgen, the external genitals differentiate as female genitals, with a vagina and a clitoris. These men later develop normal-sized breasts and look like normal females, although they are in-fertile. When raised as females, they are quite "feminine" in typical in-tellectual patterns (good verbal ability) and female behavior.[22]

Thus, we are intrigued by questions about possible hormonal influ-ence, but we are not really certain that hormones played a part in the "different" behavior of either the androgenital girls or the other groups studied. It is also possible that androgen has an effect on factors relating to behavior, such as increased activity level and energy expenditure, but not on more complex behaviors. One well-known researcher sums up the doubts as follows:

> To think that hormones have a direct effect on desire for functional clothes, intention to have a career, choice of playmates, engaging in fights, etc., makes little sense when one looks at the behavior of boys in cultures where male role behavior is very different than in our own. . . . Are we to think that the androgens found in these other cultures are of different types or that their effects are somehow thwarted or that the effects of socialization are somehow greater in these other cultures?[23]

In fact, studies on hormones are new and experimental, and we do not know enough about sex hormones to know which ones, if any, are acting in particular situations. The picture is even more unclear because we do know that, at least in rats, hormones convert into one another (andro-gens undergo transformation into estrogens at the cellular level in the brain). We also know that low levels of hormones may be present in hu-mans or animals when their primary source, the ovaries or testes, has been removed.[24]

Gender Identity and Gender of Rearing

Gender identity, or what sex a person thinks he or she is, may also differ from the physical manifestations of gender. This matter of gender iden-tity is often the focus of the heredity-versus-environment controversy. Money and Earhardt, and others who have done extensive research in this area, firmly believe that psychosexual identity, or gender identity, is a learned factor. It is a matter of the sex assigned the child and how she or he is reared. In their studies of all the possible contradictions between chromosomes, hormones, physical appearance, and the way a child is reared, the sex of rearing is almost always the winner. Even in the dra-matic instance where external genitals contradict the sex of rearing, Money and Earhardt report that twenty-three out of twenty-five patients believed themselves to be the sex as which they were reared.

To support Money and Earhardt's assertion, several dramatic in-stances have been reported in research where sex reassignment has taken place following a decision about indeterminate sex or following an accident. These instances point up how important the influence of those around us may be. The parents of seven-month-old twin boys had their sons circumcised by means of electrocautery. The current used on one of the twins was too strong, and his penis was burned off flush to the abdominal wall. The parents agonized over what to do and decided to sex reassign the damaged boy so he would not have to compete with his normal brother. The child was reassigned as a female at seventeen months of age and given a new name, new clothing, hair ribbons, and feminine toys. The parents and all others interacting with the child made every attempt to treat her as a girl from that time forward. By the age of five the little girl was helping her mother around the house, exhibited motherly behavior toward her twin brother, and had asked for a doll house and doll carriage for Christmas. However, the little girl still exhibited a high activity level and a great deal of dominance behavior.[25]

In a similar case, a genetically normal boy was born with a very small penis, so his parents decided to reassign the child as a girl. Again, a new name, clothes, toys, and behavior different from the parents and older brother followed. The girl imitated her mother but was still showing signs of dominant behavior and seemed to be louder, more aggressive, and more energetic than other girls her age.[26]

Money believes that children acquire their gender identity from the age of six months to the age of three or four years. It is difficult after two years, he states, to change a child's primary orientation without severe emotional trauma and permanent damage.

Yet even in the case of gender identity, we cannot be certain that environment is the factor operating alone without physical influences. Some evidence exists for the fact that hormones, especially those that pass through the body in the fetal stage, may help determine the sex in which one feels comfortable after birth. In 1972 two villages in the Dominican Republic were discovered where eighteen of the males had an enzyme deficiency. They could not metabolize testosterone properly, so that at birth their external genitals looked female. These boy babies were thought to be girls and were raised as girls in the household: they did chores, babysat and stayed close to their mothers. At puberty, however, they made testosterone normally, so their testes descended, their clitorises grew into penises, their voices deepened, and their muscles developed.

The conflict between hormones and rearing has left two of the eighteen villagers confused. One knows he is a male physically, but he feels like and dresses like a woman. The other, who also feels like a female, married a man and wants a sex-change operation. In these cases, we see the influence of sex of rearing. However, the remaining sixteen who had been raised as girls easily assumed male identities.[27]

What do these cases tell us? How could the "girls" have changed gender identity so easily? One critique states that the children may have had enlarged clitorises, which made them and their families question their sexual identities from birth, especially in a town where gender changes were known. However, the author of the original study, Imperator-McGinley, said that she had studied older people who had not known about the disease and, in the rare cases found in other countries, those people also converted to the identity and behavior of the other sex without problem.[28]

Another question we might raise is whether the male role was one that was decidedly preferable in Dominican Republic society. Some have claimed that this is likely to have been the case and that the "girls" who found themselves "boys" at the age of twelve may have been relatively pleased to give up the restrictive nature of the Latin woman's role. It would have been difficult to continue in the role of women anyway, as they now had the bodies of men.[29]

Hampson, another authority on gender identity, has suggested that there may be some "imprinting" of sexual identity on the brain during the critical periods of fetal development. This imprinting, or predisposition to feel or behave in a certain way, may develop later—possibly under the influence of more hormones. Yet Hampson clearly believes in the importance of sex of rearing and says that although there may be some imprinting of sexual identity during critical periods of fetal development, "psychologic sex . . . appears to be learned . . . we can [postulate] a concept of psychosexual neutrality in humans at birth."[30]

How do we reconcile the possible roles of fetal hormonal imprinting, later parental action, and environment in determining gender identity? For the moment, we have no firm evidence for the degree of importance of any of these factors. Although the proponents of sex of rearing seem to have more evidence on their side, we cannot discard the possible effects of hormones. Thus, evidence seems to exist that refutes the total nature of biological or environmental determinism. The twin study shows us the effects of socialization; the Dominican Republic example reminds us that sex of rearing alone does not always determine gender identity. It is likely that both biological and environmental factors and their interaction influence gender identity and the subsequent development of sex-typed behavior.

Physical Characteristics of Infant Boys and Girls

Clearly evoked by sex hormones are the physical characteristics of males and females. However, other than the obvious physical differences of different genitalia, boy and girl babies are extremely similar in characteristics like height, weight, and general behavior. Yet some minor differences do exist that may later become accentuated by interaction with the environment. The hormone androgen facilitates the synthesis of proteins from amino acids, helping muscle and bone development in males. At birth the average male infant exceeds the average female baby by 2 percent in height and 5 percent in weight, although the average male baby has less body fat from birth onward. Male infants also have a consistently higher average basal metabolism after the age of two years, which is partially accounted for by this larger bone and muscle mass. As one might expect with the larger mass, they also tend to develop larger hearts and lungs and have a lower resting heart rate.[31] The male infant grows faster before birth and after birth for about seven months.

The development of the internal organs of the average girl baby is ahead of that of the average boy baby. After eight months girls grow faster than boys, and they reach the limits of their growth an average of one to two years sooner.[32] The estrogens in the infant girl, which are activated at puberty, help reduce serum cholesterol and protect her against heart attacks, although they encourage tissue deposits of fat, particularly in the hips and thighs.

Infant boys, on the average, seem to have greater use of the large muscles, whereas most infant girls have more developed use of the fine muscles and show more manual dexterity immediately after birth. Female infants, on the average, spend more time in reflex smiles, rhythmical mouthing, and moving mouth to objects.[33] There is usually no difference in activity level during the first year of life; after this findings vary, but when differences exist, boys are usually found to be more active. One recent study found that male infants were awake more often than females, displayed considerably more facial grimacing, and engaged in more low-intensity movement. In this study, the experimenters did not know the sex of the infants they were watching—an elimination of an important source of bias.[34]

Heredity and/or Environment

In other areas the sexes do not seem to have well-established differences. Where differences do occur, it appears that heredity interacts with environment.

Other Physical Characteristics: The Sexes and the Senses

For many years people have believed that boy and girl babies differ in their use of sight, hearing, smell, taste, and touch, as well as in the physical characteristics described above. Maccoby and Jacklin tried to make sense out of the many contradictory studies and findings and concluded that boy and girl infants are much more similar in their use of the senses than had been believed.

Hearing. It was originally believed that newborn females responded more intensely than newborn males to auditory stimulation. It was also believed that such auditory stimulation as speaking softly at girls could be used to reinforce or reward other behavior. However, Maccoby and Jacklin's review of the relevant research does not support this belief. Although girl infants respond slightly more when some measures of response to sound are used, they do so only during a very limited age span.[35] We do not know why these beliefs about the hearing of infants developed. Perhaps because girl babies use the small muscles around their mouths more than boys do and give reflex "smiles," parents thought their daughters were responding to them. Parents seem to react to the belief that their daughters hear them better, as they talk more to infant girls than to infant boys.

Adult women in our culture do seem to have statistically a higher sensitivity to sound than men do. They seem to hear better in the higher ranges, but are less tolerant of loud noises. At eighty-five decibels and above, any sound is twice as loud to them as it is to a man. Women are also less tolerant of repetitive sounds. Thus, there seem to be some differences between men and women in response to sound, although these differences are not readily apparent in infants.[36]

Vision. No consistent difference had been found between newborn males and females in vision. However, adult men on the average are reported to have better visual acuity from age eighteen to seventy, and men are supposed to have better daylight vision while women have better night vision.[37]

Touch. In a similar fashion, newborn boy and girl babies seem equally sensitive to touch. If soothed with a blanket or soft fabric, both sexes quiet equally well. Neither sex shows any real differences in touch sensitivity when meters measure their skin responses. For older adults, however, there does seem to be a statistical difference showing that women are more sensitive to the stimuli of touch. In one experiment, women reported greater sensitivity to pressure than men did, but the discrimination differed according to body part.[38]

Smell. Most studies have found little difference in the sense of smell among newborn babies.[39] However, several studies on adults have shown differences between men and women in sensitivity to odors, with women showing more sensitivity to musk and various urinary odors. While some of this response may be a learned sensitivity (women wearing perfume), there is also evidence that changes in estrogen levels are associated with sensitivity to smell. The difference in sensitivity appears only after puberty and may decline after menopause.[40]

Taste. The female of the species seems to have more of a sweet tooth than the male. Girl babies increase their sucking rate for sweet solutions, while boy babies do not. Sex hormones also seem to directly affect preference for food, possibly through the mediating factor of blood sugar level. In the premenstrual period, females often report an increased urge for carbohydrates and sweets. Men, in contrast, generally seem to prefer more sour and bitter tastes, such as quinine.[41]

Let us look now at some of the similarities and differences in older boys and girls and men and women. Studies on similarities and differences between the sexes often concentrate on the areas of cognitive abilities and behavior.

Possible Differences in Cognitive Abilities

Verbal Ability. Almost all the research on verbal ability agrees that the average girl exceeds the average boy in verbal ability after about age ten or eleven and scores higher on both simple verbal skills and higher-level tasks, including vocabulary, listening, speaking ability, comprehension of difficult material, creative writing, fluency, and spelling.[42] However, the average differences between the sexes are small. Many of the studies use large samples to establish a statistically significant difference; on the average, girls score only about 5 percent higher than boys.[43]

Research differs on whether or not this verbal advantage develops in early childhood. Maccoby and Jacklin surveyed more than a hundred recent studies and found almost no difference in male and female infants in verbal ability, although females develop their ability sooner.[44] Girls acquire phonemes (the basic speech sounds out of which mature language is built) before boys do and, according to rigorous studies, talk sooner than boys.[45] Girls also lead in developing more complex speech constructions, such as the passive voice, reflexives, and subordinate clauses.[46] Some research indicates that girls talk more than boys and outscore boys on word fluency tests,[47] although this research is dated. Girls seem to articulate more clearly than boys and have many fewer speech disorders. Boys have more speech defects, including stuttering, and more boys than girls have difficulty in learning to read.[48] Girls outperform boys on measures of verbal comprehension and reasoning, and there is some evidence that language plays a greater part in girls' intellectual development.[49] Data from two longitudinal investigations indicate that female-infant scores on various language measures correlate substantially with their subsequent scores on general intelligence measures at ages three to twenty-six.[50] As no such relationship was observed for males, these findings suggest that linguistic skills may be more important in females' than in males' thinking, problem solving, and general intellectual ability.

While this earlier acquisition of language and seemingly greater use of it does not necessarily mean a difference in verbal ability before puberty, in adolescence girls seem to have slightly greater verbal ability. This higher verbal ability helps them on tests like the Scholastic Aptitude Test (SAT) and the Graduate Record Exam (GRE). Interestingly enough, a significant mean difference does exist between how women and men do on the verbal portion of the GRE aptitude test. A recent mean for women was 503, while for men it was 493. Although the difference is small, it is significant at the 0.001 level of probability. Beginning in the 1950s an attempt was made to balance the content of these tests, particularly the SAT, by including items in which males might be more interested. This was done in the hope that the scores might be more balanced between the sexes. However, no attempt was made to balance the even larger difference between the scores of men and women on the mathematical part of the SAT.[51]

Environmental influence seems to affect verbal ability in the same way that it does other specific abilities and general intelligence. Infant girls are talked to and vocally reinforced more often than boys.[52] Mothers may respond to the stereotype of girls talking more. Conversely fathers, and possibly mothers, may spend more time with their boys in physical activity than in verbal interaction. The "mutual socialization" that occurs may shape future skills. Girls who are more independent of their mothers seem to have higher verbal scores, just as independent girls seem to have higher IQ scores.[53] However, boys who are more protected also seemed to have higher verbal ability. This difference in the environment producing greater verbal ability is hard to explain unless we postulate that mothers of children with high verbal abilities give their children more verbal stimulation. Perhaps the protected boy spends more time with his mother and gets this stimulation. In contrast, independent girls not only spend time with their mothers but also have expanding outside experiences that may increase their IQ as well as other abilities.[54]

Cultural expectations with respect to abilities also seem to play an important part in the performance of verbal skills. Johnson reports that girls score higher than boys in reading skills in the United States and Canada, but that boys outscore girls in reading skills in England and Nigeria. In these latter nations, the teachers say they *expect* boys to be better readers.[55]

Mathematical Ability. Boys and girls do equally well in mathematics in the early years; when differences are found, girls outperform boys. However, beginning at about age thirteen, boys seem to increase their mathematical performance more than girls do. As with verbal ability, the difference between the average girl and the average boy is small and depends greatly on two factors: (1) whether the number of math courses taken is accounted for and (2) the general attitude conveyed in the learning situation about math being a male domain.

When older boys and girls are compared without controlling for the number of mathematics courses taken, males do far better than females on measures of performance.[56] However, some of the studies may be based on questionable measures or assumptions. One study that reported large differences in mathematical ability was Benbow and Stanley's 1980 study. They used the SAT and gave this instrument, which measures achievement in high school seniors, to a group of highly talented seventh and eighth graders. They reasoned that the younger children would show potential math ability by their scores. Boys and girls did equally well on the verbal test, but boys scored far better on the math test. To this point the boys and girls had taken the same courses in high school, and both boys and girls scored highly on the tests even when they did not like math. Because of these results, Benbow and Stanley concluded that "sex differences in achievement in mathematics result from superior male mathematical ability, which may in turn be related to greater male ability in spatial tasks."[57] Their conclusions were published in *Science*, excerpted in the *New York Times*, and generally given publicity.

In a critique of the study, Fausto-Sterling points out that (1) the test results were based on a test designed to measure achievement, not aptitude, and (2) attitudes about sex roles might be equally important. She reports that in the research fewer of the talented girls than boys enrolled in accelerated classes, and those that did enroll said they found the classes dull.[58] She also suggests that the conclusion drawn goes far beyond the results of the research, as Benbow and Stanley emphasize inborn factors as a strong cause of the sex differences.

Other studies show that the number of courses taken greatly influences performance in all these tests. The National Assessment of Educational Progress (NAEP) mathematics study done in the spring of 1978 found a significant sex difference in enrollment in and completion of such elective advanced math courses as trigonometry, precalculus, and calculus. The College Entrance Examination Board reported in 1978 that approximately 63 percent of college-bound males, but only 43 percent of the females, had taken four or more years of high school mathematics.[59] Wise, Steel, and MacDonald did a longitudinal study of 400,000 high school students in 1979 to determine differences when controlling for the effect of taking math courses. They found no differences between ninth-grade boys and girls who had had similar amounts of math at that grade level; but three years later the males and females differed significantly. Boys' gains on the test were twice that of females in the three-year period. However, when the number of math courses was held constant, sex differences in "ability" disappeared.[60] In other research, if the number of math courses was controlled, the differences in ability between boys and girls was very small, with boys exceeding girls by only 5 percent, a matter of two test items.[61]

Whether or not mathematics is considered a male domain also influences test score. Fennema and Sherman studied 1,000 boys and girls who were ninth to twelfth graders at four different public high schools in Wisconsin. In two of the schools, boys and girls performed equally well on tests of math and spatial ability, but at the other two schools, the boys performed about 5 percent better than the girls in math. In the two schools where sex-related differences appeared, there were significant differences in parent and teacher attitudes toward math, confidence in ability to learn math, and attitude toward math as a male domain.[62] Fausto-Sterling says, "In fact, if all of the variables affecting math performance were taken into account, less than 2 percent of the achievement difference remained unaccounted for and might, therefore, be considered by some to represent "pure" sex differences (although they too might disappear if earlier childhood experiences were factored in)."[63]

The significance of general background affecting the ability to do math may possibly be seen in the results of the National Assessment of Educational Progress in the spring of 1978. Significant sex differences were found among samples of thirteen- and seventeen-year-olds on some of the subtests in the mathematics achievement assessment. At age thirteen, boys scored higher on the practical applications subtest, but girls scored higher on the computation subtest. No sex difference was found on the computation subtest for seventeen-year-olds, but boys continued to outperform girls on the applications subtest.[64]

Thus, there are many questions about the small (5 percent) difference usually found between boys and girls in mathematical ability after puberty. Several studies have found that achievement test items are biased in favor of boys in terms of content or sex appropriateness and that bias does indeed relate to differential achievement on such tests. The learning and application of mathematical skills outside of school may also be greater for boys than for girls, and boys are likely to improve their achievement scores by taking more and more advanced mathematics classes.[65] In addition, the attitude that math and related occupations such as engineering or physics are male domains may influence the attitude of girls toward enrolling in math classes and doing well in them.[66]

Visual-Spatial Ability.   One of the differences in ability between the sexes that Maccoby and Jacklin believed they established in their review of the literature was the slight superiority of males in being able to manipulate three-dimensional objects in space visually or to perceive differences between a figure and its surrounding background. The second part of the ability is known as *field independence*. A field-independent person can focus on a particular problem and ignore extra elements. Thus, to give an example from a child's puzzle book, such a person could "find the three lions in the picture that are hidden in the forest." It is hypothesized that one of the reasons males may have an edge in advanced mathematics courses is that some of these courses, like geometry and trigonometry, rely on three-dimensional spatial concepts. Boys are also more likely to learn to handle three-dimensional space early in childhood. They have toys that are large and can be manipulated, such as erector sets or various kinds of building tools, and they deal with movement through space when they use sports equipment. In school courses, boys may continue this kind of experience as they do things like put picture frames together in shop.

Various kinds of tests measure the ability to visualize three-dimensional figures. Some of these tests involve mental rotation of objects and description of what a hypothetical third side might look like. In the rod-and-frame test, the subject sits in a totally darkened room and tries to place a lighted rod on the vertical in a tilted frame, ignoring the context of the frame to place the rod vertical in the room. Other tests are tests of embedded figures, like the "lions in the forest."[67]

In most of these kinds of test, men show a slight superiority or there is no difference between the sexes.[68] However, the degree of training in skill-related areas is not held constant in most measures, so it is difficult to know the true degree of difference between males and females in the ability to visualize space. Studies on the performance of first-grade children on embedded figures and blocks tests show small sex differences if the children have not practiced the tasks. With practice, the girls improve their scores much more than the boys do.[69] Children who are allowed more independence, who have varied kinds of experiences, and who have less verbal interaction are more likely to develop strong spatial skills. These criteria dovetail much more with the childhood experiences of boys than with those of girls. Girls who are independent and tomboyish tend to have higher spatial skills than the average girl. Such ability also improves with practice. Teenagers, in one study, show a positive relationship between visual-spatial skill and the number of courses such as drafting and mechanical drawing that they had taken.[70]

Whether the cultural environment demands such skills also seems to be important. Berry compared the ability of the Eskimos, Scots, and Temme people of Sierra Leone in this regard. In the Eskimo culture, where spatial skills are important for survival in a snow-covered environment, no differences between the sexes are found in spatial ability. Where there is no need for high development of these skills (as in the

Temme culture) or where there are distinct male and female role separa-
tions (as in urban-industrial society), differences do exist in the skill displayed by men and women, with men showing a general superiority. The
encouragement of responsibility, self-assertion, and curiosity in a child
also seems to relate to field independence or spatial skills, whereas the
repression of aggression and a stress on discipline and conformity seem
to relate to lack of such ability.[71]

Thus, we can speculate that the environment plays a great role in
the development of visual-spatial skills and that in urban-industrial society the masculine sex role, with its greater manipulation of the physical
environment and encouragement of curiosity and responsibility, gives
more practice in the use of those skills.

Actually, only a few studies have been done on the role played by
the environment in the acquisition of spatial skills. Most studies have
concentrated on the possibility that spatial abilities and related mathematical ability are genetically carried, linked to sex hormones, and/or
linked to the way in which information is processed by the brain. These
theories, which are discussed below, have gained great popularity but
have received little substantiation by research.

Theories Explaining Sex-Differentiated Cognitive Abilities

The X-Linked Gene Theory. Stafford proposed a theory of sex-linked
inheritance of intellectual abilities in 1961. He postulated that two different genes, one for high spatial ability and one for mathematical ability,
were placed on the X chromosome. As in the case of recessive disorders
like hemophilia, the female can carry the gene but not evidence the ability or the disorder. This is because the female's other X chromosome,
which lacks the gene, is powerful enough to mask the ability or disorder
carried on the recessive X. The female must inherit two recessive X chromosomes (those with the gene) to evidence the trait. In contrast, the male
needs to inherit only one recessive X chromosome to evidence the ability
or the disorder, as the more fragile Y chromosome will not mask the recessive gene. If Stafford's hypothesis that math and spatial ability are
"recessive" traits and carried on genes is correct, then we would expect
more males than females to have high math and spatial ability because
they would have a greater chance of demonstrating a recessive trait. We
could make certain mathematical predictions of parent-child *correlations* in
ability if this hypothesis were true. However, research has failed to sub-
stantiate the predicted correlations. The one study that shows a high
father-son correlation in mathematical ability could easily be explained by
noninheritance factors.[72] Some other small studies done before 1975 seem
to support the X-linked hypothesis, but recent research with larger sam-

ples has failed to do so. Fausto-Sterling quotes one researcher as concluding, "Since the previous evidence from small studies cannot be replicated, it appears that the X-linkage hypothesis is no longer tenable."[73] She also points out that if the hypothesis were correct, girls with Turner's syndrome and only one X chromosome should show a higher than average female incidence of spatial ability. In fact the opposite is true: those with Turner's syndrome have noted deficits in spatial ability.[74]

Hormones and the Abilities. Theories about hormones and the sexes are divided into two categories: those that link hormones to activating a particular gene, such as the one described in Stafford's inheritance hypothesis, and those that deal with the activating nature of hormones by themselves. Theories postulating that sex hormones activate sex-linked genes are called *sex limited*, as the trait is limited to those who possess high levels of a particular sex hormone as well as the gene in question. (An example of a sex-limited trait is baldness, which is almost only found in men because its expression depends on high testosterone levels *and* a "baldness" gene.)[75] According to this theory as applied to sex-differentiated abilities, math and spatial abilities are carried on the genes of both sexes but activated only by male hormones. However, in androgen-insensitive patients, those raised as males score above the normal range on spatial tests, while those raised as females score lower, though in the normal range. If the expression of spatial ability depends on high levels of male hormones, then the patients who were raised as males but are insensitive to male hormones should have low scores.[76] Thus, we can probably safely discard theories about hormones activating genes that express math or spatial ability.

Hormones and Intelligence. What about the role of sex hormones in facilitating the particular abilities in which each sex may show a slight superiority? Some researchers have hypothesized that the varying verbal and spatial abilities of the sexes are linked to sex hormones because these abilities seem to spurt ahead at puberty, when the hormones are activated. When Money and Lewis studied androgenital syndrome patients, they discovered that many of their patients had an IQ significantly higher than the population average and that this higher IQ was present in spite of sex, class, or treatment differences. They postulated that the higher IQ might result from the circulation in the blood of high levels of androgen during the time of fetal development. (As males usually have higher circulating levels of prenatal androgen, one could assume that males are predisposed to be more intelligent, although Money and his colleagues drew no such conclusions.) Other studies using control groups seemed to support their conclusion and pointed to the possible effect of androgen on the behavior of the girls studied as well.[77]

Finally, Ehrhardt and Baker designed a reexamination of androgenital patients in which they used sisters and brothers of the affected children as *controls*. In this study, they found that for some reason whole families scored above the general population norm for IQ. They also showed that the androgenital patients scored lower on a general test of mathematical skill than their sisters and brothers, although they scored equally well on verbal and visual-spatial tests.[78]

Thus, in the case of girls and boys with androgenital syndrome, sex hormones do not seem to be linked to spatial ability. We know, in addition, that males who have high mathematical ability frequently do not appear to have the masculine body build that might be linked with high hormone levels, and that very masculine-appearing males have high verbal-fluency scores but not necessarily high math scores.[79] In addition, the male with high mathematical ability may evidence a number of characteristics that are not congruent with the masculine sex role as it is usually conceived. He is usually low on dominance, aggression, and autonomy and high on the need for affiliation.[80]

In contrast, field-independent boys and girls in another study both showed characteristics often associated with the masculine role. Aggression was highly correlated with field independence. Field-independent boys were rated by their teachers as being the toughest and most aggressive boys, and field-independent girls played boys' games. However, if boys were field *dependent*, they were likely to have extreme cross-sex interests, such as playing with dolls. In an interesting sidelight to the experiment, Nash found that the more masculine view an adolescent boy or girl had of himself or herself, the better his or her spatial performance. The spatial ability of the girls who preferred to be boys was equal to that of the boys.[81] Thus, there may be a real question of whether hormones are acting or whether preference for the male role and experiencing male type of activities influence field independence.

A second theory relating hormones and sex differences is the one proposed by Broverman and his colleagues. They postulate that there are two different and opposite cognitive styles. In the *automatization* style, a person can do very well on practiced, or learned, tasks that require a minimum of conscious effort to perform. The second style, called *cognitive restructuring,* requires the inhibition of automatic responses to familiar stimuli in order to respond to something new. In this style, one might not repeat an old way of doing a puzzle but might try a new one instead. Broverman and his colleagues believe that individuals who do well on one kind of task do poorly on the other. They theorize that the sex hormones, estrogen and testosterone, aid an automated style of cognition, but that estrogen is more potent, so that women do better on these kinds of tasks; conversely, men do better on restructured, creative kinds of tasks. This theory, of course, has led many people to infer that men are more creative and should do creative work, while women are best limited to repetitive, overlearned tasks like typing.[82]

The theory is not supported by experimental evidence and has other problems as well. Few data support the influence of hormones. Tasks grouped in the categories of automatization and cognitive restructuring hardly seem to reflect the automatization or restructured style. Automatization style, for example, includes women's verbal skills, reading, and writing, which are hardly repetitive, overlearned tasks. Males also do better only on visual-spatial restructuring tasks; in verbal restructuring tasks, like anagrams, females excel.[83]

In another study designed to test hormone levels and performance on visual-spatial and verbal tasks, Peterson compared the performance of thirty-five males and fifty females on both types of task with their degree of secondary sex development. She compared each subject at ages thirteen, sixteen, and eighteen. She found no relationship between performance and secondary sex characteristics for the subjects at the younger ages, but at age eighteen she found that males who had highly masculine secondary sex characteristics (deep voices, body hair) had high verbal fluency and poor spatial ability. For females the results showed highly developed secondary sex characteristics related to poor spatial ability but not to verbal ability.[84] Thus, *if* you can assume that levels of hormones are consistent with developed secondary sex characteristics, there may be partial support for Broverman's theory in Peterson's study: high levels of hormones seem to inhibit spatial ability. This does not, however, directly relate to automated or restructuring styles of cognition, and even if secondary sex characteristics are consistent with certain abilities, it is also possible that social norms are operating to develop abilities consistent with gender role.

Sex Hormones and Brain Development. A division of the sex hormone theory is that hormones influence abilities by influencing the development of the brain. When we talk about the possibility that sex hormones (and other hormones) affect brain development, we are often dealing with new and untested theories. Many theories about the development of male and female brains are connected to the fact that the human brain has a right and a left hemisphere, each of which processes information in a slightly different fashion. In nearly all right-handed people and in about two-thirds of left-handers, the right hemisphere specializes in spatial or nonlinguistic operations and in general, overall "gestalts," or total pictures, when processing information. The left hemisphere specializes in logical, analytical analysis of information, with verbal labeling and taking into account details and time variables. The similarity of the different hemispheric modes of processing information to the slightly different verbal and spatial skills of women and men has led researchers to hypothesize that gender, through the medium of hormones, is related to slightly different development of the hemispheres of the brain in each sex.

Hypotheses regarding gender and intellectual ability are based not only on studies of human behavior, like the ones described above, but also on animal and brain research. Some studies show differences in nerve connections in male and female rat brains. Others show that animals of one sex, when given injections of hormones from the other sex, develop skills different from those of similar animals of their own gender. In humans, there is new information about electrical wave differences in male and female brains as a response to certain stimuli.[85] Let us look briefly at some of these studies.

Research on Animals. An English team of scientists found differences in the nerve connections in male and female rat brains, and they traced this development to the influence of hormones. When newborn male rats were castrated during the critical period when sex hormones circulate in the fetus, they developed a female pattern of nerve connections. When newborn female rats were given testosterone during the critical period, they developed a male pattern of nerve connections.[86]

Other research seems to indicate that these nerve connections and later brain development may have an effect on abilities. Male rats run mazes better than female rats. However, when female rats were given male hormones during their critical period (and developed a male pattern of nerve connections in the brain), they ran the mazes like male rats.[87] Female rats usually learn other behaviors faster than the males. One researcher taught rats to go to the other end of a box when a light went on; otherwise, they would get an electric shock. Females picked up the trick sooner than males.[88] If the females received the male hormones during the critical period, however, their performance got worse; similarly, castrated male rats learned as rapidly as females. Thus nerve connections in the brain and abilities of rats may be linked to their sex hormones.

Research on Human Brains. A study at the National Institute of Mental Health used electroencephalographs and computers to analyze the brain's electrical response to stimuli of light and sound. These responses to stimuli can be seen in brain wave form and size, which vary according to the intensity of the stimulus and the degree of interest that the stimulus arouses in the individual. Buchsbaum discovered that women in general have a greater response to stimuli (lights, sounds, or shocks) than men do; this holds true for every sense tested, especially at the higher levels of intensity. Women's brains react more to all stimuli. It is believed that this more intense reaction to stimuli in women is related to high levels of estrogen, which in turn supress another hormone, monoamine oxidase (MAO). Low amounts of MAO mean more nerve transmission and more response to stimuli. The difference is not great, but it accounts for some of the differences in amount of reaction to stimuli.[89] One group of researchers base their contention that hormones cause differential male and female brain development on other differences in the growth patterns of boys and girls. Because the left foot is larger than the right in females, and the right foot is larger than the left in males, the researchers have proposed that the right and left sides of the brain might develop differently in males and females. There has been little research, however, to support their theory directly.[90]

In another study, Marylou Reid of the University of Massachusetts has used tests of neurological performance to determine verbal and spatial abilities in boys and girls five and eight years old. Right-handed girls developed the left hemisphere of their brains more quickly than their right and moved ahead in verbal skills. Right-handed boys developed their right hemispheres more quickly than their left and advanced in spatial abilities. However, in left-handers the reverse was true. The maturation pattern was the same: girls developed the left hemisphere more quickly, but in this case spatial skills developed first. Boys developed the right hemisphere more quickly, but verbal skills developed first.[91]

Abilities and Brain Lateralization. There is a general agreement that the two hemispheres of the brain are not specialized at birth and that specialization—and subsequent transfer of information—occurs later. Some believe that such specialization is complete by the age of five;[92] others, that it is not complete until adolescence. Some believe that the age of maturation (puberty) affects the degree of specialization and the use of subsequent verbal and spatial skills.[93]

The theory that the brain processes information in slightly different ways in men and women is connected to the idea of *brain lateralization;* that is, the ability of the brain to transfer information from one side to the other. In normal people, the two hemispheres are connected by a membrane called the corpus callosum. Messages received in one hemisphere can be transferred to another to aid in the processing of information. Occasionally as a treatment for extreme epilepsy, the corpus callosum is surgically cut. In people treated this way, messages cannot be sent from one hemisphere to the other. We have learned a great deal about the specialization of each hemisphere of the brain from such people and from others who have specific hemispheric damage.

The Old Theory: Women Specialize More. Many theories have developed to suggest that men and women combine the use of the hemispheres of the brain differently. Some of the theories, however, contradict each other on how the combination of information takes place. Buffer and Gray originally posited a theory that women develop their left hemispheres sooner than men do and specialize in interpreting verbal information in the left hemisphere and spatial information in the right hemisphere. They believed that if this specialization occurred, it would hurt spatial performance but help verbal abilities. They claimed that linguistic skills required "rapid associations which could most efficiently occur if all the nerve cells involved lay close together," as in the supposed left-hemisphere specialization of women. They also claimed that spatial skills were more efficient if information was shared between the hemispheres, but the reason why this should be so is not clear.[94] However, this theory describing the supposed hemisphere specialization by women and its consequences has largely been discredited as new experimental evidence seems to show that, on the contrary, women specialize less in the functions of the brain hemispheres than men do.

The New Theory: Women Specialize Less. Several pieces of new research have supported the theory of *less* specialization by women. In one study of accident victims, only men showed specific verbal deficits after left-hemisphere damage or specific spatial deficits after right-side damage to the brain. Women showed less severe losses in either verbal or spatial skills no matter which side of the brain was damaged. Jennette McGlone at University Hospital in Ontario thus believes that a woman's spatial and verbal abilities are more likely duplicated on both sides of her brain, while a right-handed man is more likely to have his speech center on the left and spatial skills on the right.[95]

Another experiment tested 200 right-handed boys and girls between the ages of six and fourteen and found that the girls did equally well recognizing spatial objects with both hands, while the boys did significantly better with their left hand. (The right side of the brain operates the left side of the body, and vice versa.)[96] Studies of braille learning seem to indicate that girls have more *bilateral representation* of spatial processing than do boys.[97] There are also higher correlations between verbal and spatial performances in females than in males.[98]

If one accepts the findings that women process both visual and spatial information on both sides of the brain, whereas men are more specialized, many inferences can be drawn. Several different theories have been put forward, but many of these theories are incompatible with one another.

Jerre Levy has suggested that this *lack* of specialization by women, or their supposed tendency to transfer information from one hemisphere to another, may be the reason for women's slightly poorer spatial abilities. She suggests that the dual processing of information may mean that the primary function of the hemisphere is interfered with; in particular, women may have poorer processing of spatial information because of the "spillover" of verbal processing into that hemisphere. However, as in the case of Buffrey and Gray's theory, there are inconsistencies. Even if one accepts the idea of more processing of information on both sides of the brain in women, the second part of Levy's hypothesis—that the primary function of a hemisphere may be interfered with by a secondary function—has no support. Levy's theory would not account for the greater verbal skill of women; it would imply that women are less skilled in both verbal and spatial areas.[99]

One study attempted to relate hemispheric specialization and the cognitive abilities in boys and girls directly to the rate of body maturation. Waber found that late maturers of both sexes were better at spatial tasks than early maturing children of the same sex; no relationship existed between verbal skill and time of maturation. She hypothesized that the difference in spatial ability was related to degree of specialization of the brain hemisphere and that late maturers had more specialization. In diotic listening tasks designed to measure whether one or both hemispheres were functioning, she did find that late maturers were more specialized than early maturers. Boys are more likely to be late maturers and thus have more specialization of function in brain hemispheres. However, she found no sex differences among children who were early or late in maturation.[100] In other words, if some girls were late in maturing, they were also more likely to be specialized in hemisphere functioning.

Still More Theories.   Still other theories suggest that dual processing of information does not necessarily occur in women.[101] The theories postulate that females may simply develop a preference for a left-brained verbal approach and use linguistic strategies to solve spatial problems.[102] This belief conflicts somewhat with our evidence from accident victims or the way that male and female children transfer sensory information about three-dimensional objects to the brain. The truth is that we still do not know whether each sex uses the hemispheres of the brain differently or, if they do, whether this difference relates to any type of verbal or spatial skill.

Therefore, at present, while there may be some effect of sex hormones on the brain, we do not know whether sex hormones are really affecting the brain and, if they are, how they are exercising their effect. We do not know whether any effect begins at birth, is activated at puberty, or never exists at all. We do not know whether any kind of hemispheric brain specialization is related to hormones or to the ability to perform different kinds of tasks. We do not know for certain whether such brain specialization even exists or is different for each sex. As one researcher stated, "One must not overlook perhaps the most obvious conclusion, which is that basic patterns of male and female brain asymmetry seem to be more similar than they are different."[103]

The effects of environment certainly seem to be greater than any biological predisposition. If brains are specialized, it is the environment that increases the repertoire of skills for each sex; it is also the environment that gives us reinforcement for and practice in using various kinds of information. As Kimball has pointed out, a disproportionate amount of energy seems to have been spent on biological explanations that have very little evidence to support them.

Are There Behavioral Differences?

Aggression. It is frequently asserted that the one sex difference that has been established is aggression. Yet discussing aggression as a sex difference is difficult because even defining aggression is a problem. Aggression can be physical, verbal, or ritualized, as in the playing of a football game. Even when we limit the definition to physical aggression, it is difficult to differentiate things like rough-and-tumble play from actual aggressive acts. This definition problem affects any determination of sex differences or similarities in aggression. Boys may be more likely to engage in physically active behavior and thus are more likely to be defined as aggressive. Aggression also varies according to what a culture defines as aggressive and whether one includes "ritualized" aggression. The degree of behavior defined as aggressive is almost certain to vary as well according to whether or not a particular culture rewards aggression for one gender or the other.[104]

In spite of these problems, Maccoby and Jacklin claim that, with the exception of maternal aggressiveness, the male of all species is, on average, more likely to engage in almost all kinds of aggressive behavior. They believe this is true in all human societies for which evidence is available and that differences in aggression are often found early in life, at a time when there has been little chance for much differential socialization. Aggressive behavior seems to be related to levels of sex hormones, and the degree of aggressive behavior can be changed by changing the level of these hormones. Many researchers concur with Maccoby and Jacklin that there is a sex difference in aggression in all species, including humans; that this difference is particularly influenced by prenatal sex hormones and again by sex hormones at puberty; and that the male of each species tends to be more aggressive under more conditions than the female.[105]

Animal Studies. Much of the research on aggression as a possible sex difference has been done on animals because of the problems of separating out the effects of socialization in humans. We must remember that humans are much more complicated organisms than are mice or monkeys, and all findings in animals will not be applicable to humans; but some animal studies raise intriguing questions for us about the relationship between hormones and aggressive behavior.

In the animal kingdom, prenatal androgens seem to program aggressive behavior in both the female and the male of several species, particularly rodents. There is a critical period when the androgen must circulate in the brain and exert its effect. This period varies for each species. Usually, aggressive behavior is not evident until puberty, when additional doses of the male sex hormone "activate" the behavior. Female rats prenatally treated with androgens during the critical period will not develop aggressive behavior unless they are also treated at puberty. Female rats that do not receive prenatal hormones but are treated at puberty increase in aggressiveness, but not as much as those that are treated both times.[106] In one experiment, male rats that did not produce testosterone did not develop aggressive behavior. When testosterone pellets were implanted in them, aggressiveness appeared; when the pellets were removed, it disappeared again.[107] Excessive doses of estrogen will have the same effect of stimulating aggression in female rats, but the effect will not appear in male rats. In male rats, the administration of estrogen seems to significantly reduce aggressive activity.[108]

Interaction effects may also occur between behavior and levels of hormones. It was found that low-dominance male rats placed with rats they could dominate developed higher levels of androgen. Conversely, after an animal was defeated in a fight, the androgen level went down and stayed low. Thus, aggressive behavior seems to stimulate a higher level of male hormones.

Some who have studied primates have also concluded that aggression is related to hormone levels, not to socialization. Other researchers, however, believe that aggression and dominance are not universal; they cite many problems with the primate studies, including the small number of monkeys used in many studies and the difficulties in defining dominance and dominance-related behavior as well as in connecting such behavior to hormones. For example, in many cases of dominance, body size rather than hormones may be operating.[109]

In addition, some of what is defined as aggression in the animal kingdom may be ritualized behavior to establish territory, sexual rights, and other kinds of dominance. Among fallow deer, rival stags may engage in vigorous fighting. Their encounters are antler-to-antler charges, however, and the attack is never directed against other vulnerable body sections. In the same way, giraffes may engage in neck-to-neck pushing and shoving matches, but they reserve their sharp hooves for defense against predators.[110]

Human research on hormone level and aggressiveness has been limited. Frequently, hormone levels are inferred by degree of secondary sex characteristics rather than directly measured. In other studies where levels have been measured, a particular environment may have influenced aggressiveness. For example, studies on prisoners found no connection between hormone levels of prisoners and their verbal aggressiveness or fighting behavior in prison. Yet prisoners with higher androgen levels had committed more violent crimes during adolescence.[111] In studies such as this one, aggressiveness may have been influenced by the environment, and the studies lack comparison control groups.

It is also difficult to control for the influence of a particular cultural environment. Although Maccoby and Jacklin claim that differences in aggression are found in children too young to be exposed to socialization pressures, this claim has been disputed. Fausto-Sterling points out that in the studies with children up to the age of five, half the studies showed no sex-related differences, and that the observers knew the sex of the children and the behavior they were looking for. In addition, it is difficult to separate out particular cultural influences.[112] Thus, substantiating observational evidence about aggressiveness in humans with clinical studies and experiments poses serious problems.

Female Aggression. While more males of all species are aggressive under more conditions, in maternal situations females of many species demonstrate an unusually high degree of aggression. A few days before giving birth, the female mouse may be so aggressive that she will kill any males invading her territory. Female grizzly bears with cubs account for 82 percent of all bear attacks on hikers and campers in the national parks of Canada and the United States, and many other species also show ferocious maternal behavior. Usually the maternal aggression is in response to some sort of perceived threat to the young. As the mother gets farther from her young, the tendency to be aggressive diminishes. It also changes as the levels of hormones associated with birth and nursing change.[113]

Some Questions About the Relative Influence of Heredity and Environment

Male Hormones and Cycles

Some of the fascinating information gleaned from studies like those on aggression and other behavior concerns the cyclical nature of moods and the relationship of those moods to hormones. Many of the studies have attempted to document the variation of male moods, including aggressive behavior, with the ebb and flow of hormones. In Denmark, a careful sixteen-year study was conducted in which the subjects showed a fluctuation of hormone levels that approximated a thirty-day cycle.[114] Other studies have shown twenty-one-hour peaks and lows in testosterone. Although men tend to deny that their moods fluctuate in a cyclical way that may be connected to hormone levels, other studies seem to indicate that they do. A study done on factory workers that included physical examinations, four-times-a-day interviews, and interviews with families showed that emotions varied within a twenty-four-hour cycle and within a larger monthly cycle of four to six weeks. High periods were marked by a feeling of well-being and energy, while low periods were marked by apathy, indifference, and a tendency to see little problems as disproportionately large.[115] Mary Brown Parlee, in a small sample of fifteen men, found variations in moods that were remarkably consistent for each man over a three-month period. The cycles, however, varied in length from man to man and according to the mood measured. Unfortunately, in the two experiments cited hormone levels were not measured, so connections of mood to various hormone levels could not be assessed.[116]

One experiment by a team of medical researchers at Stanford in 1975 examined the relationship between testosterone cycles and possible accompanying moods. Testosterone levels in twenty men were measured for sixty days, and the men filled out self-reports of moods every other day. The experiment found cycles in testosterone levels ranging from three to thirty days; for several of the men, the cycles were clustered around the twentieth- to twenty-second-day mark. The study found no correlation between hormone cycles and moods, however.[117] Thus we know that men do have cycles of hormones and cycles of moods. How much the two cycles interact and how much they are affected by other things like circadian, or time, cycles or environmental factors are still open questions.

Female Hormones and Cycles

Over history, the menstrual cycle has caused strong cultural reactions. Many societies look upon the menstruating woman with fear, thinking that she somehow has at this time evil or magical powers. Many societies isolate menstruating women and prohibit them from preparing food or dealing with hunting implements. Fausto-Sterling reports that as recently as 1940, Frenchmen barred menstruating women from picking mushrooms for commerical use, from handling fermenting wine, or from working in perfumeries.[118] More recently still, the personal physician of a president of the United States said that the "raging hormones" of women at this time of the month make them unfit for holding high governmental office. As we will see in chapter 6, our contemporary culture still holds many negative ideas about the menses. Women call it "the curse," several religions forbid husbands to have intercourse with a menstruating wife, and a whole list of symptoms is associated with the menstrual period and the days just before it begins. Among the commonly reported symptoms are water-retention, cramping, fatigue, irritability, anxiety, paranoia, and the likelihood of crying more easily.[119]

Because the menstrual cycle is a cycle of hormone highs and lows, many researchers have associated premenstrual symptoms with the level of hormones in the body. They have asked women to keep daily diaries of their moods or list all the symptoms they have encountered during the premenstrual days and have concluded that women have more elated, positive moods at midcycle, when estrogen and progesterone are high, and depressed moods during the premenstrual days, when levels of progesterone and estrogen fall dramatically.

However, findings about the supposed levels of female hormones confuse us. Women in the early months of pregnancy, when estrogen levels are high, also experience symptoms similar to the premenstrual "blues" when estrogen is low. Women taking the contraceptive pill (which keeps these hormones levels from fluctuating so widely) still report mood cycles. Girls who have not yet begun to menstruate also report twenty-eight-day cycles of moods.[120]

The studies that give us our information about premenstrual symptoms also have many problems. One major problem is that hormone levels are always inferred and not measured. Few studies offer control populations, and most studies rely on self-reports of their subjects. Many direct questionnaires use mainly negative items to measure premenstrual mood. Thus, it is not at all clear whether premenstrual symptoms are directly related to hormone levels and/or whether the negative cultural expectations for that time of the month lead women to experience symptoms in line with the negative expectations.[121]

In addition, gynecology texts state that behavioral events may affect the menstrual cycle, as in the case of stress delaying or precipitating it.[122] Alice Rossi seems to confirm that behavioral events can affect the menstrual cycle in her study of forty college women. She found that the periods of sexually experienced women seldom began on the weekend. In contrast, the periods of inexperienced women began on the weekend much more often than chance alone would have predicted. Many of the sexually inexperienced women said they had not expected their period on the weekend, but it had come early or late, perhaps conveniently in time for them to fend off any sexual advances, guesses Rossi.[123]

In the same study Rossi found that some of the women demonstrated mood cycles that correlated with their menstrual cycle, but that the great majority of women showed no consistent pattern of mood connected with menstruation. In fact, there is a question of what cycle was operating for many of these women. Rossi found that weekly cycles operated for both men and women, with highs on the weekends and lows in the middle of the week.[124]

Thus, moods of both men and women may be influenced by factors other than hormones alone, such as environmental conditions and daily time cycles. The interaction among age, daily cycles of temperature and hormones, and weekly cycles connected with work and play and hormones has never been fully explored. Future research should add fascinating information about such interaction.

Influence of Heredity and Environment on Other Possible Differences

Activity level. Other physical differences may be related to physical states and possibly to the behavior of aggression itself. Some of the evidence about possible sex differences in activity level has been contradictory. Such differences do not show up in infancy, but when significant results are found after the age of social play, boys are usually found to be more active than girls. Boys also seem to show more curiosity and exploratory behavior, according to Maccoby and Jacklin.[125] Whether this is because of higher metabolism rates and greater energy expenditure and/or because of social reinforcement for exploratory behavior among boys is an interesting question that has not been settled by research.

Dominance and Competition. Dominance and competition are two other social behaviors that have been linked to aggression and have sometimes been considered to show differences between the sexes. While dominance can stem from aggression, there are many kinds of dominance. For example, one can dominate by greater skill or by manipulation. Maccoby and Jacklin report that while there are no significant sex differences in dominance, dominance seems to be more of an issue in boys' groups, and boys make more attempts to dominate each other. However, because younger children usually play in sex-segregated groups, boys make fewer attempts to dominate girls. Maccoby and Jacklin report that in adult groups, formal leadership tends to go to males in the beginning of any interaction, but as the relationship continues, influence becomes more nearly equal between the sexes. Thus, there is a real question of whether any legitimate difference in dominance exists between the sexes. Any differences that do appear seem to be highly influenced by cultural norms.[126]

There is mixed evidence about any sex differences in competition. Some studies show boys to be more competitive, but many studies show the sexes to be similar in competitive level. Boys seem to need a stimulus to compete, but when aroused, they sustain a higher level of competition than girls. Girls seem to care less about competition but will try hard when put into a competitive situation. Some studies have postulated that girls avoid competitive situations because they do not want to disrupt social relationships, but this hypothesis has received only mixed support. Girls seem to try equally as hard as boys in the presence or absence of supportive comments, as well. Much of the observed difference in competitiveness may be due to social role. Traditionally in our culture, boys have been expected to compete; this competition is part of the masculine sex role and masculine self-image. Girls, in contrast, have not until recently been urged to enter much competition and have not received rewards for competing.[127] With the growing popularity of sports for women and as women enter varied occupations, this picture may change.

Fear, Timidity, and Anxiety. In observations of fearfulness, researchers do not usually find that girls are any more fearful than boys; however, girls are more willing to admit fear and anxiety. Some have suggested that this greater willingness to admit fear leads to avoidance of situations where the conquering of fear could result. The girl who stands at the top of a ski slope and says she is afraid to go down may never try the slope and conquer her fear; the boy who cannot admit his fear and must go down the slope to preserve his self-image may find that the fearful situation is not so bad. Boys and girls both report boys as more exploratory and assertive than girls.[128] Girls have also been reported as more anxious for social approval. The evidence supporting this social-anxiety hypothesis is mixed, although girls score higher on measures of social desirability and compliance to adults at younger ages. Block suggests that this may "be an effective strategy for warding off anxiety due to the possible disapproval of peers or adults."[129]

Nurturance and Maternal Behavior. The question continues as to whether the ability to nurture and care for young infants is an area where inheritance and instinct play a dominant role or whether nurturing behavior is primarily learned. With the recent changes in sex roles and the controversy about whether men are able to care for children as well as women do, looking at research on maternal behavior is particularly important.

No evidence exists for a maternal *instinct* of any sort, although hormones may play some role in stimulating maternal behavior (at least in animals), as may critical periods of interaction with a newborn. Recent studies of human infants and their mothers and fathers seem to show that mother/father–child bonds are strongest when the parents can hold the child and care for it immediately after birth.[130] However, most researchers believe that the response to infants is learned rather than instinctive, because not all mothers exhibit this maternal behavior, even when in constant contact with their infants after birth. History has recorded many cases of mothers killing unwanted babies, and child-abuse cases have always been frequent and are coming more and more to public attention today.

Researchers also believe that nurturing is learned because males may exhibit this behavior. While male rats are often initially cannibalistic, they will frequently develop nurturing behavior if given successive litters of baby rats to care for. While little research has been done on the nurturing potential of human fathers, men who care for infants seem to establish the same close bonds with them that females do,[131] and many men seem willing to exhibit nurturing feelings if they can do so without public disapproval. In one experiment on androgyny, men who did not define themselves as "macho" were quite willing to play with a small kitten or a baby; in fact, they played more with the kitten or baby than women who defined themselves as "stereotypically feminine."[132]

The fact that maternal, nurturing behavior is probably learned can also be inferred from cross-cultural studies. Such behavior is not usually found in very young children of either sex, and when it does occur it does not differ by sex. In one cross-cultural study that compared children in Kenya, India, Okinawa, the Philippines, and Mexico, there was no difference in nurturing behavior among three-to-six-year-olds. In seven-to-eleven-year-olds, however, the girls offered more help to younger children and gave them more emotional support.[133] "This additional nurturing behavior evidenced by females seems to be a result of our society's encouragement of nurturance as a feminine quality." In the Gurin, Veroff, and Feld study of a national sample of American women, many women mentioned nurturance as a desirable feminine trait that they would like in their personalities.[134] Nurturing by men has been regarded in our culture as somewhat unmasculine, at least until recently.

Myths About Differences

In certain instances, societal myths perpetuate belief in specific differences between the sexes, such as the belief that women are sociable rather than rational or that they are not as creative as men are. Such beliefs, however, have been thoroughly disproved by research.

Intelligence, Creativity, and Styles of Analytic Behavior

As noted above, no difference exists between the sexes in overall intelligence or in analytic ability. Whether one defines males or females as more analytic or more creative depends on the kind of test used. While men excel in visual-spatial restructuring, women excel in verbal problem-solving tasks. There is no evidence to support the contentions that women are better at overlearned, rote kinds of tasks and that men do better in creative, analytical situations. Nor does either sex seem to differ in inhibiting impulsive responses and building on past experiences.[135]

Are girls less rational or logical than boys? We often hear that females are not logical; yet neither sex seems to have an advantage in terms of reasoning and concept mastery. Only in tests directly using mathematical processes do males seem to have any edge in reasoning. In creativity tests measuring the "ability to produce unique and novel ideas," girls seem to show a slight superiority to boys from age seven on, but this may be because of verbal fluency.[136]

Achievement Orientation and Self-esteem

Women seem to have as great an achievement motivation as men do and to be as persistent in attempts to achieve their goals. However, the goals that motivate achievement may be different for the sexes. To some degree women may be more interested in goals that relate to social interaction, and the basis for women's self-esteem also seems to be in different areas. Women are more likely to feel good about their interpersonal skills rather than about concrete achievements.

Although women's general self-esteem seems to be as high as that of men, some evidence shows that women do not feel as good as men do about their specific abilities. They do not expect to do as well as men on problem-solving tasks, in spite of past ability. They rate masculine qualities higher than those considered feminine, and they rate work believed to be done by men as better than work believed to be done by women. When women fail, they are more likely to blame their failures on lack of ability, while males blame their failures on lack of motivation or bad luck. Men who succeed believe they have done so by virtue of their own ability, while women who succeed often believe they have been lucky.[137] Block reports that over the period from age eighteen to age twenty-six, "females studied longitudinally lost self-confidence, while males at the same age developed a greater sense of competence."[138]

Sociability

Little evidence seems to support the contention that girls are more sociable than boys. At early ages, girls have no more preference than boys do for being with people or for toys representing faces or people. Girls are also more likely at slightly older ages to play in smaller groups than boys, and while their friendships seem to be based on more intimacy than those of most boys, girls are equally likely to exclude strangers from their group.[139]

Although Maccoby and Jacklin did discover that girls and women were more interested in social activities than males and that girls devel-

oped an earlier interest in the other sex, girls and boys were equally interested in social stimuli and equally responsive to social rewards. They
were also equally sensitive to social cues. When asked to examine a series
of pictures and to tell what the central character was feeling, girls were
better at identifying the feelings of female characters; and boys, the feelings of male characters.[140]

However, some researchers have found that girls seem to be more
emphathetic than boys, that they seem to be able to interpret nonverbal
cues and discern emotions more accurately.[141] Bem also found in her androgyny studies on college-aged women that women who accepted beliefs concerning traditional female roles were more likely to be able to de-
code feelings in others.[142] Perhaps because of the social stereotypes that
women are empathetic and more social, traditional women believe that
knowledge of and sympathy for the feelings of others are what they
"ought" to have and thus are more tuned in to obtaining these feelings.
Females are also probably rewarded more than males for empathetic
behavior.

Some of the "myth of sociability" may lie in how much emotions
are shown. Girls seem to learn to suppress their negative emotions more
than boys do so that they may seem more "sociable." After eighteen
months, boys show more anger than girls, because girls decrease the
number and intensity of their outbursts.[143] Boys may be allowed to express more anger and frustration because parents believe this to be evidence of their spirit and strength, while girls are taught to suppress anger
and act in nice, sociable ways.

Suggestibility and Passivity

There is no evidence that girls are more suggestible than boys, in spite of
pervasive myths to that effect. Maccoby and Jacklin find that "the two
sexes are equally susceptible to persuasive communications, and in face-
to-face situations where there is a social pressure to conform to a group
judgment about an ambiguous situation, there are usually no sex
differences."[144]

Maccoby and Jacklin point out that although boys and men seem to
be more aggressive, females are not passive victims of aggression. When
faced with aggression action, they do not withdraw any more in childhood than males do. While boys seem on the average to be more likely to
have strenuous bursts of physical activity, girls are not idly sitting by (in
spite of what the school books tell us); they are playing more quietly, but
in an organized and planned fashion. Maccoby and Jacklin point out that
girls impose their own ideas on the environment as much as boys do.
When both sexes are given equal freedom to explore a new environment,
they are both likely to do so. The great majority of evidence seems to

show little difference in passivity between females and males, at least in the early years.[145]

Thus, we see that many of the differences that we have over the years attributed to men and women are nothing more than well-established social myths. In other cases, some possible differences may exist in personality traits or in abilities of one kind or another, but the differences seem to be based almost completely on social learning. Only in the cases of aggression, verbal ability, and mathematical and visual-spatial abilities is there any consensus that some differences exist between the sexes; and even here, the differences are "average" differences and are very small. Similarities in these areas are much larger than any differences. In many cases where a difference is found, it is largely based on what society expects and rewards—as in the case of boys doing well at math and girls doing well at verbal tasks.

A classic example of how cultures can influence behavior by their definitions of what is masculine and what is feminine is given in Margaret Mead's book *Sex and Temperament*.[146] Her description of three "primitive" cultures in New Guinea shows us how their concept of the ideal sex role varies drastically from ours. In the Arapesh culture, both men and women are raised to be nurturant. The dominant ethic of the culture is to "grow" things, and this includes young human beings. The responsibility for such growing is shared among men and women in the culture. While the women do more of the actual child care, the men are expected to be nurturing and maternal/paternal in nature. Even before a child is born, the father is considered to be participating in the growth of the fetus by contributing his sperm to the mother's blood, and he participates in pre- and postbirth rituals. Neither sex is supposed to demonstrate aggression, competition, or even assertive behavior. The ideal is cooperation and peace. The role of the authority figure is repugnant to those in the tribe, but they have ways of selecting leaders and training them to be more aggressive. The role of leader is not envied in this group; in fact, his contemporaries pity him for having to be assertive and to display asocial traits.

Here we have a tribe where both sexes follow the norms for behavior that we would call "feminine" in the American culture. Those who are not passive, cooperative, and nurturant are considered abnormal, and they are outcasts as surely as those in our culture who do not respond to the appropriate sex role.

At the opposite extreme is the culture of the Mudugamor, where both sexes exhibit in an exaggerated way the kind of characteristics we might call masculine. Both men and women are expected to be violent, competitive, jealous, aggressive, and sexual and to enjoy display, action, and fighting. The culture is structured to evoke these very characteristics.

Mother, daughter, and co-wives are pitted against each other for the attention of the father in an incestuous family structure. Sexual jealousies establish the pattern of distrust, which is continued through imagined insult and severe fighting and carried over into the culture. In the culture, competition to display one's status and material goods is rampant, and aggression is common. Until fairly recently the Mudugamor were actually cannibalistic.

The third culture, the Tchambuli, does show differences between the sexes, but reversed from what we would expect to find in our own culture. It is the women who take care of the most important economic affairs and are considered rational, practical, and good providers. They have control of the important property in spite of existing patrilineal institutions. They also are considered to be the gender with the strongest sex drive. In addition, they take on most of the child care and also manage practically all the economic activities in the group.

In contrast, the Tchambuli men are considered weak, inefficient, and even childish. They are very much concerned with personal ornamentation and sit by the hour in "club houses," primping and gossiping and giggling. They are known for their artistic ability, sensitivity, nervousness, emotional dependence, and petty jealousy.

Thus, we can see that any physical predispositions toward behavior seem to be overcome by cultural training. Margaret Mead, herself a student of human nature and cultures for over forty years, says, "Many, if not all, of the personality traits which we have called masculine or feminine are as lightly linked to sex as are the clothing, the manners, and the form of head-dress that a society at a given period assigns to either sex . . . the evidence is overwhelming in favor of the strength of social conditioning."[147]

When all the evidence about physical similarities and differences between the sexes is examined, we must assert that there are far more similarities than differences. We can also see that many of the abilities and behaviors believed to be inherited and "natural" for a particular sex are actually learned cultural behavior. We see that in some cases there may be a physical predisposition toward a certain behavior, but that this behavior is expected and rewarded for a particular gender, such as higher levels of aggression in boys. In other cases, a culture's definition of sex-role behavior may be largely responsible for a person acquiring a trait and maintaining it, such as empathetic behavior in women. The society also gives greater opportunities for one sex or the other to learn and practice certain abilities, as in the case of spatial ability in males. When differences between the sexes are found, they are usually small, and variation within one gender is far more pronounced than the differences between the genders. In all cases, the part played by the socializing agents—parents, cultural reinforcers, and social institutions—is of the utmost importance in shaping behavior.

Essay Questions

1. Identify the aspects of gender as discussed in the first part of the chapter and tell a little bit about each one.
2. Discuss how chromosomes match at fertilization to form males and females. Identify and tell a little about at least three chromosomal abnormalities that may occur.
3. Discuss hormonal "imprinting" during the critical period. How do we know that hormones can affect male and female brains in different ways during this period?
4. Contrast and compare the hormonal abnormalities of androgen insensitivity and androgenital syndrome with the case of pregnant diabetic women who receive extra estrogen. How is the fetus affected in each of these cases?
5. What is the opinion of most researchers about hormonal imprinting and later behavior? What part do they believe environment plays? Use the case of the Dominican Republic girl/boys as an example.
6. Discuss the nature of sexual identification and how it relates to sex of rearing. Use as examples the children discussed in the chapter who, because of accident or indeterminate sex, had a switch in sexual identity.
7. Compare and contrast the physical characteristics of infant boys and girls. Be very specific. Be sure to include a comparison of how they differ in regard to the five senses.
8. Discuss what we know about hormones and aggressiveness. Why, in the case of aggressiveness particularly, do researchers believe that there is an inborn tendency for males to be more aggressive, when they do not believe that inborn tendencies shape other behaviors?
9. Discuss the difference in male and female brains and later behavior in regard to verbal and spatial abilities. How might the knowledge that female and male brains may differ in the development of these abilities (we do not yet know this with certainty) affect the teaching of reading and mathematics?
10. Discuss the whole area of mathematics ability for women in terms of the interaction of physical tendencies and environmental reinforcement of these tendencies.
11. How do the three tribes discussed by Margaret Mead in *Sex and Temperament* show us that male and female sex roles are indeed learned? Be complete in your comparison of the three tribes.

Exercises

1. Have you ever noticed what you believe to be hormone cycles in yourself or your friends? Discuss when you think they occurred and why.
2. Discuss whether or not you believe that all men are inherently more aggressive than all women. If you believe they are, what are the implications of this conclusion for society? If you do not believe they are, what are the implications of this state of affairs?
3. List some stereotypes in our culture that deal with verbal and mathematical abilities for men and women (for example, women can't balance their checkbooks). Are there equal numbers of positive and negative stereotypes for each sex? Discuss.
4. What examples in your experience would make you think that verbal and mathematical abilities differed for men and women? Discuss reasons why you think this may have been true.

Notes

1. S.A. Shields, "Functionalism, Darwinism, and the Psychology of Women: A Study in Social Myth," *American Psychologist* 30 (1975):739–754; D.M. Broverman *et al.*, "Roles of Activation and Inhibition in Sex Differences in Cognitive Abilities," *Psychological Review* 75 (1968):23–50; A.D. Landers, "The Menstrual Experience" in E. Donelson and J.E. Gullahorn, eds., *Women: A Psychological Perspective* (New York: Wiley, 1977).
2. Jeanne E. Gullahorn, "Sex-Related Behaviors: Historical and Psychological Perspectives," pp. 1–7, in E. Donelson and J.E. Gullahorn, *op. cit.*
3. Jessie Bernard, "Sex Differences: An Overview," in Alexandra Kaplan and John Bean, eds., *Beyond Sex Role Stereotypes: Readings toward a Psychology of Androgyny* (Boston: Little, Brown, 1976).
4. Inge K. Broverman *et al.*, "Sex Role Stereotypes: A Current Appraisal," *Journal of Social Issues* 28, no. 2 (1972):59–78.
5. Meredith M. Kimball, "A Critique of Biological Theories of Sex Differences" (Unpublished paper).
6. M.B. Parlee, "The Premenstrual Syndrome," *Psychological Bulletin* 80 (1973): 454–65.
7. Eleanor Maccoby and Carol Jacklin, *The Psychology of Sex Differences* (Stanford, Calif.: Stanford University Press, 1974), pp. 169–77.
8. Jeanne Block, "Issues, Problems, and Pitfalls in Assessing Sex Differences: A Critical Review of *The Psychology of Sex Differences*," *Merrill Palmer Quarterly* 22, no. 4 (1976):284–308.
9. *Ibid.*

10. Kimball, *op. cit.*, p. 3.

11. Katherine B. Hoyenga and Kermit Hoyenga, *The Question of Sex Differences* (Boston: Little, Brown, 1979).

12. Ashley Montague, *The Natural Superiority of Women* (London: Macmillan, 1968).

13. Jarrick F. Lissey, "Sex Differences in Longevity," in Hugo G. Beigel, ed., *Advances in Sex Research* (New York: Harper & Row, 1963), p. 156.

14. John Money and Anne Earhardt, *Man and Woman, Boy and Girl* (London: Johns Hopkins, 1972), pp. 96–103.

15. E.B. Hook, "Behavioral Implications of the Human XXY Genotype," *Science* 179 (1973):139–50.

16. Witkin *et al.*, "Criminality in XYY and XXY Men," *Science* 193 (1976):547–55.

17. "New Research on Criminals with an Extra 'Y' Chromosome," *New York Times*, December 21, 1976, Sec. 4, p. 7.

18. Hoyenga and Hoyenga, *op. cit.*, p. 112.

19. *Ibid.*

20. Money and Earhardt, *op. cit.* pp. 93–103.

21. J.M. Reinish, "How Prenatal Exposure of Human Fetuses to Synthetic Progestin and Estrogen Affects Personality," *Nature* 266 (1977):561–62.

22. *Newsweek*, November 26, 1979, p. 100.

23. Leonore Giefer, "The Context and Consequences of Contemporary Sex Research: The Feminist Perspective," in McGill, Devesburn, and Sach, eds., *Sex and Behavior* (New York: Plenum Press, 1978), pp. 363–85.

24. Alice Rossi, "The Missing Body in Sociology: Closing the Gap" (Presidential address, Eastern Sociological Society, Philadelphia, April 6, 1974).

25. Money and Earhardt, *op. cit.*, pp. 11–15.

26. *Ibid.*, pp. 123–25.

27. J. Imperato-McGinley, L. Guerrero, T. Gautier, *et al.*, "Steroid 5 Alpha Reductase Deficiency in Man: An Inherited Form of Male Pseudohermaphrodites," *Science* 186 (1974):1213–15; J. Imperato-McGinley *et al.*, "Androgens and the Evolution of Male-Gender Identity among Male Pseudohermaphrodites with a 5 Alpha Reductase Deficiency," *New England Journal of Medicine* 300, no. 22 (1979):1233–37.

28. "Research News," *Science* 205, no. 7 (1979).

29. Imperato-McGinley, quoted on p. 28 of Anne Fausto-Sterling, "Hormones at the Helm, Part I" (Unpublished draft chapter).

30. J. Hampson, quoted in Bernard Rosenberg and Brian Sutton-Smith, eds., *Sex and Identity* (New York: Holt, Rinehart and Winston, 1972), p. 27.

31. John Traverse, *The Growing Child* (New York: Wiley, 1977).

32. Daniel Goleman, *Psychology Today*, November 1978, p. 48.

33. Sheridan Phillips, Suzanne King, and Louise DuBois, reported in "Newsline," *Psychology Today*, September, 1978.

34. J.E. Garai and A. Schoenfeld, "Sex Differences in Mental and Behavioral Traits," *Genetic Psychology Monographs* 77 (1968):191.

35. Maccoby and Jacklin, *op. cit.*, pp. 17–38.

36. Diane McGuiness and Karl Pribram, "The Origins of Sensory Bias in the Development of Gender Differences in Perception and Cognition," in Morton Bortner, ed., *Cognitive Growth and Development: Essays in Honor of Herbert G. Birch* (New York: Brunner/Maxel, 1979).

37. Goleman, *op. cit.*

38. Hoyenga and Hoyenga, *op. cit.*, pp. 323–27.

39. Maccoby and Jacklin, *op. cit.*, pp. 17–38.

40. Hoyenga and Hoyenga, *op. cit.*, p. 324.

41. Maccoby and Jacklin, *op. cit.*, pp. 17–38.

42. Hoyenga and Hoyenga, *op. cit.*, p. 237.

43. Gullahorn, *op. cit.*

44. Maccoby and Jacklin, *op. cit.*, pp. 75–87.

45. F.F. Schacter *et al.*, "Do Girls Talk Earlier? Mean Length of Utterance in Toddlers," *Developmental Psychology* 14 (1978):388–92.

46. D. Horgan, "Sex Differences in Language Development" (Paper presented at meetings of the Midwestern Psychological Association, Chicago, May 1976), in Gullahorn, *op. cit.*, p. 10.

47. S. Goldberg and M. Lewis, "Play Behavior in the Year-Old Infant: Early Sex Differences," *Child Development* 40 (1969):21–32.

48. Stanford Research Institute, "Follow-through Pupil Tests, Parent Interviews, and Teacher Questionnaires," appendix C, 1972, cited in Maccoby and Jacklin, *op. cit.*

49. Maccoby and Jacklin, *op. cit.*; J.P. Gullford, *The Nature of Human Intelligence* (New York: McGraw-Hill, 1967).

50. J. Cameron, N. Liason, and N. Bailey, "Infant Vocalizations and the Relationship to Mature Intelligence," *Science* 157 (1967):331–33.

51. Hoyenga and Hoyenga, *op. cit.*, p. 238.

52. L.J. Harris, "Sex Differences in the Growth and Use of Language," in B. Donelson and J.E. Gullahorn, eds., *Women: A Psychological Perspective* (New York: Wiley, 1977).

53. Maccoby and Jacklin, *op. cit.*, pp. 70–71.

54. Hoyenga and Hoyenga, *op. cit.*, p. 238.

55. D.D. Johnson, "Sex Differences in Reading across Cultures," *Reading Research Quarterly* 49 (1973):67–86.

56. Maccoby and Jacklin, *op. cit.*, pp. 119–20.

57. C.P. Benbow and J.C. Stanley, "Sex Differences in Mathematical Ability: Fact or Artifact?" *Science* 210 (1980):1262–64; "Are Boys Better at Math?" *New York Times*, December 7, 1980, p. 102; "The Gender Factor in Math," *Time*, December 15, 1980, p. 57.

58. Anne Fausto-Sterling, "Hormones at the Helm, Part II" (Unpublished draft chapter), p. 65.

59. Lynn H. Fox, *The Problem of Women and Mathematics* (Report to the Ford Foundation, March 1980), p. 13.

60. *Ibid.*, p. 10.

61. A. Sherman and E. Fennema, "Distribution of Spatial Visualization and Mathematical Problem-Solving Scores: A Test of Stafford's X-Linked Hypothesis," *Psychology of Women Quarterly* 3 (1978):157–67.

62. *Ibid.*

63. Fausto-Sterling, *op. cit.*, p. 68.

64. Fox, *op. cit.*, p. 11.

65. *Ibid.*

66. Fausto-Sterling, *op. cit.*

67. *Ibid.*

68. Maccoby and Jacklin, *op. cit.*, pp. 126–27.

69. Fausto-Sterling, *op. cit.*, p. 27.

70. *Ibid.*

71. J.W. Berry, "Ecological and Cultural Factors in Spatial Perception Development," *Canadian Journal of Behavioral Science* 3 (1971):324–26.

72. Fausto-Sterling, *op. cit*; Kimball, *op. cit.*

73. Fausto-Sterling, *op. cit.*, p. 48, quoting D.R. Bock and D. Kolakowski, "Further Evidence of Sex-Linked Major Gender Influence on Human Spatial Visualization Ability," *American Journal of Human Genetics* 25 (1973):1–14.

74. *Ibid.*

75. *Ibid.*, p. 41.

76. *Ibid.*

77. J. Money and V. Lewis, "Genetics and Accelerated Growth: Androgenital Syndrome," *Bulletin of Johns Hopkins Hospital* 118 (1966):365–73.

78. A.A. Ehrhardt and S.W. Baker, "Fetal Androgens: Human Central Nervous System Differentiation and Behavior Sex Differences," in R.C. Friedman, R.M. Richart, and R.L. Vandewiele, eds., *Sex Differences in Behavior* (New York: Wiley, 1974), pp. 33–51.

79. Hoyenga and Hoyenga, *op. cit.*, pp. 240–42.

80. *Ibid.*, p. 239.

81. S.C. Nash, "The Relationship Between Sex-Role Stereotyping, Sex-Role Preference, and the Sex Differences in Spatial Visualization," *Sex Roles* 1, no. 1 (1975):15–32.

82. D.M. Broverman, E.L. Klaiber, Y. Kobayashi, and W. Vogel, "Roles of Activation and Inhibition in Sex Differences in Cognitive Abilities," *Psychological Review* 71, no. 1 (1968):23–50.

83. J. Sherman, *Sex-Related Cognitive Differences: An Essay on Theory and Evidence* (Springfield, Ill.: Thomas, 1978); M.B. Parlee, "Comments on Roles of Act . . . by Broverman *et al.*," *Psychological Review* 71 (1972):180–89;

A. Singer and R. Montgomery, "Comments on Roles . . .", *Psychological Review* 76 (1969):325–27; D.M. Broverman *et al.*, "Reply to Singer and Montgomery," *Psychological Review* 76 (1969):328–31; Kimball, *op. cit.*, pp. 7–8.

84. A.C. Peterson, "Physical Androgyny and Cognitive Functioning in Adolescence," *Developmental Psychology* 12 (1976):524–33.

85. D. McGuiness, "Sex Differences in the Organization of Perception and Cognition," in B. Lloyd and A. Archer, eds., *Exploring Sex Differences* (London: Academic Press, 1976); D. McGuiness and K. Pribram, "The Origins of Sensory Bias in the Development of Gender Differences in Perception and Cognition," in Bortner, *op. cit.*

86. Research News, "Sex Hormones and Brain Development," *Science* 205, no. 7 (1979):83.

87. "Science News," *Newsweek*, November 26, 1979, p. 104.

88. *Ibid.*

89. Goleman, *op. cit.*

90. J. Levy, "Cerebral Lateralization and Spatial Ability," *Behavior Genetics* 6 (1976):171–88; J. Levy and J.M. Levy, "Human Lateralization from Head to Foot: Sex-Related Factors," *Science* 200 (1978):1291–96.

91. J. Levy and M. Reid, "Variations in Writing Posture and Cerebral Organization," *Science* 194 (1976):337–39.

92. G.L. Carter, and M. Kinsbourne, "The Ontology of Right Cerebral Lateralization of Spatial Mental Set," *Developmental Psychology* 15 (1979):241–45; M. Hiscock and M. Kinsbourne, "Selective Listening Asymmetry in Preschool Children," *Developmental Psychology* 13 (1977):217–24.

93. R.G. Rudel *et al.*, "The Functional Asymmetry of Braille Learning in Normal, Sighted Children," *Neurology* 27 (1977):160–64; S.F. Witelson, "Sex and the Single Hemisphere: Specialization of the Right Hemisphere for Spatial Processing," *Science* 193 (1976):425–27; D.P. Waber, "Sex Differences in Mental Abilities, Hemispheric Lateralization and Rate of Physical Growth at Adolescence," *Developmental Psychology* 13 (1977):29–38.

94. A.W.H. Buffery and J.A. Gray, "Sex Differences in the Development of Spatial and Linguistic Skills," in C. Ounsted and D.C. Taylor, eds., *Gender Differences: Their Ontology and Significance* (Baltimore: Williams & Wilkins, 1972).

95. Jennette McGlone and A. Kertesz, "Sex Differences in Cerebral Processing of Visual-Spatial Tasks," *Cortex* 9 (1973):313–20.

96. Witelson, *op. cit.*

97. Rudel *et al.*, *op. cit.*

98. C.K. Bennet, H.G. Seashore, and A.G. Wesman, *Differential Aptitude Tests,* 3d ed. (New York: Psychological Corp., 1959), cited in Gullahorn, *op. cit.*, p. 23.

99. Jerre Levy, "Information Processing and Higher Psychological Functions in the Disconnected Hemispheres of Commsurotomy Patients" (Ph.D. diss., Pasadena California Institute of Technology, 1970, Dissertation Abstracts International 1970, 31, 1542B); Levy, "Psychobiological Implications of Bi-

lateral Asymmetry," in S. Diamond and J.G. Beaumont, eds., *Hemispheric Function in the Human Brain* (London: Paul Elek, 1974); Levy, "Cerebral Lateralization and Spatial Ability," *Behavior Genetics* 6 (1976):171–78.

100. Waber, *op. cit.*

101. J. Sherman, *Sex-Related Cognitive Differences: An Essay on Theory and Evidence* (Springfield, Ill.: Thomas, 1978), pp. 129–33.

102. *Ibid.*, p. 130.

103. J. McGlone, "Sex Differences in Human Brain Asymmetry: A Critical Survey," *The Brain and Behavioral Sciences*, 1980, pp. 3215–63, cited in Fausto-Sterling, *op. cit.*, p. 62.

104. Kenneth Moyer, "Sex Differences in Aggression," in Friedman *et al.*, *op. cit.*, p. 340.

105. Maccoby and Jacklin, *op. cit.*, pp. 242–46.

106. *Ibid.*, p. 246.

107. Moyer, *op. cit.*, p. 338.

108. Maccoby and Jacklin, *op. cit.*, p. 246.

109. Moyer, *op. cit.*, p. 338; Anne Fausto-Sterling, "The Molecular Connection: Hormones at the Helm (Part III)" (Draft chapter).

110. *Ibid.*

111. Maccoby and Jacklin, *op. cit.*, p. 246.

112. Fausto-Sterling, *op. cit.*

113. Moyer, *op. cit.*, p. 351.

114. Estelle Ramey, "Men's Cycles: They Have Them Too, You Know," *Ms.*, Spring, 1972.

115. *Ibid.*

116. Mary Brown Parlee, "The Premenstrual Syndrome," *Psychological Bulletin* 80 (1973):454–65.

117. Ramey, *op. cit.*

118. Fausto-Sterling, *op. cit.*, chap. 3, p. 8.

119. Parlee, *op. cit.*

120. Therese Benedict, "The Psychobiology of Pregnancy," in J. Bardwick, ed., *Readings on the Psychology of Women* (New York: Harper & Row, 1972), pp. 246–250.

121. Parlee, *op. cit.*, p. 132; Fausto-Sterling, *op. cit.*, pp. 17–20.

122. Parlee, *op. cit.*, p. 127.

123. Rossi, *op. cit.*, p. 122.

124. *Ibid.*

125. Maccoby and Jacklin, *op. cit.*, pp. 169–77.

126. *Ibid.*

127. Eldon Snyder and Elmer Spreitzer, *Social Aspects of Sport* (Englewood Cliffs, N.J.: Prentice-Hall, 1978).

128. Maccoby and Jacklin, *op. cit.*

129. Block, *op. cit.*

130. Carol Travis and Carole Offer, *The Longest War* (New York: Harcourt, Brace, Jovanovich, 1977), p. 126.

131. David Lynn, *The Father: His Role in Child Development* (Monterey, Calif.: Brooks/Cole, 1974).

132. Sandra Bem, "Probing the Promise of Androgyny," in Kaplan and Beam, *op. cit.*

133. Beatrice Whiting, *Six Cultures: Studies of Child-Rearing* (New York: Wiley, 1963).

134. Gerald Gurin, Joseph Veroff, and Sheila Feld, *Americans View Their Mental Health* (New York: Basic Books, 1960).

135. Maccoby and Jacklin, *op. cit.*, pp. 91–105.

136. *Ibid.*, p. 108.

137. *Ibid.*, p. 154.

138. Block, *op. cit.*

139. Maccoby and Jacklin, *op. cit.*, pp. 203–14.

140. *Ibid.*, p. 213.

141. M. Hoffman, "Sex Differences in Empathy and Related Behaviors," *Psychological Review* 84 (1977):712–22.

142. Bem, *op. cit.*

143. Maccoby and Jacklin, *op. cit.*, p. 180.

144. *Ibid.*, pp. 211–19.

145. *Ibid.*, pp. 166–67, 189–90.

146. Margaret Mead, *Sex and Temperament* (New York: Dell, 1963).

147. Margaret Mead, quoted in Janet S. Chavitz, *Masculine, Feminine, or Human?*, 2nd ed. (Itasca, Ill.: Peacock, 1970), p. 260.

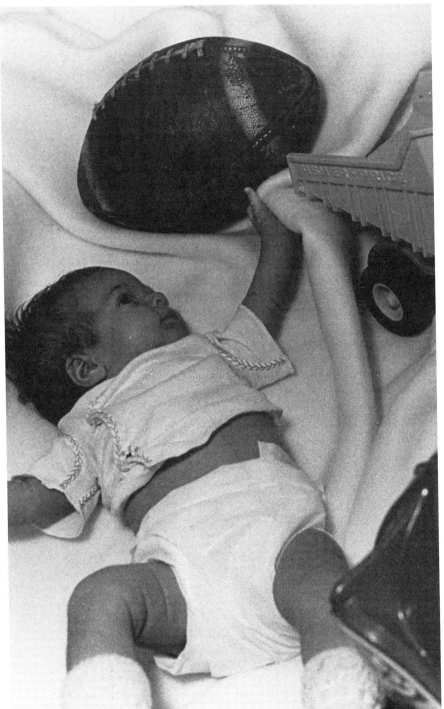

Chapter Three

Early Socialization into Sex Roles

The infant years are the crucial years for development, when patterns of personality and behavior are established. These early years are also critical in establishing beliefs about appropriate masculine and feminine behavior. Learning sex-role norms and behavior is a complex process. The infant, toddler, and young child are socialized into, or taught, appropriate sex-role beliefs and action in many ways. Such vehicles as language provide very subtle but important messages because they are constantly being used. Other means of socialization, such as toys, games, television, or books, convey much more direct messages about appropriate masculine and feminine behavior. Parents and the school contribute both subtle and overt messages about the correct way to act as a boy or as a girl.

The combined force of all these sources of beliefs and behavior is very strong. The young child has no previous knowledge to bring to bear in evaluating what he or she hears and sees. The tendency, therefore, is to accept the values that are set forth. Until recently there has been little questioning of the masculine or feminine behavior a child learns in these formative years. Indeed, until recently few were aware of the extent to which children *are* socialized into male and female roles during this period. But it is crucial to be aware of what values a child is learning. Thus in this chapter we examine in detail the major influences on the sex-role socialization of a child from infancy through elementary school.

Parents and Children

Parents are the earliest and probably the major influence on the sex-role socialization of young children. The emotional content of their interaction with their children gives their input great significance. How and why do parents consciously or unconsciously influence the sex-role beliefs and behavior that their children develop?

Children's Stimulation of Parents

Parents may treat their children differently because boys and girls seem to stimulate their parents differently. We have seen that little girls may stimulate their parents to talk more to them because they use the small muscles around their mouths more often.[1] Parents may think their baby daughter is smiling and thus vocalize more to her. Conversely, boys may stimulate their parents to pay more attention to them because of their somewhat higher activity level. Some evidence indicates that male infants tend to sleep less and are more irritable than female infants; thus they are held and soothed more. One recent study also shows that parents interrupt the play of male toddlers more often than they do that of female toddlers—perhaps because the play is noisier and more boisterous.[2]

Parents' Expectations of Children

Another reason that parents may react differently to boys and girls is because they have different expectations for the sexes. In one hospital study of thirty pairs of new parents, fifteen with boys and fifteen with girls, the parents were asked to describe the characteristics of their infants. In some cases, the parents had not even held the newborn but had only looked at him or her behind the nursery glass. The new fathers and mothers tended to describe their children according to typical stereotypes of the culture; fathers, in particular, described children in these terms. Boy babies were described as firmer, large-featured, more alert, and stronger. Girls were described as delicate, fine-featured, softer, and smaller.[3]

A fascinating replication of this study showed that it is not only parents who are willing to attribute sex-typed characteristics to newborn infants. In other research, kindergarten children were introduced to a four-month-old baby boy. Some of the children saw the infant dressed as a boy and called John, while others saw him dressed as a girl and called Laura. After playing with the baby for five minutes, the children were asked to rate the infant on scales that described it as big or little, cuddly or not cuddly, noisy or quiet, and so on. Most of the children rated the baby as cuddly and friendly whichever sex they saw. On the other adjective pairs, however, they differentiated according to what sex they thought the baby to be. As a boy he was described as big, tough, and fussy, and as a girl the baby was pictured as little, cheerful, and gentle. Neither sex stereotyped more than the other.[4] But if at five years children have distinct ideas of what babies will be like, no wonder much older parents have strong feelings about the gender characteristics of their infants.

Apparently these stereotyped beliefs about infants are merely extensions of those that parents generally hold about boys and girls. Parents describe boys as rough at play, noisy, able to defend themselves, physically active, competitive, and enjoying mechanical things. Girls are described as more likely to be helpful around the house, neat, clean, quiet, reserved, sensitive to the feelings of others, well mannered, and easily upset and frightened.[5]

There seems to be some difference in the sex stereotyping done by fathers and mothers. Fathers stereotyped more than mothers in all cases. In addition, the fathers of boys stereotyped the most, and the mothers of both boys and girls were more traditional than mothers of only girls.[6] In general, parents seemed to specify more traditional traits for their sons than for their daughters.

Parents' Treatment of Boys and Girls

Parents are also more likely to treat male and female infants and children in ways consistent with how they view either sex. In general, fathers are reported to roughhouse with boys and to be more gentle with girls.[7] Both mothers and fathers are more likely to speak softly to girls.[8] Parents also openly encourage sex-stereotyped behavior in their children. In one recent study that points to early differences in treatment, mothers of young babies were asked to play with a six-month-old "actor" baby. Two female infants and two male infants appeared equally often as actor babies, sometimes dressed as their own sex and sometimes as the other sex. In the mother-baby play period, the toy that the mothers chose for the infant varied with the perceived sex of the child. In addition, boy babies were verbally encouraged to engage in large-muscle motor activity, such as crawling, more than girls were, and the mothers responded more to the boys' activity.[9]

As infants become toddlers, parental interaction with them continues to be sex differentiated. In certain studies, both parents emphasized achievement for boys and urged them to control their emotions. Both parents characterized their relationship to their daughters as having more warmth and physical closeness. They believed the daughters to be more truthful, and they showed a reluctance to punish them. They discouraged rough-and-tumble play for girls and doll play for boys.[10] They were more likely to reward girls for dependent behavior, although girls had more freedom to do cross-sex things. After age seven, they were also likely to let boys be more independent.[11] Differential treatment particularly showed up for aggressiveness and dependency. In one study, girls asked for help three times as much as boys did and almost always received a positive response for this, while boys were likely to get a nega-tive one.[12] Other studies show that mothers will take more angry behav-ior from boys and even humorously encourage it.[13]

One classic study seems to show that dependence is encouraged in girls and independence in boys. Perhaps it shows the results of the kinds of parental behavior where girls get three times more help from parents than boys do. In this particular study of independence, Goldberg and Lewis studied the willingness of very young children to be independent of their mothers. A mother and her toddler were placed in a room marked off in squares. The mother sat in one corner, and the researchers kept track of how far the baby wandered from its mother and how often she or he returned for reassurance. At one point a barrier was placed be-tween the mother and the baby, and the baby was left to find a way around it. Girl babies stayed closer to their mothers and returned more times for reassurance. They were also more upset by the barrier and tended to hold on to it and cry, rather than actively seek a way around it.[14]

In other cases, parents may consciously teach their children some of the stereotypic norms. We have reported that boys are specifically dis-couraged from playing with dolls, especially by their fathers. They are also told specifically that ''big boys don't cry,'' and many fathers refrain from hugs and intimate physical contact with their sons as they get older.

For Better or For Worse by Lynn Johnston

© 1981 Universal Press Syndicate. Reprinted by permission.

Fathers are particularly likely to discourage feminine behavior in their boys. Maccoby and Jacklin quote one father who represents the strong feelings fathers often have about finding feminine behavior in boys. When asked if he would be disturbed by indications of femininity in his son, he said, ''Yes I would be, very, very much. Terrifically dis-turbed—couldn't tell you the extent of my disturbance. I can't bear fe-male characteristics in a man. I abhor them.''[15] Conversely, fathers are likely to encourage and enjoy feminine and coy behavior in their daugh-ters. Goodenough reports half the fathers in her study describe their daughters as ''soft, cuddly, and loving,'' saying, ''She cuddles and flatters in subtle ways. I notice her coyness and flirting. . . .''[16] The fathers obviously like the feminine-typed behavior and reinforce their daughters for it.

As children get older, parents may also attempt to teach actual sex-appropriate skills. A father may throw a ball with his son, and a mother may teach her daughter how to sew or to bake cookies. While some cross-sex behavior may be taught—for example, the boy to cook or the girl to fish—it is unlikely that it is stressed unless the father is looking for a substitute son in his daughter or the mother for a substitute daughter in her son. (Interestingly enough, some of the women who rose into the managerial ranks in the 1950s and 1960s were women who were only children and treated by their fathers like boys, taken hunting and taught to shoot.)[17]

Parents as Models for Children

Finally, children learn from their parents by seeing what their parents do. Nothing may be said directly, but children pick up many important messages by watching. If the mother is the one to always do the cooking and grocery shopping, the implication is that this is women's work. If the father is always the one to climb on the roof to clean the leaves out of the gutters, children soon learn that this is a man's job. It is significant that in households where the mother works outside the home, the children have less stereotyped sex-role perceptions.[18] This modeling of sex-role stereotypes by parents can be very subtle. The author can think of one equal home where both mother and father worked outside the home and shared the housework, but a daughter had picked up the idea that men were better drivers because the father always drove the car if the couple went out in the evening.

Thus we see that parents may engage in actions that, for a number of reasons, influence their children's sex roles. Parents may be stimulated by the boy or girl baby to behave in a specific way, they may have special expectations of boys and girls that cause differential treatment, they may consciously or unconsciously attempt to teach a child appropriate sex-role behavior, or they may model sex-role behavior for the child to imitate. Any kind of parental action is a strong influence. It is combined with the other influences of childhood to make this a crucial period in forming sex roles.

Toys

Toys also influence the growing child. The young child learns to differentiate at an early age between toys appropriate for boys and those appropriate for girls. The media play a major role in stimulating a child's desire for certain kinds of toys. As we have seen, parents also play a role here by the toys they give their children.

When children are very young, both boys and girls receive many of the same kinds of toys. The very young may receive a stuffed animal, rings that stack on a pole, blocks, a pull toy, and the like. Even at a very early age, however, some of the toys are likely to be designated as appropriate for the sex of the particular child. Thus a girl might get a doll and a boy a truck. One study of twenty-month-old children showed that they already knew the appropriate toys for their sex and preferred to play with them. Only one child out of twenty-four preferred a toy usually given to the opposite sex.[19]

After two years of age, toys for each sex differentiate markedly. Girls are more likely to get passive toys, such as dish sets, clothes, and coloring books. They may get toy ovens, irons, and sewing machines. The more elaborate models of these toy household applicances actually work, and girls can start ironing and baking at early ages. Many of these toys are a realistic representation of the things that the girls might do later in life. They may also get doll houses, where they can move the furniture and play house. Their dolls are frequently ones that can be handled like real babies: they can be fed, diapered, and even bathed.

Boys are more likely to get mobile toys, action toys (such as guns or bows and arrows), and sports equipment. The toys that boys get are often connected with action and exciting occupations, such as being a cowboy, a policeman, or an astronaut. For the most part, however, these toys do not represent occupations likely to be entered by most young men. Thus boys may learn, unrealistically, that the world of men is a world of excitement and toughness. Seldom does a boy get a toy briefcase and a bunch of papers to shuffle in an imitation of a father's likely role.

Boys are also far more likely than girls to get sports equipment. Boys are given bats, balls, basketballs, footballs, hockey sticks, and the like, and encouraged to use them. The sports equipment given to girls is different and often includes such things as a jump rope or skates. Parents in one study said that a baseball glove and similar items would be appropriate toys for either sex, but they gave their children only toys considered appropriate for that sex.[20] We can see that the different kinds of equipment encourage more active play and more team play by boys than by girls.

Boys seldom get dolls to play with after they are two or three years old. Although a young boy may want to cling to the comfort of his stuffed animal, dolls and stuffed animals are considered babyish or sissy for him. Yet a girl may continue to have her stuffed animals on her bed through her college years. Male dolls do exist (one catalog shows about 68 male dolls in contrast to 356 female ones), but they are justified in terms of supermasculinity or activity. A little boy can choose a GI Joe with a Kung-fu grip that can chop a board in the pressing of a button or an Action Jackson with his rescue rig. The dolls all emphasize action, and accessories include scuba outfits, mountain-climbing equipment, and spaceships.

The contrast with the dolls for girls is striking. After their baby dolls, slightly older girls often get Barbie dolls and their counterparts. These dolls are supposed to be models of the appropriate feminine body and activities for the older girl. What do girls see as an appropriate model? The Barbie doll, with its unrealistically big breasts and long slender legs is made to be dressed up in expensive and elaborate outfits, complete with wig and high heels. Barbie has an escort, Ken, who is also a clotheshorse. Barbie's little sister, Skipper, may express the ultimate idea of how to grow up in a hurry. In one version of the Skipper doll, a child can rotate Skipper's arm and she will grow breasts and develop a thinner waist—truly a model of how to quickly become a desirable sex object. None of the Barbie, Ken, and Skipper accessories emphasize action; rather, they are examples of dressing up and quiet family roles.

Toys as gifts for boys and girls continue to be differentiated as children grow older. While research on toys is limited, two Yale sociologists surveyed forty-two boys and forty-two girls to see which toys they received. While the boys and girls received almost exactly the same number of gifts, 73 percent of the boys' gifts were toys and only 57 percent of the girls' gifts were toys. Girls were much more likely to get clothing and jewelry instead. Later, advertising seems to stimulate people to buy different toys for each sex. Pictures on the covers of boxes for chemistry sets or weaving sets show the "appropriate" sex using the equipment. Toy salespersons also recommend sex-stereotyped toys. Recent research has found that they recommend sex-stereotyped toys for boys, in particular.[21]

Boys also get more expensive toys and toys they can manipulate and that stimulate creativity. Thus boys will get microscopes, chemistry sets, erector sets, and model planes. Even similar items for boys and girls, such as doctor and nurse kits, can actually be very different. Goodman and Lever report that a doctor kit marketed for boys had "stethoscope with amplifying diaphragm . . . miniature microscope . . . blood pressure tester . . . prescription blanks, and more, while the nurse kit came equipped with nurse apron, cap, plastic silverware, plate, sick tray, and play food."[22]

Even unisex equipment, such as bicycles, differentiates in style, price, and use between boys and girls. Boys' equipment is usually more expensive, more intricate, and sturdier. It is also different in kind and designated intent. A boy will get hockey skates, and a girl will get figure skates. The subtle message is not lost: boys skate fast and play rough games, whereas girls do graceful figure eights. As children get older, the presents given boys and girls tend to converge somewhat, and both sexes get more clothes, records, and books.

The toys given children are partly in response to their own wishes, which have been stimulated by the media. The toys given are also partially a result of parental expectations. For example, in one experiment, eleven mothers played with a six-month-old child who was variously dressed as "Adam" and "Beth." When the mothers thought that the child was a boy, they were significantly more likely to give it a train, and when they thought it to be a girl, they gave it a doll.[23]

The message about appropriate toys is absorbed by young children. By twenty months of age, they know which toys are for which sex and prefer those for their own sex. For a while it was believed that girls would be willing to play with boys' toys even when they knew they were not appropriate. (And who could blame them, as boys' toys are so much more exciting!) Some recent studies show, however, that girls are equally sex typed in regard to toys.[24] Indeed, boys were more likely to play with a sex-inappropriate toy if an older, same-sex model played with it first.[25] This study does not mean that boys are ready to start playing with dolls. It does show, however, the importance of a model who encourages or discourages certain play interests. Thus, parents who are actively encouraging only sex-appropriate toys in both boys and girls help perpetuate sex stereotypes.[26]

Games

The sex-role messages implied in girls' and boys' toys may be further emphasized in the games they play. Young boys play more fantasy roles than girls do and imitate exciting, creative people. Boys may play cowboys and Indians or cops and robbers, but girls often imitate their future household roles as they play house or take care of their dolls.

Boys and girls also learn to relate in different ways to those around them when they play. Girls are more likely to play in smaller groups. They may play jacks or jump rope in twos and threes.[27] They are also likely to play in a more unstructured way. While there are some rules to their games, they are minimal. The emphasis is on cooperation and taking turns, and not necessarily on winning. Even some of the competitive sports that girls engage in, such as horseback riding, skating, and swimming, put more emphasis on individual than on team competition. Lever, in a study of the nature of boys' and girls' play, showed that only 47 percent of girls' activities were competitive, compared to 65 percent of the activities for boys. Even if we eliminate team sports for both sexes, only 30 percent of the girls' activities are competitively structured, compared to 54 percent of the boys' activities. Girls are also more likely to join large, affiliative groups like Girl Scouts in the course of their play.[28]

In contrast, boys are more likely to play in larger groups and often in teams where performance is related to the role of the whole group. Boys are also more likely to engage in games of greater complexity, with rules and strategy. They learn to combine competition and cooperation, and they learn to play with those whom they may not like so that they will have the required number of players for the game. In *Games Mother Never Taught You*, Betty Harragan points out that many of the lessons learned on the playground stand a boy in good stead when he is later working his way through the corporate world. He learns to "play his position," "not to talk back to the coach," and to "play by the rules."[29]

One of the striking aspects of boys' play is the pressure to be good or to win. The boy who learns skate boarding must equal or surpass the others on the street in the number of tricks he can perform. If he plays hockey, shoots baskets, or throws a baseball, he must do it well enough so that he will be chosen for the neighborhood and school teams. While we have mentioned cooperation in these team sports, strong competition is also encouraged. Boys learn early that they must be tough and willing to play in spite of injury or difficult conditions. It is all too common to see high-school coaches putting players into the game with pulled tendons, broken wrists, and other relatively severe injuries. Even when boys engage in affiliative activities, competition and toughness is emphasized. Many fraternities emphasize team sports and painful initiations, and even the Boy Scout works to become an Eagle Scout.

Clothing

Clothing is another influence on sex-role behavior, although it is a very subtle one. Now little girls are much more commonly seen wearing the jeans, shirts, and sneakers that active boys have enjoyed for so long. However, it is still not unusual to see girls who wear dresses and slick-soled shoes in both preschool and elementary school. One can observe the same children dressed in that fashion day after day. Often these little girls are unable to run, climb, and be truly active, at least if they are going to obey the injunction to be modest and "not let your panties show." Even for the girl in slacks there may be disadvantages. In contrast to boys' clothes, girls' slacks are often made without pockets. Young girls must awkwardly carry a comb and tissues in their hands or begin to carry a purse.

As girls get older and enter junior high school, other styles of dress inhibit their movement. Even in junior high schools, girls often wear high heels and hose. They may also begin to wash, blow-dry, and curl their hair every day and to wear makeup. If a purse was not carried before, it now becomes necessary, as makeup and other elements of a good appearance must be portable. The clothes worn are often uncomfortable and unhealthful and inhibit active motion; yet they are "the style," and girls and women who do not wear the appropriate feminine dress may be reproved. It is in late elementary school, too, that a girl starts spending more time and money on her appearance. Girls of ten or eleven frequently have their ears pierced and start acquiring earrings and other kinds of jewelry. They may spend time curling their hair—and later bleaching it—and applying makeup. They may worry about the length of their fingernails or how their hair will look if they engage in sports like volleyball or swimming. Many girls and women spend a great deal of time and money attempting to improve their appearance, and their interest in and desire to engage in more active pastimes may be limited by this fact.[30] While boys are certainly interested in their appearance and spend considerable time picking out clothes and washing and blow-drying their hair, too, the emphasis is not as extreme. The young male seems to gain most of his approval from what he does, while the young female often tries to gain her approval from how she looks.

Some changes have occurred. The emphasis on clothes and appearance is recognized by some as artificial, and the natural look that started in the 1960s has persisted to some degree. Women have access to more comfortable styles of clothing, although they may not choose to wear them. Where changes have been made, many of the men seem to have taken on women's styles rather than the reverse. We now see men wearing pants without pockets, carrying purses, and blow-drying their razor-cut hair. Yet, although some convergence toward a unisex mode in clothing has occurred, there is still great differentiation. Both sexes are also still learning to wear clothing that is uncomfortable and inhibiting. While women suffer in high heels and hose, men suffer in ties and three-piece suits. Both sexes learn that on many occasions it is important to dress "appropriately" for their sex, whatever the discomfort.

Thus we see in some of the early actions of parents as well as in the way they dress their children, in the toys they give them, and in the games children are encouraged to play, the subtle pressure on children to behave in what are deemed sex-appropriate ways. Even parents who hope to avoid pushing their children into sex-stereotyped behavior may unconsciously pass on subtle messages about "appropriate" actions.

The Black Family

It is very difficult to discuss the black family, because when you do so, you are immediately setting a group apart and saying it is different. On the other hand, if you don't discuss black families, you are saying that they are just like white families—which, of course, is not true either. We hope to discuss differences in the black family's socialization of their children in a way that will simply show that there are differences and that these differences are no more right or no more wrong than any other way of raising children.

We must begin by saying that there is no one black family. The upper- and middle-class black families are very similar to white families in their sex-role socialization. Mednick and Weston say that the black middle class "outmiddle-classes" the white middle class or, in other words, is very eager to adopt white norms for sex-role socialization. Of course, in all black families a socialization occurs that must deal with being black in a predominantly white society, but it is in the working- and lower-class (or ghetto) black families that the great differences in sex-role socialization are found.

While much of what we have said about the sex-role socialization of white children also applies to black children (parental expectations, stimulation of parents by infants, and parental teaching), a few differences do exist. In the working-class black home, sex roles may be handled in a somewhat different fashion from the middle-class black home. For one thing, more adult models may be present with whom a young child can identify. Sometimes several generations of women live together. Teenage girls will bring their babies home for their mothers to watch while they continue to go to school or to work. Sometimes the father of the baby moves in and out of the household for periods of time. Men in the household may take some care of young children, and children may also be cared for by siblings as much as by parents. Very young children are often watched closely until around the age of three or so, usually by the grandmother or other kin. They are then given more freedom and often put almost completely in the care of an older sister or cousin. Older girls almost always have child and home-care responsibilities, while boys are usually free from these. Boys and girls learn early that sex roles are divided in this way, although the older men may "help out."

In addition, black boys may be particularly pressured to be strong and unemotional. It may be physically necessary to fight—or to show oneself capable of fighting—almost every day in some living situations. Strength may also be shown in being able to "rap" well or in being good at "sounding" or "playing the dozens" (see section on language). A certain degree of "street savvy" or "street smartness" is a necessary skill. Thus, there is heavy pressure to learn a traditional male role in the working-class black family and little toleration of those who deviate from this role.[31]

Young black girls are given more responsibility and taught more independence than their white counterparts. They have early and extensive responsibility for child care and are taught that they are capable and strong and must take care of themselves. Later they are also taught that they must depend upon themselves for future economic survival, and they may be encouraged in academics even more than their brothers are. They are expected to be "street smart" and able to take care of themselves, but are warned about being hustled and cautioned about being respectable. Thus, the young black female learns an androgynous conception of sex roles. She learns to care for children while she learns to be independent, capable, and assertive. In contrast, the young black male usually learns an exaggerated male stereotype.

Theories of Sex-Role Learning

We need to pause at this point and to look at some of the theories that have attempted to describe how a child comes to use certain sex-role behaviors. At some point in the interaction among the child, significant others, and the environment, the child decides what sex he or she actually is (that is, establishes a sexual identity) and then comes to practice behavior the culture says is appropriate for that sex. Each of the theories about this phenomenon emphasizes different stages in acquiring the behavior and different reasons for its acquisition. The controversy over heredity versus environment, biology versus cultural conditioning, has been focused in some of the more popular theories.

Freudian Theory

The biological side of the controversy has largely been taken over by Freud and his followers. Freudian theory emphasizes the physical and biological differences between the sexes and states that "anatomy is destiny."[32] Freud believed that each infant goes through a series of physical and psychosexual stages that follow in a definite sequence and are based on physical growth. These stages are linked to the child's level of mental or social development and to his or her feelings about parents.

In the oral stage, which lasts from birth to about one year, the child is largely an instinctual being, and the id, or primitive and impulsive part of the mind, is in control. The child derives pleasure and information largely by putting things into his or her mouth.

The anal stage follows from one to three years, and the child is concerned with the other end of her or his anatomy. This is the time when parents try to institute toilet training, the first necessity for the child to take control over id impulses. As the child begins to gain some of that control, a new section of the mind, the ego, or rational, conscious mind, begins to develop. With the developing of the ego, the child might reason that if she goes in her appropriate potty chair, mom will be pleased with her, she won't get a scolding, and she might even get a reward. Therefore, the child begins to operate through reason and not just through impulse. During these first two stages, both male and female children are identified with their mothers. They see them as sex and love objects and imitate some of their actions.

The phallic, or genital, stage takes over from about three to seven, and here the sexes begin to differ in their development. During the genital stage, both boys and girls become aware of their genitals and their own similarity to or difference from their mother and father. The little boy is still very close to his mother but, according to Freud, he begins to see his father as a rival for his mother's affections. This scares him, as his father is big and powerful, and he develops what is called an Oedipal complex. He is in love with his mother and afraid of his father. He may also have a sister whom he sees without a penis, and he develops fears that he could be castrated if he competes with his father. He resolves this fear by identifying with his father and recognizing his own similarity to this strong male. In this way he feels secure. He is no longer afraid of his father; he can love his mother; and he can turn to other women later and obtain their love as his father has obtained the love of his mother.

The little girl goes through this genital stage in a different way, according to Freud. She sees that boys have penises and blames her mother for not getting her one (penis envy). She may transfer her love to her father and be very angry with her mother for a while. In time, however, she realizes her own similarity to her mother and replaces her wish for a penis with a desire to have a child. She begins to identify with her mother partly out of fear of her mother's jealousy, but also out of recognition of similarities to her.

Thus, according to Freud, both sexes identify with the same-sex parent and acquire some of the parent's personality characteristics. The two sexes then enter the period of latency, where they sublimate sexual urges in activities like collecting frogs or string. Then at puberty, the stage of adolescence begins and each sex becomes attracted to the opposite gender, firming up sexual identity and sex role.[33]

Problems with Freud's theory are many. We have not even discussed some of the more "far out" parts of the theory because they are not directly relevant to sex roles. Three problems are directly relevant to our concerns, however: (1) Freud's insistence that two parents need be present if the child is to go through the stages correctly and develop appropriate sexual identity and gender-role behavior, (2) his view of women, and (3) his idea of fixed stages of development.

First of all, it is evident that children develop firm sexual identities in the many single-parent families found today.[34] Second, Freud's view of women as inferior men who wish to have a penis also seems by more modern standards to be erroneous and probably reflects only women's envy of the masculine sex role. While young boys and girls both rate their own sex-appropriate roles as being more fun, older girls are more willing to say they wish they were a boy. Cross-cultural evidence also shows that some men envy women's child-bearing capacities and that, indeed, there may be a "womb-envy" that Freud has not touched on. (However, it is certain that men are not as likely to envy the feminine sex role and its limited privileges as women are to envy the masculine sex role.) Finally, Freud's view of biological stages as fixed and unchangeable is open to question. In one study, children were given figures of boys and girls and men and women cut into three pieces each. The children were told to assemble the four figures of a man, woman, boy, and girl from the twelve pieces given. As long as the figures were dressed in sex-appropriate clothes, the children made few mistakes. However, when the figures were undressed, 88 percent of the three-year-olds made at least one error, 69 percent of the four-year-olds made an error, and 31 percent of the six-year-olds made an error. Thus, children may reach different stages of awareness about their bodies at different times.[35] Freud's theory has been important in developing our ideas of children's stages of development and the later behavior of adults, but it does not take into account important differences in families, environments, and cultures.

Social Learning Theory

Mischel, Bandura, and Walters have developed a theory of learning sexual identity and sex-role behavior known as social learning theory. In this theory, imitation and reward and punishment for correct and incorrect behavior play very important roles. The young child is told that he is a boy or she is a girl and is treated in ways parents think are appropriate for dealing with that particular gender. A father may come home from work and say, "How's my big boy tonight?" and toss the infant son into the air. Conversely, he may come home and say, "How's my sweet little girl?" to his infant daughter while tickling her under the chin and saying, "Come on, now, give daddy a smile." The child thus usually learns to think of himself or herself as a boy or a girl; he or she identifies others who are similarly called boys and girls and notes how they are alike. Usually, these noted similarities in gender characteristics are such obvious external things as "girls have longer hair than boys" or "boys are bigger than girls." Children notice, too, that boys and girls in general are treated differently and are expected to behave differently.

The young child learns the behaviors of both sexes by such observation but is much more likely to imitate the behavior of his or her own sex. Thus, a little girl may be more likely to dress up in her mother's high heels in imitation of her mother (in whom she sees a similarity); but she could, if pushed, imitate her father puffing on a cigar. The child not only imitates because the behavior is associated with the appropriate sex, but because he or she is reinforced or rewarded for sex-appropriate behavior. Thus, the little girl who dresses up in mother's high heels may be told that she is "cute and quite a little female," but the little boy who tries the same thing is not likely to get approval. He may even be told directly that "boys don't do that, and go outside and play."

Thus, by reactions to their own behavior, by seeing how others are treated, and by imitation of the behavior of older models, children learn sexually appropriate behavior. They learn to generalize this behavior to other situations as well. They do not have to experience the behavior personally to know whether it is appropriate or not for their own sex: the young boy knows that for a man to dress in women's clothes and walk down the street is not appropriate behavior, even though women may wear the equivalent of men's clothes in public. Children also have to learn that reinforcement for the behavior is determined by the content of the situation. A boy may be teased for sewing or cooking, but it is all right to sew a patch on a tent on a camping trip or to cook over a camp fire.

As children are responded to in terms of a particular gender and as they learn to act in gender-appropriate ways, they develop gender identities as boys or girls. Thus, according to this theory, children acquire sex-role stereotyped behavior before they acquire gender identities.

Parents are the primary models for young children and the primary reinforcers of sex-appropriate behavior. Models who are the most imitated are nurturant, but they are also seen as successful. The strong influence of parents can be seen dramatically in the case of children who have had sex-reassignment surgery: the parents' behavior toward such children clearly influences the children's subsequent identification as the other gender. However, peers are also strong reinforcers of "appropriate" sex-role behavior. In one experiment, the behavior of nursery school children was analyzed and divided into "male-stereotyped" and "female-stereotyped" kinds of behavior. Researchers then looked at teachers and peers to see how much sex-appropriate behavior was reinforced. The teachers actually preferred more feminine behaviors and rewarded them more in both sexes, but the peer groups almost completely rewarded sex-appropriate behaviors. The one boy who exhibited some feminine behaviors had fewer playmates and was criticized more than any other boy.[36]

There are some specific problems with social learning theory. In particular, the insistence on models being present, imitation of the same sex, and the insistence on reward and punishment as learning mechanisms present difficulties in accepting the theory totally. Children do not necessarily resemble their same-sexed parents. Girls, especially, imitate both parents more than boys do. Some sex differences persist in spite of seeming lack of reinforcement or even punishment. Boys are consistently punished more for aggressive acts than girls are, but they continue to exhibit more aggressiveness, whereas girls do not learn, necessarily, to aggress more in this situation. Of course, boys are also rewarded subtly for aggressive behavior, but this theory does not emphasize such reward systems as peer approval or a personal feeling of what is right. The theory emphasizes specific, tangible rewards, although it is clear that other kinds of rewards may be just as important. Boys in one experiment would not change their toy preference to dolls in spite of a reward system.[37] Nevertheless, the idea of modeling and reward is obviously important in learning sex roles, and the theory has had a great impact.

Cognitive Development Theory

Kohlberg proposes that gender identity and sex-role behavior are acquired in stages. These stages are consecutive like the ones Freud proposed, but they are mental rather than physical. They are based on Piaget's stages of cognitive development and the readiness of the child's mind to handle certain concepts. According to this theory, at the appropriate stage when the child's mind is ready to handle the concept, the acquisition of certain kinds of information and behavior takes place without external reinforcement being necessary.

While the stages of Kohlberg's theory are consecutive, they may not occur at the same time in all children. Some children may reach one stage of development before others and can handle sex-role identity concepts sooner. This progress to a different level of handling concepts may depend on intelligence and also on physical maturation. At the appropriate stage, the child must, however, also have the necessary experience—or information—to learn.

For example, the very young child may call everything that is warm, fuzzy, and small "kitty." Later he or she learns to differentiate "puppy," "kitty," and "squirrel." In a similar way, the young child may differentiate between men and women on the basis of external cues, such as long hair, wearing lipstick, and wearing a skirt, or behavior such as cooking dinner and feeding the baby. Even when the differentiation is finer and the child recognizes genital differences, he or she may not believe they are permanent.

At one family gathering at which the author was present, a five-year-old boy had just been told by his parents that boys had penises and that girls did not and this was the way you told one from the other. He went around the room of fully clothed adults and tested his new knowledge by pointing to each one in turn and saying, "You are a boy, so you have a penis; you are a girl in a skirt, so you don't have one." He waited until each person gave the answer that told him he was right, and when he had made the full circuit of the room, he walked off satisfied. Later, the mother confessed that he was still not sure of the permanence of these characteristics. He had told her that afternoon, "When you grow up, you can be a boy and ride a bicycle like daddy."

The stages in cognitive development theory roughly correspond to the age of the child, although children differ in their progress through each stage. From about birth to three, the child differentiates the sexes according to external cues or differences in observed behavior like cooking or mowing the lawn.

At about three, the child begins to label himself or herself as a particular sex. In keeping with a strong value of self, this is seen as good. Thus, at this stage one's own sex and its activities are preferred because the self is valued. One boy, when asked why he liked a particular boy baby-sitter, replied, "Why, because he's a boy, of course!"[38] Thus, a boy might also say, "I'm a boy; therefore, I want to do boy things, play with boy toys," and the like. Discrimination has taken place so that children are indeed able to tell what toys are appropriate for them to play with, although they may not be sure of what toys are appropriate for the opposite sex. However, in this stage from three to four or so, the child does not yet realize that gender cannot be changed. He can label himself as a boy and still say he's going to grow up to be a mommy.

In the period from about four to six, children acquire the knowledge that gender cannot be changed. They achieve this knowledge at about the same time that they learn certain facts about the constancy of objects—for example, that you don't change a quantity of water by pouring it from one shaped container to another, or that a kite doesn't shrink when it gets farther away.

Stereotypes and behavior around the stereotypes become very important at this stage. Children want to imitate adults who are like themselves and also who are seen as powerful and competent. After about eight, children stop imitating adults in general and then selectively only model themselves after skills or other things they see as relative to their own competence. According to Kohlberg, sex typing does not increase much after this age.[39] Thus, according to this theory, the child learns his or her own gender identity at the proper time and then does appropriate sex-role behavior because it is "right and good." Models provide clues to this appropriate behavior, but rewards come mainly from the child knowing that he or she is doing the right thing.

Most of Kohlberg's work has been done on boys, but the implications for girls are frightening. The girl who wishes to value her own gender but also to associate with a powerful model who has prestige is going to have difficulty finding one. Many same-sex models will not have this power or prestige; those who do may not display the "appropriate" behavior for women. Thus, the girl is left in a double bind. If she accepts the female stereotype, she does not have power; if she does not accept it, she is not doing sex-appropriate things. Either choice is disturbing. Hoyenga and Hoyenga tell of a four-year-old girl whose mother was a doctor and who still insisted that only boys become doctors.[40]

This conflict shows up in girls' attitude toward their own gender at this stage. Children of both sexes say that fathers are bigger and stronger than mothers, that they have more social power. Girls show themselves as liking their own sex less often than boys do. At five, although both sexes are sex stereotyped, girls show less preference for their own sex role.[41] They frequently cite boys' activities as more fun and exciting, and quite a few say they would like to be a boy. However, cognitive development theory has some positive things to recommend it, which the other theories do not. First, while it is based on consecutive stages of development, these stages can vary from child to child according to physical development and IQ. The idea about how the child develops sexual identity is also consistent with single-parent homes, because in this theory the father is not the only model for boy children. In addition, some of the present research about sex typing and parental identification seems to support the theory. Research shows that sex typing is positively associated with father identification in both boys and girls, which Kohlberg would have expected as he emphasized the modeling of a competent, powerful model. Masculinity in boys is also associated with a nurturant, warm father figure. Neither girls nor boys identify with a passive father, and behavior shows an increasing similarity to that of the dominant parent as the children grow older.[42]

Theories of Learning Sex Roles: A Choice of Emphasis on Heredity and/or Environment

While all three of these theories are still very important, there has been a progression in the degree to which each has been accepted, which may well reflect the progression in our societal views about heredity and environment determining sexual differences and behavior. Freud's theory, which emphasizes the anatomy-is-destiny perspective and bases sexual identity and sex-role behavior on moving through a series of fixed, physical stages, has lost a great deal of credibility. Although many aspects of the theory are still valued and used, the totally hereditary perspective has been mostly discarded by the greatest proportion of the social science community. In a similar way, elements of the almost totally environmental theory of Mischel, Walters, and Bandura have been discarded. It has been recognized that some physical tendencies toward sexual differences and behavior cannot totally be accounted for by an environmental theory alone, especially one that puts such a strict emphasis on modeling and reward and punishment. The Kohlberg theory of cognitive development has come to be regarded to some degree as a mixture of the physical or hereditary and the environmental. Its concept of mental stages of maturation and readiness to accept gender identity allows individual differences. It also establishes the importance of the environment and, in particular, it shows the importance of societal models beyond the family.

In looking at these three theories about the development of gender identity and acquisition of knowledge about gender-appropriate behavior, we see that there are no certain answers about the relative role played by heredity and environment in shaping identity and sex roles. At the moment, it seems that accepted theories emphasize the role of the environment. This environment is not just the one provided by the immediate family. It includes the values developed and reinforced by many cultural institutions. For example, the early messages about appropriate masculine and feminine behavior that are developed in childhood games and toys are strengthened and reinforced in the playing fields of the elementary school. Language provides children with other subtle messages, and the masculine and feminine stereotypes are repeated and reemphasized by books, television, and school. We will look at the specific influences of the media and educational institutions in the next chapter.

Essay Questions

1. Many people say that sex stereotyping begins at the cradle. What evidence can you cite to support that statement?
2. In what ways do parents model sex-role stereotypes to their children (list at least four or five) and how do they directly teach their children "sex-appropriate" behavior?
3. How do the toys given to little girls and to little boys differ after about two years of age? What implications does this difference have for the activity of the boys and the girls?
4. In what way are the different toys given to boys and girls realistic or unrealistic representations of their future occupational roles? Why do you suppose a middle-class little boy doesn't get a briefcase and papers to shuffle, and how do you think he may be affected by a lack of a realistic view of his future occupation?
5. How do the games played by little boys differ from those played by little girls in terms of their structure and the number of players?
6. What does Betty Harragan mean in *Games Mother Never Taught You* when she says that the games boys and girls play affect their future attitudes and behavior in the work world?
7. Briefly discuss Freud's beliefs about the physical stages through which children pass and their relationship to sexual identity. What are some of the problems with Freud's theory as it applies to learning appropriate masculine and feminine behavior?
8. Discuss the importance of modeling and reward and punishment in

social learning theory. How does the importance given to these ideas affect the application of this theory to the learning of masculine and feminine behavior?

9. Discuss Kohlberg's beliefs about stages of cognitive development and their relationship to the establishment of sexual identity and appropriate sexual behavior. What do you see as any problems with the theory in terms of applying it to the learning of sex-role behavior?

10. If you were to pick a theory to describe the learning of sexual identity and appropriate sex-role behavior in single-parent families, which of the theories in questions 7, 8, or 9 would you choose, and why?

Exercises

1. Make a list with two columns headed "Baby Girls" and "Baby Boys." List things you have heard or believe about the characteristics of each in the appropriate column. Discuss where you have heard or learned each belief. Do you think the belief is accurate?

2. Discuss any evidence you have from your own experience (watching your parents, an older sister with a baby, and so on) that parents treat boy and girl infants differently. If you have found a difference in treatment, why do you think it occurs?

3. Make a list of privileges or activities that you think, feel, or know about for each sex. Do it as if you were a young child. Divide them by male and female. Title your list, "My Parents Let Me or Treat Me. . . ." Examples:

Male	*Female*
My brother can go hiking alone.	My sister can baby sit and I can't.
My dad plays catch with my brother.	My mother shows my sister how to cook.

4. Discuss whether you think your parents treated you differently from your sisters and brothers when you were a child. Do you think this has influenced your attitude toward masculine and feminine behavior?

5. Pretend you are going to visit an old college friend whom you haven't seen in six years and who now has a child four years old. You do not remember the sex of the child and are embarrassed to ask. You want to bring a nice present to the child ($10 variety). What will you pick that would be appropriate for either sex? Try to list at least ten possibilities.

6. Make a list of toys for boys and girls that are actually different in kind (like boys' bicycles and girls' bicycles). Why do you suppose toys are made with these kinds of differences?

7. Imagine that you are a parent who wants to raise *your* child in a nonsexist way, but that you do not want to make your child unhappy by having him or her teased by friends. What toys could you give a fifth or sixth grader that would be nonsexist and yet acceptable to the child's peer group?

8. Do you believe that the competition and rules of Little League baseball or hockey, or whatever sport, are good for little boys? Discuss in some detail why or why not. Do you think little girls should have a similar experience? Should boys and girls play on the same team?

9. Pretend you are a girl going to a job interview and that you want to be "appropriately" dressed. Would you be willing to wear slacks rather than a skirt? Why or why not?

10. If you are a girl, have you ever rebelled against wearing hose and high heels to a dressy occasion? Do you think women should give up wearing hose and high heels? Why or why not?

11. Do you remember your parents doing any behavior that was an unconscious modeling of sex roles (such as your mother sliding over to let your father drive the car when she picked him up)? Do you remember them consciously telling you what was appropriate masculine or feminine behavior? Discuss your answers.

12. How do you *feel* about parents teaching their children appropriate masculine or feminine behavior? What do you think would happen if they didn't? (Would the children learn such behaviors anyway? Would they be less sex stereotyped? What do *you* think?)

Notes

1. Eleanor Maccoby and Carol Jacklin, *The Psychology of Sex Difference* (Stanford, Calif.: Stanford University Press, 1974), pp. 309–11.

2. Beverly J. Fagot, "The Influence of Sex of Child on Parental Reactions to Toddler Children," *Child Development* 49 (1978):462.

3. J. Rubin, F. Provenzano, and Z. Luria, "The Eye of the Beholder: Parents' Views of Sex of Newborns," *American Journal of Orthopsychiatry* 44 (1974): 512–19.

4. Caroline Smith and Barbara Lloyd, "Maternal Behavior and Perceived Sex of Infant: Revisited," *Child Development* 49 (1978):1263–65.

5. W.E. Lambert, A. Yackley, and R.N. Hein, "Child Training Values of English-Canadian and French-Canadian Parents," *Canadian Journal of Behavioral Science* 3 (1971):217–36.

6. Leonard M. Lansky, "The Family Structure Also Affects the Model: Sex-Role

Attitudes in Parents of Preschool Children," *Merrill-Palmer Quarterly* 13 (1967):139–50.

7. Maccoby and Jacklin, *op. cit.*, pp. 310–11.

8. *Ibid.*

9. Smith and Lloyd, *op. cit.*

10. J.H. Block, "Assessing Sex Differences: Issues, Problems and Pitfalls," *Merrill-Palmer Quarterly* 22 (1976):283–308.

11. Maccoby and Jacklin, *op. cit.*, p. 319.

12. Fagot, *op. cit.*

13. Maccoby and Jacklin, *op. cit.*, p. 347.

14. S. Goldberg and M. Lewis, "Play Behavior in the Year-Old Infant: Early Sex Differences," *Child Development* 40 (1969):21–31.

15. E.W. Goodenough, "Interest in Persons as an Aspect of Sex Differences in the Early Years," *Genetic Psychology Monographs* 55 (1957):287–323.

16. Maccoby and Jacklin, *op. cit.*, p. 329.

17. Margaret Hennig and Anne Jardim, *The Managerial Woman* (Garden City, N.Y.: Anchor Press/Doubleday, 1977).

18. Richard Perloff, "Some Antecedents of Children's Sex-Role Stereotypes," *Psychological Reports* 40 (1977):463–66; P. Weston and M. Mednick, "Race, Social Class, and the Motive to Avoid Success in Women," *Journal of Cross-Cultural Psychology* 1 (1970):284–91.

19. Greta Fein, David Johnson, Nancy Kosson, Linda Stork, and Lisa Wasserman, "Sex Stereotypes and Preferences in the Toy Choices of 20-Month-Old Boys and Girls," *Developmental Psychology* 11, no. 4 (1975):527–28.

20. M. Richmond-Abbott, "Sex-Roles in Single-Parent Homes" (Paper presented at the National Council on Family Relations, Portland, Oregon, October 1980).

21. Nancy Kutner and Richard M. Levinson, "The Toy Salesperson: A Potential Gatekeeper for Change in Sex-Role Definitions" (Paper presented at the annual meeting of the American Sociological Association, New York, August 1976).

22. Letty Cottin Pogrebin, "Gifts for Children," *Ms.*, December 1974, p. 63–68 and 76–79.

23. J.A. Will, P.A. Self, and N. Daltan, "Maternal Behavior and Perceived Sex of Infant," *American Journal of Orthopsychiatry* 46 (1976):135–39.

24. Fein *et al.*, *op. cit.*

25. Thomas Wolf, "Influence of Age and Sex of Model on Sex-Inappropriate Play," *Psychological Reports* 36 (1975):99–105.

26. Sheila Fling and Martin Mansovitz, "Sex-Typing in Nursery School Children's Play Interests," *Developmental Psychology* 7, no. 2 (1972):146–52.

27. Maccoby and Jacklin, *op. cit.*, p. 207.

28. Janet Lever, "Sex Differences in the Complexity of Children's Play and Games," *American Sociological Review* 43 (1978):471–83.

29. Betty Harragan, *Games Mother Never Taught You* (New York: Warner Books, 1977).

30. Marie Richmond-Abbott, *The American Woman* (New York: Holt, Rinehart and Winston, 1979), p. 115.

31. David A. Schultz, *Coming Up Black: Patterns of Ghetto Socialization* (Englewood Cliffs, N.J.: Prentice-Hall, 1969).

32. Hoyenga and Hoyenga, *op. cit.*, p. 278.

33. Calvin Hall, *A Primer of Freudian Psychology* (New York: World, 1954).

34. David Lynn, *The Father: His Role in Child Development* (Monterrey, Calif.: Brooks/Cole, 1974).

35. Katherine H. Hoyenga and Kermit Hoyenga, *The Question of Sex Differences* (Boston: Little, Brown, 1979), p. 182.

36. Walter Mischel, "A Social-Learning View of Sex Differences in Behavior," in Maccoby and Jacklin, *op. cit.*, pp. 56–81.

37. L. Kohlberg, "A Cognitive-Developmental Analysis of Children's Sex-Role Concepts and Attitudes," in Maccoby and Jacklin, *op. cit.*

38. *Ibid.*

39. *Ibid.*

40. Hoyenga and Hoyenga, *op. cit.*, p. 189.

41. P.H. Mussen, "Early Sex-Role Development," in D.A. Goslin, ed., *Handbook of Socialization Theory and Research* (Chicago: Rand McNally, 1969), pp. 707–29; Mavis Hetherington, "A Developmental Study of the Effects of Sex of the Dominant Parent on Sex-Role Preference, Identification, and Imitation in Children," *Journal of Personality and Social Psychology* 2 (1965):188–94.

42. Kohlberg, *op. cit.*

Chapter Four

Early Socialization Into Sex Roles: Language, Media, and the Schools

Some of the most pervasive and influential messages about sex-appropriate behavior are given children in language and in the sex-stereotyped behavior portrayed by books and television and reinforced in school settings. Language and the institutions that produce the media and educate children in the United States reflect American cultural values about sex-appropriate behavior.

Language

The following quote from Thomas Mann's *The Magic Mountain* illustrates the importance of language in our social interaction.

> Conversation is the bonding agent between ourselves and our society. It enables us to reaffirm our own existence. Speech is civilization itself . . . it is silence which isolates.[1]

Language is a subtle but extremely important socializer of sex roles. It is the lens through which we see our culture; it may set limits on our thoughts or on our ability to describe things. In some cultures, there is no past or future tense; this lack imposes immediate limits on expressing one's imagination. In other cultures, there is no word for "I"; there is only the tribal "we." You can imagine how difficult it would be to develop a separate self-identity without the word *I*.

In our own culture, the sexes are conceived of as distinct and separate. We will see that different adjectives are used for men and for women and that different occupations, different behaviors, and even different ways of standing and sitting are designated as masculine or feminine. Adjectives or implied meanings about things shape how we feel about men and women. When people are defined in this fashion and when they learn the definitions of self at a very young age, they come to believe the definitions and to act in accordance with the labels given them.[2]

It is even easier to come to believe in the labels and definitions that are part of language because the meanings are very subtle and one is not always conscious of stereotyping taking place. Language is also one part of our lives that is always with us, so we are continually exposed to its influence. Language does not always have to be verbal; it can include facial expressions and gestures as well as general body posture and the use of space.

Language Differentiation

Sexism is perpetuated in language in many ways. Women are frequently excluded totally or else are assumed to be part of the male gender. As one example, in the state of Michigan pronouns of the female gender are absent from the first two readers in first grade. The excuse is that the word "she" does not appear high enough on word lists. Therefore, if "he" and "it" are talked about more in print, they must continue to be talked about first, and so we perpetuate a cycle of females being ignored.[3] Women learn, also, that they are assumed to be part of mankind (shortened to "man"), that they are part of the "brotherhood of man," and that they have been freed to enjoy "liberty," "equality," and *"fraternity."* They also learn that important and exciting jobs are referred to by masculine terms such as *fireman* and *policeman*. While progress has been made toward more neutral terms like *firefighter* or *police officer,* many occupations are still defined in masculine terms. Doctors, dentists, and pilots are almost always referred to as "he," while nurses, dental technicians, and elementary-school teachers are referred to as "she." Certain occupational titles that are differentiated for women carry a slightly inferior implication, such as *poetess* (not quite a poet?) and *authoress.* (It is interesting that this differentiation is perpetuated in other languages; in French, for example, a professor is always "le professeur," the masculine article *le* being used, even when the professor is a woman.) Another area where achievement or honors are defined in masculine terms is educational degrees. One gets a Bachelor of Science or a Master of Arts degree. The thought of a Spinster of Arts seems absurd. This, however, is because of the different implications of the words *bachelor* and *spinster.*

The implication of certain words is as important as their actual meaning. Language differentiates between the sexes both obviously and more subtly by such implication. For example, the term *bachelor* implies a carefree, sociable playboy; the term *spinster*, however, implies a withered old crone. The title *master* implies dominance or power, as in "the master of his trade." However, the parallel word for woman, *mistress*, implies being dominated by a man and giving him sexual favors, although it may also imply being in charge of the household. In like manner, *gentleman* has positive implications of high social status or at least of being mannerly, while its counterpart, *lady*, can be used much more freely. Someone might yell out, "Hey, lady!" One may also use *lady* in the context of "ladies of the night," or prostitutes.[4] Other pairs of titles or words are not as obvious in the differences between the masculine or feminine versions, but the masculine version usually carries a more positive implication. Compare words like *patron* and *matron*, *wizard* and *witch*, for example.

The difference in verbs or adjectives applied to men and women may also show a difference in positive or negative implication. Women chatter or engage in "girl-talk" (which is assumed to be inconsequential talk), while men "discuss" or simply "talk." She will "nag" while he "reminds," she "bitches" when he "complains," and she is "picky" when he is "careful."[5] The worst insults for a man are those inferring that he has feminine characteristics. Thus he can be called a "sissy" (diminutive of sister) or be told he "swings a bat like a girl." Other insults tie a man to his mother and insult him by questioning his mother's sexual character. Someone with whom you are extremely angry is often referred to as a "son-of-a-bitch." (It is true we have probably forgotten the original meaning of the term, but the demeaning implication and the tie to a female relative are still there.)

Many terms that refer to both men and women have sexual meanings. Thus men become "studs" or "jocks," and women become "broads," "dogs," or "chicks." Somehow the terms applied to men imply more power and success, while those applied to women imply promiscuity or being dominated. And why is it that the term *promiscuous* is applied only to women, although its literal meaning is really applied to either sex? Actually, there are 220 words and phrases for a sexually promiscuous woman, and only 22 for a sexually promiscuous man.[6] While it may seem a bit picky to complain about being called an animal such as a "dog" or a "chick," the following excerpt shows the cumulative effect of such characterization:

> In her youth she is a "chick" and then she gets married and feels "cooped up" and goes to "hen parties" and "cackles" with her women friends. Then she has her "brood" and begins to "henpeck" her husband. Finally, she turns into an "old biddy."[7]

Women are referred to by their gender when the gender is not appropriate to the subject at hand. Compare the following statements and see which ones you would be likely to see in a newspaper headline: "Widow opens real-estate office"; "Widower opens real-estate office"; "Grandmother runs for office"; "Grandfather runs for office." Women are also referred to by their relationship to men. A woman is "Ed's widow," although it would be rare for a man to be referred to as "Vera's widower." Women are known as "Miss" or "Mrs." according to their marital status (although the term *Ms.* is finding favor); one cannot differentiate a single from a married man by the title *Mr.* Women may also become "the senator's wife" or "the first lady." If a husband and wife are described together, it is likely that he will be described in terms of what he does and she will be described in terms of what she is physically: "Ralph is a brilliant young lawyer, and he has a beautiful, blond wife."[8]

Finally, behavior can even be inferred from style of language. Men are often described in the active voice: "He romanced her"; "He took her in marriage," while women are described in the passive voice: "She was romanced by him"; "She was given to him in marriage." We may learn subtle messages from this language style.[9]

Styles of Speech

In addition to differentiation through language, men and women differ in their styles of speech and what they talk about. Men tend to talk about external things and to use straight, factual communication. In particular, they talk about sex, sports, politics, work, and other men. They talk louder, employ stronger statements, and press their arguments on their listener.

Women are more likely to talk about feelings and people. They tend to talk about their physical and psychological states and say that they are cold, tired, hungry, or feeling good or bad. The talk more softly and use more expression than men do. Their talk is more polite and indirect. They use qualifiers to keep from imposing their beliefs on others. Women tend to agree with statements in conversation with others and to build on those statements, while men tend to dispute a person's argument. Each sex sees the other's style of speech as uncomfortable. Men see women's speech as illogical recitals of feelings, and women see men's speech as wearing and competitive.

The sexes also differ in talking in mixed groups and in how much they talk. Contrary to the old stereotype of women chattering away while silent men try to get a word into the conversation, men talk more in mixed groups. Indeed, in a mixed group where everyone is taking turns talking, men not only talk more but take their turns unfairly by interrupting women and answering questions not addressed to them. When there are overlaps—that is, two people starting a sentence at the same time—it is almost always the man who continues and the woman who drops out.[10]

It is women who tend to do the listening and try to keep the conversation going. They say more positive, reinforcing things like, "That's a good idea" or, "Go on," to keep the speaker happily telling *his* tale. They are the ones to laugh at the jokes the men are telling and to nod agreement (even when they do not agree!). In contrast, men may use techniques like the "delayed response" to keep from actively encouraging women to speak. The woman says something like, "You'll never guess what happened to me today." Only after a long, long pause will her male companion say, "Oh, what?" At other times the pause extends, so that the only response to the woman is silence. Thus, the woman is discouraged from talking further. This happens in spite of the fact that the man may have talked at some length himself.[11]

If a woman keeps talking and insists on attention in a group, she may find herself simply not listened to. Indeed, she may hear an idea that she suggested and that was ignored taken up later by a man and suddenly found to be worthwhile. Specific studies show that women students are not listened to as much in the classroom, either by their male peers or by their professors.[12] It is likely that the same pattern occurs in social relationships. If women persist in trying to talk, they may be seen as pushy or radical.

The words that women use and their style of speech may have something to do with the difficulty in commanding attention, although it is likely that the stereotypes of proper roles for men and women are really more important. We have noted that men use stronger statements than women. In addition, women may use words that imply a certain sense of silliness or weakness or trivialize what they are trying to say.[13] Notice the difference in impact between "Oh, my, such a lovely idea!" and "Damn, yes, that's a tremendous idea!" It is not hard to guess the sex of the person saying each phrase. Women, however, are caught in a double bind: if they use weaker expletives or exclamations, they diminish the power of what they want to say; if they swear or speak assertively in expressing feelings, they are condemned for doing so.

Some studies indicate that women and men may also use a somewhat different vocabulary. Women are more likely to make finer color distinctions and use words like chartreuse or ecru. Their adjectives are also ones that men are unlikely to use: sweet, lovely, cute, pretty, darling, charming, and the like. While there is no basic difference in a man saying that something is "good looking" while a woman says it is "pretty" or "lovely," women's adjectives tend to sound more frivolous or trivial.

Women also use qualifiers that make their speech less forceful.

These qualifiers are such phrases as "I guess that"; "I could be wrong, but"; "I guess this is silly, but"; "Don't you think we should"; and so on. While the woman may be trying to soften what she is saying so that it is not offensive or imposed upon anyone, the qualifiers give her statements an unsure, apologetic air. Indeed, women tend to hesitate, apologize, and disparage their own statements. In addition, women may phrase things in a tentative way that asks for others' cooperation or opinion. Such phrases as "It seems to me that . . ." or "Why don't we . . ." are weaker than they could be. Compare the phrase "Perhaps you shouldn't do that" with "You shouldn't do that!" A woman is more likely to say the first phrase and a man the second.[14]

Although the results of studies vary, there is also some indication that women use tag questions. A tag question is something that is added at the end of a regular statement. While there are legitimate uses for tag questions, such as in starting conversations ("It's fun here, isn't it?") or in getting confirmation ("You're going to clean your room, aren't you?"), for the most part such tag questions indicate uncertainty. They are often used to leave oneself open to agree with others. Thus, a young girl might say, "That's a pretty good album, isn't it?" if she isn't sure of how her listener might respond and she wants to leave herself a way of backing off from her statement.[15]

While some might say that women will be taken less seriously no matter how they speak, the difference in actual vocabulary and style of speech may contribute to the lesser impact of women's speech. Male speech reinforces the male role of being assertive and dominant, while female speech reinforces the stereotype of the female sex role: to be polite, supportive, and reinforcing. At the same time, however, we should recognize that the active listening and interpersonal interaction in female speech are communication strengths.

Thus, at present the sexes learn not only different styles of speaking but even different vocabularies. Books, television, and spoken language all reinforce these differences that help perpetuate sex roles. If this section appears to be biased in favor of change for women, it is because language is biased in favor of men. As language is continually a part of our lives and influences us so strongly, it is important for us to recognize this male bias. We will continue to perpetuate sex-role stereotypes until we make some basic changes in the language that we live.

Body Language

Women and men continue their pattern of different styles in their body language. Women use more facial expressions and show their emotions in gestures and movements. They smile more than men and often smile not only with their mouths but with their eyes. Smiling is a submissive gesture often seen in the animal kingdom among apes and chimpanzees. "The smile is women's badge of appeasement," say Henley and Thorne. Other submissive gestures are also found in the body language of women. When confronted with a stare, women will avert their eyes and drop their eyelids. They also tilt their heads when talking, the beginning of a submissive gesture.[16]

In addition, women and men have different postures. A woman's space is more restricted than a man's. Women are supposed to be compact, not sprawled out. They sit with their legs crossed at the ankle or thigh; they may have their arms folded and they keep their elbows at their sides. By contrast, a man will usually sit with his legs crossed so that one ankle rests on the opposite knee or thigh, a much more open position. He may sprawl backward as he sits, with his arms along the back of a couch. When standing, there is a similar pattern. Men stand with their legs apart, firmly planted. Women stand with their legs together, sometimes to the point of crossing one ankle over the other, so that the outside edges of their feet are together. (While the author did not believe that this was a posture women were likely to use often, she was surprised to find one day, while standing waiting for an elevator, she had assumed exactly that pose.)[17]

Part of the concept of body language is the element of space. There seems to be a direct association between the amount of space surrounding a person and that person's dominance.[18] Executives have the largest desks; the rich have large yards separating them from their neighbors; professors stand behind lecturns on raised platforms; and in some Oriental countries, one must not sit in a way that will make him or her higher than the chief.

In this application of the principle of the higher the status, the greater the space, females have lower status than males. Walum reports a study by Willis where 800 experiments showed (1) women have more tolerance for invasion of their personal space than men have; (2) women stand closer to other women than men to other men, and when women get as close to males as they do to other women, the males retreat; (3) when men get as close to other men as they normally do to women, the male subjects "fight" (accuse the experimenter of being pushy or homosexual); and (4) both men and women stand closer to women than to men.[19]

As higher-status people touch lower-status people significantly more, women are also more likely to be touched by others rather than to initiate touching. Not only do males touch first, but they are allowed to touch in an intimate way (an arm around the shoulders) without necessarily implying actual sexual advance. Women cannot do the same things. However, women still use affectionate touch more, especially with other women; men use more status touch, such as ritual handshakes.

In the touch situation, there are certain things that point out the inferior position of women. We have only to think of the poor waitress to realize that women are subjected to many gestures usually used with children: cheek tweaking, hair mussing, pinching, or a spank on the bottom. Many hostile and painful touches are used on women in the guise of affection. Women are swung painfully at square dances and are chased by gangs of men and thrown in the water, spanked, or dunked at the beach. They are sometimes passed up the stands at football games. At the University of Michigan games, the practice of "passing up" got increasingly out of hand when games were boring. Sometimes hundreds of women students were sent up hand over hand. Among the injuries were a dislocated shoulder, a broken arm, internal injuries of various sorts, and many severe bruises.

Women are also more likely to move out of men's way if women approach men in a narrow passage. While chivalry would seem to dictate that men would step off a narrow walk into soggy ground and let the woman pass, the opposite actually happens. One study in Atlanta, Georgia, also showed that women are more likely to move out of the way if their space is invaded while they are waiting for a traffic light.[20] Women's space is actually invaded by others in a common and general way. In particular, children invade their mother's privacy and life space in a way that they would not duplicate for their fathers. A woman's reaction to the invasion of her space is to usually give way, to move, or to answer the interrupter; thus, the event occurs again.

Women's time is also invaded in a similar fashion. They are expected to tolerate interruptions or to wait patiently. Women's time is more likely to be controlled; for example, there are usually more curfews for girls and women. Almost all body language suggests that women's role is that of the person of inferior status. It is the boss who touches his employee first (the boss with higher status), and it is the lower-status employee who steps aside, who nods in agreement when he does not agree, who looks away, or who is interrupted. Body language thus becomes a further extension of the sex-role stereotypes of dominance and submission in our culture.[21]

In a final perspective on body language, space, and active and passive roles, let us briefly consider the etiquette that prevails between males and females. While we often think of such matters as opening doors and other forms of chivalry and etiquette as trivial, they are important in reinforcing the passive and active nature of feminine and masculine roles. It is the man who is expected to do the active things: he opens the door, lights the cigarette, hails the cab, or takes the woman's arm to help her on a slippery sidewalk. The male is in control (of the door or cigarette). In contrast, the female waits to be helped. She waits to have the door opened, to have her cigarette lit, to be helped in dangerous territory.[22]

The nonverbal communication indicates that she needs to be helped in everyday life. Thus the man practices his control and the woman her helplessness every time this type of etiquette ritual occurs. Usually, the man and woman "feel" much more masculine or feminine because they have acted out their stereotyped roles.

Thus, whether the language message is conveyed through words or body language or is learned by imitation or the more sophisticated rules of etiquette, language sends us different messages about the roles for females and males. These messages are particularly important because language in some form is always with us. The messages may be subtle and not easily recognized. The different styles and vocabulary of each sex can be assimilated without question. Yet this vocabulary and the language styles may influence a person's behavior and opportunities throughout life. Language is thus one of the most potent of the sex-role socializers, especially for young children.

Black English

Black Americans may learn a special variation of English. In some cases the variation is distinct enough even to be considered a dialect or second language. One black professional mother said that she distinctly attempted to teach her child to distinguish between standard English and black English as it was spoken in most of the black community. Black English was also seen as different enough from standard English that the school systems in Ann Arbor, Michigan, were sued to provide bilingual education for black students. A special teacher-training program resulted, and apparently rapport, understanding, and learning were promoted between teachers and students as a result of the teachers' awareness of the different terminology used by their students. Walum describes black language in the following way:

> [It] is structurally complex, grammatically ordered, action-oriented, and capable of finely honed double-entendres. Talk is . . . expected to be intense in entertaining and skills . . . are . . . understood as a necessity for personal and community survival. To speak excellent "soul" is to achieve prestige and status. . . . [23]

Black English is complex and subtle. It has different forms and varies by social class. In the working class, one form of talking is "rapping," which is a lively way of talking where the speaker describes real or fantasized activities to impress his or her audience. Another form is "signifying," where the speaker goads, begs, or boasts by indirection, particularly by "loud-talking," or talking loud enough for the object of the insult, or whatever, to overhear. A third form is "sounding," where one insults another person or that person's family directly. Distinctions are also made between "street talk" and "sweet talk." "Sweet talk" is associated with the home and is expected to be used by women, with the exception of some of the years in the teens and twenties. This talk is less public, less loud, and closer to standard English. Women are more likely to use the form of talk known as "signifying," as well. However, it is pointed out that a woman must also be capable of "street talk," "rapping," and even "sounding" if necessary. Apparently, to earn respectability she must control the talk in her presence. Only when that is done—by insult or whatever—is she free to talk seriously about a subject or perhaps to use more standard English.

Men apparently use "sweet talk" for hustling women and others who may not be familiar with the interactions in black English. However, "the usual male language style is combative, aggressive, argumentative, and hostile," says Walum.[24] The male speech is louder and also has more syllable stress, total change, and rhythmic variation than are found in black women's speech or in that of standard English.

Language has a special role to play for the black male, especially in the working class. He establishes his reputation with his ability to "rap" and "sound." Using a style of speech that is differentiated from that of women also means that he has separated himself from home, mother, and feminine things. "Sounding," or "playing the dozens," is frequently done and is often cruel and destructive—deliberately. The aim is to get someone so mad that they will fight or even cry. (Perhaps this had appropriate survival significance in days when a black man did not get mad at a white man.) The insults are usually aimed at the physical, mental, or sexual prowess of the person or at their family, particularly at their mothers. Some examples quoted in Kochman are, "Nigger, Bell, you smell like B.O. Plenty," or "Your mother is so black she sweat chocolate," or "At least my mother ain't a railroad—laid all over the country."[25]

Thus, black male and female speech roles are similar to those in the white community. Males use direct and aggressive forms of speech and are louder and more uninhibited in their use of language. While women can use these stronger forms of speech, nice girls are expected not to and to rely mostly on "sweet talk" or on standard English. Thus, black women are constrained much as white women are by the language they are taught, though not to such a degree as their white counterparts.

Television

Television is also an extremely important influence that molds children's views of how the sexes should behave. It is estimated that between kindergarten and sixth grade, children watch from ten to twenty-five hours of television a week. Preschoolers usually begin watching television when they are about three years of age, and a high level of watching continues until around twelve years. During the teenage years, television viewing declines, but it increases again in the young-adult years after marriage. *Children spend more time watching television than they do reading books, listening to the radio, or going to the movies.* They begin by watching children's shows like "Sesame Street" and "Captain Kangaroo" and move on to detective shows, sit-coms, movies, and the like. They see approximately 250 commercials during a week's television watching where the set is turned on about six hours and eighteen minutes a day. The average child has spent fifteen thousand hours in front of a set by the time he or she is sixteen. That is four thousand more hours than the child has spent in the classroom. What does this "classroom of the air" teach children about their roles in the world?[26]

In spite of some recent improvements, television portrays overwhelmingly stereotyped masculine and feminine roles. A study by Women on Words and Images ranked sixteen of the top-rated programs of the 1973–74 viewing season in terms of occupations and positive and negative behaviors.[27] The study reported that the television programs appear to present a distorted view of family life, and many of them are unremittingly violent. About 75 percent of the male roles in prime time represent tough, cool, American males who are unmarried and without responsibility. These men engage in violent, mobile occupations and have numerous female admirers. Women, in contrast, are usually shown as the person being rescued or as someone playing a peripheral role, such as secretary or researcher. Women are the objects of victimization by men and are sexual objects or mates in marriage rather than responsible individuals acting on their own. Even in more recent prime-time shows that attempt to show women in action roles, such as "Charlie's Angels," the women not only have to be beautiful sex objects, but the show usually portrays them as subservient to a man (Charlie) or rescued by one. In "Policewoman," Angie Dickinson is continually rescued from situations by her male colleagues.[28]

In prime-time television, children not only see six times as many men as women, but these men work at many more occupations and they support families. In the family show, the male is almost invariably shown as the provider. For example, in "The Brady Bunch," the father supported six children, a wife who stayed at home, and a domestic employee. "All in the Family" showed Edith Bunker as a totally dependent housewife. The Waltons, who were barely scraping along, never thought of having mother take a job; the father supported them all. Although women are shown working, as on "Maude," they are not shown as contributing in a meaningful way to family support. "Mary Tyler Moore" was the notable exception of a show showing a woman working as an equal with men, but Mary was portrayed as a single woman. Only about

25 percent of the married women in prime-time shows work, and both married and single women usually work in traditional female occupations. In soap operas, women workers are shown, but they are subservient to men. "The Doctors" shows surgery being performed by male physicians, and the female physicians fill out forms. Male lawyers try cases, and female lawyers research them.[29]

The studies report that in comedy shows males are portrayed as worldly, self-confident, and showing leadership. Women seldom show these behaviors unless they take over in situation comedies, and then they are twice as likely as the men to be cast showing bungling behavior. Even in the "educational" shows, women are often shown in negative ways. The female puppets on "Sesame Street," for example, portray strident, loud-mouthed types.[30] Children's cartoons include even fewer women or female characters than adult prime-time shows do. The studies conclude that the television message is women don't matter much and are inferior in many ways to men.

Television commercials portray even more stereotyped roles. Out of 2,750 commercials in one study, 94 percent used a male narrator, although over 50 percent of the products portrayed were typically used by a woman.[31] The man's voice would frequently be heard over the action telling the woman how to cook, clean, or wash with the particular product. Men told women what laundry soap or bleach to use, what cleaner to use on the floor, and how to wash their windows. The implication is that even in their own domestic center of work, women are too dumb to know how to do things correctly.

Women and men were also portrayed in different kinds of advertisements. Seventy-five percent of all the ads using women were for products found in the kitchen or in the bathroom. Fifty-six percent of the women were judged to be homemakers, while men were significantly more likely to be shown outdoors or in business settings.[32]

How do black men and women fare in this television world of make-believe? Of 2,226 characters surveyed in one research study, 75 percent were white, 19 percent were black, and 5 percent were nonblack minority members. Of all spot messages, only 40 percent had black characters and 10 percent had nonblack minority characters. Within each minority group, however, the representation of male and female characters was much more nearly equal than it was for whites. Of all the male characters, 22 percent were black and 6 percent were nonblack minority members; of all the female characters, 16 percent were black and 4 percent were nonblack minority members.[33]

Thus, the percentage of blacks and other minorities appearing on television is fairly close to these groups' percentages in the population. Indeed, the black female is portrayed more favorably in her roles than the white female in hers. In all-white family interactions, men are more dominant than women; in all-black family interactions, women are more dominant. Black women are also shown more forcefully than white women. In fact, situation comedies present black women as dominant more frequently than they do any other group—however, only within the context of all-black interactions. The one negative aspect of the portrayal of the black woman is that she is always shown within the family (thus reinforcing myths about black matriarchy).[34]

While these data on the percentages of black men and women show that blacks are being represented approximately in proportion to their percentage of the population, we must not forget that whites fill 70 to 80 percent of the parts on the screen. They also predominate in newscasters' and other important roles. We must also remember that blacks, both men and women, are cast in the stereotyped roles that we have identified above.

Relatively recent information from the Screen Actors' Guild sums up the roles of women and minorities in prime time quite succinctly. In a content analysis of all prime-time network shows during the month of February 1974, 71.8 percent of the roles were played by men. Men outnumbered women 3 to 1 on ABC and NBC and 2 to 1 on CBS. Minorities played in 12.7 percent of all roles: blacks in 5.8 percent, Asian-Americans in 1.6 percent, American Indians in 0.29 percent, Mexican-Americans in 18.3 percent, and others in 4.2 percent. In a week of general adult programming on Public Broadcasting, female participants totaled 15 percent in twenty-eight programs, while another eleven programs had no females.[35]

How much of an effect does television really have on the children who see it? Research shows that what children watch *does* affect their view of the world. In one study, children who watched the most television had the most traditional sex-role development, even when compared within social classes. As one study reported, "modeling occurs simply by watching others, without any direct reinforcement for learning and without any overt practice. The child imitates the model without being induced or compelled to do so."[36] This was true for both boys and girls and did not change with increasing age.[37] Seventy-six percent of the heavy viewers, compared with 50 percent of the moderate viewers, selected stereotyped careers for themselves. In one report of sixty-three interviews with boys and girls between three and six, some of the girls had abandoned their ambitions. When asked what they wanted to be, they replied that they would really like to be a doctor or a milkman, but sighed and said they would never do it because they were not boys. In contrast, one boy said, "Oh, if I were a girl, I'd have to grow up to be a nothing."[38] The pervasive influence of the "tube" is shown in a 1977 murder trial in

Miami, Florida, where the young criminal's defense was that he had been so indoctrinated by the violence in one television show ("Kojak") that he had been driven to kill.[39]

However, it seems that children are aware and able to learn non-sex-stereotyped behaviors as well as traditional ones. In one study where girls viewed three programs showing traditional, neutral, and liberal sex roles, the girls showed very different attitudes when tested. Girls who viewed the low-stereotyped program received a significantly lower sex-role stereotype score than did girls in the high or neutral conditions.[40] Other research also shows that exposure to televised behavioral models makes it more possible for girls to learn cross-sex behaviors. Children exposed to programs where opposite-sex careers were shown were significantly more likely to pick such careers. Children exposed to female police officers, for instance, were more likely to state that a woman could be a police officer than children who watched more traditional fare.[41] The message here is that television does not have to be a force for maintaining rigid sex-role stereotypes: children are pliable enough to imitate an androgynous model as well as a sex-stereotyped one. However, if all they see is sex stereotypes, then that is what they will learn.[42]

Finally, some other research may be encouraging. One study compared how much children learned from televised models and how much they learned from their own parental models and discovered that parents had more impact on sex-role stereotyping. In particular, the study pointed out that children whose mothers were employed outside the home had less stereotyped sex-role perceptions than children whose mothers did not work outside. This may ease the burden of guilt carried by working mothers when they think of their children sitting home watching all that television.[43]

However, we must not become complacent. Sexism continues blatantly on television. A recent study shows that male voice-overs in commercials have actually increased. When children spend more time in front of a television set than they do in school, television is a powerful influence. The message of cartoons, commercials, and prime-time shows is that there are more men around and that these men are important, smart, and interesting, while women are relegated to traditional housekeeping and nurturing roles. Thus, we should not be surprised that traditional sex roles are reinforced.

Books

Another influential element in the teaching of sex roles is books. Although children may not spend as much time today reading as watching television, books are particularly important because they may be one of the first contacts an infant or a very young child has with a depiction of sex roles. From nursery rhymes onward, the stereotyped roles are clearly shown. Books are also important because the written word implies a certain truth or authority. This authority is often accentuated when the book is picked out by a parent or read by a mother or father. Finally, the older child may not have much choice about reading certain books. Children could only escape a required school book by refusing to open it, with the possible consequences of that action.

Sex stereotyping starts in books for the very young. Adult roles in both preschool and elementary-school books show men as providers and women at home. In one study of preschool books, seventeen male characters were shown as providers, but only one female (a schoolteacher) was shown as having an occupation. In contrast, eighteen female characters were shown doing domestic things, and only three male characters were shown in the home.[44]

One picture book entitled *I'm Glad I'm a Boy; I'm Glad I'm a Girl* makes one wonder if the girl really is glad. The book depicts appropriate occupations and roles for each sex. It tells us that "boys are doctors; girls are nurses"; "boys are pilots; girls are stewardesses"; "boys are football players; girls are cheerleaders"; boys are presidents and girls are first ladies." Perhaps worst of all in terms of dealing with competence, it tells us that "boys fix things and girls need things fixed; boys build houses and girls keep houses." How can a child help being affected by such a strong portrayal of sex roles![45]

Competence and activity seem to be traits reserved only for boys in all these books. In play activity, boys are overwhelmingly shown as active and girls as passive (watching, sitting, admiring). Boys are shown talking and girls, listening. Boys are also shown as logical and realistic, while girls are illogical and idealistic.[46] Even the animated characters in educational books like the Dr. Seuss series reflect a difference in the presentation of males and females.[47] For example, boys are always riding the bicycle, while girls are the passengers. In most other stories, the inanimate objects that are personified as achievement oriented (Toot the Tugboat) are male, and male animals are portrayed as exciting tigers or horses, while female animals are sloths, geese, or squirrels.[48]

In school books, the pattern is continued. Boys far outnumber girls, and adult males outnumber adult females. As we saw in the discussion of language, pronouns of the female gender were totally absent from the first two readers in the first grade in the Michigan schools. (The excuse was that the word *she* does not appear high enough on word lists.) Thus, females who have been talked about less will continue to be ignored.[49] An even greater proportion of male characters appears in books as one progresses to higher elementary grades. In the later grades, the characters are increasingly adults with whom the children identify, and they are adult males. In one series of Lippincott readers, thirteen books showed the following tallies:

59 stories featuring boys	11 stories about girls
28 stories featuring men	2 stories about adult women
39 male folk fantasy	10 female folk fantasy
24 male biographies	8 female biographies
36 stories about male animals	3 stories about female animals [50]

The roles in which boys and girls or men and women are shown also imply characteristics of the sexes that go beyond simple occupational stereotyping. Girls are not only ignored but are shown as passive, fearful, vain, and unable to make friends. They are told that they are not good at sports and are silly and boring. They usually watch the boys in action or are at home helping with household chores, caring for pets or for other children, or doing things to improve their appearance. They are so clumsy that they drop dishes when they are drying them, and they fall down when they try to skate. They frequently must be rescued (by boys), and they cry a lot. [51]

Boys, in contrast, do active and interesting things. They are school crossing guards, they play sports, and they help their fathers build things. They form friendships easily and have great camaraderie with each other. However, boys are not allowed to express emotion. They are never shown crying, and they are seldom shown hugging animals or playing with younger children. There is an implied pressure on them to enjoy being active and to be good at the things they do. While boys are shown indoors playing with chemistry sets and erector sets, they are still being active. There is no picture of the boy who would like to sit quietly and read or perhaps help cook.

Girls also learn early that it is a boy/man's world. One frequently quoted phrase from an elementary-school reader advises girls to "accept the fact that this is a man's world and learn to play the game gracefully." [52] When the message isn't that explicitly stated, it is often implied. In one story, Kristen, a newcomer who has been ostracized by a group of girls, bakes Danish cookies for the school fair and wins their approval. When complimented on her cooking, she says, "It's easy. Even I can do it and you know how dumb I am." The story seems to be a nice one but again manages to convey that girls are mean and exclude newcomers; that the way to gain acceptance is to do something feminine, like cooking; and in spite of everything, at least one girl is dumb—or excessively modest. [53]

Unfortunately, mathematics books also present this stereotyping. Girls are presented as not very good at math and confused by complicated problems. In some books, girls are shown earning lower salaries than those of boys, even when doing the same work. They are also shown as using mathematics for typically female tasks such as buying hair ribbons or grocery shopping. One wonders if these comparisons would be allowed if they were made between races.

Adult men and women are also shown in extremely stereotyped roles. The limited range of career options shown for women is striking. In one large survey, men participated in 213 different occupations and women in only 39 (one-fifth the number). Only seven of the female occupations were shown in more than one book, and the ones most commonly shown were nurses, librarians, elementary-school teachers, seamstresses, secretaries, mothers, and (!) witches.[54] Frequently these women were shown working only if they were single. Married women were not shown contributing to the income of the household, although in fact 50 percent of them now work. The way occupations and roles are divided between men and women is dramatically shown in these poems published for children:

What Boys Can Be

A fireman who squirts water on the flames
and a baseball player who wins lots of games,
a bus driver who helps people travel far or
a policeman with a siren in his car,
a cowboy who goes on cattle drives
and a doctor who helps save people's lives,
a sailor on a ship that takes you everywhere and
a pilot who goes flying through the air,
a clown with silly tricks to do
and a pet tiger owner who runs the zoo,
a farmer who drives a big red tractor and
on TV shows, if I become an actor,
an astronaut who lives in a space station and
some day grow up to be President of the nation.

What Girls Can Be

A nurse with white uniforms to wear or
a stewardess who flies everywhere,
a ballerina who dances and twirls around or
a candy shop owner, the best in town,
a model who wears lots of pretty clothes or
a big star in the movies and on special TV shows,
a secretary who will type without mistakes or
an artist, painting trees, clouds and lakes,
a teacher in nursery school someday or
a singer and make records people play,
a designer of dresses in the very latest style or

a bride, who comes walking down the aisle,
a housewife someday when I am grown,
a mother with children of my own.[55]

Fathers are shown working in a variety of occupations but almost never
doing anything in the house, unless they "help" the mother with the
dishes. Fathers are almost always shown outside, and they do fun things
with their children.[56] In contrast, mothers seldom do anything that is fun
with their children. They are frequently shown scolding or harrassing,
and they are shown in very limited roles. It is clear that their main role is
to be a homemaker, to cook, to clean, and to take care of children. (One
story asks where the mother is if she is not in the home at three in the
afternoon when the children get home from school.) While motherhood
is portrayed relatively positively, the books show no realism at all about
the approximately 50 percent of married women who are in the paid
work force. Single-parent families are almost never shown, although one
in six children will spend some time in a single-parent family. Finally, the
books do not deal with any of the real problems in families. They present
a peaceful and happy ideal that would be impossible to live up to in fact.
This raises unrealistic expectations in children who read the books, and
children who do not have these "ideal" families are bound to feel different and excluded.

How do minorities fare in this world of preschool and elementary-
school books? The textbook world is a world primarily for the white male.
In one series, whites are 81 percent of the illustrations; only 8 percent are
black and even fewer are American Indian, Latin, Chicano, or Asian.
While there are a few books about black and white boys together, almost
no black women are portrayed.[57]

In another analysis of a textbook series, blacks were in 10 percent of
the illustrations, American Indians in approximately 5 percent, Asians in
2 percent, and Latins in about 1 percent. When the characters portrayed
in textbooks are shown by race and by sex, we see that 18 nonwhite
males are shown for every 100 males. In contrast, only 7 nonwhite females are shown for every 100 females. As the percentage of females is
much lower to begin with (31 percent), this means that nonwhite females
comprise only a little over 2 percent of all the characters depicted.[58]

Thus, the question of representation in textbooks is not so much
one of race as it is of sex. While black males are represented in numbers
that approximate their percentage of the population, black females are
not depicted anywhere nearly as often. Black boys and white boys are
shown together as friends, but black girls and white girls are seldom, if
ever, shown together. The double whammy for black females is clear.

While we do not have exact figures on the kinds of environments
shown in the textbooks, it would clearly be difficult for many nonwhite
students to relate to the kinds of homes, schools, and environments

(ranches, suburbs) portrayed. These children do not get a chance to see the kind of family they live in portrayed, and they also find information about their cultural heritage missing.

Thus, we see that one of the most authoritative sources of sex roles—books—reinforces traditional stereotypes. The limited range of occupations shown for women depresses their aspirations, and the ones shown for men are often unrealistic, although exciting. The implication that the sexes have other kinds of attributes is even more insidious. It is bad enough that girls are ignored and shown as passive and doing only household chores. However, when they are shown as dumb, clumsy, vain, incompetent, and unfriendly, the chances for a low self-image are greatly increased. The characteristics for boys are more positive, but boys are denied quiet pastimes or expression of emotion. Most of the books now available are hurting our children by the depiction of sex-role behavior in this rigid manner.

There have been courageous attempts to correct these depictions of girls and boys and women and men. Unfortunately, good intent is not enough. One book that talks about "mommies at work" ends with "all mommies loving the best of all to be your very own mommy and coming home to you."[59] The intent of depicting working women is admirable, but the impression left is that women are not serious workers and that motherhood is their primary job. In another book entitled *The Snake in the Carpool*, a little girl finds a snake and fearlessly handles it. However, in the end the rightful owner of the snake is a boy who must show the girl how to feed the snake and how to build a house for it.[60] Again, the intent is good, but the message clearly comes through that boys know more about these things.

The sexism and racism depicted in many of these books can be eliminated. Pressure can be brought on publishers, school boards, PTOs and others who are instrumental in designing and adopting books for the schools. Parents need education so they can pick the right books for their children at an early age. The checklists that follow this chapter are helpful for evaluating children's books for racism and sexism. Take a look and see what children have been reading recently. You may be surprised at the hidden messages!

Schools

Schools reinforce traditional sex roles in many ways. Differences between boys and girls and their behavior are often stressed very early. In preschool, little boys and girls usually line up separately, use different bathrooms, and may even have recess or physical education at different times. Gender may also be used as a way to separate teams for spelling bees and other activities. Boys' groups are frequently chosen for physical activities like carrying chairs or washing blackboards, and girls' groups may be the ones to pass out cookies. Even pictures around the classroom may illustrate sex roles in one way or another. This author saw one classroom where the days of the week were illustrated by the old sayings, "Monday's wash day, Tuesday's baking," and so on, all using female models to do the household chores.

Segregated classes are another way in which boys and girls are encouraged to maintain separate roles. While these are not as prevalent in elementary school where most classes are mixed, the girls frequently get a chance to take an extra craft, sewing, or cooking class, whereas the boys are directed toward extracurricular classes such as woodworking or sports. As we noted earlier, differentiation between boys' and girls' activities on the playground comes early.

The authority structure of the elementary school itself is also a model to the children. While 85 percent of all elementary-school teachers are women, 79 percent of all elementary-school principals are men. The difference in status is quite clear to the pupils. As the grades get higher, the percentage of female teachers also gets smaller, and men have correspondingly more influence.

Female and male children are also affected by the expectations of teachers. At the nursery-school level, teachers react differently to boys and girls. Girls are rewarded for neatness, docility, obedience, passivity, and following instructions both inside and outside school. Boys are rewarded for obedience and docility in school, as well, but teachers also subtly encourage more aggressive behavior. There is a feeling that "boys will be boys." In one study, female teachers were explicitly shown to encourage independence and assertion in boys, although they rewarded dependency in both sexes.[61] For example, the teachers would often give attention to nearby, dependent girls. They would praise and assist them. They would also praise nearby, dependent boys, but then would send them off to work by themselves.

However, with the passive nature of much elementary education, boys get into trouble and become discipline problems more often than girls do. Therefore, boys get reproved by teachers more often. In one study, teachers responded to boys' class disruptions three times as often as they did to similar disruptions by girls. This disapproval was primarily for violation of rules, however. When disapproval was for lack of attention, the sexes were treated approximately equally, and when disapproval was for lack of knowledge or skill, girls were criticized more than boys.[62]

In addition, although teachers disapproved of boys more, they also listened to them more, gave them more instruction, and approved of them more. In one nursery school, boys received more directions from the teacher and were twice as likely to get individual instruction on how to do things.[63]

In one poignant example quoted by Serbin and O'Leary, a teacher helped the children in the classroom to make Easter baskets. The class had progressed to the point where they were stapling the paper handles on the baskets they had made. The teacher approached each girl in turn, took her basket, and stapled the handle with the comment, "Here, dear, let me do that for you." With the boys, the teacher gave them the stapler and showed them how to staple the handle themselves. In another example, a girl and two boys were learning Piaget's concept of "conversion." In demonstrating this concept, water is poured from one container to another to show that different shapes of containers can hold the same amount of water. The teacher let one of the boys try to pour the water himself. When the girl asked to try, she was told to wait her turn. The teacher then let the other boy try and the period ended. The materials were put away without the girl getting a chance to actually handle the containers and practice using the concept.[64]

Research about elementary school agrees that teachers see girls as less creative than boys, give less attention to girls, and reward girls for conformity.[65] One exception to the general pattern of teachers giving boys more attention was when classes engaged in explicitly feminine, sex-typed activity such as cooking; then the teachers paid more attention to the girls.

Boys are also rewarded more than girls. When Torrance asked teachers to describe situations where they had rewarded creative behavior, 74 percent of the children rewarded were boys. However, this high percentage of boys may be the result of different perceptions of who is creative. When boys and girls played with science toys and suggested uses for them, the girls suggested many more interesting and creative uses. Yet, when the students were asked whether boys or girls had contributed the ideas, they all replied that the boys had done better.[66] It seems more likely that teachers will share this perceptive bias and see boys as more creative whether they are or not.

As teacher expectations may become self-fulfilling prophecies, these data are important. While teachers are often not aware of what they are doing and may even be opposed to it in theory, they still exercise a powerful influence on the sex-role behavior of their students.[67]

Surprisingly, male and female teachers do not behave a great deal differently. In one study of 128 teachers of grades five through eight, both male and female teachers approved of dependency (a "female" behavior) for both boys and girls. Male teachers showed even greater approval of dependency than did female teachers. However, in another study male teachers also approved of masculine behavior in boys more than female teachers did. Therefore, while both boys and girls are getting a message to be passive and dependent in elementary school, boys are also being rewarded by their peers and by some teachers for operating in assertive, masculine ways.[68]

What may be the results of this type of interaction with teachers during the early years of school? One effect is that boys may get lower grades. Although boys seems to achieve as high or higher than girls on standardized tests of achievement, their grades are significantly lower. The sex of the teacher giving the grades does not seem to be as important as whether the child receiving the grades is a boy or a girl.[69] Why the lower grades for boys? Perhaps teachers expect more of them or they grade them more severely because they are not as neat or have disrupted the class more often.

Will boys suffer from the excessive amount of disapproval that they receive? Judith Bardwick, a well-known psychologist, speculates that boys learn they can get attention from disruptive behavior; thus teacher criticism, although it may seem negative, may actually lead boys to greater independence and autonomy. Boys learn how to take criticism and to assert themselves. They also seem to be more realistic about their achievement.[70] Indeed, educators speculate that boys are more likely to develop more independent, autonomous behavior as they are disapproved of, praised, listened to, and taught more by the teacher. Many educators believe that adults respond as if they find boys more interesting and attention provoking than girls. This message is not lost on either sex.

Judith Bardwick speculates that as the criticism a girl gets is more general and personal, it may lead to an oversensitivity to criticism and a tendency to do tasks only to get social approval rather than for the joy of achievement.[71] It is also speculated that girls may have lower ambition from being relatively ignored and from being criticized for lack of skill. Indeed, one study does find bright fifth- and sixth-grade girls to be lower than equally intelligent boys in self-concept and estimate of their mental abilities.[72] Even girls who do consistently well in subjects and get high grades will estimate their future grades lower than boys who get similar grades. When the girls do achieve, they attribute their success to luck, while boys who are successful attribute their success to their own skill and ability.[73] Girls seem to be less willing to take risks, less likely to try creative solutions to problems, and less willing to risk failure of any kind.[74] Girls seem to accept a negative stereotype of their abilities, often unnecessarily. At least some studies show that their opinions of themselves become lower as they progress through school, while the self-evaluations of boys become higher.[75]

Patterns of motivation are set early in elementary school. By the time girls reach ninth grade, only 3 percent of the girls, compared with 25 percent of the boys, are considering careers in science or engineering.[76] This trend continues throughout the school years and beyond into adulthood. In a longitudinal study of gifted children begun in 1920, 86 percent of the "highly gifted" men achieved success in professions, but 61 percent of the young women who were tested as "highly gifted" while young ended up being full-time homemakers rather than achieving prominence in professional fields.[77] While stereotypes and motivation have changed to some extent over the years, statistics still show that women do not achieve the career success that would be predicted on the basis of their IQ and education. We should also be reminded at this point that the sex-biased interaction with the teacher may be reinforced because the students are also probably reading the kind of sex-stereotyped books discussed above.

You might be interested in turning to the exercises at the end of this chapter and seeing whether your elementary-school teacher (or the one that your children now have) acted in the ways we have described. If he or she did, do you believe that this has affected you?

The cure, of course, does not lie in reversing the pattern. Instead, children of both sexes need to learn to be independent as well as not disruptive in class. Teachers, especially elementary-school teachers, are a very important link in the chain of sex-role stereotyping. Both sexes need equal amounts of time and attention in teaching skills and, hopefully, equal amounts of praise and disapproval.

The Black Child in School

The black child in the school setting faces some of the same sex-role stereotyped environments as the white child but often faces many other problems as well. One is that the language used by the teacher and by other children may be anywhere from slightly to considerably different from his or her own. If the black child has been brought up using street talk or black English and is now faced with the problem of talking, reading, and writing standard English, he or she is facing a language barrier as well as a typical elementary-school situation. For the male black child, in particular, to revert to standard English may be to revert to what is considered feminine in his culture. His resistance to using standard English may thus hinder his learning.[78]

In a similar fashion, playing the role of the quiet, docile student may be particularly difficult for the male black child who may base his masculinity on being "bad" or "tough." While the same problem exists for the male white child, the black boy experiences even greater conflict between the definitions of masculinity and good student.

In all cases, for working-class black students, the elementary-school environment is likely to be a distinct departure from the more active street environment where initiative and daring count. Lining up, sitting quietly and listening to stories, and concentrating on passive work for long hours may be extremely difficult for a black child who happens to come from an urban "street" environment.[79]

The female black child, however, probably is free from many stereotype problems experienced by her white counterpart. As female children in the black community are encouraged to be self-sufficient and are expected eventually to be their own support, female black children are likely to be more assertive and independent in the school setting. Indeed, if they are in an all-black school or have a female black teacher, they may be the ones getting the extra attention instead of the boys. If they are in integrated schools or with white teachers, the lack of attention that they may receive relative to the boys in the class probably doesn't hurt their self-image as much as it might hurt that of their female white classmates.[80]

On the other hand, the difficulty for many black children, both male and female, is that school subjects and materials are not relevant to their environment. While many white children will also have trouble identifying with readers depicting "mom, dad, Jane, Dick, and Spot (all white) living in a nice little white house with a picket fence in a small town with Mr. Smith, the postman, delivering letters," black children will probably find no responsive cues in the story at all. Indeed, black children will find they are treated as much as white girls are treated in the school textbooks and various readers: they are underrepresented or totally ignored. When they are shown, only the skin color may be changed, so that mom, dad, Dick, and Jane have black skins, but the environment is still one with which many black children would be unfamiliar.[81] The message is the same one that white females receive: if you are not shown, you must not be important. At the very least, this kind of school material will be irrelevant for the black child.

Summary

We have seen that children receive sex-role socialization from the cradle onward. Some of this socialization is subtle and indirect, as in the role of language; but direct influences such as the messages sent by television, books, and school teachers about appropriate sex-role behavior reinforce other subtle pressures. The early pressure to conform to traditional roles limits the potential for both sexes, particularly in regard to the emotional expression of men and the achievement potential of women.

Psychologists are now beginning to call attention to the great damage done to both men and women by our narrowly defined role models. In a statement to the American Psychological Association in September 1970, the Association of Women Psychologists said:

> Psychological oppression in the form of sex-role socialization clearly conveys to girls from the earliest ages that their nature is to be submissive, servile and repressed, . . . the psychological consequences of goal depression in young women—the negative self-image, emotional dependence, drugged or alcoholic escape—are all too common. In addition, both men and women have come to realize the effects on men of this type of sex-role stereotyping:

the crippling pressure to compete, to achieve, to produce, to stifle emotion, sensitivity, and gentleness, all taking their toll in psychic and physical traumas.[82]

Many individuals would be happier and more creative if they could choose a wider range of behavior.[83] If children are to see more kinds of behavior as sex appropriate, socialization and the institutions that perpetuate sex-stereotyped norms will have to change.

Essay Questions

1. Discuss several examples of how the same kind of word may have different implications when applied to men or to women (example: *master* or *mistress*). Discuss the different styles and vocabularies of men and women when they use language and when they respond to one another. How may this differentiation affect the way they are treated by others?

2. How are "rapping" and black English different from standard English, and why are they used?

3. It is said that a smile is "women's badge of submission." Discuss other forms of body language that imply submissiveness on the part of women.

4. How are men and women portrayed in the three different areas of television: prime-time viewing, commercials, and children's programs? Comment on occupational roles and behavioral characteristics as well as numbers. How are blacks shown in these three areas?

5. Boys and girls are portrayed quite differently in children's books. What is the relative number of boys and girls shown in these books? How are they portrayed in occupational or work roles? And (very important!) what kind of characteristics are boys shown as having? What kind of characteristics are girls shown as having?

6. How are adult men and women shown in children's books? Are women and men limited in their chosen occupations or in the behavior they are allowed to express? Give examples.

7. How can the different amount and kind of attention paid by the teacher to boys and girls affect the kind of achievement motivation they will have in the future?

8. List ten different ways in which a teacher could differentiate between boys and girls in an elementary-school classroom, (for example, different games at recess). How could these differences be eliminated?

9. Why may school seem irrelevant for many black children? (Mention at least three or four reasons in your answer.)

10. Of all the early childhood areas that teach and reinforce sex-role stereotypes, which one do you think is the most influential?

Exercises

1. Develop a list of "parallel adjectives" that are used about men and women. If men are called "absentminded," then women are called . . . ("scatterbrained"), and so on. After you have done this, talk about your feelings.
2. Take a newspaper. Count the number of men and women both in news stories and in advertisements. Make a list of important, positive images versus unimportant, negative images. How do men and women show up on these lists?
3. Watch several hours of television. Write down all the putdowns or insults to men or women ("men can't cook; women can't drive"). Would any of them not have been allowed if aimed at ethnic groups? Hint: it is extremely interesting to watch children's cartoons.
4. Watch several hours of television again and develop nonsexist commercials for all the sexist ones you find. Is it possible to have nonsexist commercials for some of the products that are advertised?
5. Read three or four children's picture books. Compare the number of aprons your mother (or you) own and wear to the number shown in the books. What is the message?
6. The following checklist is designed specifically for books (although it might also be used for television programs). Take one preschool book, one early-elementary book, and one later-elementary book and evaluate them in terms of the checklist.

Checklist for Nonsexist Socialization

- Are both men and women shown in the nurturing role and also sharing responsibility for children?
- Are both men and women shown as doing a wide range of jobs free from sex stereotyping?
- Are both boys and girls shown in active and passive play; does the play encourage physical development?
- Are both boys and girls showing a full range of emotions, from gentleness to anger?
- Are both boys and girls shown as having skill and independence?
- Are boys and girls being friends with each other?
- Are alternatives to the nuclear family shown?
- Are all ethnic and racial groups represented?

7. Evaluate classroom materials, books, television programs, and the like, in terms of the checklist.

8. Develop nonsexist materials that could be used with young children or elementary-school classrooms. For example:

> Make a jigsaw puzzle where the opposite of usual sex stereotyping is shown (examples: a girl in a job associated with the opposite sex; a father feeding a baby). After you have found the pictures, paste them on heavy cardboard and have them cut with a jigsaw. In putting the puzzle together, the idea that the baby is associated with fathers becomes reinforced.
>
> Develop a lotto game where boys and girls do the same activity (girls can be running track, for example). The idea can be modified to fit any kind of game. Just be sure that girls as well as boys get a chance to be doctors, and boys as well as girls get to do housework.
>
> Make a flannel board where you play out men and women in community roles such as officers, doctors, nurses, letter carriers, and so on.

Checklist for Classroom Teachers

- Level with students. Point out racist or sexist bias in books or materials. Help them learn to identify sources of bias and important omissions.
- Develop classroom activities around identifying bias found in television, textbooks, movies, library books, magazines, and so on.
- Incorporate the development of critical reading skills in all your teaching.
- Identify or develop supplementary materials that help correct some of the bias.
- Assign student papers, themes, term papers, or other activities on topics or persons not usually covered in textbooks or materials.
- Ask students to rewrite materials, write their own materials on subjects omitted from the textbook, or rewrite the material from another person's point of view.
- Use bulletin boards, posters, pictures, magazines, and other materials to expose students to information commonly excluded from traditional materials.

9. When students have completed review of sexist or racist materials, have them write letters and send reports to administrators, publishers, community groups, and organizations working to reduce bias.

Checklist for Classroom Teachers:
Are You Treating Boys and Girls Differently?

- Do I tend to discipline girls verbally and leniently but boys physically and strictly?
- Do I ask girls to do the housework type of tasks and the boys to do the executive duties or heavy work?
- Do I find myself taking a different tone of voice with a boy than with a girl?
- Do I notice when there are more sports activities for boys than for girls?
- Do I react when I find that there are limited activities for boys in art, drama, and dance?

Notes

1. Thomas Mann, *The Magic Mountain* ("Der Zauberberg"), translated from the German by H.T. Loul-Porter (New York: Knopf, 1949).

2. Laurel Richardson-Walum, *Dynamics of Sex and Gender: A Sociological Perspective*, 1st ed. (Chicago: Rand McNally, 1977), p. 14.

3. Michigan Women's Commission, "Sex Discrimination in an Elementary Reading Program," Lansing, Mich., 1974.

4. Barbara Eakins and R. Gene Eakins, *Sex Differences in Human Communication* (Boston: Houghton-Mifflin, 1978).

5. *Ibid.*, p. 131.

6. Julia P. Stanley, "Paradigmatic Woman: The Prostitute" (Paper presented at the South Atlantic Modern Language Association, 1972, quoted in Eakins and Eakins, *op. cit.*, p. 113).

7. Allen Nilsen, "Sexism in English: A Feminist View," *Female Studies VI* (Old Westbury, N.Y.: The Feminist Press, 1972), quoted in Eakins and Eakins, *op. cit.*, p. 123.

8. Eakins and Eakins, *op. cit.*, p. 117.

9. *Ibid.*, p. 121.

10. Nancy Henley and Barrie Thorne, "Womanspeak and Manspeak: Sex Differences and Sexism in Communications, Verbal and Nonverbal," in Alice Sargent, ed., *Beyond Sex Roles* (St. Paul, Minn.: West, 1977).

11. Eakins and Eakins, *op. cit.*, pp. 66–72.

12. Gael O'Brien, "Male Professors Found Cool to Women's Issues," *American Association of University Professors Bulletin*, April 5, 1976, p. 1.

13. Eakins and Eakins, *op. cit.*, p. 31.

14. Henley and Thorne, *op. cit.*, p. 207.

15. Eakins and Eakins, *op. cit.*, p. 39.

16. Nancy Henley and Jo Freeman, "The Sexual Politics of Interpersonal Behav-

ior," in Jo Freeman, ed., *Women: A Feminist Perspective* (Palo Alto, Calif.: Mayfield, 1975), pp. 481–82.

17. Eakins and Eakins, *op. cit.*, pp. 115–76.
18. Robert Sommer, *Personal Space: The Behavior Basis of Design* (Englewood Cliffs, N.J.: Prentice-Hall, 1969).
19. Walum, *op. cit.*, p. 22.
20. Henley and Freeman, *op. cit.*, p. 480.
21. Nancy Henley, *Body Politics: Power, Sex, and Nonverbal Communication* (Englewood Cliffs, N.J.: Prentice-Hall, 1977).
22. Eakins and Eakins, *op. cit.*, p. 171.
23. Walum, *op. cit.*, p. 30.
24. *Ibid.*, pp. 31–32.
25. *Ibid.*; Thomas Kochman, " 'Rapping' in the Black Ghetto," *Transactions* 6 (1969):106–13.
26. Women on Words and Images, *Channeling Children: Sex Stereotyping on Prime Time TV* (Princeton, N.J., 1975).
27. Nancy Tedesco, "Patterns in Prime Time," *Journal of Communication* 24 (1974):119–24.
28. *Ibid.*
29. Jane Bergman, "Are Little Girls Harmed by Sesame Street?" in Stacey *et al.*, eds., *And Jill Came Tumbling After: Sexism in American Education* (New York: Dell, 1974), pp. 110–16.
30. *Ibid.*
31. Gaye Tuchman, "The Symbolic Annihilation of Women by the Mass Media," in Gaye Tuchman, Arlene Kaplan Daniels, and Jane Benet, eds., *Images of Women in the Mass Media* (New York: Oxford University Press, 1978), pp. 3–38.
32. Joseph R. Dominick and Gail E. Rauch, "The Image of Women in Network TV Commercials," *Journal of Broadcasting* 16 (1972):259–65.
33. Judith Lemon, "Dominant or Dominated: Women on Prime Time Television," in Tuchman, Daniels, and Benet, *op. cit.*, p. 73.
34. *Ibid.*, pp. 60–61.
35. Screen Actors Guild, "Documentary Use of Minorities and Women in Prime-Time TV Shows," (Press release, October 31, 1974); see Paul Sargent, 7750 Sunset Blvd., Hollywood, Calif.
36. Muriel Canton, "Where Are the Women in Public Broadcasting?" in Tuchman, Daniels, and Benet, *op. cit.*, pp. 78–89.
37. Terry Frueh and Paul E. McGhee, "Traditional Sex-Role Development and Amount of Time Spent Watching Television," *Developmental Psychology* 11, no. 1 (1975):109.
38. Ann Beuf, "Doctor, Lawyer, Household Drudge," *Journal of Communication* 24, no. 2 (1974):142–45.
39. "Miami Murder Trial," *Detroit Free Press*, October 17, 1977, p. 11.

40. Emily S. Davidson, Amy Yasuna, and Alan Tower, "The Effects of Television Cartoons on Sex-Role Stereotyping in Young Girls," *Child Development* 50 (1979):597–600.

41. Muriel Cantor, "Children's Television: Sex Role Portrayals and Employment Discrimination," in K. Mielke *et al.*, eds., *The Federal Role in Funding Stereotypes on TV Children's Television Programming*, vol. 2 (Washington, D.C.: U.S. Office of Education, 1975), OEC 074–8674.

42. Thomas M. Wolf, "Response Consequences to Televised Modeled Sex-Inappropriate Play Behavior?" *The Journal of Genetic Psychology* 127 (1975): 35–44.

43. Richard M. Perloff, "Some Antecedents of Children's Sex-Role Stereotypes," *Psychological Reports* 40 (1977):463–66.

44. Janice Chavetz, *Masculine, Feminine, or Human* (Itasca, Ill.: E.E. Peacock, 1974), p. 84.

45. Whitney Darrow, Sr., *I'm Glad I'm a Boy; I'm Glad I'm a Girl* (New York: Simon and Schuster, 1970).

46. Lenore J. Weitzman, Deborah Eitler, Elizabeth Hokada, and Catherine Ross, "Sex-Role Socialization in Picture-Books for Pre-School Children," *American Journal of Sociology* 72 (1972):1125–50.

47. Women on Words and Images, *Dick and Jane as Victims: Sex Stereotyping in Children's Readers* (Princeton, N.J., 1972).

48. Elizabeth Fisher, "Children's Books: The Second Sex, Junior Division," in Stacey *et al.*, *op. cit.*, pp. 116–23.

49. Michigan Women's Commission, *op. cit.*

50. Women on Words and Images, *op. cit.*

51. Fisher, *op. cit.*, pp. 121–77.

52. *Ibid.*

53. Lenore Weitzman and Dianne M. Rizzo, "Images of Males and Females in Elementary School Textbooks" (Slide program produced by NOW Legal Defense and Education Fund, New York).

54. Fisher, *op. cit.*

55. Dean Walley, *What Boys Can Be*, Hallmark, no date; Walley, *What Girls Can Be*, Hallmark, no date.

56. *Ibid.*

57. Fisher, *op. cit.*, pp. 116–23.

58. Weitzman and Rizzo, *op. cit.*

59. Eve Merriman, "Mommies at Work," quoted in Elizabeth Fisher, "Children's Books: The Second Sex, Junior Divison," in Stacey *et al.*, *op. cit.*, pp. 116–23.

60. Miriam Schlein, *The Snake in the Carpool* (London and New York: Abelard, Schuman, 1963).

61. Claire Etaugh and Valerie Hughes, "Teacher's Evaluations of Sex-Typed Behaviors in Children," *Developmental Psychology* 11, no. 3 (1965):394–95.

62. P.S. Sears and D.H. Feldman, "Teacher Interactions with Boys and Girls," *National Elementary Principal* 46 (1966):30–35; also in Stacey *et al., op. cit.*

63. Lisa A. Serbin and K. Daniel O'Leary, "How Nursery Schools Teach Girls to Shut Up," *Psychology Today,* December 1975, pp. 57–58 and 102–03.

64. Serbin and O'Leary, *op. cit.*, p. 102.

65. W. Meyer and G. Thompson, "Sex Differences in the Distribution of Teacher Approval and Disapproval among Sixth-Grade Children," *Journal of Educational Psychology* 47 (1956):385–96.

66. E.P. Torrance, *Guiding Creative Talent* (Englewood Cliffs, N.J.: Prentice-Hall, 1962).

67. L. Good and J.E. Brophy, *Looking in Classrooms* (New York: Harper & Row, 1973).

68. Claire Etaugh, Gene Collins, and Arlene Gerson, "Reinforcement of Sex-Typed Behaviors of Two-Year-Old Children in a Nursery School Setting," *Developmental Psychology* 2 (1970):255.

69. Sears and Feldman, *op. cit.*, p. 153.

70. Judith Bardwick, *Psychology of Women* (New York: Harper & Row, 1971), p. 113.

71. *Ibid.*, pp. 112 and 158.

72. Sears and Feldman, *op. cit.*, p. 150.

73. Maccoby and Jacklin, *The Psychology of Sex Differences* (Stanford, Calif.: Stanford University Press, 1974), p. 154.

74. *Ibid.*

75. *Ibid.*

76. W.R. Looft, "Vocational Aspirations of Second-Grade Girls," *Psychological Reports* 28 (1971):241–42.

77. L.M. Terman and M.H. Oden, *Genetic Studies of Genius. The Gifted Child at Mid-Life. Thirty-Five-Year Follow-Up of the Superior Child* (Stanford, Calif.: Stanford University Press, 1959).

78. John U. Ogbo, "Black Education: A Cultural-Ecological Perspective," in Harriette McAdoo, ed., *Black Families* (Beverly Hills, Calif.: Sage, 1982), pp. 146–49.

79. Charles Silberman, *Crisis in Black and White* (New York: Random House, 1964).

80. *Ibid.*

81. Women on Word and Images, *op. cit.*

82. Association of Women Psychologists, "Statement Resolutions and Motions" (Statement presented at the American Psychological Association Convention, September 1970), quoted in Women on Words and Images, *op. cit.*, p. 43.

83. Janice P. Gump, "Sex-Role Attitudes and Psychological Well-Being," *Journal of Social Issues* 28, no. 72 (1972):79–92.

Chapter Five

Adolescence: A Time of Change

The adolescent boy or girl is faced with carving out an individual identity separate from parents and peers. The freedom of childhood and the comfort of being an unthinking part of one's family are left behind. Boys and girls of this life-cycle stage are faced with new norms and values, new tasks to learn, and a resultant concern about whether they are doing well in the new, freer environment. Changing bodies, combined with uncertainty about identity and behavior, too often make adolescent boys and girls anxious. Pressures for certain kinds of sex-role behavior may be intensified, such as boys being pressured to control their emotions even more rigidly than before. In other instances, prescriptions for sex-role behavior are modified; for example, the girl who was a tomboy in elementary school may find pressure on her to be more "feminine" and increased emphasis by her peers on being pretty and popular rather than on being active.

Uncertainty about appropriate behavior may be increased because our society has few rites of passage to mark the transition from boy to man or from girl to woman. In many cultures, when girls can bear children and boys are large enough to hunt game and provide for a family, they are considered adults. The adult roles and responsibilities that they take on are well known, and their passage to adult status is usually marked with some kind of ceremony. But the transition from childhood to adult status is not easily marked in our own society. With our prolonged adolescence, marriage may be deferred until ten years or more after puberty. Because there is no strict definition of the transition from boy to man or from girl to woman, the adolescent years may be marked by uncertainty and conflict as boys and girls try to separate from parental attachments. The question of just when you become a man or a woman is always there. Is it when you can bear or father children? Is it when you have your first sexual experience? Is it when you can earn a living? Is it when you are old enough to vote or to be drafted? Is it when you can drink legally or get your driver's license? There are no pat answers to these questions. While some general norms do exist, they vary by region, by size of home town, and by one's friends and family. Thus, individuals must develop their own answers to such questions as, "When are you old enough to set your own curfews and to decide how you want to spend your time?" "How much can you be seen with your parents or do things with them and still have an identity of your own?"

Some have even characterized adolescence as a time of crisis and considerable emotional pain. Douvan and Adelson say, "Most of us find it so painful to recover the emotional quality of our adolescent years . . . [that] the emotional intensity of this period comes under repression, where it is blocked out, muted, or misremembered."[1] Hall uses the German expression *Sturm und Drang,* or "storm and stress," to characterize the psychology of adolescence.[2] Anna Freud suggests that the psychic structure "dissolves" during adolescence and leaves "psychological chaos, with the adolescent a slave to his impulses and subject to anxiety, depression, poor reality testing, and a search for immediate gratifications."[3] In other literature, dramatic terms such as *turmoil, turbulence, tremendous changes,* and *chaos* are frequently used to describe this period.[4]

However, many others disagree that adolescence is a crisis and question the universality of the storm-and-stress theory. Gesell found his adolescent subjects pleasant, easy to get along with, and living in relative harmony with their environment. Others believe that adolescent crisis is created by the form of our culture.[5] Offer feels that a compromise terminology can be used to define this period more clearly. He suggests that we use Erikson's concept of "normative crisis," or the somewhat unsettling change of any transitional period. Thus a normative crisis, or transitional period, is a time of some emotionality, with changes in identity and new tasks to learn.[6] It may include rebellion or changing *reference groups,* those others to whom one looks for approval. We find that this concept of normative crisis best applies to adolescence, and we would like to use it as we discuss the changes of this time.

The most tumultuous period in adolescence seems to be early adolescence, or junior-high age. Simmons and Rosenberg, in their study of 1,917 children in grades 3 through 12, point out that early adolescents show heightened self-consciousness, greater instability of self-image, slightly lower self-esteem, and less favorable views of the opinions that others hold of them.[7] These findings agree with those of Offer, who studied a slightly older group and reported that parents and adolescents both agreed that the greatest turmoil in their lives occurred between the ages of twelve and fourteen.[8]

We also agree with Douvan and Adelson when they say:

There is not one adolescent *crisis* [italics added], but two major and clearly distinctive ones—the masculine and feminine. . . . The tone and order of development that begins in adolescence and concludes in maturity . . . differ sharply for the two sexes. . . . The areas of achievement, autonomy, authority, and control focus and express boys' major concerns and psychological growth; the object relations—friendship, dating, popularity, and the understanding and management of interpersonal crisis—hold the key to adolescent growth and integration for the girl. . . .[9]

Thus, because boys and girls face different problems in dealing with the adolescent years, we will look at their situations separately until we deal with dating and sexuality. (For convenience, we will refer to males and females as boys and girls through the high-school years and as men and women after that time. This distinction is not entirely arbitrary, as the transition to college or to the labor force usually marks the time when boys and girls move out of their parents' homes and are partly or fully their own support.)

The Masculine World in High School

In many ways, the values for adolescent boys are simply intensified versions of values already learned in early childhood. In particular, masculine, or "macho," themes intensify. The young boy was always expected to be tough and scrappy; now it is absolutely essential to hold one's own in fights and to be physically tough enough to "take it" while participating in sports. The young boy ideally was expected never to cry or show emotion; however, some leeway was allowed. Now it would be a disaster to cry or get upset in any but an angry fashion. The young boy was always supposed to be good at sports or other activities; now that pressure is increased. In addition, there are new pressures to be good (but not too good) at activities that will lead to occupational success and to be good at sex and heterosexual relationships. These pressures are intense and continually present. The penalty for not living up to the norms of being tough, being "cool," and being good is severe: rejection or simply being ignored. Let us look at each norm in turn to see how pressures are applied. While there is individual variation according to family, social class, and area, most of what we say will apply in some degree to all adolescents in American society.

Being Tough

Physical toughness is an important norm for males and can be expressed in a variety of ways. It can mean having a good body build and being in shape. A good body build is an obvious way for a boy to show he is tough and able to use force if necessary.[10] John Gagnon notes that for older middle-class men, the appearance of being tough is usually enough. It is not usually necessary to prove one's toughness by fighting or engaging in contact sports. This is not so true for blue-collar men, who may get into more physical confrontations; nor is it true for adolescents. While some boys may get through high school without any actual fights, most boys have some, and some boys have many. Fights are a way to prove that one is tough, that one's ego cannot be stepped on, that one is "a man." Fights may be picked over inconsequential things for just that reason. In addition, any confrontation over an issue may end in a fight. My son has told me that junior high school is the worst time for confrontations and fights, and I imagine that he is right, at least for middle-class boys. In other words, here are kids with big bodies but little social maturity to guide them as to when and how to use those bodies. One can also imagine the trauma of spindly seventh- and eighth-grade boys who have not yet undergone their growth spurt but must deal with adolescent norms of toughness. During this period, many boys begin to lift weights or engage in body building of some type. It is important to be tough enough to protect oneself and to look as though one can't be "messed with."

For working- and lower-class boys, the pressure to be tough is greatly intensified. Because these boys will probably not compete as much for academic and occupational success as middle-class boys, toughness is the primary field of competition, besides competition for women. Working- and lower-class boys are likely to engage in many more fights than their middle-class peers. Staples points out that fighting may be a means of gaining status among youths in the black community.[11] In the lower class, fights may actually become institutionalized with confrontations between gangs.

Body Build.   A good body build not only is a vehicle for proving toughness but also enhances a boy's social prestige. For boys, popularity is associated with strength and athletic skills.[12] In particular, a strong, heavy, athletic body build is preferred and seems to lead to popularity.[13] Physical attractiveness often determines interpersonal acceptance. Indeed, studies show that people are less likely to make negative assumptions about attractive individuals. When subjects in one study were asked to identify a person with epilepsy from two different photos, 83 percent chose the less attractive one.[14] In contrast, attractive people are described as having socially more desirable personalities and are seen as likely to be successful both professionally and maritally.[15] The importance of physical attractiveness as a factor in determining acceptance does not diminish even when a person has been known for a long time.[16]

Body build also seems to influence a boy's attractiveness to the

THE RYATTS　　　　　　　　　　　　　　**by Jack Elrod**

other sex. In a 1975 study, traditional women preferred very masculine physiques, with broad shoulders and chests and tapering hips; less traditional women preferred more moderate builds. However, even women with liberal views of sex roles rejected body builds that seemed unmasculine.[17]

The popularity enjoyed by attractive boys leads to greater self-esteem for them. Attractive boys are seen as having greater social power, and they perform more successfully within their groups.[18] Successful group performance enhances self-esteem, which is also related to high masculine role identification for males.[19] Therefore, we may at least partially agree with Gagnon's statement that "the primary power the young male has is his own body."[20] His attractiveness and body build seem to influence his popularity, his social prestige, and his ability to conform to such prescriptions for the masculine role as being tough and being good at sports, and these in turn affect his self-esteem.

Sports. Participation in athletics goes hand in hand with a good body build as evidence of toughness. Coleman states that athletic or sporting ability for boys is directly associated with high status and membership in the adolescent elite, and that the adolescent's position in relation to this elite has a direct bearing on his self-image, his adjustment, and his general development.[21] Athletic achievement is thus directly linked to prestige for males.[22] It seems to be the single most important factor for a male adolescent's social standing in high school.[23]

There are social-class differences in the emphasis on body build and some indication that competitive sports are less valued in middle- and upper-class high schools,[24] but schools still give overwhelming emphasis in time and financial support to sports.[25] A great deal of the social life of the school is organized around participating in or watching sports events. Boys are told that they should participate in sports and are encouraged—even pressured—to do so. Offer tells of one young man who was a very good athlete but was not particularly interested in sports. He liked music. The coach made fun of this student in front of the whole gym class and even some of the bigger boys pin him against a wall and threaten to "cut your long hair and make you a real man if you don't join the group and fight for your high school."[26] Luckily the student had a good deal of self-confidence, his own group of friends, and supportive parents, and so he was able to withstand this kind of pressure.

The pull to the sports world is reinforced by the fact that many of the teachers who are highly respected by faculty and students alike are also coaches.[27] Students often see these coaches as confidants and among the few teachers who treat them as individuals. Offer points out that the adolescent emphasis on athletics may be partially a reflection of the adult emphasis on sports. Boys frequently see adult males who are fanatic followers of all kinds of sports and teams, from the hometown league to professional players.

While there is some variation by social class, contact and team sports probably contribute the most to masculine prestige; general team sports (baseball) or general contact sports (wrestling) are next; and sports that are neither team nor contact (track) are last in the hierarchy. Snyder and Spreitzer suggest that within the lower rung of the hierarchy, track would be more prestigious than gymnastics for men in most regions and social classes, because sports like track involve endurance and the projecting of the body through space with some force, while sports like gymnastics or tennis involve less force and more grace, although as much or more skill.[28]

Thus, the best way for a boy to gain prestige in the junior-high or high-school world of sports is to play football. The sacrifices boys will make to play are mute testimony to the need for this prestige. Smaller boys who get clobbered by their classmates in the running of every play will still go out for the team and take the punishment. Boys will endure brutal training techniques and three or four hours of practice a day, giving up their weekends, giving up dating and drinking during the season, giving up summers for football camp or training—all to be a member of the team. In this way they show that they are tough enough and skilled enough to be accepted.

There are negative aspects to this overemphasis on toughness and work in sports. It has been documented that much of the spontaneous fun associated with childhood sports is eliminated in overorganized athletic leagues for children at an early age. Clearly, children become more negative about sports as the fun dimension is gradually replaced by emphasis on skill and success.[29] The high degree of organization and consequent lack of fun are certainly evident in sports in junior and senior high school. They are not fun, at least not very much fun; they are work. What they are all about is proving yourself.

The emphasis on group conformity as being part of the team may also be excessive. Although group identity provided by team membership may ease the transition to manhood[30] and even be a rite of passage, belonging may have a price. Some teams have special "initiations" to show that the boy has arrived or has been accepted as a member of the team. Needless to say, these rites emphasize that the boy must be a man among men, that he must be tougher than the tough. If he takes his initiation without complaining, he is a member of the team. While some teams do this informally by "making it tough" for the new guys and others have mild initiations, one seriously difficult initiation was recently described in the *Ann Arbor News*. Several members of the University of Michigan hockey team kidnapped a new team member from his dorm room, stripped him (in twenty-degree weather), and shaved his body hair in front of the dorm. They then poured alcohol into the still-naked young man, stuffed him in the trunk of a car, and drove around for three or four hours in the freezing weather. When they finally dumped the initiate on his dorm steps, he could neither walk nor talk and had to be treated for exposure at the hospital. In spite of great pressure from administrative officials, he never told who had initiated him.[31] Fraternity initiations in college have similar functions of strengthening ties to the in-group, of course, but the physical-toughness element is stressed in initiations for teams.

Violence. Another element of being tough in sports is the violence that is an illegal but common accompaniment of most sports. Hockey certainly has enough legitimate body contact, but it is believed that many fans really relish the extra checking against the boards, the fights that break out, and the general violence that goes beyond the sport itself. One researcher reports that young hockey players perceive that their illegal behavior in hockey is supported by their coaches, parents, and nonplaying peers.[32] In one court case involving hockey professionals, Boston's Dave Forbes was charged with aggravated assault with a dangerous weapon—his hockey stick. His victim, Henry Bourcha, almost lost an eye. Forbes claimed that Bourcha had hit him first and that he had to retaliate. He stated that if he didn't fight back, he would be an easy mark from then on. He pointed out that fighting back is an integral part of the game, taught to players as youngsters. "Before the trial (which ended with no verdict), National Hockey League president Clarence Campbell defended fighting as a well-established safety valve for players, and even as an essential ingredient for the economic well-being of the game. . . . 'Insofar as fighting is part of the show, certainly we sell it, he said.' "[33]

Sports are not just an area in which the adolescent can prove toughness. They are a reflection of the dominant values of the society. The values of being tough, working hard, winning at all costs, and working with the team continue into adult male life. While the majority of adult males may be watchers rather than participants in team sports, they still live by the values. Sports are a way, therefore, to socialize adolescents to learn the values of the adult male world. Betty Harragan, in *Games Mother Never Taught You*, has pointed out how the rules of the team player carry over into the corporate world. She notes that one learns to play by the rules, to play one's own position, to take criticism, and not to talk back to the coach. The player learns that you can't win them all and sometimes the crowd will be against you, that you must play with those you don't like, and that you must cooperate and compete at the same time.[34] These rules stand a boy in good stead later in the business world.[35]

The slogans frequently used for athletics show how other adult male values of effort, coolness, noncomplaint, aggressiveness, and competition are socialized in sports:

> It's easier to stay in shape than to get in shape.
>
> It takes a cool head to win a hot game.
>
> The guy who complains about the way the ball bounces usually dropped it.
>
> The harder I work, the luckier I get.
>
> No one ever drowned in sweat.
>
> Anyone can be ordinary, but it takes guts to excel.
>
> A gentleman winning is getting up one more time.
>
> A quitter never wins; a winner never quits.
>
> When the going gets tough, the tough get going.
>
> Winning isn't everything; it's the only thing.
>
> They ask not how you played the game, but whether you won or lost.
>
> If it doesn't matter whether you win or lose, why keep score?
>
> There is no "I" in team.
>
> Who passed the ball to you when you scored?
>
> An ounce of loyalty is worth a pound of cleverness.[36]

The emphasis on sports, then, is on achievement and success through competition, hard work, and discipline. Sports socialization also tells the young man that he must adopt certain behavior patterns to win: he must be cool and he must keep trying.[37]

For the working- or lower-class boy, success in sports becomes extremely important. Although often a false promise, it can be a possible occupation or a way out of the ghetto. It is also a way to gain acceptance by the larger society. Some black leaders have become worried about the overemphasis on sports for the black child. Arthur Ashe, the tennis star, points out in "An Open Letter to Black Parents: Send your Children to the Library" that while black athletes comprise 60 percent of the National Basketball Association, blacks are less than 4 percent of the doctors and lawyers in the United States. Few can qualify at the top of the athletic heap, and the period of earning a high salary is a short one.[38] Nevertheless, sports are a route to achievement for some black youths.

For all young males, sports represent a chance to prove themselves masculine and, if they are really good, to be sports heroes. There are few other paths to adulation for the adolescent male. Success in sports means approval of both peers and parents, it means social success, and it may even mean a future occupation.

The emphasis on toughness and athletic ability is especially difficult for the boy who does not have a spectacular body build or athletic skills. If what he can do physically determines to a great extent his social acceptance by others and his own self-esteem, the boy who is nonathletic may suffer. He is less likely to be a leader[39] and is more likely to doubt his masculinity.[40] For the boy who is physically large, strong, and talented, sports may provide an avenue toward a masculine identity. For the boy who is not athletically inclined, not playing sports deprives him of a culturally defined route to masculine identity.

Therefore sports and toughness influence the lives of most young males in one way or another. The following quotes from a recent book emphasize this all-pervasive influence:

> I went out for three sports in high school because I needed to stabilize myself and to possibly raise my self-esteem. I eventually gained some stability but was on the whole unsuccessful in all three sports, though I felt I had the determination and the desire to be great. My low self-concept did not help me out at *all* in sports, which demanded quite the opposite.

> It was during seventh and eighth grade that I had mad crushes on girls, but the hope of achieving as much as a kiss seemed to me a dream too remote to hope for. By my eighth-grade year, I had started to play football as I had already achieved my six-foot height was beginning to get myself straight.[41]

Being Cool

Not showing the emotions, being cool, is an element of the "ideal" male role that carries over into many other areas than just the emotional realm. Part of the image of being tough is to be cool. The person who maintains a calm exterior during an exciting sports competition or during a physical encounter is also being tough. Lack of emotion is supposed to signal many things: that the person is not afraid of danger (as in skiing a steep slope) or is keeping a cool and reasonable mind in the face of hot competition (during a basketball game). Being cool is also interpreted as not expressing tender emotions, at least not expressing them in public. This part of being cool may be a denial of the tender and gentle side of men, but it is also a denial of what are considered "feminine" characteristics.

Thus, the man who is cool has a perpetual poker face and keeps his feelings to himself.

The Inexpressive Male.   The epitome of the "cool dude" is the actor John Wayne, whose dialogue consisted primarily of "yup" and "nope" while acting in death-defying roles. Actually, John Wayne epitomizes a particular kind of inexpressive male: the "man's man," who is rugged, tough, and quiet.[42] He enjoys men's activities and the outdoors and is a little uncomfortable around women. Although he respects them and always treats them politely, he is more likely to spend time and use tender words with his horse (car, boat) than with a woman. My high-school-aged informants tell me that a more modern version of the John Wayne role described by Balswick and Peek is the type of man portrayed by actor Clint Eastwood. He has played a role in several recent movies where he has not spoken a word but is tough and handy with a gun. Women obviously have their place as mothers and housekeepers and should be respected, but they are not really a part of these men's intimate worlds. The male gangs of football players and others in high school may come the closest to fulfilling this image. While many of these high-school boys date girls, they do not spend much time with them and do not really relate to them in other than a sexual way. One quote from a high-school boy shows this:

> I don't allow myself to get involved with girls in any kind of meaningful relationship. I see girls as a softening agent to guys like me who can't afford to soften up in a love thing. The reason I can't afford to soften up is that I'm in sports and a degree of meanness and toughness is needed for me to excel.[43]

For this kind of male, the worlds of males and females are separate. We will see this style again in the blue-collar marriage.

Another type of inexpressive male is not so quiet, although he rarely reveals his emotions either. This type is epitomized by the James Bond character in films. Such a man relates to women and spends time with them. He is verbal and articulate, but he relates in an artificial way; he uses a "line." He does not really express his emotions or actually get involved in a relationship. He is not respectful of females but sees them as sex objects and is more likely to use them.[44]

While most high-school boys and adult men do not fall completely into either category of "cool man," the models are there to copy. When men must keep quiet if they are scared, if they are disappointed or hurt, if they have tender feelings, not much is left for them to talk about that has deep, personal meaning. It is hard for them to get intimate with anyone, in the sense of revealing themselves, without breaking the code of "being cool." Douvan and Adelson report that significantly more boys than girls worry about control of their emotions, especially over the emotion of anger.[45] Offer also reports that boys spent a great deal of time and effort curbing aggressive tendencies. Most of the boys used sports to cope with aggression, and they coped with feelings of sexuality by ignoring them on the whole—by denying and repressing them during the first year or so of high school.[46] Sermat reports that males who disclose a great deal of personal information to another male are less well liked,[47] and rejected male adolescents in one study are characterized by other males as pesky, noisy, conceited, silly, and effeminate.[48]

Researchers have taken different perspectives toward the inexpressive male. Some have suggested that learned inexpressiveness is good later in life. A man will modify inexpressiveness somewhat with a wife, but it keeps him away from other women.[49] Others, who have taken a dimmer view of such inexpressiveness, have said that it is not a help to marriages and is often used as a weapon against women. In our discussion on language, we saw that men will frequently not answer women and will cut off a woman's conversation. They also use their own silence to frustrate women and make them feel there is something wrong with them.[50]

Homophobia.   Another reason it is difficult for men to get close to other men is because of the homosexual taboo. Too close a relationship with another man—perhaps one in which the other man may cry or tell of fear and self-doubt—may make his friend fear that this man will abandon masculine role behavior. It is unnerving and frightening to many men when a man does reveal himself, and a frequent response has been, "Get yourself together, man." If the man has sought physical comfort, if he has cried in his friend's arms, if he has been given a hug at some point, the problem is further compounded. Now there is a fear that latent homosexuality exists and may come out. It has been proposed that this excessive fear of homosexuality among men may occur because of the excessively strong prohibition against doing anything feminine like hugging when they were small. As young boys must be weaned from their identification with their mothers and taught to identify with the male role, the prohibition against doing anything "feminine" is often extremely strong. In the stereotype, to be "feminine" means not being "masculine." Any departure from aggressively heterosexual masculine role behavior is also seen as not being masculine, and "feminine" characteristics in a male become equated (however erroneously) with being homosexual. Thus, the boy who looks effeminate in childhood may be called a "girl" or a "sissy," but he may also be called a "fag" or another derogatory homosexual term.[51] (We will say more about homophobia later.)

The result of this homosexual taboo is that men often fear real closeness with one another. They fear possible homosexuality. They fear losing status if they reveal themselves. The way to not get close is to be cool. Oh, you can be friends, but there is a limit to the emotions expressed and the topics discussed. There is also a limit to when and where you can touch. Because one male touching another can imply homosexuality and is thus taboo, at least in our culture, touch between men seems to have evolved with some ritual. While men would never think of giving each other a pat on the fanny in any other situation, have you noticed what happens when a football player makes a particularly good play or the hockey lineup skates onto the ice? As each successive player skates onto the ice, for example, the player before gives him a pat on the rear with his stick. Athletic events are the few times you will also see men holding hands, often in the huddle of a football game, or hugging each other in joy after some triumph. It is OK to do these things on the field; it would not be OK to do them any other place. The hugs, and even the hand holding, are symbols of achievement in a competitive male domain; the athletic mystique and its connection to the masculine role protects men from charges of homosexuality. In a similar fashion, one of the few times tears are allowed for men is when their team has lost an important game. No one will fault a player or a coach for a few quiet trickles down the cheeks or for burying his face in his hands; but the same tears would be unacceptable at a movie or even at the loss of a job.

We will return below to this whole idea of men experiencing discomfort in their friendships with other men. It is enough to say here that the prescription to be cool is one of the dominant ones of adolescence, and it means that adolescent boys keep a certain distance from their male friends and from their female ones. Being cool is also a difficult thing to do with the problems and stresses of this period, and in his struggle to be cool, a boy may become oversocialized to be inexpressive.

It is interesting that when men do disclose themselves and talk about their feelings and their troubles, they usually talk to a woman. Frequently they talk to a woman who is a friend rather than a girlfriend. A woman is more likely to listen supportively and not to "put them down" for emotions like fear or self-doubt.[52] In contrast, it is very difficult for men to talk intimately with other men. They can be friendly, but it is hard for them to be friends. To admit to doubt, fear, or strong feelings may make them lose status with other men. Thus, many male conversations center around sports, business, war stories, or personal stories of achievement in the physical realm or with women.

Being Good at Something

After being tough and being cool, the next prescription for the adolescent boy is to be "good." This means to achieve at something. Preferably, the "something" will include physical prowess in sports. It can also include "being good" at sex or, to some extent, being good in school. We have already looked at the need to achieve and to be good in sports, and we will look at sexual "achievement" below.

Career Plans.   When Douvan and Adelson asked the boys in their sample what gave them high self-esteem, the boys talked about work and skill. In particular, many mentioned contributing to a work group and achievement in school. When they were worried, they seemed worried about realistic problems such as doing well in school and going to college. Interestingly enough, most of the boys seemed to feel quite happy with their lives; 38 percent said they would not change anything about themselves or their situations.

Douvan and Adelson believe that boys anchor much of their identity in occupational choices. They say that the boy "is made to feel, however much he may doubt it deep down, that his identity is in his own hands, that the choice of a vocation and with it, a life style, will define him."[53] Douvan and Adelson report that when boys are asked about the future, they are consistently concerned about their work role. Fifty percent of the boys mention a professional or semiprofessional job they want to reach; 30 percent think they will be skilled laborers, and only 20 percent say that they will do unskilled work. While half the boys choose jobs that are higher in skill and status than those of their fathers, they seem to plan realistically to work toward those jobs. Few name glamour jobs; rather, they name a wide variety of jobs and some highly specific ones. They also choose colleges and courses with a rough idea of the jobs they will enter. Most choose work that has a high interest level for them.[54]

Others support Douvan and Adelson's finding that a boy's identity and self-esteem come largely from high achievement. Beech and Schoeppe found, in a survey of 739 New York City pupils in grades 5, 7, 9, and 11, that boys exhibited a unitary theme of increasing achievement orientation (in contrast to girls, who exhibited dual themes of achievement and stereotyped feminine roles).[55] Offer also mentions that boys name school and study as their most important areas of concern and conflict.[56]

Academic Success.   In the academic area, Coleman notes ambivalence in the boys about achievement, as peers pull the boys away from academic success to some extent:

> The average boy, as an individual, appears to be more oriented to scholarship than is the social system of the high school. The norms of the system constitute more than an aggregate of individual attitudes; they actually pull these attitudes away from scholarship. The implication is striking: the adolescents themselves are not to be held accountable for the norms of their adolescent culture. As individuals, they are less oriented away from scholarship than they are as a social system.[57]

Yet the pull away from academics is not just the collective pull of peer attitudes but is also influenced by ambivalence in adult cultural values as well. Offer believes that if adolescents and their parents were asked to choose between going to a football game and listening to a lecture by a famous scientist, the same percentage in both generations would choose each event. Therefore, while the peer norms that give little emphasis to academic achievement are present, they do not necessarily represent any kind of adolescent subculture, but rather reflect the ambivalence about scholarship and its connection to success in the real world.

Thus, while middle-class boys are expected to do well enough in school to get into college, they are not necessarily supposed to be "brains." It is shameful to flunk, but it may also not be appropriate to get too many A's. Although it is acceptable to study for the big test or for exams, turning down a chance to go out with the boys just to study may be difficult. As Hoffman and Hoffman point out, the prevailing tone in the public high school, at least, is somewhat anti-intellectual.[58] The praise goes to the athletes; those who are rewarded for academic achievement may be considered a little strange. Another factor may be the more recent recognition of the costs of success and fame, which often come only after spending many youthful years in professional school. As we will see below, boys have increasingly shown a fear of success, citing stress, health problems, and lack of time for individual pursuits.[59] Others have suggested that this unwillingness to work very hard may reflect the tone of the "me generation" of the 1970s: it's time to have fun; life is too short to work so hard. There seems to be less willingness to defer gratification and to use discipline to study and work.

Therefore, being good is a qualified ideal. In sports and in social and sexual interaction, the commandment is clear that the adolescent boy should do his absolute best. However, in academics and the future occupational world the prescription is not so definite.[60]

Other Areas of Being Good.   For the adolescent male, being good also extends into a variety of other areas. It may mean being a good driver, knowing about cars, and knowing something about woodworking or cameras and other things. It is very difficult for a boy of this age to admit lack of knowledge in an area. It is part of being good and being cool to always be competent. Obviously, this is an impossible goal. However, the fact that the goal exists keeps a terrific pressure on the boy. He may feel the need to "act smart" even when he isn't. He may attempt to relieve the pressure by weeding out areas where competence would not be considered absolutely necessary or might even be considered feminine— like dancing. While some boys might gain prestige from being good dancers, many boys can keep from learning without penalty.

Being good also means being good at sex. It is up to the boy to initiate social and sexual overtures and to be successful in his interaction with women. This is one other pressure added to the many already mentioned. We will talk more about sexuality in the next chapter.

By late adolescence, most boys are working at part-time jobs. They need to support cars and dates and perhaps to buy clothes or save for college. They may gain competence by means of these jobs. They also gain social power by having money. Thus work may be a bonus way to gain skills. In this and other areas, the pressure for being good is very real, and the adolescent boy may figure out ways he can be good, tough, and cool in as many areas as possible.

The Feminine World in High School

Sources of Self-Esteem

Maccoby and Jacklin report that high-school girls have the same level of self-esteem as boys, but the sources of that self-esteem seem to differ. It seems more difficult for girls to gain self-esteem from concrete achievements that they control. About 60 percent of American girls under age fourteen mention sports and physical activities as things that are in the male domain—that is, they are things that boys, not girls, do for the most part.[61] Certainly athletic facilities and support for girls' sports are different and inferior. Girls may even learn that they "should not be athletic."[62] We will look at how girls are moving more into sports today and how this is affecting their self-image, but sports still are probably not a primary source of self-esteem for girls. In the same fashion, academic achievement may be limited for girls. Douvan and Adelson report that few girls are highly invested in school or work *per se*.[63] We will examine below some of the reasons for their lack of investment in academics.

Being Pretty.   Much like boys, girls gain a great deal of self-esteem from their physical appearance. Douvan and Adelson also found that about 60 percent of the girls they surveyed believe that their physical appearance is crucial for their popularity with boys.[64] To some extent they are probably correct. In a study done by Coombs and Kenkel, 500 men and women filled out a questionnaire on what they wanted in a date. Attractive physical appearance was a very important quality for the boys to find in their female companions.[65] Good-looking females also seem to influence males more than good-looking males influence females.[66] Both women and men are happier with a "computer date" if that date is attractive.[67] We might think that this is superficial and that personality becomes more important as someone is known better; however, the influence of attractiveness on the desirability of the person as a date does not diminish as the person becomes better known.[68] Therefore, girls may perceive accurately that physical attractiveness is very important to their popularity and dating success.

In spite of the importance of physical appearance and popularity, many girls report themselves as unhappy with thier looks or social skills. Douvan and Adelson report that 60 percent would like to change their looks (compared to 27 percent of boys in the same sample), and 33 percent would like to improve their social skills. Many report themselves as dissatisfied with their bodies in other ways. Seventy-three percent worry about the acceptance of their peers, and all the girls in Douvan and Adelson's sample say they would like some change in themselves (compared to 60 percent of the boys), but few are working specifically toward any changes.[69] This lack of control over important aspects of self-image can create anxiety, and as Rosenberg points out, anxiety can lead to lower self-esteem.[70]

Related to concern about appearance may be concern for the "right kind of dress." The right kind is the kind that is popular among peers at any particular school. There may even be several different peer groups in the school, each with its own proper style of dress. It is a matter of dire necessity for both male and female adolescents to dress in "the right way" and to be approved of. Any small deviation is a disaster. Shoes, shirts, and pants have to be the right brands and even the right colors. Students who deviate from the norm may be made fun of or even rejected, unless they have a great deal else going for them in the way of personality and personal support. There is some variation in the appropriate feminine clothing, at least in the early years of adolescence. A young girl may go off to school one day wearing jeans (designer jeans), top, and low shoes (name brand). The next day, she may wear a skirt, hose, and heels. This variation in style may be part of the testing out of various self-images.

Thus, dissatisfaction with self and the need for approval come together and become translated into preferred conformity of physique and dress style as a way of winning approval. It is important to stress that this approval is the approval of one's peers, not of one's parents. (They just pay the bills!)

Being Popular and Being Nice.   Girls also base a great deal of their self-esteem on interpersonal relations. Douvan and Adelson report that the self-esteem of girls is anchored in interpersonal relations rather than in achievement, work, or skill. Seventy-three percent of the girls that they studied worried about acceptance by their peers, compared to 29 percent of the boys in their sample.[71] Rosenberg also stresses that girls consistently give high priority to being liked. They stress the values of interpersonal harmony and of such desirable personality traits as being likable, easy to get along with, friendly, sociable, pleasant, and well liked.[72] These values are very similar across all social classes (in contrast to the differing achievement values of boys in the working class and the middle class). Girls seem to increase in their social orientation during the period between sixth and twelfth grades (in contrast to the boys' increase in achievement orientation).[73] Another study of 24,000 students showed females as more consistently cooperative in their attitudes during adolescence, while males were consistently competitive in theirs, with the greatest difference between the sexes in grades 8 through 10. Females jump in their orientation toward cooperation in grades 8, 9, and 10.[74] Linger, in a 1971 sample of almost 4,500 tenth and eleventh graders, also found that females were more congenial and more likely to display strong affiliation than were males.[75] Girls and boys both agree that the most acceptable girls are good-looking, tidy, friendly, likable, enthusiastic, cheerful, quiet, and interested in dating.[76] Being popular for girls is inextricably tied up with "being nice." We will examine the whole idea of "being nice" in our discussion of the dating personality in chapter 6.

Sources of Stress

Good Looks As A Mixed Blessing. There is some indication that good looks in a female may be a mixed blessing. While good looks give girls more social power and lead to popularity, good-looking girls may be feared by men[77] and are often perceived as less intellectually competent, although good looks and intelligence are not correlated in any way.

As being pretty and popular is so important to many female adolescents, good looks may also become associated in a girl's mind with being worthy as a person. The girl who is not attractive or popular may even develop low self-esteem. Judith Bardwick believes that the connection between good looks and worthiness may last in a female's mind throughout her life and make her excessively dependent on approval.[78]

Lack of Control over Outcomes. Girls may see being pretty and popular as the route to femininity. But because they are operating in the realm of interpersonal relationships rather than of concrete achievements, girls have much less control over areas that are important to them. While beauty can be faked to some extent, it is difficult to charge one's basic appearance. To be popular, a girl must also have someone respond to her: someone must call her, talk to her, or ask her out. While a girl may do everything in her power to elicit the response she wants, she does not have the ultimate control over getting it.

Ambiguous Definitions of Femininity. The definition of what is feminine has also become less clear, and this ambiguity leads to stress. The adolescent girl may find her mother critical of her dress and of how she displays her body. At the same time, she sees actress Brooke Shields in a sexy jeans ad saying, "Nothing comes between me and my Calvin's." On a magazine cover she sees a pretty woman backpacking, but she hears her father say that he really likes to see women in skirts and high heels. This lack of a specific definition for being "feminine" may lead to some confusion and feelings of lack of control. One study that looked at the possible stress caused by the ambiguity in contemporary feminine sex-role norms reported that women who allow their identities to be defined or molded by their relationships with others are in a very vulnerable position that may affect their health and well-being.[79]

Femininity and Future Roles

Douvan and Adelson point out that the goals girls hold for the future are more ambiguous and less consistent than those of boys. They say, "We must teach the girl the attitudes and skills for her central feminine goals and at the same time give her the kind of training that will permit her to choose appropriate individual or egoistic goals as well."[80] These two sets of goals are often in conflict. If the girl makes a clear-cut choice in either direction, they point out that she is likely to feel uneasy. For example, if she remains single and chooses a professional career, she may feel that she has somehow failed as a woman. If she decides on a wife-and-home-maker role, she does not have total control over adopting that role and may feel guilty about not working. With this kind of conflict, girls tend to keep both options open when they answer questions about their future plans. They talk about educational and job-related goals for the future, although only about 30 percent mention marriage goals.

Career Orientations and Academic Success. It is clear that most girls have not realistically and definitively considered job choices. Their aims may be inappropriately vague in terms of the needs and training required for occupations they wish to enter. For example, one girl mentions wanting to be a nurse or doctor as though the two were equivalent choices in terms of preparation. Girls' job choices are usually centered around a narrow range of highly visible and traditionally feminine occupations. Thirty-four percent of the girls mention being a secretary; 21 percent being a nurse; and 17 percent being a teacher. They also choose glamour jobs, such as modeling and being a stewardess, that may actually be unrealistic for them to pursue. They seldom choose any kind of manual labor jobs as appropriate to aim for, and they are much less interested in the content of the jobs they choose and much less aware of what is necessary to train for them than boys are. Girls are more likely to consider subsidiary aspects of jobs when they make their occupational choices. Twenty-three percent of the girls, but only 6 percent of the boys, desire social service; 17 percent of the girls and 6 percent of the boys mention nice co-workers; and 11 percent of the girls but none of the boys mention a desire to work with children.[81]

Most of the girls in Douvan and Adelson's sample have educational aspirations that are almost as high as those of boys. Ninety-seven percent of the fourteen-to-sixteen-year-old girls plan to finish high school; 34 percent of the girls as compared to 46 percent of the boys plan to go on to college. The girls are not as certain as the boys, though, as to how college will fit in with their future occupational plans. In fact, a third of the girls who plan to go to college want to enter occupations for which they will not need college training. Douvan and Adelson suggest that for most girls the primary purpose of college is to broaden their interests and sharpen their focus. It is not seen directly as an avenue to achieving occupational aims. In fact, Douvan and Adelson point out that very few of the girls are interested in work or school *per se.*[82] In contrast to older boys, older girls do not seem to plan more realistically for the world of work during the college years. Few of the girls choose any sort of career that involves strong commitment. Some want to achieve but do not mobilize the skills and efforts needed to do so. Although they want social status, most of the middle-class jobs they choose require little skill and will lead to little prestige.

Marriage is a major goal for many girls. Although few mention it directly in future plans, 96 percent in one study answer a direct question and avow that they want to get married. They want a middle-class style of life and seek a cooperative and congenial marriage partner in a companionship marriage. (Only 7 percent want husbands who work in factories or at trades; and only another 5 percent want husbands who work at blue-collar jobs.) Interestingly enough, Douvan and Adelson point out that this image of marriage is middle class, but the acceptance of such an image spreads over all the social classes.[83] Rosenberg also found that girls are more likely than boys to hold similar values whatever their social class.[84]

In girls' fantasies, the themes that dominate are those of femininity, personal attractiveness, and popularity. The stress on femininity can also be seen in the qualities that girls admire in others; 76 percent admire such qualities as kindness, generosity, and thoughtfulness, compared to 34 percent of the boys. When they choose adult ideals, girls are less likely than boys to mention character traits like responsibility and resourcefulness (18 percent of the girls compared to 28 percent of the boys); they seldom mention work skills (22 percent of the girls and 40 percent of the boys do so). Girls are also less likely to name personal achievement as a source of self-esteem (25 percent of the girls; 36 percent of the boys). Girls mention popularity, acceptance by others, and adult recognition as the qualities that make them feel "important and useful."[85]

Thus, girls seem to show a desire for stereotypically feminine traits and roles in addition to some orientation toward middle-class status and individual achievement. Beech and Schoeppe, in a 1974 study of 739 New York City pupils in grades 5 through 11, also found that boys exhibited a unitary theme of increasing achievement orientation, whereas girls showed a dual theme of achievement and stereotyped feminine roles as their values developed through adolescence.[86] Several factors may influence girls to be less specific about their future occupational identities than men are. Let us look at some of them now.

Negative Stereotypes. The stereotype of women includes some unflattering ideas about their ability and competence. They are known as "terrible" drivers; they are told they are not logical; they hear that they cannot balance their checkbooks or do math; and they are told that they swing (at baseballs) like "rusty gates." Most of these stereotyped ideas, of course, are untrue. For example, one only has to check with insurance companies about the rates quoted for young male and female drivers to know which sex has the better driving record. These stereotypes, however, are very prevalent in our everyday culture: we hear them on television, we read them in books, we see them in the movies. Women may actually come to believe that they are not good at many of these things.

Even when women do not actually believe they are so unskilled, they may find themselves trying to fool the men in their lives about their abilities or holding back so that they will not seem unfeminine to the world in general.[87] This game means that they are not realizing their own potential, that their relationships may be dishonest, and, finally, that they reinforce the original notion that they cannot be admired for their concrete accomplishments—that they must be admired only for what they *are*, not what they *do*.

The irony is that some evidence shows that men *do* admire competent women, even women who are competent in masculine specialities. Some men admit to being threatened by intellectual women, but they usually find ways to compensate for this threat. They may pick an intellectual woman who is less attractive than the average woman or has few social skills.[88] Other evidence shows that men truly admire the woman who can stand on her own without leaning on them—the woman who can balance her own checkbook or who can hold her own in a game of tennis. One study showed both men and women liking best a woman who was competent and had masculine interests. The one exception was very traditional men, who liked incompetent, feminine women the best.[89] Ironically, men seem to admire masculine skills in women, and women seem to admire feminine traits like sensitivity and understanding in men.[90]

Yet women may come to believe elements of the negative stereotype. Although girls make better grades in schools than boys do until late high school, some research seems to show that girls' opinions of their own abilities grow worse with age and their opinions of boys' abilities get better. Boys also develop better opinions of themselves and worse opinions of girls' abilities.[91] Unfortunately, these data are from the late 1950s, and little recent data bear directly on the topic. One other study done by

Philip Goldberg and its replications do seem to indicate that women and men may not value the abilities of women as highly as those of men. Goldberg gave a college class of women a series of professional articles dealing with material in male- and female-dominated fields of study. Some of the articles listed the author as John McKay and others as Joan McKay. Students were asked to rate the articles on value, writing style, and the like. The male authors came out ahead in every case, even in the female-dominated fields like dietetics.[92] Replications of the study with classes of both men and women have had mixed results. Some of the research showed devaluation of women's work and other studies did not.[93]

We should not be surprised that this devaluation of women's work is supported by some studies. The fact that women do have lower social status in our culture and are often devalued by themselves and others is not hard to document. Both sexes seem to value the characteristics, values, and activities of men more highly than those of women.[94] They may also see success and achievement as male traits.[95] Mental health professionals characterize the mentally healthy adult as having the characteristics that we associate with a "masculine" man. By contrast, "feminine" characteristics such as dependency and passivity are connected with adults who are deemed mentally unhealthy.[96]

In addition, when girls do succeed, they do not give themselves credit and thus feel better. They attribute their success to luck or to hard work rather than to innate ability. When they fail, however, they believe it is because of their innate characteristics. Thus, they seldom feel better when they do a good job, but always blame themselves when they don't perform.[97]

School and Messages about Ability.   Girls may get other messages suggesting they are not able. In a continuation of the pattern of the elementary-school years, teachers pay more attention to boys. Many high-school girls and college women claim that they are ignored or taken less seriously when they speak out in class, particularly in male-dominated academic areas. Surveys show they are right: their teachers take them less seriously, and the girls get the subtle message that they are not worth listening to.[98]

We have seen in chapter 2 that mathematics is one area in which girls are taken less seriously and that high-school girls may often feel incompetent in math compared to high-school boys. We have also seen that when they are encouraged to take math courses and given a supportive climate, the mathematical skills of girls are equal to those of boys.[99] Yet in spite of equal skill, boys are much more likely to be advised to take advanced mathematics because they are expected to enter such diverse occupations as engineering or physics. Girls, in contrast, are seldom counseled into math classes and have been subject to cultural stereotypes that tell them they cannot balance their checkbooks, much less do advanced mathematics. Even mathematics books reinforce these negative stereotypes. For example, elementary-school math books usually show girls as less skillful at math than boys. Finally, girls may genuinely fear being successful in a masculine field. They have been taught most of their lives that they should not surpass men in what is defined as a masculine area.

Counseling and Tracking. In all areas, most boys are counseled to take the proper sequence of courses, "just in case." Girls, in contrast, may be counseled to take something like the slower introductory algebra that stretches over two years. This may throw off the whole cycle of courses a girl has to take, so that she is not then prepared for advanced work. Counseling women out of engineering or other careers may not be a conscious decision, but it is an unconscious implementing of the stereotype that women do not need to be as serious about or as prepared for their careers as boys do. The stereotype persists even though over half of today's high-school girls will work full time for thirty years or more, and 90 percent of these girls will work for other long periods of time.[100]

Counseling in high school has been largely passive rather than active and has not reflected changing roles for women. The counselors often wait for girls to ask for help and do not understand the problems of possible poor self-concept and ambivalence about careers.[101] Yet counselors could publicize opportunities available for men and women in all fields. The fact that a counselor encourages a high-school girl to go for an interview with a business or computer firm may be all that is needed to set her on the right career path.

Fear of Success. There has been a continuing debate about whether women's self-devaluation and early socialization not to surpass men actually lead them to fear success in masculine areas. This fear of success is *not* a fear of inability to achieve in an area stereotyped as masculine, but a fear of the negative consequences of *success*. One argument in favor of fear of success stems from the belief that female achievement behavior is often motivated by a drive to please rather than to really succeed. If success and pleasing someone else conflict, a girl may give up success.[102]

On the other hand, some have disagreed with the idea that girls are motivated by social approval. Maccoby and Jacklin believe that boys and girls respond in similar ways to the need for such approval and that their similar levels of self-esteem show no differing needs for societal praise.[103] Still other researchers emphasize that girls *are* motivated to achieve and that the basis for learning is the same in boys and girls: social approval.[104]

One possible reason for these differing views is that boys and girls may get different amounts of approval for different kinds of achievements. Boys are approved of for concrete academic, athletic, or occupational achievements, and girls are approved of for personal qualities, family relationships, or "feminine" traits like being "nice."

While research documenting this differential approval is scarce, certainly the stereotypes of what is appropriate masculine and feminine behavior emphasize different areas of achievement. One may then speculate that if someone succeeds in an area that is not appropriate for his or her gender, that person may be uncomfortable and fear stigma or other negative consequences.

This is an important concern in looking at sex roles, as women's occupational and cultural success may depend on being able to achieve in areas previously stereotyped as masculine. We will see, as we examine the research in this area, that the passage of time and changing societal norms for women's roles affect any fear of success that might exist.

In 1965 Matina Horner, in her classic experiment, had female students complete sentences about a woman, Anne, who finds herself ranked at the top of her medical-school class, and had male students complete stories about John in a similar situation. The content of the stories was coded to find stories that anticipated positive or negative results from the academic success that Anne or John was having. Horner found that women wrote many negative responses based on their perception of the feminine role in society and the negative consequences that would ensue if Anne pursued her goal.[105] A typical comment was: "Anne is happy she is at the top of her class, but now she will have to make a decision about whether or not she really wants to be a doctor or get married." One revealing comment suggested that "Anne is not happy with her position at the top of her class because she now fears she will be teased and excluded by the other students." Approximately 65 percent of the women wrote themes that showed fear of success for Anne. In contrast, male students showed little such fear for John. Only 10 percent expressed negative feelings about John's success.[106]

In this and similar studies that followed, the most sex-typed (feminine) women showed the highest fear of success, particularly when competing with males. Very-high-ability women, who had a good chance of succeeding, also showed a high fear of success.[107] In some of the research men, too, wrote stories portraying negative results for successful women, although neither men nor women wrote stories that portrayed negative results for sucessful men. Thus, it was not just women who saw women's success in negative terms.[108]

Lois Hoffman attempted to replicate Horner's study five years later. She used the same story cue as Horner but also tried to look at several other aspects of the fear of success, particularly whether Anne's fear of success would be reduced if the medical-school class had equal numbers of men and women. The difference in the setting for success did not significantly diminish fear of success for women. Approximately 62 percent of the women still showed fear of success in the medical-school setting. Thus, there was no significant diminishing of fear of success between Horner's study in 1965 and this replication in 1971. In spite of the women's movement, these students perceived that very real negative consequences would result from being a successful woman in a man's field.[109]

The group that had changed in their perceptions since Horner's study were the men! Horner reported only 8 percent of the males tried to avoid success, and Hoffman's study showed 77 percent of the men tried to do so. They were equally likely to show fear of success in all-male settings as in settings where both sexes functioned professionally.[110]

For both men and women, mean scores of "desire to achieve" had gone down significantly between 1965 and 1971. However, women's reasons for fear of success remained much as they had been earlier, whereas men's reasons seemed linked to a diminished desire to achieve at all. Hoffman points out that the content of the men's stories was different from that of the women's. The men seemed to question the value of success itself. They also mentioned health dangers and family problems that came with being successful. A typical male quote said, "He graduates with honors and hates being a doctor. He wonders what it was all for." In contrast, the women respected success but saw continued problems for women.[111]

Other more recent studies that have duplicated Horner's show much less fear of success among women but a continuing fear among men.[112] The fall in women's fear of success probably reflects changing cultural norms about successful women. The amount of fear of success shown certainly varies with the area of achievement, geographic region, and the like.[113] In addition, one researcher hypothesizes that one factor that may make a difference in women's fear of success is whether or not they accept achievement as female appropriate. There seems to be evidence that bright, academically oriented girls show achievement patterns and attitudes similar to those found in males, while underachieving girls or mixed samples like Horner's do not.[114]

Thus, we see that achievement efforts may be lowered in adolescence for many women partly because of pressure to adhere to feminine role definitions and partly because females internalize the low expectations of the culture for their achievement. These reduced achievement efforts may stem from a fear of failure and sometimes also from a fear of success. While some women have internalized achievement as part of the feminine role, and while fear of success may be receding for females and accelerating for males, women are still faced with ambivalence about their success.

Thus, many women may deliberately narrow their own options and choose fields stereotyped as feminine. Their choices are also narrowed for them by their socialization. By high school, women have learned a repertoire of behaviors and attitudes that make it easier for them to function in some careers than in others. It is no accident that women have traditionally gone into the nurturing fields: nursing, social work, teaching. Not only do they receive less flak if they choose such appropriately feminine fields, but they also have the behavioral characteristics that are necessary to do well in such areas. It is much more difficult for them to do well in business or entrepreneurial jobs that require aggressive, competitive behavior.[115] Thus, the combination of the pressures of early socialization, discouragement by teachers and counselors, ambivalence about their own abilities, fear of success, and cultural values may discourage many women from choosing a nontraditional career or even preparing early for any career. While these generalizations do not apply to all women, they still apply enough so that we must be worried about some of the influences in high school.

Happily, the bottom line is good news. Studies show that the views of adolescents were significantly less stereotyped about what occupations were sex appropriate in 1975 than in 1973. The views of male adolescents had liberalized the most, although this liberalization was mostly among middle- and higher-income students.[116] Women are also becoming more and more aware of the opportunities available in traditional male fields; the greater rewards of money and status are increasing their numbers in business and allied fields.

A New Emphasis on Sports for Women

Adolescents' perception of the role of women in sports is also changing. The advent of Title IX and other legislation guaranteeing women equal opportunities in the schools has increased the funding, personnel, and equipment available for girls' sports, and girls have had unprecedented opportunities to participate and compete. (However, this flourishing arena of women's sports may not last. As I write this, a court ruling has held that schools do not have to spend equal amounts on men's and women's sports or treat them equally in terms of personnel, time allotted, or equipment. Many schools may see this an opportunity to funnel money away from women's sports again.[117] President Reagan has also come out against implementation of Title IX legislation.) As prestige has increased, sports for girls have become more popular. Many girls who would not have participated before and would have considered sports unfeminine are now joining teams. Some women's sports have become extremely popular with spectators as well. Women's basketball is well on its way to becoming a spectator draw to rival women's tennis. Women are beginning to have an opportunity to achieve recognition by participating in these physical, competitive activities. More important, they have a chance to experience achievement personally as they learn physical skills and use their bodies.

How does participation in sports actually affect the teenage female? Some stigmatizing of girls who participate in sports still seems to occur, although the stigma varies according to the sport. The most "acceptable" sports for women are aesthetically pleasing and do not involve direct body contact. Fifty-six percent of women involved in basketball reported stigma, 50 percent of those in track, 40 percent of those in swimming and diving, and 31 percent of those in gymnastics.[118] Men who were questioned saw soccer, basketball, field hockey, fencing, track and field, and softball as the least desirable sports for women.[119]

Part of the stigma seems to come from a perception that women who engage in these sports are less "feminine" to begin with or become less feminine as a result of their participation.[120] The research on whether or not this is true seems to be quite contradictory. While the characteristics of the sports participants and their "femininity" are not necessarily important in and of themselves, it is important to know whether women who play sports suffer stigma and loss of self-esteem.

In one study, no differences in self-esteem were found between those who participated in what were considered acceptable or unacceptable sports for women.[121] Indeed, the self-image and feelings of self-satisfaction of women athletes are exceptionally high. While stigma does exist, it does not seem to make participation in athletics psychologically stressful for women. Positive feedback and concrete achievements seem to outweigh negative sanctions. Measures of psychological well-being seem to show that female athletes stack up very well against the population as a whole.[122] Girls who participate in sports feel better about themselves and their bodies than girls who do not participate. They report themselves as having more energy and better health and being in good spirits or satisfied with life considerably more of the time than nonathletes do. Female athletes in one study also seemed to be more independent, creative, and autonomous than nonathletes.[123] Other studies showed that they tended to have slightly higher grade averages and educational goals than nonathletes. It has been hypothesized that their achievement may depend on the discipline and commitment learned in athletics.[124]

Therefore, participation in sports may be an important way for women to change their self-image. They are able to get a sense of mastery by control over their physical achievements. In addition, they learn the cooperation and competition that are so valuable later in life.

The Experience of Black High-School Girls

Differences exist between the races in expectations for kinds of masculine and feminine behavior. We saw that the black man may have to put a special emphasis on toughness and being cool. The black female may also be socialized with different expectations for feminine behavior than her white sister.

One of the things that distinguishes the behavior of white girls is their desire to get married. Marriage is desired by almost all, and career plans may be relatively unformed by many.[125] In contrast, the black girl may not have as many chances to get married. By the time black adolescents reach their late teens, there are only 85 men available for every 100 black women.[126] This difference is due to greater infant mortality and greater sickness and accident rates among black boys.

While marriage may be an ideal to many black women, they may also be less eager to marry because they have alternative options for working and are not likely to need to depend on a man for support.[127] In the past, it has been difficult for many black men to get jobs and support families. Black women have usually had to work outside the home and often contribute a great deal of the income for their families. Because it is known that they may have to support themselves, black girls are encouraged by their families to get a good education and to have career ambitions. The black woman is also more likely to have a strong female-relative support system and may not feel the need for the companionship and emotional support of marriage.[128]

The black girl who has alternative possibilities and is less eager to marry does not need to depend on being pretty and popular. She has very little anxiety about these areas and feels self-assured about her looks and social interaction. It is noteworthy that studies show that black girls put much less emphasis on being liked and on desiring to get married. Forty percent were also "satisfied with their looks." Both attitude toward popularity and satisfaction with looks lead to higher self-esteem for black girls.[129] In addition, black girls are usually socialized to be self-sufficient and independent.[130]

Thus, fear of success does not seem to be as evident among black girls as among white girls, although here we find differences by social class and political values. In several studies that combined lower- and middle-class black girls, fear of success was very low, although fear of success was present for the black high-school boy.[131] It has been suggested that fear of success does not tend to exist among these black girls because they have been socialized to think of themselves as being independent and their own support, and it is necessary to succeed. It has also been hypothesized that a successful black woman creates a special situation: such women are so few in number that nobody knows how to treat them, and they are not subjected to the same discrimination that a black man or a white woman might face.[132]

The assertion that black women show less fear of success because they are more dominant and independent and because they have had to succeed and support themselves seems to vary with social class. Mednick and Weston describe the black middle class as "out-middle-classing" the white middle class in terms of values. They hypothesize that as middle-class life is usually male dominated and family life is more stable, black middle-class women may be less aspiring and less dominant than black lower-class women. Although their study did not directly support this hypothesis, other studies with upper-middle-class sorority black women at the University of Michigan did show fear of success. Perhaps, higher up the social ladder, fear of success appears for black women when they have less need to be successful themselves.[133]

The political views of black women may also have some bearing on their fear of success. In *Black Macho and the Myth of Superwoman*, Michelle Wallace describes the dilemma facing the modern black woman. The woman is asked to hold back and to help her man advance for the greater betterment of her race. If she does this and scuttles her own ambitions, she may be left with nothing, as there are not enough black men to go around, nor can stable marriages always be counted on.[134] Puryear and Mednick believed that this holding back would be particularly evident in black women with militant political values. As a result, they hypothesized that militant black women would show more fear of success. Their study bore this out and showed that it was particularly true for women who were not attached to a man at that time. Therefore, black women who feel that men should be dominant or who are insecure about their relationship with a man may show fear of success even when the great majority of black women do not.[135]

Thus, the experience for black high-school girls is different from that for white girls. The black high-school girl is likely to have higher self-esteem and to be more satisfied with her looks. She is not likely to depend on getting married and thus feels less pressure to be pretty and popular. In social interaction she is expected to be independent and self-reliant; she does not have to take a passive role. She can define her own identity rather than having it defined for her. She gets help in defining that identity because she is valued in her family, trained to be assertive and independent, and expected to be her own support.

Summary

We have seen that the teenage years with all their growth and excitement are still a time of both pain and pleasure. The adolescent boy who must be tough, cool, and good at things is under constant pressure to prove himself. Being tough and cool also means repressing emotions and finding it difficult to relate to other men or to women in an intimate and open way. Being good may mean the constant push to initiate social and sexual relations whether one feels like such interactions or not. The equation of being tough, cool, and good with being masculine means that boys are pressured to succeed at being these things in spite of any adverse consequences. Yet many boys cannot succeed in these ways and thus they feel inferior.

While the feminine stereotype does not affect the experience of all girls in the same way or to the same degree, it can lead to anxiety for girls as they learn to value such things as looks and popularity over which they have little control. They may have to define their success as females by the extent of others' approval. Stereotypes of women as incompetent in many areas, less smart than men, poor at mathematics, unable to do well in male occupations, and uncoordinated in sports may be internalized by high-school girls, and they may limit their career and recreational choices. While girls seem to be overcoming their fear of success and going into more occupations where men have predominated, the problems of early socialization and peer and teacher pressure may mean they do not prepare early or seriously enough for a career. However, girls are participating more in sports, which seems to raise their self-esteem as they realize more concrete achievements. Black girls who are less eager to marry show higher self-esteem, more independence, and much less fear of success than do white girls. Thus, high school is a time of testing oneself, of trying new experiences, and of developing socially. Unfortunately, the rigid sex stereotypes that are enforced by peer and cultural pressure limit the options of both boys and girls, so that they often become less than what they could be.

Essay Questions

1. Discuss the intensification of macho themes in the male adolescent years. In what ways is the boy expected to act tough and cool?
2. Discuss the role of sports in high school as a way for a boy to show he is tough, cool, and good. What part do team initiations play in defining the male role in sports? What significance do gestures like tapping another player from the team with a hockey stick as he skates onto the ice have for a hockey player; or holding hands in the huddle, for a football player? How many sports help a boy play his part later in the corporate world?
3. Discuss the kinds of inexpressiveness a boy may be socialized to have. How is homophobia related to such inexpressiveness?
4. What does Coleman mean when he says that the high-school boy is ambivalent about high-school success? How do adolescent peer pressures for "being good" conflict with adult expectations of "being good"?
5. Why does Gagnon say that "the primary power the young male has is his own body"? How does appearance fit in with the other prescriptions for male behavior?

6. Discuss the relationship between appearance and self-esteem for girls in high school. Why may good looks be a mixed blessing?
7. Why is the need to be popular a problem in terms of a girl's sources of self-esteem?
8. What factors influence girls' feelings about academic success in high school? In particular, discuss stereotypes about ability, hidden messages, expectations for careers, and counseling and tracking practices.
9. What is fear of success and how does it differ from fear of failure? Has the degree of fear of success changed in recent years for females? For males? What groups show the greatest and the least fear of success and why?
10. Discuss the relationship between participation in sports and self-esteem for high-school girls.
11. Discuss the particular nature of the black girl's feelings about prettiness, popularity, and career success and their relationship to her self-esteem.

Exercises

1. Pretend that you are a 140-pound male who would like to go out for the football team in high school because the girls all look up to football players. Discuss your feelings about this possible choice.
2. In what way does high-school commitment to sports show in the physical atmosphere and social activities of schools? Do you believe that sports for males are treated differently from sports for females?
3. Suppose you want to be a biologist and you have a big test in high-school biology coming up. The guys have also called and want you to go to a party that night when you need to study. How do you feel and what kind of decision will you make?
4. If you are a male, discuss your feelings about being a future "breadwinner." Do you ever wish that you could work part time, stay home and take care of children, or do other things that many women are able to do?
5. List five times that you—or a male you were with—have chosen to be inexpressive and to hide personal feelings. How did you feel underneath? Or how do you think he felt?
6. List all the qualities you associate with your own sex. List the qualities you associate with the other sex. Put a plus before the qualities you think are positive and a minus before those you think are negative and discuss your choices. Are there some qualities of the other sex you would like to have? Are there some qualities in the other sex that you fear?
7. List five times that you (if you are a girl)—or a girl you were with—

have chosen to hide anger and to act "nice" in a group or dating situation. How did you feel underneath? Or how do you think she felt?

8. As a girl, discuss how you feel about your appearance. If you were given the choice of being extremely pretty or extremely bright and successful, which would you choose?

9. As a girl, discuss how you feel about being "popular" or not being so. Would it bother you if you didn't have dates? Why?

10. As a girl, discuss your future career plans. What courses are you taking now and what else are you doing toward those plans? If you are not working toward your career plans or have not made any such plans, do you expect to work. If so, full time?

11. As a girl, discuss your feelings about succeeding in a field that is not a traditional one for females. Do you believe that "fear of success" is something that affects you or your friends? If not, why not? If so, why?

12. For the boys and girls in the class to do separately: Discuss how you will (or how you do) combine career and marriage roles. After each sex has discussed this separately, compare your answers. Are males planning a different combination of these roles than females are? Discuss.

Notes

1. Elizabeth Douvan and Joseph Adelson, *The Adolescent Experience* (New York: Wiley, 1966), p. 3.

2. Stanley Hall, quoted in Daniel Offer, *The Psychological World of the Teenager* (New York: Basic Books, 1969), p. 175.

3. Anna Freud, quoted in Offer, *op. cit.,* p. 177.

4. Offer, *op cit.,* pp. 180–81.

5. Dorothy Rogers, "Stage Theory and Critical Period as Related to Adolescence," in Dorothy Rogers, ed., *Issues in Adolescent Psychology* (New York: Appleton-Century-Crofts, 1969), pp. 173–75.

6. Albert Bandura, "The Stormy Decade: Fact or Fiction?" in Rogers, *op. cit.,* p. 195.

7. Roberta Simmons and Florence Rosenberg, "Disturbance in the Self-Image at Adolescence," *American Sociological Review* 38 (1973):553–69.

8. Offer, *op. cit.,* chapter 11.

9. Douvan and Adelson, *op. cit.,* p. 350.

10. J.C. Gledewell, M.B. Kantor, L.M. Smith, and L.A. Stringer, "Socialization and Social Structures in the Classroom," in L.W. Hoffman and M.L. Hoffman, eds., *Review of Child Development Research,* vol. 2 (New York: Russell Sage, 1966).

11. Robert Staples, "Masculinity and Race: The Dual Dilemma of Black Men," *Journal of Social Issues* 34, no. 1 (1978):173.

12. Y.H. Clarke and D.H. Clarke, "Social Status and Mental Health of Boys as Related to Their Maturity, Structural, and Strength Characteristics," *Research Quarterly of the American Association of Health and Physical Education* 32 (1961):326–34.

13. H.H. Clarke and W.H. Greene, "Relationships Between Personal-Social Measures Applied to Ten-Year-Old Boys," *Research Quarterly of the American Association of Health and Physical Education* 34 (1963):288–98.

14. R.C. Hansson and B.J. Duffield, "Physical Attractiveness: Attribution of Epilepsy," *Journal of Social Psychology* 99 (1976):233–40.

15. K.K. Dion, E. Berscheid, and E. Walster, "What Is Beautiful Is Good," *Journal of Personality and Social Psychology* 24 (1972):285–90; K.K. Dion and E. Berscheid, "Physical Attractiveness and Peer Perception among Children," *Sociometry* 37 (1974):1–12.

16. N. Cavior and P.R. Dokecki, "Physical Attractiveness, Perceived Attitude Similarity, and Academic Achievement as Contributors to Interpersonal Attraction among Adolescents," *Developmental Psychology* 9 (1973):44–54.

17. P.J. Lavrakas, "Female Preferences for Male Physiques," *Journal of Research in Personality* 9 (1975):324–34.

18. J. Mills and E. Aronson, "Opinion Change as a Function of the Communicator's Attractiveness and Desire to Influence," *Journal of Personality and Social Psychology* 1 (1965):173–77; H. Sigall and E. Aronson, "Liking for an Evaluator as a Function of Her Physical Attractiveness and the Nature of the Evaluations," *Journal of Experimental Social Psychology* 5 (1969):93–100.

19. D.M. Connell and J.E. Johnson, "Relationship Between Sex-Role Identification and Self-Esteem in Early Adolescents," *Developmental Psychology* 3 (1970):268.

20. John Gagnon, "Physical Strength, Once of Significance," in Deborah S. David and Robert Brannon, eds., *The Forty-Nine Percent Majority: The Male Sex Role* (Reading, Mass.: Addison-Wesley, 1976), p. 173.

21. J.S. Coleman, *The Adolescent Society* (New York: Free Press, 1961).

22. *Ibid.*

23. Laurel Walum Richardson, *The Dynamics of Sex and Gender*, 2nd ed. (Boston: Houghton-Mifflin, 1981), p. 69.

24. Gagnon, *op. cit.*

25. Terry Saario, Carol Jacklin, and Carol Tittle, "Sex-Role Stereotyping in the Public Schools," *Harvard Educational Review* 43 (1973):386–416.

26. Offer, *op. cit.*, p. 43.

27. E.Z. Friedenberg, *Coming of Age in America* (New York: Random House, 1965).

28. Eldon Snyder and Elmer Spreitzer, *Social Aspects of Sport* (Englewood Cliffs, N.J.: Prentice-Hall, 1978), pp. 106–07.

29. *Ibid.*, p. 65.

30. Shirley Fiske, "Pigskin Review: An American Initiation," in Marie Hart, ed., *Sport in the Sociocultural Process* (Dubuque, Iowa: William C. Brown, 1972), pp. 241–58.

31. *Ann Arbor News*, Winter, February 28, 1981, p. C–1.

32. Snyder and Spreitzer, *op. cit.*, p. 130, quoting Smith, 1976.

33. *Ibid.*, p. 132.

34. Betty Harragan, *Games Mother Never Taught You* (New York: Warner Books, 1977).

35. Gary Shaw, *Meat on the Hoof* (New York: Dell, 1972).

36. Snyder and Spreitzer, *op. cit.*, p. 26.

37. Fiske, *op. cit.*

38. Snyder and Spreitzer, *op. cit.*, p. 83, quoting Arthur Ashe.

39. Coleman, *op. cit.*

40. Julius Lester, "Being a Boy," in Joseph Pleck and Jack Sawyer, eds., *Men and Masculinity* (Englewood Cliffs, N.J.: Prentice-Hall, 1974), p. 270.

41. Eleanor Morrison, Kay Starks, Cynda Hyndman, and Nina Ronzeo, *Growing Up Sexual* (New York: Van Nostrand, 1980), p. 158.

42. J.O. Balswick and C.W. Peek, "The Inexpressive Male: A Tragedy of American Society," *The Family Coordinator* 20, no. 4 (1971):363–83.

43. Morrison *et al.*, *op. cit.*, p. 145.

44. Balswick and Peek, *op. cit.*

45. Douvan and Adelson, *op. cit.*, p. 113.

46. Offer, *op. cit.*, pp. 69 and 212.

47. V. Sermat, "The Effect of Some Dimensions of Verbal Communication on Self-Disclosure, Liking, and Sexual Attraction," (Paper presented at the meeting of the American Psychological Association, Honolulu, September 1972).

48. M.R. Feinberg, M. Smith, and R. Schmidt, "An Analysis of Expressions Used by Adolescents of Varying Economic Levels to Describe Accepted and Rejected Peers," *Journal of Genetic Psychology* 93 (1958):133–48.

49. Balswick and Peek, *op. cit.*

50. Barbara Eakins and R. Gene Eakins, *Sex Differences in Human Communication* (Boston: Houghton Mifflin, 1978); Jack Sattel, "The Inexpressive Male: Tragedy or Sexual Politics," *Social Problems* 23 (1976):469–77.

51. George K. Lehae, "Homophobia among Men," in David and Brannon, *op. cit.*, pp. 66–88; Don Clark, "Homosexual Encounter in All-Male Groups," in Pleck and Sawyer, *op. cit.*, pp. 88–93; Alan Gross, "The Male Role and Heterosexual Behavior," *Journal of Social Issues* 34, no. 1 (1978):87–107; Robert Lewis, "Emotional Intimacy among Men," *Journal of Social Issues* 34, no. 1 (1978):108–21; Stephen Morin and Ellen Garfinkle, "Male Homophobia," *Journal of Social Issues* 34, no. 1 (1978):29–47.

52. Sidney M. Jouard, "Some Lethal Aspects of the Male Role," in Pleck and Sawyer, *op. cit.*, pp. 21–29.

53. Douvan and Adelson, quoted in Pleck and Sawyer, *op. cit.*, pp. 169–70.

54. *Ibid.*

55. Robert Beech and Aileen Schoeppe, "Development of Value Systems in Adolescents," *Developmental Psychology* 10, no. 5 (1974):644–56.

56. Offer, *op. cit.*, p. 42.

57. Coleman, *op. cit.*, p. 305.

58. Hoffman and Hoffman, *op. cit.*, p. 496.

59. Sherry W. Morgan and Bernard Mardner, "Behavior and Fantasied Indicators of Avoidance of Success in Men and Women," *Journal of Personality* 31 (1973):457–70.

60. Eleanor Maccoby and Carol Jacklin, *The Psychology of Sex Differences* (Stanford, Calif.: Stanford University Press, 1974).

61. Douvan and Adelson, *op. cit.*

62. Jack H. Wilmore, "They Told You, You Couldn't Compete with Men and You, Like a Fool, Believed Them. There's Hope," *Womensports*, June 1974, pp. 40–43.

63. Douvan and Adelson, *op. cit.*, p. 38.

64. *Ibid.*, p. 211.

65. R.H. Coombs and W.F. Kenkel, "Sex Differences in Dating Aspirations and Satisfaction with Computer-Selected Partners," *Journal of Marriage and the Family* 28 (1966):62–66.

66. D. Krebs and A. Adinolfi, "Physical Attractiveness, Social Relations, and Personality Style," *Journal of Personality and Social Psychology* 31 (1975): 245–53.

67. E. Walster, V. Aronson, D. Abrahams, and L. Rottman, "The Importance of Physical Attractiveness in Dating Behavior," *Journal of Personality and Social Psychology* 4 (1966), 508–16.

68. E.W. Mathes, "The Effects of Physical Attractiveness and Anxiety on Heterosexual Attraction over a Series of Five Encounters," *Journal of Marriage and the Family* 37 (1975):769–73.

69. Douvan and Adelson, *op. cit.*, pp. 46–50.

70. Morris Rosenberg, *Society and the Adolescent Self-Image* (Princeton, N.J.: Princeton University Press, 1965).

71. Douvan and Adelson, *op. cit.*, p. 46.

72. Rosenberg, *op. cit.*, p. 254.

73. Rae Carlson, "Stability and Change in the Adolescent's Self-Image," in Marvin Powell and Allen Frerick, eds., *Readings in Adolescent Psychology* (Minneapolis: Burgess, 1971), pp. 24–30.

74. Andrew Ahlgren and David Johnson, "Sex Differences in Cooperative and Competitive Attitudes from Second through Twelfth Grade," *Developmental Psychology* 15 (1979), 45–49.

75. Quoted by Russell Curtis, "Adolescent Orientations toward Parents and Peers: Variations by Sex, Age, and Socioeconomic Status," *Adolescence* 10 (1975):483–94.

76. N.E. Gronlund and L. Anderson, "Personality Characteristics of Socially Accepted, Socially Neglected, and Socially Rejected Junior High School Pupils," *Educational Administration and Supervision* 43 (1957):329–38.

77. T.L. Huston, "Ambiguity of Acceptance, Social Desirability, and Dating Choice," *Journal of Experimental Social Psychology* 9 (1973):32–42.

78. Judith Bardwick and Elizabeth Douvan, "Ambivalence, the Socialization of Women," in J. Bardwick, ed., *Readings in the Psychology of Women* (New York: Harper & Row, 1971), p. 19.

79. Ronald Burke and Tamara Weir, "Sex Differences in Adolescent Life Stress, Social Support, and Well-Being," *The Journal of Psychology* 98 (1978):277–88.

80. Douvan and Adelson, *op. cit.*, p. 33.

81. *Ibid.*, pp. 37–50.

82. *Ibid.*

83. *Ibid.*, p. 233.

84. Rosenberg, *op. cit.*, p. 258.

85. Douvan and Adelson, *op. cit.*, p. 45.

86. Beech and Schoeppe, *op. cit.*

87. Morton Hunt, "The Direction of Feminine Evolution," in Farber and Wilson, eds., *The Potential of Women* (New York: McGraw-Hill, 1963), p. 264.

88. Mirra Komarovsky, "Cultural Contradictions and Sex Roles," in J. Bardwick, *Readings*, p. 61.

89. J.T. Spence and R. Helmrich, "Who Likes Competent Women?" *Journal of Applied Social Psychology* 2 (1972):197–213.

90. P. Hawley, "What Women Think Men Think: Does It Affect Their Career Choice?", *Journal of Counseling Psychology* 18 (1971):193–99.

91. S. Harris and S.C. Tseng, "Children's Attitudes toward Peers and Parents as Revealed by Sentence Completions," *Child Development* 28 (1957):401–11.

92. P. Goldberg, "Are Women Prejudiced against Women?" in J. Stacey *et al.*, *And Jill Came Tumbling After* (New York: Dell, 1974).

93. G.K. Baruch, "Maternal Influences upon College Women's Attitudes toward Women and Word," *Developmental Psychology* 6 (1972):32–37; L.S. Fidell, "Empirical Verification of Sex Discrimination in Hiring Practices in Psychology," *American Psychologist* 25 (1970):1094–97.

94. R. Brons, *Social Psychology* (New York: Free Press, 1974), p. 162.

95. A.H. Stein and M.M. Bailey, "The Socialization of Achievement Orientation in Females," *Psychological Bulletin* 80 (1973):345–66.

96. Inge K. Broverman *et al.*, "Sex-Role Stereotypes: A Current Appraisal," *Journal of Social Issues* 28, no. 2 (1972):59–78.

97. E. Crandall, "Sex Differences in Expectancy of Intellectual and Academic Performance, in C.P. Smith, ed., *Achievement-Related Motives in Children* (New York: Russell Sage, 1969).

98. Gael O'Brien, "Male Professors Found Cool to Female Issues," *AAUP Bulletin*, April 5, 1976.

99. E. Fennema and J.A. Sherman, "Sex-Related Differences in Mathematic

Achievement, Spatial Visualization and Affective Factors," *American Educational Research Journal* 14 (1977):51–72; E. Fennema and J.A. Sherman, "Sex-Related Differences in Mathematic Achievement: A Futher Study," *Journal for Research in Mathematics Education* 9 (1978):189–203; L.H. Fox, D. Yahin, and L. Brody, "Sex Role Socialization and Achievement in Mathematics," in M.A. Witteg and A.C. Petersen, eds., *Sex-Related Differences in Cognitive Functioning: Developmental Issues* (New York: Academic Press, 1979); L.H. Reyes, "Attitudes and Mathematics," in M.M. Lindquist, ed., *Selected Issues in Mathematics Education* (Berkeley, Calif.: McCuthan, 1980).

100. S.S. Algrist and E.M. Almquist, *Careers and Contingencies: How College Women Juggle with Gender* (New York: Dunnellen Press, 1975).

101. Iris M. Tiedt, "Realistic Counseling for High School Girls," in Stacey *et al.*, *op. cit.*, p. 236.

102. L.W. Hoffman, "Early Childhood Experiences and Women's Achievement Motives," *Journal of Social Issues* 28 (1972):157–76.

103. Maccoby and Jacklin, *op. cit.*

104. Stein and Bailey, *op. cit.*

105. Matina S. Horner, "Sex Differences in Achievement Motivation and Performance in Competitive and Noncompetitive Situations" (Ph.D. diss., University of Michigan, 1968), p. 58.

106. *Ibid.*

107. L.A. Peplau, "The Impact of Fear of Success, Sex-Role Attitudes, and Opposite-Sex Relationships on Women's Intellectual Performance: An Experimental Study of Competition in Dating Couples," (Ph.D. diss., Harvard University, 1973).

108. L. Monahan, D. Kuhn, and D. Shaver, "Intrapsychic vs. Cultural Explanations of Fear of Success Motive," *Journal of Personality and Social Psychology* 29 (1974):60–64.

109. L.J. Hoffman, "Fear of Success in Males and Females: 1965 and 1972," *Journal of Consulting and Clinical Psychology* 42 (1974):353–58.

110. *Ibid.*

111. *Ibid.*

112. Adeline Levine and Janice Crumrine, "Women and the Fear of Success: A Problem in Replication," (Paper presented at the American Sociological Meeting New York, August 1973.

113. Sherry W. Morgan and Bernard Mardner, "Behavior and Fantasied Indicators of Avoidance of Success in Men and Women," *Journal of Personality* 41 (1973):457–70.

114. Thelma Alper, "The Relationship Between Role Orientation and Achievement Motivation in College Women," *Journal of Personality* 41 (1973):9–31.

115. Angrist and Almquist, *op. cit.*

116. Sharon Rakowski and Jonelle M. Farrow, "Sex-Role Identification and Goal Orientation in Teenage Females," *Psychological Reports* 44 (1979):363–66.

117. Roger LeFievre, "Judge Deals Blow to Women's Sports," *Ann Arbor News*, February 25, 1981, p. 1.

118. Snyder and Spreitzer, *op. cit.*, pp. 108–09.

119. *Ibid.*, p. 113.

120. D. Kanders, "Psychological Femininity and the Prospective Female Physical Educator," *Research Quarterly* 41 (1970):164–70; T. Malmumphy, "Personality of Women Athletes in Intercollegiate Competition," *Research Quarterly* 39 (1968):610–20; Eldon Snyder and Joseph Kivlin, "Perceptions of the Sex Role among Female Athletes and Nonathletes," *Adolescence* 12 (1977):23–29.

121. T. Malmumphy, "The College Woman Athlete: Questions and Tentative Answers," *Quest. Monograph* 14 (1970):18–27.

122. E. Snyder and Elmer Spreitzer, "Correlates of Sports Participation among Adolescent Girls," *Research Quarterly* 47 (1978):804–08.

123. B. Ogilvie and T. Tutko, "Sports: If You Want to Build Character, Try Something Else," *Psychology Today* 5 (1971):61–63.

124. *Ibid.*

125. Douvan and Adelson, *op. cit.*, pp. 33–42.

126. Robert Staples, *The Black Women in America: Sex, Marriage, and the Family* (Chicago: Nelson Hall, 1973); LaFrances Rodgers-Rose, "Some Demographic Characteristics of the Black Woman from 1940 to 1975," in La Frances Rodgers-Rose, *The Black Woman* (Beverly Hills, Calif.: Sage Publications, 1980).

127. Carol Stack, *All Our Kin* (New York: Harper & Row, 1974).

128. Harriet Pipe McAdoo, "Black Mothers and the Extended Family Support Network," in Rodgers-Rose, *op. cit.*

129. J. Ladner, *Tomorrow's Tomorrow: The Black Woman* (Garden City, N.J.: Doubleday, 1971); M. Rosenberg, "Race Ethnicity and Self-Esteem, in S. Guterman, ed. *Black Psyche* (Berkeley, Calif.: Glendessary Press, 1972) pp. 87–99; M. Wright, "Self-Concept and the Coping Process of Black Undergraduate Women at a Predominantly White University," (Ph.D. diss., University of Michigan, 1975).

130. Ladner, *op. cit.*

131. P. Weston and M.T. Mednick, "Race, Social Class, and the Motive to Avoid Success in Women," *Journal of Cross-Cultural Psychology* 1 (1970):284–91.

132. C.F. Epstein, "Explaining the Success of Black Professional Women, the Positive Effects of the Multiple Negative," *American Journal of Sociology* 78 (1973):912–35.

133. Diane K. Lewis, "The Black Family: Socialization and Sex Roles," *Phylon: The Atlanta University Review of Race and Culture* 36, no. 3 (1975):221–37.

134. Michelle Wallace, *Black Macho and the Myth of Superwoman* (New York: Dial, 1978).

135. Gwendolyn Puryear and Martha Mednick, "Black Militancy, Affective Attachment, and the Fear of Success in Black College Women," *Journal of Consulting and Clinical Psychology* 42, no. 2 (1974):263–66.

Chapter Six

Adolescence: Friendship, Dating, and Sexuality

As we have seen, much of the early interaction between boys and girls is on a platonic basis, in which they engage in activities together and see each other as friends rather than as persons of the other sex. At some point, however, comes a recognition that there is indeed another sex, and persons of the other sex cannot be as easily included in plans as before. "Dear Abby" recently ran a letter from a concerned father whose sixth-grade son was having a birthday party and inviting the members of his baseball team to spend the night. One of the team members was a girl. Although the boy wished to invite her, the father was dubious about having her spend the night with all the boys. "Dear Abby" agreed with the father that it would not be appropriate for the girl to be invited. One can only imagine the feelings of the girl who was left out; but the boys, too, were made aware that a difference existed and that their former pal could not always be included.[1]

Another story in a popular magazine told of a girl who had routinely played baseball on Saturday mornings with a group of neighborhood boys. Every Saturday morning, some of the "gang" would come by her house and whistle to get her up, and they would all head off to the nearby sandlot field. She awakened one Saturday morning when the sun was up high in the sky and realized that it must be mid-morning. She wondered why no one had come by, figured that there had been some mistake, threw on her clothes, and ran down to the field. The game was in progress and another boy was playing her usual position. When she yelled and asked them what was going on, her former pals responded that they didn't want any girls on their team, that "girls swing like rusty gates." Up until this morning, however, she had been considered one of their most valued players.

In the preteens and early teenage years, it is frequently the girl who is excluded from previously coed activities, which are no longer considered suitable for females. Boys also face prohibitions that are even stricter than before about not doing anything "sissy"—that is, feminine. Thus, the members of the two sexes give up their few shared activities and move further apart into same-sexed groups.

Yet at the same time, perhaps absence does spark interest. With the beginning of puberty comes a stirring and awakening of interest in the other sex, just because they *are* the other sex, not because they are Mary or John or a former pal. We can think of sixth-grade or junior-high girls gathered on a corner giggling and talking about boys as they pass by. The boys, who are often considerably shorter and smaller at this age, strut by self-consciously, ignoring "those silly girls," poking one another, and trying to be cool. Or some of the boys may still be unconscious of the girls' attention and uninterested in them. I remember my sixth-grade daughter coming home from school one day and announcing that a certain boy was her boyfriend. Thinking it would be nice to meet her first boyfriend, I suggested that she bring him by some day after school. Her reply was, "Oh, mom, *he* doesn't know he's my boyfriend!"

The first tentative steps made in interacting with the other sex can be anxious ones. In the stylized heterosexual interaction of early puberty, boys and girls are testing themselves and their social skills and seeking a confirmation of whether or not they are being appropriately "masculine" or "feminine." The reactions that each individual gets from the other sex may greatly affect ego and self-image. One colleague tells of his sixth-grade daughter who was upset when he picked her up from an after-school mixer. When he asked her if she had danced, she burst into tears. It seems the boys she had asked to dance had refused her but had danced with other girls.

All these early interactions are also wrapped up with feelings about the adolescent's changing body, with budding sexual desire, and with cultural norms for what is appropriate appearance and behavior. It is little wonder that in the years from eleven to thirteen or so, both boys and girls prefer coed groups where they can get the reinforcement of their same-sexed peers while taking tentative steps toward the other sex. Interaction between the sexes varies by individual, by social class, by ethnic background, and even by geographic area,[2] but research seems to show that some commonalities occur in the experiences that young people share in the adolescent years.

Friendship

Boys' Friendships

Friendship patterns are somewhat different for each sex. Douvan and Adelson found that boys in early adolescence are less sophisticated about friendship and less eager for intimacy than are girls of the same age. The gang, collectively, is important to the boy, rather than close friendship. Boys say that they want a friend who controls his impulses, makes few demands for closeness, and has some special traits such as athletic ability or good looks. In contrast to girls, boys at this age do not seek loyalty and empathy in their friends and they are not so threatened by the loss of a friend. A friend is seen primarily as a person to do things with, and the friend must "go along with the crowd."[3] Coleman also points out that boys are behind girls in sympathizing with the individual and that they tend to identify with the group. While most eleven-year-old girls express sympathy for the individual, 50 percent of eleven-year-old boys identify with the group. Not until age fifteen do most boys identify with the individual rather than with the group.[4]

Coleman also finds that while boys seem more able than girls to rebel against parents at an early age, they seem to need the support of the peer group in their quest for independence. In contrast, girls seem more capable of handling solitude with recourse to a peer group. The dependence of boys on the peer group has been supported by the Cornell study of student values, which assessed nearly 6,000 undergraduate men and women in Cornell and ten other universities. E.S. Suchman quotes the study as saying, "Much of the student's development during four years in college does not take place in classrooms. The conformity, contentment, and self-centered confidence of the present-day American students are not academic values inculcated by the faculty but rather the result of a highly organized and efficiently functioning extracurricular social system."[5] In a survey of ten high schools selected at random from schools in New York State and stratified by size of community, Rosenberg also found that high self-esteem among boys depends on their ratings with their peers and a feeling that their peers think them "good enough."[6] However, another large study did not find boys as dependent on friends approval as girls were.[7]

For both boys and girls, friendships progress in stability between the ages of five and eighteen. Boys, however, show less conflict in their friendship relations at every age but fifteen.[8] The ages of fourteen and fifteen seem to be critical for friendship for both boys and girls, probably because they spend more time with their friends then, than at any other time.

Both boys and girls seem to experience a feeling of possible rejection at all ages when they are a part of odd-numbered groups. Two examples of quotes from fifteen-year-old boys in Coleman's study are typical: "Often when three people are together they argue and two are dominant over one. Often when three people are together one is left out; make sure it isn't you."[9]

As age goes up, conformity to the peer group seems to go down,[10] and the relationship with friends changes as well. In the early ages of adolescence, friends are mostly same sex people to do things with. By middle adolescence, same-sex groups are common, but more interaction occurs with the other sex. By late adolescence, the boy is doing more with girlfriends than he is with the same-sex friends.[11]

Girls' Friendships

In early adolescence, Douvan and Adelson find that girls choose friends for companionship—people to do something with. The focus is more on the activity than on the friend. Girls mention at this time that they want a friend who is amiable, easy to get along with, cooperative, and fair. Leisure time is spent more often with the family than with friends, and boys do not yet have much importance at this age, at least for the girls in the sample.[12]

When girls are fourteen, fifteen, and sixteen, their friendships seem to be different in content, the researchers report. Girls spend more time with friends at this point, and they want a friend in whom they can confide and who will offer emotional support. They particularly want a friend who will be loyal and trustworthy, who will not abandon them in a crisis or gossip about them behind their back. Douvan and Adelson believe that girls at this age want a friend who will be like them in terms of the trials and tribulations suffered and with whom they can identify. The girl looks for response from friends to help her form her own identity and self-evaluation. Loyalty is important because this is a time when a girl reveals her fears and doubts—particularly in the area of sexuality. A friend must be someone she can trust not to use information against her or abandon her in favor of boys. In Douvan and Adelson's sample of girls aged fourteen to sixteen, boys are not yet seen as close friends and intimates, although the girl of this age wants to be popular with boys because it affects her appraisal by her peer group of girls.[13]

The later adolescent of seventeen and eighteen seems to establish calmer friendships. She is more secure about herself and less insistent that the loyalty of a friend be a prime consideration. The girl of this age is also more secure with boys and can turn to them as intimates and friends. In all of their friendships, girls seem to have more intimacy than boys do.[14] However, they also have more conflict, possibly because of dating and jealousy. They show about the same degree of conformity to the peer group that boys do, with the greatest degree of conformity at ages eleven to thirteen for both sexes and increasing autonomy and ability to withdraw from the group at later ages.[15]

Conformity to the group is shown by such quotes as, "If someone is not part of the group, they aren't worth knowing"; "If someone is not part of the group, you don't let them join in the fun."[16] However, in a way that is different from boys, girls seem able to empathize with the individual at early ages and are more likely to express a thought like, "If someone is not part of the group, I feel sorry for them and help them join in."[17]

Dating

Douvan and Adelson believe that for both boys and girls, dating is a way of "measuring the self through the other's appraisal." This measurement may be a somewhat tense one, as "sexual anxiety and tenuous self-esteem" give dating an emotional tone. Because dating behavior is somewhat formal and ritualized, at least for younger ages, it may keep the couple from too much intimacy but also discourages them from getting to know one another.[18] Just as boys and girls differ in the way they perceive friendships, they also see dating (or heterosexual interaction of various kinds) from a different perspective.

Dating from a Boy's Perspective

To start with, boys start dating later than girls do. In one study, although 95 percent of the male students had reached puberty by the end of their high-school freshman year (as judged by the fact that their voices had changed and they were getting facial hair), only 45 percent had started dating by the end of that year. By the end of the junior year, 77 percent had started dating and 30 percent were heavy daters. By the end of the senior year, 95 percent were dating and girls occupied a prominent place in their lives.[19]

Offer points out that a typical attitude toward girls was expressed by one of his subjects who was on the football team and who, by the end of his sophomore year, had never dated. He stated that he did not feel that anything was wrong and that he would have a lot of time for "that sort of thing" in college. Yet when the interviewers pointed out to him that his level of anxiety went up even while he was expressing this indifference, he admitted that he simply did not understand girls and wanted to be left alone by them.[20] In contrast, by the end of the senior year, not only were 95 percent of the boys in this research project dating, but they liked their dates and enjoyed their relationships to girls. Those who were not dating stated that they wanted to do so but lacked the courage to try to get a date.[21]

Therefore, for the first two years of high school, dating was not a major issue for boys in this research group. Later it became more important: if a boy was not dating, he could not exchange experiences; he was not part of the social group. Asking the girl out was apparently very painful for these boys.[22] Indeed, dating emphasizes the active, "need to perform" role of the boy. First of all, the boy had to perform by making the social overtures of asking for the date. While girls would call the boys and ask for rides to parties and the like, it was almost always the boys who did the asking on actual dates. They, of course, were anxious about what to say, wondered if the girl would say yes only out of politeness or would reject them, and wondered what the girl would say to others about them. (Given the difficulty of this "asking" role, it is little wonder that many boys develop some bravado and thick skins about rejection.) However, the boys' curiosity about girls and their desire to be part of a social group enabled them to overcome their fear of girls. They reported great satisfaction from their dates and enjoyed the social sharing of experiences with their peers afterward.

Offer believes that the "minute dissection" that goes on among the boys telling each other what they did right or wrong is extremely helpful and suggestive. They try to do better the next time, not so much because they enjoy kissing or petting, but so they can tell their boy friends about it. As their anxiety diminishes in their relationships with girls, they begin to enjoy the encounters more and eventually can look forward to a date simply because they like the girl and want to share their experiences with her and her alone. (Hallelujah!)[23]

Boys also have to take an active role in dating in the sense of providing the transportation and planning the entertainment. It is usually considered preferable to have one's own car, and this preference has far-reaching consequences. It means that by the time a boy is dating on a regular basis, he may have to work many long hours to pay for the support of a car. At the very least, he must pay for gas, and if it is his own car, he may have to make car payments and pay for repairs and insurance as well. As the boy is also usually expected to pay for many of the expenses of a date, dating can become a heavy financial burden. While the situation may vary by locality and social class, middle-class boys may even attempt to outdo each other in entertainment for their dates. At one local tenth-grade dance, boys not only got corsages for their dates but took them out to dinner at a nice restaurant and out for pizza later. As some of the boys could not yet drive, they used taxis for transportation! The senior prom at the same school involved the necessity of a rented tuxedo and more elaborate after-dance entertainment and was estimated by the boys to cost at least $150 per couple. Many boys opted to stay home rather than pay out that kind of money.

The boy gets certain power to decide what to do and to set certain behavior standards on a date, but with this power comes responsibility. He may make the decision about where to go on the date, but he must live with the results of that decision. If he has displeased his date, he may feel like a fool. He may also have to perform by having to protect his date under certain circumstances. If they go to a rowdy rock concert, or if someone makes remarks to her on the street, it is up to him to defend her and possibly fight on her behalf. He is also expected to be in charge and to know what to do. If the car breaks down, he is expected to know what is wrong. There is, in addition, a subtle expectation that he will be smarter than his date and can "tell her" about things. This is, of course, what makes bright girls threatening. It is not surprising that boys often date girls who are a year or two younger. The traditional roles are more easy to establish with that age difference.

Dating from a Girl's Perspective

The active role for the boy in dating is paralleled by a passive role for the girl. While she may make herself available and give every indication that she would like to be asked out, she usually has to wait for the boy to do the asking for a formal date. She can, however, arrange to "accidentally" be at a place where the boy will be and she can even, under some circumstances, ask him to do things.

As popularity with boys is part of general popularity and builds esteem with peers, the girl is eager to be asked out again. To this end she may, some hypothesize, develop a "dating personality." The female "good date" is amiable and verbal; she should be gay and bright, but not too serious and intellectual. She is the boy's audience for his offerings of entertainment; she must be polite and, if possible, enthusiastic about his plans.[24]

Dorothy Pearce, in intensive interviews with girls of fifteen and sixteen, describes the dating personality even further. The girls make themselves available and look interested in the hope that the boy will ask them out. They try to respond to his moods. "If he is quiet, they attempt to remain low key and ladylike; if he is interested in sports, the girls quickly develop an interest in sports."[25] In certain situations, they adjust their behavior to that of their date. For example, if a girl is unsure that a boy is going to open the car door for her, she uses a ploy. As one says, "You just sort of walk along and if he walks the other way, you know you are going to open it yourself." These girls learn to manage unwanted attentions and to turn down dates gracefully. They try not to embarrass the boy unless he is too persistent. They agree, however, that if he is persistent, it is all right to be rude. They also try to encourage shy boys by moving over or saying something like, "Gee, don't I get a goodnight kiss?'' They agree that the right words and the right behavior come with experience. One says, ''I change my behavior and manners according to the date I am with and the kind of date I am on. There are times you can do things and times you can't.''[26]

Douvan and Adelson believe that such a dating personality may become a social role that takes the place of the girl's real personality and as such is restrictive and leads to no real friendship or intimacy.[27] However, others believe that the American girl knows the social role to such a degree that she can be an individual within it.[28]

In spite of the restrictions, girls report that they really like dating. It enables them to establish separate identities in the eyes of their parents, although parents have some influence on their choice of dates. Pearce believes that it also represents to many a first visible step toward sexual behavior.[29] Douvan and Adelson report variations in dating patterns with age, social class, and region, but they profess that dating has certain functions that are similar for most girls. They believe that it is a testing of identity and a training in social graces, as well as an early stage in the filtering through of various possible mates.[30]

American girls start dating sooner than boys, at about fourteen for most girls and a year or so later for boys, although there are ethnic and class variations. (Young people in Europe and other areas begin their dating much later.) As the young girl is likely to be ahead of boys her own age in social maturity and secondary sexual characteristics, she is likely to date boys a few years older. In the early years of dating there is a preference for coed activities in groups. During this period, real friends continue to be same-sex friends. However, by seventeen or eighteen most girls are dating regularly, and Douvan and Adelson report that the perceived danger and the defensiveness have gone out of the dating relationships. Most young people have found genuine relationships with give and take.[31]

The fourteen- and fifteen-year-old girls in Pearce's study saw the qualities of preferred male dates as (in order) physical attractiveness, good personality, good physique, and sincere and considerate behavior.[32] We have no longitudinal study to see whether these desired qualities change as girls get older. One thing that does change is that girls tend to spend more time with their dates than with their girlfriends. Girls are not as likely to retain a number of ''girls only'' activities as boys are to retain ''boys only'' activities.[33] While it is acceptable for a male to enjoy the company of other guys, a girl who goes out with other girls is seen, in many cases, as one to be pitied: she doesn't have a date tonight; she has to go out with ''the girls.'' We see the reflection of a cultural standard suggesting that men are more important than women and men's company is more valued.

Because girls wish to be popular, there is some pressure for them to develop the appropriate dating personality, which includes a submissive, passive pattern of reaction. One of the most disturbing studies is the one by McDaniel in which he discusses how women change their attitudes and behaviors as dating relationships become more serious. "Girls who were studied in the first stage of random dating tended to be assertive, achievement oriented, autonomous, dominant, and desirous of status. They justified the dating relationship primarily in terms of recreation. When they went steady, their behavior shifted to assertive-receptive and during the final stage—when they were "pinned" or engaged—they became . . . wholly receptive: deferential, concerned about helping others, . . . and more anxious."[34] There has been a regression from autonomy to submission. Why so? It has been shown that a dating relationship may not move forward if the girl does not change in this fashion. McDaniel reports that men said they strongly disliked women who were assertive in the later stages of dating.[35]

Thus the dating scene reflects the other pressures of adolescence in pushing the female into "feminine" stereotyped behaviors. If you want male companionship and such behavior is what males expect, then there is great pressure to conform. The pressure may be accentuated because the average age of boys dated is a few years older than that of the girls. The older boy with his experience may intimidate the girl and make it hard for her to move beyond a dating personality. The whole dating situation, and to some extent general heterosexual interaction, reflects the pressure to be feminine by being pretty, popular, nice, and unassertive. There are negative sanctions for those who don't conform: they can't go to the prom without a date; if all their girlfriends are dating, they may sit home without anyone to do something with; and they may be excluded from parties and other social events.

Douvan and Adelson point out that there are also some special problems for girls who are very early or late daters. As they point out, the girl who is "out of phase" with her peers will probably suffer special anxieties and a sense of isolation.[36] Early dating may mean a girl does not have a chance to establish long-term, intimate same-sex friendships and loses valuable training in relating to other girls. The late dater may find less in common with other girls who have started dating and may worry about her physical attractiveness or become self-conscious.

Certain progress has been made in equalizing the dating or social relationship. For one thing, the casual dating that goes on today is not just in couples. Sometimes it is a form of group dating that seems to be somewhat of an extension of early adolescent co-ed activities. As Reiss describes it, "a group of several males and females will be at a party, a dance, or a bowling alley together, but not as couples. As the evening wears on, some of the males and females may pair off."[37] When couples start going out with each other steadily or exclusively, however, more formal dating still takes place. Even in this formal dating, however, girls have a few more social options. They can telephone boys without stigma today and they are more likely to pay for some of the expense of certain kinds of date, which gives them some leverage as to what they do on the date.

On the other hand, a great deal has not changed. Boys still do most of the asking, decide where to go, and initiate sexual activities. The male is still, to a great extent, the guardian of the girl's social life and her reputation. Many girls still try to be "nice" and develop a dating personality so that they will be popular. A recent letter to Joyce Brothers shows the continuing lack of control of the social situation experienced by many girls. The writer, a teenage girl, described herself as "not a raving beauty," but said, "My friends tell me that I'm pretty," and went on to say that she almost never had a date. She continued that she was particularly perplexed about her unpopularity because she "tried hard to always be sweet and nice."[38]

Sexuality

Changing Bodies

We have discussed the concern about physical appearance shared by many girls and boys during adolescence. This concern about physical appearance is accentuated by the development of secondary sex characteristics and by the norms about what is an appropriately "feminine and beautiful" or "masculine and tough" body. Unfortunately, the ideal male and female physiques seem to have been generated by the "Action Jackson" and "Barbie" dolls of childhood. While they may try their best to live up to the ideal of rippling biceps or big breasts and slim legs, it is difficult for most teenagers to come close to this ideal.

As we have seen, girls seem to feel particularly discontented about their appearance. Sixty-three percent of the girls in one study rated themselves below their peers in personal appearance, and only 12 percent desired no change in their appearance.[39] Height and weight are a major concern of many teenagers. In one large-scale study of tenth graders in California, 55 percent of the girls expressed concern about their weight compared to 13 percent of the boys.[40] While this is a 1950 study, a more recent study done in 1967 seems to show that the concern with weight continues. About 60 percent of the girls had been on diets by the time they were seniors; in contrast, although 19 percent of the boys were obese, only 24 percent of these heavy boys had ever dieted and only 6 percent were currently on diets. Half of the girls who felt themselves to be tall also expressed concern about their height.[41]

The beginning of puberty also means the acquiring of secondary sex characteristics. The bodily changes that occur at this time can be socially painful and anxiety-producing for many adolescents. Life is particularly difficult for the adolescent who does not reach puberty at the same time as his or her friends.[42] The girl who starts developing her figure early may be unmercifully teased or even accused of being overly interested in sex. One teacher was overheard to remark about a young girl who had developed early, "With that figure, she'll be the first one in seventh grade to get pregnant." The girl who develops late may be teased about her flat chest. She may feel unattractive and different and wonder whether she is really feminine. The passage through early puberty seems to be easier for some than for others, but in all cases, it is marked with some degree of uncertainty and anxiety about the changes taking place.[43]

Menstruation. During early adolescence, the young woman also begins to menstruate and may feel some ambivalence about her role as a female. Many reach menarche (their first menstruation) without knowing anything about it. Some studies show that as many as 17 percent of girls from upper socioeconomic brackets may experience their first menstrual period without having been told about it.[44] Many more learn only minimal facts from parents, from friends, or from "the movie" shown in sixth grade. Even then, the information communicated is seldom completely accurate.

However, the adolescent girl does learn *attitudes* about her body and about menstruation. These attitudes are seldom positive and bear all the negative weight of cultural tradition that we described in chapter 1. They hear the menstrual period called "the curse" and are told to hide their tampons or napkins. They may hear negative references to raging hormones or unstable premenstrual moods or overhear a male saying with disgust that a girl "has her period" or is "on the rag." At the very least, it is a messy business, and they may suffer cramping and some discomfort. Menstruation may carry with it a feeling of periodic uncleanliness and unattractiveness.

On the other hand, there is an element of delight and of having achieved an aspect of adulthood when a girl has her first menstrual period. This may be particularly true if she is one of the last in her group to begin. In any case, the ambivalence about this new biological part of her life may fit in with her general ambivalence about being female.

Changes in Boys. Boys are as much concerned with the changes in their bodies during this time as girls are. There are outward, visible signs of the many inward changes taking place. Facial and pubic hair begins to grow, voices change and become unreliable at the worst times, and acne often appears on the faces of these early adolescents. Sexual arousal may mean unwelcome erections during classes or at other inappropriate times. (Boys are usually very much concerned with their ability to have erections and to ejaculate. They may compare notes and even have contests about who can ejaculate the first or the farthest.) Boys are frequently concerned with penis size, and a large penis becomes equated with virility and masculinity. Interestingly enough, this concern with size seems to be only a male preoccupation. Linda Lovelace and "Deep Throat" to the contrary, females are very little concerned with the size of male genitals.[45] The following quotes are typical of male feelings at this time:

> About seventh grade these impromptu erections became more frequent, though, and I would always dread having to get out of my seat in class when I had one. It usually happened when the class was boring, and would sometimes last the whole hour. I was afraid that everyone would notice. Luckily nobody did. . . .
>
> Junior high was a rather god awful time in the life of most guys I know, myself readily included. What a drag puberty was. . . . I had greater questions . . . When am I going to get pubic hair on my genitalia? Junior high locker rooms were particularly grotesque, especially when some of the more physically mature dudes, who were not always the most intelligent, made fun of the younger, less physically mature guys.
>
> When I was thirteen I had my first ejaculation which was kind of a shock since at this time I still didn't know anything about sex.[46]

When Sexuality Means Sex

For teenage girls, sexuality is as tied up with cultural taboos and stereotypes about the nature of males and females as much as it is with their own bodies and desires. The cultural Madonna (good girl) and Eve (bad girl) images can be clearly seen at this time. Through the 1950s and into the early 1960s, "good girls" were not supposed to have sexual intercourse until they got married. Actually, many of the girls of this period did have intercourse in late high school or in college. However, they didn't tell people; they often didn't even tell their best friends. As contraceptives could not be openly bought and used, they frequently got pregnant. When they did, they had a quiet wedding, had the baby in a home for unwed mothers, or possibly had an illegal abortion. Legal abortion was not an option at that time, and many women died from having an illegal abortion or trying to abort themselves. You remained a "good girl" as long as you did not get a "bad reputation" (that is, your boyfriend did not talk) or as long as you did not get pregnant and stayed unmarried.

Stereotypes about female sexuality went along with the good-girl image. A "nice girl" wasn't that interested in sex and tried to fend off a boy's advances. She was not supposed to respond strongly even when aroused, and no one worried about females having orgasms.

Unfortunately, the stereotype of masculinity demanded then and demands now that boys be "on the make." Boys who try to live up to the stereotype or to fulfill their own desires attempt to have dating include as much sexual activity as possible, starting with kissing and petting and ending with intercourse. Pressure is put on the girl to give in and to allow sexual liberties. The female adolescent is thus put in a very delicate position. Dating and male companionship are rewarding to her, and she wants to gain the approval of her date and to keep her partner around. In addition, she may be very much sexually aroused and want to have sexual activity with her partner. On the other hand, if she is "easy," she will get a bad reputation. This means she will be increasingly pressured for sex and treated with little respect by the boys she dates. She may also be shunned by many girls and by the "nice crowd." Sadly, many girls get these bad reputations without deserving them when boys brag falsely to their friends about how they "scored."

Boys and girls seem to enter relationships for different reasons. In the Simon, Berger, and Gagnon study of 1972, 46 percent of the young men were not emotionally involved with their initial sexual partner; only 31 percent said that they were in love with the girl or were planning to marry her. However, 59 percent of the females planned to marry their first coital partner.[47] Other subsequent research by Gagnon and Simon also showed that females were more likely to grant sexual access to serious suitors with some feeling that they would secure a commitment to marriage by so doing.[48]

Whether she does or does not allow sexual liberties, the girl may be faulted. If she protects her reputation and is totally cool about sex, she may be labeled as "frigid." If she gives in (or even if she doesn't), she may get a bad reputation. The path between these two extremes is very narrow. A girl can neck or pet with rather casual dates, but if she wants to have intercourse, she had better wait for that very special boyfriend, who, as a special boyfriend, is not as likely to talk about her. For boys indeed do talk. In the Simon, Berger, and Gagnon study, 60 percent of the males, but only 40 percent of the females, had shared information about their sexual experience with someone else within a month after the experience took place. Apparently, a double standard still exists, as well. Eighty-six percent of the males compared to 67 percent of the females got an approving audience.[49]

Margaret Mead has pointed out that because the dating pattern leaves the control of impulse largely to the young couple, there may be later problems enjoying sex. The girl who is accustomed to fending off the boy's advances and controlling her own sexual feelings may find as a bride that it is difficult to get rid of the habit of constraint and feel free to enjoy sex.[50]

A recent study shows the ambivalence that females may feel about sexual touch. Forty male and female undergraduates were questioned to see how they felt about touch on different body areas. For females, "the more a touch was associated with sexual desire, the less it was considered to imply friendliness, warmth, friendship, and pleasantness." Thus, while touching should be pleasurable, such sexual touching may raise warning flags because of the need to exercise control. In contrast, men saw a sexual touch by a woman as being loving, warm, and pleasant.[51] Women must worry not only about reputations but about pregnancy or even the use of physical force by the male. To add to her ambivalence, it is unlikely, in the early years of adolescence at least, that a girl will be able to get total physical satisfaction from sexual intercourse. It is usually several years after menarche before young girls are likely to achieve orgasm.[52] On the other hand, the girl may enjoy the love, warmth, and intimacy associated with sex and also want to please her partner. Her own ambivalence, combined with pressures both to have and to refrain from having sexual intercourse, make the whole area of sexual experience an emotional and anxiety-producing situation for many girls.

The boy, for his part, is pressured to perform. It is up to him to initiate any sexual action. It is also up to him to be competent and cool and to look as if he knows what he is doing. To ensure his masculine image, he must press for sexual liberties. Whether he talks about them afterward depends on the closeness of the relationship.

The boy may not know much, if any, more about sex than his date does. Still, he has to be the one to tentatively reach his hand over her shoulder and let it drop casually on her breast. He has to risk rejection at every stage. He also has to be sure that he doesn't fumble or seem unsure of himself. He is put into the role of the leader and the teacher. (The author knew of one colleague who practiced unhooking bras on his mother's dressmaker dummy. He practiced until he could separate the hooks casually with one hand. Unfortunately for this poor fellow, front-hooking bras made their appearance at just about the time he started dating.)

Whether or not sexual intercourse between the dating couple does occur, there is a great temptation for the boy to lie about his exploits. He has to prove himself with the other guys. While all the participants recognize that locker room talk is not necessarily accurate, they listen and participate. The great danger is that feminine reputations may be slurred—often without reason (and girls do still get "reputations" even in this supposedly liberated age). Another danger is the younger male who listens and believes without question that this is the way "men" behave and then wonders about himself.

A danger on the sexual scene is the temptation for the male to use force to obtain his desires. The line between persuasion and force is a fine one. A majority of girls in one study say that they had been subjected to a fairly strong degree of force in an attempt to have sex. The use of force in this situation is a dangerous enactment of the master-victim relationship, which can be a negative extension of the powerful-passive male-female stereotype. In one study of 400 unmarried male college students, 23 percent had attempted to force a girl to have intercourse on a date with a degree of physical force. A majority of 261 female college students said they had encountered some sort of physical sexual aggression of this kind. In most cases, they had felt terror, fright, disgust, and anxiety.[53] Acquaintance rape is apparently fairly widespread. It is frequently unreported, or reported rapes are unbelieved because it is thought that if the girl was in the company of the boy, she "led him on" or at least gave grudging consent to intercourse and only felt outraged after the fact.

Susan Griffiths has called rape "the all-American crime" because it epitomizes some of the power relationships in our culture's traditional sex roles.[54] Because rape is so widespread in our culture, it seems worthwhile to digress from our developmental framework at this point to say something about rape in our society.

Rape

Rape is a violent rather than just a sexual act. Rape and the fear of rape are power mechanisms by which men seek to control women or perhaps to humiliate other men. Rape has always been considered a crime more against the man to whom the woman "belongs" as daughter or wife than a crime against the woman herself. Fear of rape has meant that women have had to seek the protection of men and to be "good girls" in the hope that they will be protected from rape or at least not accused of inciting it.

There are many myths surrounding the act of rape that relate to this idea of good girl and bad girl. It is frequently believed that only "bad girls" get raped and that any woman who has been raped was probably asking for it. The truth of the matter is, of course, that women of all ages, from three-month-old babies to ninety-year-old grandmothers, get raped and that few of them did anything to provoke the crime.[55] Yet victims who are even moderately attractive continue to be treated as though they provoked their own assault. They are often not believed when they report their rape, or at the least, they are harrassed or intensively questioned by police who hope voyeuristically to hear the lurid details of the attack. Susan Griffiths even goes so far as to propose that many policemen, lawyers, and judges identify with the rapists and, while they would not personally commit rape, enjoy hearing about the reaffirmation of male potency.[56]

The corollary of the "only bad girls get raped" myth is the belief that "all men are potentially rapists and will rape if too greatly sexually aroused." This later belief is used to ensure that women remain demure, modest, and under the protection of "their" men. It is also used to excuse men who just "couldn't help themselves" and thus raped because they were sexually excited. Indeed most rapes are planned: 58 percent of rapes by one man, 83 percent of rapes by pairs of men, and 90 percent of gang rapes were found to be planned ahead of time in one extensive study of rapists.[57] Thus men are not assaulting their victims in the heat of desire, but are coolly and premeditately planning their attacks.

Most of the men who rape are not convicted of their crimes and punished for them. The rape victim is put in the unusual position of having to prove that a crime was even committed and having to show that she resisted the rape. Again, the assumption is that unless she has suffered great physical abuse other than rape, she probably cooperated in the rape attempt or did not resist enough (no matter that she was threatened with a knife or gun). One judge was known to remark that "you can't thread a moving needle," as he dismissed the case against an accused rapist. It is also assumed that if the rape occurred at any but prime daytime hours at a PTA meeting, the woman asked for it by being in the wrong place at the wrong time or by being the wrong kind of woman. A judge in Oregon recently dismissed a case in which a woman jogger had been raped while being threatened with a broken bottle. The judge held that the woman should not have been out in the early morning hours jogging and that by so doing, she incited the rapist. A lawyer defending the rapist of a cocktail waitress said the victim was "familiar with alcohol" and implied that she was an unfit mother.[58]

Thus, rape can be used as a control to keep women indoors at night (or in the early morning), to keep them out of certain occupations, to make them dress in demure and inconspicuous ways, to make them act like a "good girl" in any case, and to make them seek the protection of a man. It is an effective way for men to exercise power and to show their hostility against women or their antipathy toward other men to whom the women "belong."

In all fairness, we must say that people are becoming more aware of the myths surrounding rape, and in many areas the treatment of rape victims is changing. Many localities have established rape crisis centers and hotlines where victims can seek immediate help. Police officers have been sensitized to the problems of a rape victim and trained in a more gentle approach to questioning. Frequently female officers are assigned to help a victim. In many courts, the victim's past sexual history can no longer be used in the case (as evidence that "she was a bad girl and deserved what she got"). Women are also taking self-defense courses and becoming aware of the need to defend themselves and not just seek the protection of a man. All of these things help, but the primary fact of rape remains: it is a power move used by men in an attempt to control and subdue women.

Back to the Teenage Years

Thus, we see that adult norms regarding power and sex heavily influence the kind of sexual misunderstandings that occur between teenage boys and girls. Times have changed, however, and sexual activity for girls is not as stigmatizing as before. While the possibility of a "bad reputation" can still be used as a social control, the limits by which one can get a bad reputation are different today.

Has there really been a sexual revolution? The answer to this question depends on whom you ask and whether you are talking about attitudes or behavior. Some general patterns seem to have emerged since the mid-1960s, however, and the patterns have continued into the early 1980s. Teenagers are having their first sexual experience at slightly younger ages and are having it with more casual partners. While the norm, at least for females, is only for permissiveness with affection, one no longer has to be engaged or "going steady" to validate sexual relations. Also, the rates of permarital sexual experience are tending to converge somewhat between men and women. In two out of three recent studies of boys and girls in early adolescence (the fifteenth birthday or ninth grade), only about 10 percent of both boys and girls have had sexual intercourse.[59] The other study reports that about 25 percent of the fifteen-year-old boys and 13 percent of the fifteen-year-old girls had had sexual experience in 1970, and 38 percent of the males and 24 percent of the females in that group by 1973.[60] By tenth grade, Jessor and Jessor report that 21 percent of the tenth-grade boys and 26 percent of the tenth-grade girls have had intercourse.[61] By the age of seventeen, Miller and Simon found 25 percent of both sexes had had intercourse;[62] Jessor and Jessor report 33 percent of the boys and 55 percent of the girls (in the sample in their small Western city) had had coitus, and Verner and Stewart found about 33 percent of the seventeen-year-olds were nonvirgins.[63] Most of these studies show more experienced males in early adolescence, but almost equal numbers of experienced boys and girls by late adolescence.

Yet at the same time, we should not overlook the percentage that is not having sexual relations. Offer and Offer, in a 1975 study, found that many teenagers disapproved of sexual relations in high school. Many feared that they were not old enough to handle the situation or they feared pregnancy.[64]

The prevalence of coitus increases during the college years. In the first two years of college, most studies find about an average of 40 percent of the females and 60 percent of the males have had sexual intercourse.[65] By the senior year in college, Jessor and Jessor find 85 percent of the females and 82 percent of the males have had coitus.[66] Bauman and Wilson report 73 percent of both genders are experienced.[67] In *Sexual Behavior in the 1970s*, Morton Hunt reports that 81 percent of the women and 95 percent of the men from age eighteen to twenty-four have had premarital intercourse.[68]

Thus, by the college years, norms and behavior regarding sexual activity have become similar between men and women. Women are still not supposed to be as aggressive sexually as men, and the label "promiscuous" is still more likely to be applied to women than to men, but females are relatively free to engage in sexual activity without being labeled. Living-together arrangements, and to some extent co-ed dorms, have been open admissions of what often went on covertly in the past.

Contraceptive Use

The ambivalence of our cultural beliefs about sexual activity is reflected in the statistics on contraceptive use by teenagers. Contraceptive use among teenage girls is remarkably low. Although something like 30 percent are estimated to have had intercourse by the time they are seniors in high school (and some estimates are higher), only about 20 percent of those having intercourse regularly use contraceptives.[69] This carelessness can be traced to our feelings about "good girls" and "bad girls." If you use contraceptives, then you are obviously planning to have a sexual life. If you do not use them, you can claim to self, boyfriend, or others, that it was a moment of passion and you were overcome. The girl who uses contraceptives on a regular basis is thus risking feeling like a "bad girl." If she comes prepared for sexual intercourse, her date may wonder what she has done before. The girl who does not use contraceptives does not have this problem, but if she depends on the sporadic use of condoms by her boyfriend, on rhythm, on coke douches, or on any of the other very unsure ways of preventing conception, she is quite likely to find herself pregnant. The usual solution for this dilemma in high school is to rely on the boyfriend to use condoms. Unfortunately, condoms used without foam have a high failure rate.

There is not much evidence to show that use of contraceptives has increased greatly in spite of liberalized values. Part of the problem is the attitude of parents, educators, and legislators. Until recently, many schools that had sex education classes could not teach about contraception or preventing pregnancy. There seemed to be a feeling that it was all right to tell young people about the basic facts of life, but that to talk about sexual intercourse and its results would be to encourage experimentation with sex. Many states have even attempted to remove sex education from the schools. It is common in southern states to see billboards saying, "Remove sex education from the schools, elect —— in November," and similar signs. Other attempts to limit sexual information and access to contraception have recently increased as well. A senator connected with the Reagan administration has recently introduced into Congress a law that will require Planned Parenthood clinics to notify a parent within ten days if a minor child receives contraceptives at the clinic. The effect of the law will be to prevent many young people who do not wish their parents to know of their sexual activity from getting contraceptives.[70] Right-to-life forces have also introduced legislation that will allow states individually to ban abortion (which has been legal since a Supreme Court decision of 1973). There is a real possibility that in the future, many teenagers may not be able to get contraceptives or to terminate unwanted pregnancies.

Unfortunately, parents do not seem to do a much better job of sex education than the schools and probably teach considerably less than the schools might, especially about contraceptive use. Nancy Friday, in her book *My Mother, Myself,* tells of the different perceptions held by mothers and their daughters about what the girls were told about sex. The mothers all felt they had fulfilled their parental duty and told their daughters important information; the daughters did not feel they had been told anything at all.[71] Quotes from Morrison support the same belief that parents tell their children very little:

Female: When I was in sixth grade, a film about sex education was shown at my elementary school, but I never saw it. For some reason unknown to me, my mother felt I should not see it.

Female: When I asked a group of grown-ups what Midol was, I guess my mother decided it was time for me to be lectured on where babies come from; she provided me with "What Every Teenager Must Know" and a question-and-answer period.

Female: My mother had a pretty hard time talking about the little she did talk about. The only reason she did it at all was because my Girl Scout troop was showing a movie talking about menstruation. . . .

Male: Because sex was taboo at our house, you couldn't say that "dirty" three-letter word without somebody blushing, trying to hush it up, or giggling. . . .

Male: I thought it was tough in childhood to get information about my own sex, but there was none to be found concerning the female! A sense of guilt accompanied acquisition of information about the sexuality of women which I today attempt to deal with.[72]

Although in some cases parents may offend their children by suggesting contraceptive information before the children are ready, greater efforts need to be made by parents and children to talk about their bodies, sex, and contraceptive use.[73] In particular, there seems to be a need to talk about the emotional aspects of sex and what can be expected.

Homosexuality and Homophobia

Sexuality may sometimes mean homosexuality for the adolescent. Sexuality seems to lie on a continuum (or straight line), with homosexuality at one end and heterosexuality at the other. Most people are not totally at either end of the line, but somewhere in between. Adolescence is a time for the awakening of sexual urges and the exploration of feelings.

Some of that exploring may be to explore one's feelings toward the same sex. We will see in the quotes below examples of feelings of attraction to or arousal by the same sex. One girl writes of being "turned on" by the nude bodies of other females; a boy writes of a dream in which a friend sucks his fingers. Almost all young people go through a stage in which they explore their own bodies, often in the company or with the aid of friends of same sex. Girls may play doctor, and boys may have sessions in which they masturbate together. In a large percentage of adolescents, this type of interaction occurs earlier, and by the adolescent years they are primarily attracted to the opposite sex. However, for others the attraction to the same sex persists. It may be a mild and fleeting thing, such as that described in the following quotes, or it may be the person's primary sexual orientation:

> *Male:* Last fall . . . for the first time in my life, I faced my own homosexual feelings and the fear and terror they elicited from me. Since that experience and my new awareness, I have felt a certain disappointment that my fears have continued to prevent exploration in this area.

> *Male:* Lately I have become more scared of my (latent, thank God) homosexual tendencies. The main thing that made me worry about myself was a dream I had in which a (male) friend of mine was sucking my fingers, and giving me pleasure (pretty obvious symbolism). Intellectually, I realize that this is OK, but it still frightens me a little. Emotionally, I still feel that homosexuality is perverse.

> *Female:* Many other feelings I had I really felt were abnormal, especially for a woman. I used to see pictures of nude women or would see them in movies and get sexually excited. . . . It is good now to find out that other women also have similar feelings, and that it is OK and I am not necessarily perverted or a homosexual.[74]

We do not know what causes homosexuality or heterosexuality, but doctors and scientists have come to accept the fact that homosexuality is a part of the expression of normal sexuality for many people. We have recently discovered that a great deal more of the population is homosexual or "gay" than we ever thought before. If we include those who are bisexual, estimates range from 10 to 20 percent.[75] Our concern with homosexuality in this book is limited to its relationship to sex roles. As sex-role norms have strong things to say about sexual behavior (heterosexual, that is), identifying oneself as a homosexual may make it difficult to act in ways *society defines* as masculine or feminine. According to these norms, girls are to gain approval by seeking popularity with *boys* (not other girls) to be defined as feminine. Boys are to seek sexual prowess with *girls* (not other boys) to be defined as masculine. A person who defines him- or herself as homosexual or even worries about having homosexual interests or desires may be partially rejecting what the culture defines as masculine or feminine. The fear of many about not being "masculine" or "feminine" enough leads to strong fears about homosexuality in our culture. This is particularly true for boys, as to be masculine has been depicted as *not* being feminine, and this lesson has been carefully taught from birth onward. At the same time, stereotypic masculinity is conceived of in terms of being heterosexual. Thus, if you depart from the norm of masculinity, you may be depicted as feminine, as homosexual, or even as somewhat of both. The popular conception of a male homosexual is of an effeminate person. Thus, the boy learns by implication that to be masculine is not to be feminine *or* homosexual.

We must insert here that society's norms and popular conceptions do not represent reality in most cases. Very few gay men are effeminate in looks or behavior and most cannot be distinguished from straight males. In a similar fashion, most lesbians are not "butch" in style and they, too, can usually not be distinguished from straight females. In addition, "butch-fem," or male-female, roles are seldom played in homosexual relationships. Many homosexuals are quite comfortable with their sexual preference and feel perfectly "masculine" or "feminine," in spite of what society says.[76] The real problem from most gay people is the oppression that comes from a heterosexual norm for behavior. This norm means that many gays have to keep their sexual preference secret or face stigma and even job or housing discrimination.

The fear of not living up to the heterosexual norms of sex-role stereotypes affects many straight people and leads to a related fear of homosexuality, or homophobia. The fear of being called homosexual and thus stigmatized as not masculine or feminine enough is strong enough that people can play upon it and use it as a social-control mechanism. For example, the woman who achieves in sports or a career may be called a lesbian by those who are angry at her for not playing the female role. However, the threat or implication of homosexuality (not being feminine) is not as likely to be used against women. This is probably because our culture does not put a great deal of emphasis on the sexual nature of women, and there is an assumption that all women would really prefer a man if they could have one. This assumption is not valid, but it eases society's fear of female homosexuality, and lesbianism has been more easily accepted in this culture than has male homosexuality. This fact does not make it easier for the lesbian woman to resolve any questions she may have about herself and her "femininity," but she is not as frequently the target of open hostility as is the male homosexual. Women are also able to touch, hug, and be intimate without accusations of homosexuality.

It is the male who suffers most from intimations of homosexuality, as such hints are a threat to his masculinity. Gregory Lehne, writing about homophobia, tells us that in his childhood, leaps from trees and rocks at the swimming area became tests of masculinity. Boys who hesitated were encouraged with a taunt like, "I done it three times. Come on fellas. What are you, a fag? Jump!"[77]

Many men are willing to go to almost any lengths to avoid any such threats to their masculinity. Therefore, many repress affectionate or kind feelings toward other men. They make sure they don't touch other men or express any kind and tender feelings toward them. This repression of emotions carries over into the repression of emotions in general and fits in with the cultural prescription of being "cool." It keeps men from getting close to other men and from expressing their real feelings to another male. Along with the fear of homosexuality, such expression of emotion could also be considered sissy or effeminate, and so there is a double reason for many men to be inexpressive. While men may talk about work, sports, or sexual exploits, they seldom talk about their real feelings and problems to other men. Without talking about one's real concerns, it is hard to have good friends. Thus men have kept a certain distance from one another, although this distance is papered over with ritual work and sports talk.

The fear of homosexuality is so strong in our culture that we have to call it "homophobia." Men in particular are so afraid of the parts of themselves that are attracted to other men and so afraid of having their masculinity demeaned that they constantly deny their homosexuality—by saying how much they hate "fags" or even by looking for fights with them. The threat that one might be tagged with the homosexual label is kept alive by the teasing of other men: "You don't want to fight? What's the matter, you a fag?" The man who fears the label must attack first by proving he is straight and strong, possibly by teasing others himself or by denouncing gays.[78] When he does this, he denies an important part of his own emotional structure and cannot become close to other men. He may pass these feelings on directly and indirectly to his own male children, usually by stopping hugging or even touching them once they reach ten or eleven. Psychologists have demonstrated that we need a certain amount of touch and stroking,[79] and the lack of physical closeness between boy and father hurts both of them.

Men are thus denied an important part of their psychological well-being when they cannot touch and when they cannot express their tender feelings for other men. Needless to say, gay men are damaged by the negative implications of this homophobia. They hear their sexual preference jeered at and derided or they may be physically attacked. Adolescence is the time when young men are most strongly affected by these homophobic fears, as this is when they are trying to establish a sexual and sex-role identity. It is also the time when peer-group pressure is strongest and a young man may suffer the most by deviating from society's norms. A modification of sex-role stereotypes that would allow a greater range of behavior for both men and women would allow many more people to enjoy their real potential without penalty.

Summary

It is difficult for both boys and girls to establish an identity in adolescence. The adolescent girl is socialized to need love and approval. She forms much of her identity from a reflection of the opinions of others, which makes her uncertain about her body, her popularity, and her abilities. She may be afraid to achieve academically, in a career, or in sports because she wants to remain feminine. Yet without these concrete achievements, she may find little solid foundation on which to base her self-esteem. She must also negotiate the new and precarious world of dating and sex with the handicap of needing approval from others. While females are now achieving more in sports and in the career world, it is difficult for the adolescent girl, who is establishing her identity, to become clear about the choices that are open to her. The messages about femininity are ambiguous. What the teenage girl hears is a little like the old dictum that "any man can become president," even though the presidential campaign now demands millions of dollars and high-placed contacts. In a similar way, the adolescent girl is told that she can do what she wants, that this is the "era for women." The message is not totally dishonest, but it ignores many realities. It ignores the socialization that makes it difficult for her to fit into masculine roles and jobs; it ignores the socialized need to be loved and approved of and the fact that she may not be approved of or may feel isolated if she does not do feminine things; it ignores the real prejudice against women that is still in effect in schools and in the career world. Seward points out these problems:

> American core culture overtly offers its girls the same social role choices in the competitive status hierarchy as its boys, while covertly expecting them to decline the more challenging instrumental roles in favor of low-status domestic roles for which they are paradoxically both overqualified and untrained. Here is a case of cultural discontinuity, where preparation for adult participation in society is followed by regression to dependency upon husband and children. Her situation constitutes a double bind in which either alternative leads to frustration: if she accepts at face value the invitation to share all areas of responsibility with men, she does so at the cost of denying herself as a woman. If on the other hand, she responds to the hidden message, leaving the broader social field for the protection of the home, it is too frequently at the cost of denying herself as a person.[80]

There is evidence that many girls are now fighting these odds and valuing concrete achievement for themselves. This may mean that they will have less desire for approval from others and will develop higher self-esteem. It is hoped that changes along these lines will continue.

Adolescence continues to be a difficult time for the adolescent boy as well as for the girl. For the boy, the greatest change has been in increasing ambivalence about the demands of achievement, although the norms for success may come to be reinstated with more difficult economic times. However, most of the prescriptions of the male role still remain: be tough, be cool, be good. In this period of conformity to peer pressure, the adolescent boy learns to repress his feelings and to build his body. He seeks esteem through achievements in sports, in school activities, and in sexual prowess. As the norms push him to seek sexual activity, his interaction with girls on dates may provoke anxiety and produce conflict. Also, his fear of homosexuality makes it unlikely that he will get close to other men.

The changing roles for girls that ease the "good girl" constraints and allow for more concrete achievements may somewhat ease the difficulty of female adolescence. In a similar way, the ambivalence about career success *may* take some pressure off the male and allow him to consider other options in his life. On the whole, however, adolescence is still a mixture of pleasure and tension. It is made more difficult by the pressures to conform to nonfunctional sex-role stereotypes.

Essay Questions

1. Discuss the different approaches to friendship taken by teenage boys and girls. Why do girls put so much of a premium on loyalty? What do boys want in their friends? Do the approaches to friendship change as the teenager gets older?
2. Discuss the relationship of boys and girls to dating and, in particular, the "active" role taken by the boy and the "passive" role taken by the girl. How is the "dating personality" an example of this passive role?
3. Compare how adolescent boys and girls feel about their bodies. What things do they like and dislike and how satisfied generally are they with them?
4. Drawing on the material in chapter 1, how do cultural ideas about menstruation affect a young girl's view of herself and her developing body?
5. What general trends can you cite in sexual behavior among teenagers (for example, first intercourse at a younger age)? Why are girls' rates of nonvirginity beginning to converge with boys' rates in the later teen years?
6. What different attitudes do boys and girls have toward their first sexual partner? How are these attitudes carried over in the sexual

part of the dating relationship? Why does Margaret Mead say that the sexual nature of our dating relation may hurt marital enjoyment of sex?

7. Are teenagers using more contraceptives as they become more sexually active? If not, why aren't they? What recent trends do you see that may affect contraceptive use?

8. Why does Susan Griffiths call rape the all-American crime? How do adult attitudes about rape show up in the teenage dating culture?

9. How common is homosexuality among adolescents and how does it relate to the sex-role stereotypes of masculinity and femininity?

10. How is homophobia a social-control mechanism? What does this homophobia mean for men's relationships with one another?

Exercises

1. Discuss the rituals of dating. Do you believe that dating is still as "active" for the boy and as "passive" for the girl, and do you believe that the "dating personality" still exists? Do you think that as teenagers do more in groups, there is an effect on the relationships in dates?

2. Discuss your feelings about your body and the things you might like to change? Do you really think, in your experience, that girls are more dissatisfied with their bodies than boys are?

3. *For females:* Plan to ask someone out on a date and make plans out of your $25 weekly money to provide transportation, pay for what you will do, and so on. (Draw up exact plans.) Think of approaching your date at first and be aware of having to ask for the future if you are going to go out again. Also be aware of having to initiate any sexual overtures. During all of this, you do not know for certain whether the date likes you or not. (Note: this exercise can apply to the older person reentering the dating world as well as to young adults.)

4. *For males:* Try to show you want to be asked out on a date without saying anything about it directly. Then assume you are out on the date and, without saying anything, communicate your desire to be a nice, pleasant, "good girl." What do you do if your date gets mad at you? (Note: this exercise is also effective for the older male.)

5. To get a stronger feeling about sex-role stereotypes, complete the following exercise (for either males or females):

I feel attractive when _____

I feel angry when _____

I feel feminine when _____

Being feminine is irrelevant to me when _____
I feel masculine when _____
I feel afraid when _____
I feel alone when _____
I feel competent when _____
I feel I have control over my life when _____
I feel I have little or no control over my life when _____

6. Discuss why you think teenagers are so low in their use of contraception. Do you see any connection between this low usage and the active and passive roles of boys and girls while dating?
7. Discuss your feelings about homosexuality and homosexuals. If you have said that you are afraid of homosexuals, dislike them, or anything else that is negative, explore why you might feel that way. Is this feeling realistic in terms of what you know about homosexuals? Discuss your feelings about changing heterosexual norms (for many kinds of behavior in this society) so that homosexuals would be more comfortable in enjoying their sexual preference.
8. Complete the sentence. If I could change one thing about how I relate to the other sex, it would be _____

   Discuss what you have written. Now do the same sentence completion, but substitute "same sex" for "other sex." Compare your answers and discuss why they are different.

Notes

1. *Detroit Free Press*, January 23, 1982, p. A–3.
2. Elizabeth Douvan and Joseph Adelson, *The Adolescent Experience* (New York: Wiley, 1966), p. 210.
3. *Ibid.*, pp. 195–200.
4. John C. Coleman, *Relationships in Adolescence* (London: Routledge and Kegan Paul, 1974), p. 116.
5. *Ibid.*, p. 38; E.S. Suchman, "The Values of College Students," *Long-Range Planning for Education* (Washington, D.C.: American Council for Education, 1958), pp. 119–20, quoted in Robert Grinder, *Studies in Adolescence* (New York: Macmillan, 1963).
6. Morris Rosenberg, *Society and the Adolescent Self-Image*, Princeton, N.J.: Princeton University Press, 1965), p. 25; O.J. Harvey and Jeanne Rutherford, "Status in the Informal Group: Influence and Influencability at Differing Age Levels," in Grinder, *op. cit.*, pp. 309–18.
7. Russell Curtis, "Adolescent Orientations toward Parents and Peers: Variations by Sex, Age, and Socioeconomic Status," *Adolescence* 10 (1975):483–91.

8. J.E. Harrocks and M. Baker, "A Study of the Friendship Fluctuations of Pre-adolescents," *Journal of Genetic Psychology* 78 (1951):131–44.
9. Douvan and Adelson, *op. cit.*, p. 203; Coleman, *op. cit.*, p. 100.
10. Philip R. Costanzo and Marvin E. Shaw, "Conformity as a Function of Age Level," in John Hill and J. Shelton, eds., *Readings in Adolescent Development and Behavior* (Englewood Cliffs, N.J.: Prentice-Hall, 1971), pp. 241–46; O.J. Harvey and C. Consalvi, "Status and Conformity to Pressures in Informal Groups," in Hill and Shelton, *op. cit.*, pp. 226–33.
11. P. Wilmett, *Adolescent Boys of the East* (London: Routledge and Kegan Paul, 1966), in Coleman, *op. cit.*, pp. 90–95.
12. Douvan and Adelson, *op. cit.*, p. 186.
13. *Ibid.*, pp. 186–90.
14. J.E. Marcia and M.L. Friedman, "Ego Identity Status in College Women," *Journal of Personality* 2 (1970):249–63.
15. Coleman, *op. cit.*, p. 100.
16. *Ibid.*, p. 116.
17. *Ibid.*, p. 140.
18. Douvan and Adelson, *op. cit.*, p. 205.
19. Daniel Offer, *The Psychological World of the Teen-Ager: A Study of Normal Adolescent Boys* (New York: Basic Books, 1969).
20. *Ibid.*, p. 80.
21. *Ibid.*, p. 81.
22. *Ibid.*, p. 82.
23. *Ibid.*; Douvan and Adelson, *op. cit.*, pp. 205–13.
24. Dorothy Pearce, "The Dating Experiences for Adolescent Girls," *Adolescence* 10 (1975):157–74.
25. *Ibid.*, p. 167.
26. *Ibid.*
27. Douvan and Adelson, *op. cit.*, p. 207.
28. Ernest A. Smith, "The Date," in Rogers, *op. cit.*, pp. 378–84.
29. Pearce, *op. cit.*
30. Douvan and Adelson, *op. cit.*
31. *Ibid.*, p. 215.
32. Pearce, *op. cit.*
33. Douvan and Adelson, *op. cit.*
34. *Ibid.*, p. 215.
35. C.O. McDaniel, "Dating Roles and Reasons for Dating," *Journal of Marriage and the Family* 31 (1969):97–107.
36. *Ibid.*
37. Ira Reiss, *Family Systems in America*, 3rd ed. (New York: Holt, Rinehart and Winston, 1980), p. 102.
38. Joyce Brothers, *Detroit Free Press*, February 19, 1982, p. A–7.

39. K.E. Musa and M.E. Roach, "Adolescent Appearance and Self-Concept," *Adolescence* 8 (1973):385–94.

40. A. Frazier and L.K. Lesonbee, "Adolescent Concerns with Physique," *School Review* 58 (1950):397–405.

41. J. Dwyer, J. Feldman, and J. Mayer, "Adolescent Dieters: Who Are They?" *American Journal of Clinical Nutrition* 20 (1967):1045–56.

42. Gary Cover Jones and Paul Henry Mussen, "Self-Conceptions, Motivations, and Interpersonal Attitudes of Early- and Late-Maturing Girls," in Grinder, *op. cit.*, pp. 454–65.

43. James Elias and Paul Gebhard, "Sexuality and Sexual Learning in Childhood," in Fraiser, *op. cit.*, pp. 69–78; Simon Meyerson, "Adolescence and Sexuality," in Simon Meyerson, ed., *Adolescence: The Crises of Adjustment* (London: George Allen and Unwin, 1975); Margaret Siler Faust, "Developmental Maturity as a Determinant in Prestige of Adolescent Girls," *Child Development*, 3 (1960):173–84.

44. A. McCreary-Juhasz, "How Accurate Are Student Evaluations of the Extent of Their Knowledge of Human Sexuality?" *Journal of School Health* 37 (1967):409–12; J. H. Gagnon and W. Simon, "Prospects for Change in American Sexual Patterns," *Medical Aspects of Human Sexuality* 4 (1970):100–17; Thomas F. Staton, "The Emotions and Sex Education for Adolescents," in James F. Adams, *Understanding Adolescence: Current Developments in Adolescent Psychology*, 3rd ed. (Boston: Allyn and Bacon, 1976), pp. 268–91.

45. Eleanor Morrison *et al.*, *Growing Up Sexual* (New York: Van Nostrand, 1980).

46. *Ibid.*, pp. 63–64.

47. W. Simon, A.S. Berger, and J.S. Gagnon, "Beyond Anxiety and Fantasy: The Coital Experiences of College Youth," *Journal of Youth and Adolescence* 1 (1972):203–22.

48. J.H. Gagnon and W. Simon, *Sexual Conduct* (Chicago: Aldine, 1973); R.A. Lewis and W.R. Burr, "Premarital Coitus and Commitment among College Students," *Archives of Sexual Behavior* 4 (1975):73–79.

49. Simon, Berger, and Gagnon, *op. cit.*

50. Douvan and Adelson, *op. cit.*, p. 209.

51. T. Nguyen, R. Jeslin, and N.L. Nguyen, "The Meanings of Touch," *Journal of Communication* 25 (1975):92–103.

52. Morrison *et al.*, *op. cit.*; D. Offer and W. Simon, "Stages of Sexual Development," in B.J. Saddock *et al.*, eds., *The Sexual Experience* (Baltimore: Williams and Wilkins, 1976).

53. G. Shepman, "The Psychodynamics of Sex Education," in Rhoda Unger, *Female and Male, Psychological Perspectives* (New York: Harper & Row, 1979).

54. Susan Griffiths, "Rape, the All-American Crime," *Ramparts* 10 (1971):353–81.

55. Susan Brownmiller, *Against Our Will: Men, Women, and Rape* (New York: Simon and Schuster, 1975).

56. Griffiths, *op. cit.*

57. Amir Menachem, *Patterns in Forcible Rape* (Chicago: University of Chicago Press, 1971).

58. Griffiths, *op. cit.*

59. S. Jessor and R. Jessor, "Transition from Virginity to Nonvirginity among Youth: A Social-psychological Study over Time," *Developmental Psychology* 11 (1975):473–84; P.Y. Miller and W. Simon, "Adolescent Sexual Behavior: Context and Change," *Social Problems* 22 (1974):58–76.

60. A.M. Verner and C.S. Stewart, "Adolescent Sexual Behavior in Middle America Revisited: 1970–1973," *Journal of Marriage and the Family* 36 (1974): 728–35.

61. Jessor and Jessor, *op. cit.*

62. Miller and Simon, *op. cit.*

63. Jessor and Jessor, *op. cit.*; Verner and Stewart, *op. cit.*

64. D. Offer and J. Offer, *From Teenage to Young Manhood: A Psychological Study* (New York: Basic Books, 1975).

65. J.R. Hopkins, "Sexual Behavior in Adolescence," *Journal of Social Issues* 33, no. 2 (1977):67–85; M. Zelnick and J.F. Kantner, "The Probability of Premarital Intercourse," *Social Science Research* 1 (1972):335–41.

66. Jessor and Jessor, *op. cit.*

67. K.D. Bauman and R.R. Wilson, "Sexual Behavior of Unmarried University Students in 1968 and 1972," *Journal of Sex Research* 10 (1974):327–33.

68. Morton Hunt, *Sexual Behavior in the 1970s* (New York: Playboy Press, 1974).

69. Reiss, *op. cit.*

70. "Teenagers and Birth Control," *Newsweek*, April 5, 1982, p. 33.

71. Nancy Friday, *My Mother, Myself* (New York: Dell, 1977).

72. Morrison *et al.*, *op. cit.*, pp. 51–53.

73. Friday, *op. cit.*

74. Morrison, *op. cit.*, pp. 159–60.

75. A. Kinsey, W. Pomeroy, and C. Martin, *Sexual Behavior in the Human Male* (Philadelphia: Saunders, 1953); A. Kinsey, W. Pomeroy, C. Martin, and P. Gebhard, *Sexual Behavior in the Human Female* (Philadelphia: Saunders, 1953); John Gagnon and William Simon, *Sexual Conduct* (Chicago: Aldine, 1973).

76. Simon and Gagnon, *op. cit.*

77. Gregory K. Lehne, "Homophobia among Men," in Deborah S. David and Robert Brannon, eds., *The Forty-Nine Percent Majority: The Male Sex Role* (Reading, Mass.: Addison-Wesley, 1976), p. 66.

78. *Ibid.*, pp. 66–86.

79. Desmond Morris, "Intimate Behavior," in Earl Rubington and Martin Wineburg, eds., *The Solution of Social Problems: Five Perspectives* (New York: Oxford University Press, 1971), pp. 53–63.

80. Georgene H. Seward, "Sex, Identity, and the Social Order," in J. Bardwick, ed., *The Psychology of Women* (New York: Harper & Row, 1971), p. 153.

Chapter Seven

The "Ideal Family" of the American Dream

Love and marriage, love and marriage, they go together like a horse and carriage. . . .

We will build a family, a boy for you and a girl for me. . . .

The girl that I marry will have to be as pink and as white as a nursery. . . .

These words from popular songs tell some of the expectations for the traditional family that has been held up as an ideal in the American culture. In this traditional family, the man earns the living; the woman keeps the house and tends the nursery; there are 2.3 children and a dog named Spot; the family lives in its own home in a small, friendly town; the family members all love each other; and the children obey their parents and get good grades in school.

For most Americans, the ideal family of the American dream is just that—a dream. Few families come close to living up to the stereotype. In 1978, less than one-third of all families consisted of two parents and children under eighteen. An even smaller proportion were first marriages.[1] In over 50 percent of all two-parent families today, the wife is in the labor force; the family is also likely to have fewer children than in the stereotype and may have none. Many families are headed by single parents, and some individuals never get married at all. Most families have periods of tension and discord, and evidence also shows that many marriages are not equally beneficial to husband and wife. Yet many people believe in the "ideal family" of the American dream. The media push its desirability, and all those who do not have such a family may believe that they have somehow failed. The failure is in the idealization of a dream that never was, not in the failure of reality.

In this chapter we want to look at how stereotyped masculine and feminine roles are intertwined with and emphasized by the institution of marriage. We will first look at how changing patterns of marriage influence sex roles and how, in turn, changing sex roles influence the time when people get married. Changing sex roles also influence the pattern of interaction within marriage, although things may not have changed as much as many people believe. We will examine how the institution of marriage influences the behavior of men and women, and how the addition of children to the marriage, the occupational roles of husband and wife, and other elements of reward and tension in marriage influence sex roles and are, in turn, influenced by changing roles.

Being Single: A Newly Acceptable Alternative

The saying, "Better dead than unwed" is no longer applicable to today's young adult. As we move beyond adolescence to an examination of male and female roles in the early-twenties age group, we are struck by the increase in the number of people in this age group who are staying single. Between 1970 and 1979, the proportion of twenty- to twenty-four-year-old women who had never married grew from 35 percent to 67 percent. The twenty-five-to-twenty-nine-year-old age group also increased during this period. The median age of first marriage in 1979 was 22.1 years for women and 24.4 for men, compared to 20.3 for women and 22.8 years for men in 1960.[2]

Twenty-three percent of the men and seventeen percent of the women over eighteen have never married. When the ranks are swelled by those who were formerly married, the number of persons under age thirty-five living alone increases so that it has almost trebled between 1970 and 1978.[3]

However, the increase in *never-married* singles seems to represent a postponement of marriage rather than a denial of the institution. In the late-twenties age group, the number of singles decreases dramatically. Only 15 percent of the men and 10 percent of the women in the thirty-to-thirty-four age group have never married, although this group is joined by those who are now divorced. The time of the late twenties seems to be a time of soul-searching and of reevaluating career goals and life plans for many young people. Many who have been comfortable in the single state actively begin to seek marriage.[4]

The changing number of singles and the emphasis on a separate and distinct singles lifestyle have had an influence on traditional behavior for women and men at the same time that changing norms for masculine and feminine behavior have influenced the number staying single.

More Stay Single

Ambivalence about marriage and fear of the destructiveness of divorce have pushed both men and women toward staying single. Birth-control methods are now more available and more acceptable than before, and couples living together without marriage find greater social acceptance than before. One can have an intimate relationship without ties that bind, and the pressures to get married are not so strong. Women have also been influenced to stay single by other developments. As women have had more opportunity to engage in fulfilling careers, they have remained in school longer and subsequently been more committed to their jobs and less willing to give them up. They have also been victims of what is known as the *marriage squeeze*. The squeeze occurs because women traditionally marry men a few years older than themselves. As the numerous women of the baby-boom generation look for mates, they are looking among a smaller group of men: there are 1,321,000 more single women than men between the ages of thirty and forty-four, or about 128 women for every 100 men.[5]

The marriage squeeze also has another element. In every age bracket, women tend to marry men who not only are older than themselves but also are a little better educated and have better career opportunities. We will see later that this situation gives men a dominant position in many marriages. To put it simply, men marry down and women marry up. If you picture this situation, as in figure 1, the *marriage gradient*, you can see the results. Look who is likely to be left unmarried: the better educated and skilled woman and the poorly educated and unskilled man, who apparently finds no one who will have him.

Not only do highly educated women tend to marry less often, but they tend to marry later and have a higher probability of divorce than other women. They may find it hard to discover equals to marry, and

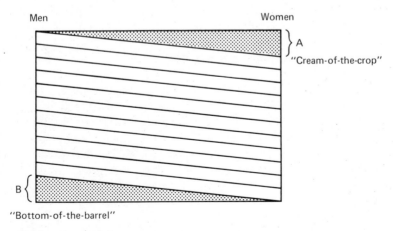

Figure 1 *Marriage Gradient*

Source: Jessie Bernard, *The Future of Marriage* (New York: Bantam, 1972).

they have interesting alternatives to marriage. In contrast, the better educated man tends to get married sooner and to stay married longer. Successful men are thus seldom available to marry their feminine equals in eduation and career. Statistics bear this out. Few educated and skilled women are able to marry equals: only 11.8 percent of all women earn as much as or more than their husbands. Many such women seem to prefer to stay single rather than marry a man with less education, occupational prestige, and income; of women in the age group from thirty-five to forty-four with some graduate education, 20 percent do not marry, compared to 5.4 percent of other women.[6] Professional women who postpone marriage further reduce their chances for marriage later, as the number of men in the upper age brackets gets smaller still. To the numbers of never-married older women is also added the competition of women who are divorced or widowed and looking for mates among these few older men.

Influences of Singlehood on Traditional Sex-Role Behavior

The marriage pattern described above influences sex roles in several ways. On the one hand, it seems to be ironically true that the adolescent rules of being pretty, popular, and not achieving too much lead women to the societal "success" of marriage. The girl who was sweet, feminine, and unachieving may well be married—and married to a well-educated, achieving husband, at that. Statistics tell us that the girl who sought education and achievement is likely to be unmarried, or at least to get married quite a bit later.

What do these professional women do? Some stay single and develop networks of friends to fill the needs of intimacy. Others prefer "live-in" relationships with women or men. Still others are willing to marry "down," to marry someone with less education and career opportunity.[7] This kind of marriage may be difficult to sustain, however, because of the more traditional sex-role norms usually held by the blue-collar man (see chapter 8).

On the other hand, adopting the traditional feminine norms of adolescence is no guarantee of a lasting marriage. As we will see, many women cannot stand the confining nature of a traditional housewife role and the dependency of not having their own money. Others who think they have done everything right are still divorced by their husbands and, with fewer skills, are left to compete among the professional women. Many traditional women still do not find appropriate mates among the decreasing numbers of men.

What we see is that the numbers ratios, the temporary nature of many marriages, and increasingly difficult economic times seem to be giving women more impetus to work outside the home before, instead of, or after marriage. Paul Secord argues that feminism has historically increased when women have outnumbered men.[8] Increasing independence may not be equated with feminism, but we have seen hints of increasing independence among black adolescent girls who make individual plans for their lives without giving marriage a high priority.[9] A similar kind of independence seems to be increasing among white girls who stay single longer or never get married.

It seems, actually, that there will be pushes both to stay single and to get married. As more and more women stay single and move into male domains, different norms for female behavior will develop. As women stay single longer, it is likely that they will learn the kinds of independence and assertiveness that make it difficult for them to revert to dependent relationships in marriage. However, other women may try to please scarce men by adopting traditional roles.

Men may also feel ambivalent about traditional roles, as seen in the increasing masculine fear of success. Men's increasing doubts about the price paid in anxiety and health deficits for occupational success may also influence their attitudes toward domesticity and their desire to support a family. The single life holds out a more attractive alternative to marriage than it has for many years in the past. Middle-class singles frequently have their own apartment complexes, clubs, and even vacation spots. They are engaging in sports activities and traveling at a level unheard of in the past—spurred on by somewhat higher incomes and a view of life that emphasizes personal pleasure rather than saving for a "nest." And at the same time, increasing inflation has made it difficult to settle down in marriage, at least in any style. Houses are priced out of the range of most young couples, two incomes are often needed for necessities, and children become a postponed luxury. Marriage becomes more a symbol of strength of commitment than a necessity. If modern contraception removes the risk of having to marry a pregnant bride, if you can have sex and companionship without marriage, then why rush to tie the knot? Many do not want to make the strong commitment that marriage implies, at least not right away.

As greater social approval makes cohabitation easier, many men are opting for living-together relationships or later marriage rather than early conjugal ties. The kind of living-together relationship varies with the age of those involved. Eighty-five percent of those who live in a romantic relationship with someone of the other sex are under thirty-five.[10] For younger college students, cohabition seems to be an extended form of going steady that includes sexual intimacy. It does not necessarily imply a desire to get married, and the cohabitation may just be drifted into, not planned. The college students studied saw this kind of relationship as a way to develop real intimacy with another person and to grow and test themselves. While the average length of such relationships was only four and one-half months, the students usually felt they had benefited from the relationship.[11] Many of the younger group who cohabit, however, are not college students; the data show that 43 percent are working class. For this group, economic necessity may pull couples into cohabitation, along with the desire to test an intimate relationship.

For the age group in the middle and late twenties, cohabitation seems to have a slightly different meaning. For some, it is a way to test a relationship and to see if they want to get married. For others, it is a more or less permanent alternative to marriage. In this age group the hopes of women and men for the relationship may diverge. Men may prefer to continue this sort of relationship without stronger ties; women may hope that it will be a step toward a traditional marriage with children. In spite of difficulties, however, the number of cohabiting couples has been increasing. In 1978, 2.3 percent of all couples, some 1,137,000 dyads, were living together without being married. That is twice the number doing so in 1970.[12] In these relationships, there seems to be some move toward equality. Couples report a sharing of chores like grocery shopping and laundry, although the woman may do more of the cooking and cleaning.[13] Thus, equality in a relationship may be practiced before marriage.

We should also note that as men and women stay single longer, they may enter marriage with different role expectations. Women have earned an income, and men may have done household chores. Will this mean a more nearly equal marriage? Both sexes state they would like to have an equal relationship. Yet in looking at dating, we saw that as the relationship became more serious, traditional behavior tended to emerge. Men may also verbalize more liberal ideals than they are willing to practice in their marriages.[14] We will see below that the pressures and structure of marriage also make it easier for traditional roles to emerge.

While modern pressures are causing people to stay single longer, the single life may soon pall for some. The insecurity of singlehood, the competition in social life, and the desire for commitment may induce many to get married. For women, the knowledge that few child-bearing years remain ahead of them may exert a powerful push into marriage. One 1975 study reported that almost all young women still expect to marry.[15]

The Ideal Marriage That Never Was

Love and Marriage

Many people do not realize that most marriages throughout history, including our own historical past, were not based on love. Marriages were arranged for economic necessity or to cement relationships between various groups. We see some arranged marriages today in our upper classes. While the marriages may not be officially "arranged" by parents, children are exposed only to the proper people and are expected to pick a mate who will enhance the family's economic and social prestige. Of course, it is hoped that the young people will care for each other, but if they do not get along well, they are expected to continue the marriage anyway.[16]

Many marriages today may continue to emphasize security and/or companionship rather than love. In Cuber and Haroff's description of five kinds of marriage, 80 percent were "utilitarian" in nature.[17] In particular, many couples had a "passive-congenial" type of marriage, in which they did not really marry for love or expect much love in the marriage. Others had a "devitalized" marriage, which once had an intimate emotional relationship but had lost it to the rigors of married life and the passage of time. Still others were "conflict-habituated," or centered around fighting. Only in "vital" and "total" marriages did the couples have a real emotional bond. However, only 20 percent of the marriages were found to be vital—to contain an ongoing, real emotional commitment—or to be total, with the couple totally absorbed in one another.

American Marriages: A Myth of Equality

Some believe that norms about equality of persons in the United States extend into the institution of marriage and mean that husband and wife are more nearly equal in this country than they are in many others. We will not attempt a cross-cultural comparison, but we should look at the supposed equality of American marriages and see whether it does in fact exist. What *is* equality? One way to think of equality in marriage is in terms of division of work.

Equality, Power, and Resources. Several well-known sociologists believe that equality of roles depends on equality of *power*, or the ability to achieve one's own desires in the face of opposition from others.[18] Sociologists Blood and Wolfe believe that power, in turn, is based on resources. They define *resources* as anything you bring to the marriage that enables you and your family to satisfy needs. Thus, the resources can be money, education, attractiveness, social status, ability to be a good hostess, and the like.[19]

The whole concept of power based on resources requires some qualifications, however. One of the first questions is, How do we measure power? Blood and Wolfe measure power by determining who makes the decisions in such areas as what job the husband should take, what car to get, where to go on vacation, whether the wife should work, what doctor to call when someone is sick, and what to fix for dinner. But there are difficulties with this type of measurement. As you can see, the decisions are not all equal in importance. A decision about the husband's job is much more important than where to go on vacation. Some decisions are also made frequently while others are made only once in a while. In addition, there are different levels of decision making. For example, who makes the decision about whether to go on a vacation at all so that someone else can make the decision about where to go?[20] There are also different kinds of power to be measured, such as coercive power, expert power, reward power, and the like.[21]

In the mid-1900s, Centers, Ravens, and Rodriguez drew a multiclass sample from Los Angeles and interviewed 776 respondents, both husbands and wives. They discovered that power differed markedly according to the area or base of power.[22] Thus, how a couple decided in a certain area would depend on who possessed the kind of power to deal with that area. For example, the husband might be seen as having expert power in deciding what car to buy. The researchers discovered that men and women differed in their bases of power and that the social classes differed as well.[23] Women saw men as having more expert power (more than the men themselves thought they had),[24] and lower social classes attributed power more to the ability to reward and coerce.

In their 1960 study of the influence of resources and ideology on power, Blood and Wolfe postulated that modern trends toward wives working and gaining resources and contemporary norms about more sharing of power meant that husband and wife were almost equal in power as they measured it.[25] However, Gillespie and other sociologists believe that things have changed little from traditional male domination of marital power. Although Blood and Wolfe demonstrated that individual resources are important in determining power, Gillespie reminds us that men have monopolized a large share of those resources. Thus, she says, men dominate in most families today as they have done historically.[26]

Gillespie makes a good case for her contention that wives have a difficult time equaling the resources of their husbands. Traditionally, men have always had an edge in possessing the most usable resources. They have been older than their wives, they are physically stronger (and can threaten the use of force), they have greater income, and they usually have more education. They also have had the advantages of social status in the world outside the home, social contacts and interaction at work, and the ability to find an attractive alternative to their marriage more easily than their wives could.[27] In addition, as we will see below, men's dominance is guaranteed by the legal system as well as by cultural norms about men "wearing the pants" in the family.

Which resources are most likely to yield power? In Blood and Wolfe's study, the man's income and occupational status were the two strongest predictors of family power. They also found that spouses who had three years or more of educational advantage over the other partner gained power, and those who had greater verbal skills and social status gained as well.[28] The spouse who was most self-sufficient and did not need a great deal of emotional support from the other partner had more power.[29] Another study demonstrated that the spouse who had the most opportunities outside the marriage (*attractive alternatives*—either social or occupational) or the least interest in maintaining the marriage also had superior power.

The alternative of working and supporting herself is particularly important for a woman. It gives her options she could not consider if she were dependent upon the support of her husband.[30] It is important to recognize, however, that the position of a single woman may still be difficult in our culture, and a "career" may not be a sufficiently attractive alternative to marriage for many women.

In all of these areas, the man is still likely to dominate in resources. Besides the obvious resources of income and occupational status, men can do the asking in the social scene and can marry women from a wide range of ages. Thus, they can find new marital partners more easily than women can. The man has an alternative source of emotional satisfaction in his work and is less likely to need his mate's emotional support; if the marriage ends, his source of financial support and his friendship network will continue.

Women have few resources that can match those of their husbands. Their traditional ones have been physical attractiveness, their homemaking and mothering skills, and sometimes the social status they bring to the marriage. While many women may be equal to their husbands in education, few exceed them by three years or more of education and few have equal occupational status. Women usually have fewer contacts outside the home and less chance to develop social status of their own. They also have less legal protection. Without these outside sources of esteem, they may be less confident and more in need of emotional support and thus willing to grasp any power that they do have. They may also find their support and friendship network gone if a marriage dissolves and thus may be willing to make more compromises to sustain the marriage. While wives may wield informal, manipulative power, they may not be willing to use this power if it threatens their marriage. Even children are not a resource for the wife. On the contrary, they detract from her power and make her more dependent on her husband.[31]

It is true, however, that wives today are likely to have more resources than in the past. They are likely to be closer in age to their husbands and are more likely to have equal education and greater incomes than they had in the past. Fifty percent of all wives now work outside the home, and they usually gain some power from contributing to family resources, especially when their income is needed by the family. Their work outside the home may also increase their status, their social skills, and even their attractiveness when they "dress for the office." Their self-confidence is likely to increase and their need for approval and attention to decrease. They are more likely to have an attractive alternative to their marriage in a career, with the possibility of supporting themselves in a single life or cohabitation. The sum total of such changes indicates a trend toward equal roles in the family because husbands and wives will have similar work roles and similar resources.[32]

The Cultural Context of Power. Hyman Rodman has pointed out that resources must be viewed in a *cultural context*. If the ideology of the particular culture does not support the use of certain resources, then their accrual by one of the marital partners grants that person little power. Conversely, a person without many resources may dominate in certain cultures. The ideology of power may differ by social class in each culture. Rodman has noted that in Yugoslavia, well-educated husbands with high-status jobs frequently do not have a great deal of marital power because they subscribe to norms regarding equal marriages. In our own working class, husbands with few resources may dominate if their families subscribe to the tradition of male dominance; the women may wield undercover power, but men are the official heads of the households.[33] One early-1970s study states that husbands in Asian-American couples have the most power, and in black couples the least.[34]

Individual attitudes toward the cultural ideology are also a factor. Lois Hoffman has shown that a working wife may accrue all kinds of resources, but if she is not sure that she should be working and making money, then she is not likely to grasp power.[35]

Other Modifications of Resource Theory. Ideology is modified by individual resources and experience as well as the other way around. Husbands of working wives and sons of working mothers are more likely to approve of a woman working.[36] Power is also modified within the confines of a family even when traditional norms are given lip service, and here we see the use of "informal power." In one experiment, Leik divided families in two ways: (1) in natural family groups and (2) in "artificial" families composed of members from two or three of the natural families. In each case, he gave the artificial and the natural families a task and watched the problem-solving process. In the artificial families, the women deferred to the men and were willing to accede to their judgment; in their natural family group, however, these same women were much more outspoken and sometimes dominated the discussion. They were much more aware of the resources of their own partners and of how much they could dominate.[37]

Husband versus Wife Resources: Ranges of Power. Despite the many possible modifications of resource power, Gillespie's point about husbands dominating resources is a valid one. A wife with strong resources still has difficulty surpassing those of her husband. Even Blood and Wolfe, who suggest that American marriages are equalitarian, believe that when wives exercise power, they do so by default, when a husband is unemployed or has given up power in general.[38]

While one would suspect that more wives than Blood and Wolfe document actually exercise power in their families, women's difficulty in gaining power was pointed up in a study of Cuban immigrant families who came to Florida in the late 1950s after the Castro revolution. Although the men had difficulty finding employment, most of the women could find jobs as maids or seamstresses. When the men did get jobs, they were almost always far below their previous status in Cuba: doctors would be working as filling-station attendants; lawyers, as janitors. Further, the women needed mobility to do their jobs and had to take buses, go out by themselves, and move about town. These were all things that most of them would not have done in Cuba. With the women gaining independence and bringing in resources that exceeded those of the men, one would think that the traditional Latin male-dominance ideology would have been modified. But while some small moves were made toward equality, the male-dominance ideology remained very strong for the Cuban families interviewed.[39] The higher-status families had the most contact with Americans and would normally have become the most liberalized. In these families, however, the resources of the husband were more likely to be equal to or to exceed those of the wife, and so she gained little power. In the lower-status families, the male-dominance ideology kept the wife from claiming the power she had gained through increased resources.[40]

Why Discuss Power?   This discussion of power makes it sound as though all marriages are battles, with people fighting for every scrap of authority. Of course, this is not true. Power considerations may be outweighed by respect, concern for the needs of others, and just plain "love" and loyalty. However, power is always an underlying factor in a marriage. Its influence may only surface in times of conflict, but both partners are aware of the underlying power positions.

The kind of power that can come from earning one's own money is illustrated by a story a barber told to one of his customers. Apparently, the barber's wife had complained for some time that their bedroom was hot in the summer, and she wanted to buy a bedroom air conditioner. The barber did not mind the heat and refused to buy one. After several years of his refusals, his wife became disgusted and went out and got herself a job. She worked just long enough to buy the air conditioner and have it installed, then she quit. The message is clear: those who control the purse strings have the power. If you don't have resources of your own, you may not be able to get what you want. The barber in this story was terribly upset. He believed that his authority had been trampled upon, but the wife had asserted her own temporary power and now had a cool bedroom. While assertions of power by women who are earning their own money are seldom so dramatic, they are certainly increasing. As women work longer periods before and after marriage and even when young children are present, power relationships seem to be modifying.

Differences in Power: Decision Making and Division of Labor

Usually decision-making power in a family changes toward the equalitarian model before the division of labor does.[41] There seem to be many reasons for this difference. To paraphrase the organized argument of Scanzoni and Fox in their review of the 1970s sex-role literature, *preference and process* are interwoven in such a way that some behaviors will change more rapidly than others. They believe that (1) a questioning of traditional sex-role arrangements and preferences is taking place; (2) this questioning causes potential conflict because some arrangements can no longer be taken for granted; (3) but behavior is not changing as rapidly as preferences are because many people—especially women—do not wish to engage in conflict to change behavior (or do not have the power, physical or otherwise, to engage in such conflict); (4) nevertheless, some behavioral change is taking place because norms are changing. Thus, if men believe that they should listen to their wives and give them some voice in decision making and the wives believe that they should have such a voice, the decision-making process may change in the family even though the wife's power has not really changed.[42] However, (5) while women increasingly prefer to work outside the home, neither men nor women have significantly changed their preference for doing household work. Thus, the division of household tasks remains more traditional than the division of power.[43]

This analysis still does not tell us *why* preferences and norms for decision-making power change more rapidly than those for the division of labor. Why are men more willing to grant decision-making power to women than to help around the house? Why are women more willing to engage in conflict about decisions than about household chores? It seems to me that the answers are rooted in the American historical past. There is a tradition in this country that all *men* are created equal. This is interpreted to mean all "persons," and while seldom lived up to in the ideal, the concept of men or men and women as equals in making decisions is still operative in our democratic political tradition. On the other hand, no tradition holds that men and women should do equal work—and certainly none states that they should do the same work. In our historical past, women and men have done different and unequal work.

Determining what is men's work and what is women's work is also tied to other concerns. As we have seen, people are defined as masculine or feminine by the tasks they perform. Many women have learned that it is feminine to do child-care tasks, to cook, to sew, and even to do housework. They may feel their femininity is reaffirmed when they bake bread or make dresses for their daughters. They may have also learned that women who do not do these things or who ask men to do them can be thought of as not quite feminine. Judith Laws has pointed out the mystique of the housewife role. It becomes an extension of *love*, therefore, it is not permissible to analyze it as an exchange of labor. If a woman does not do these tasks for her husband and her children, it may be assumed she does not love them.[44]

In contrast, most men have been socialized to believe that it is *not* masculine to do things women do. *They* are not masculine if they do them! The mythology says it is all right for a man "to help out" with the dishes or to "baby-sit," but if he is directly responsible for any household work or child care, his self-definition of being masculine may be threatened. It is no accident that men choose cooking or grocery shopping as the household chore they are most willing to perform. Great male chefs have an esteemed profession, but great housecleaners??? (Needless to say, housecleaning is also less desirable work.) The norms are enforced by peer-group pressure. Even men with good intentions can be teased out of those intentions by their friends. Researchers have shown that lack of social support was an important factor in preventing men with equalitarian attitudes from changing their behavior in helping in the house.[45]

Several other considerations also enter the picture. Men may have a vested interest in continuing women's personalized services at home so that the men are free to pursue their careers. Also, housework is not valued labor, and no one wants to do work that is not valued. General housework is seldom exciting, fulfilling or creative, so there is not much natural incentive to do it either. In addition, each sex has had more practice at doing certain tasks and may feel more comfortable doing them. Even with good intentions, both sexes have blind spots when it comes to the traditional areas of work of the other gender. A man may not notice the dust in the living room, and a woman may not notice that the lawn needs to be fertilized. Ultimately, each knows that society will blame the traditional sex if that chore goes undone. People are not likely to enter a home and think that "John sure is a lousy housekeeper," no matter how the chores are actually divided.[46]

Thus, the division of labor has changed little in most families. Feelings about doing gender-appropriate work, comfort with familiar roles, and societal pressure keep labor in traditional molds. This is true even though the wife works outside the home. In reviewing the literature,

Scanzoni and Fox say that the following conclusions seem to emerge from the research on this question: (1) working wives continue to have prime responsibility for the organization and functioning of the family; (2) the employment status of wives only minimally affects the husbands' participation in domestic tasks; (3) the length of the woman's day increases at the expense of her leisure and sleep time; (4) however, the aggregate amount of family time spent in housework decreases when the wife works—it is unclear whether this is because of an increase in efficiency, a decrease in standards, or both; and (5) to some extent, the participation of older children in domestic tasks increases when the wife works.[47]

Actually, some studies show an increase in the participation of the husband in household tasks when the wife works, and other studies do not.[48] Some show little participation by the husband,[49] while others by Blood and Wolfe and Young and Wilmott show that husbands do more.[50] Pleck says that the differences arise because husbands do almost the same amount of housework as before, but the total amount done in the family decreases when the wife works, so the husband's proportion of the housework is larger.[51] How much work is actually done by the husband seems to depend somewhat on the relative status of the couple. If the husband is very successful and earning a great deal, he may feel he has to contribute less to the household even when his wife is working.[52]

One study done in 1979 found that couples were more likely to have shared roles when the husband did not have a high income, the wife was highly educated, they had no children under twelve, and local kinship networks existed. This study also supported the previous finding that husbands with high incomes are less likely to do less around the house.[53] We can see this limited participation of men in housework illustrated in a table from Vanek's in-depth study of the division of household labor.

	Men	Unemployed women
Housework	2 hrs., 13 min.	33 hrs., 6 min.
Child care	1 hr., 57 min.	17 hrs., 17 min.
Shopping	2 hrs., 55 min.	5 hrs., 12 min.
Labor force	40 hrs.	—
	47 + hrs.	55 + hrs.

Joann Vanek, "Keeping Busy: Time Spent in Housework, U.S. 1920–1970" Ph.D.diss. U. of Michigan, 1973.

Housework and Wives in the Paid Labor Force

The division of labor between the sexes changes only a little when wives work outside the home. According to Vanek's 1973 study, wives employed for pay outside the home spent about half as much time doing housework as unemployed wives did. Women who worked at least thirty-five hours a week spent an average of twenty-five hours a week on housework. However, their husbands did not seem to increase their participation and spent only eleven hours a week on household duties, the same amount as husbands of wives not employed outside the home. Thus, wives who were employed full-time spent approximately sixty to seventy hours a week in work inside and outside the home. This means that many had little or no leisure time.[55]

Wives with part-time jobs fell in between full-time labor force participants and housewives in the number of hours of housework that they did. The ratio of more hours worked outside the home to fewer hours worked inside the home was quite consistent. One 1973 study compiled detailed records of household labor in 1,296 households in Syracuse, New York,[56] and came up with the following data:

Wives not employed outside the home	8.1 hrs. a day	(56.7 a week)
Wives employed 1–14 hrs. a week	7.3 hrs. a day	(51.1 a week)
Wives employed 15–30 hrs. a week	6.3 hrs. a day	(44.1 a week)
Wives employed over 30 hrs. a week	4.8 hrs. a day	(33.6 a week)

It is clear that even with changing norms, men are still doing very little to help. The *New York Times* reported on recent studies by advertising agencies who hoped to appeal to the househusband market but found few men who did housework. Although 80 percent of the men said husbands *should* help a working wife and 55 percent said that working couples should split chores, the *New York Times* reported that it was a case of, "All Talk, No Action." Only about 25 percent of the men did any substantial amount of housework and only 50 percent did even occasional work. The area in which they helped the most was child care. In addition, one of the studies found that 70 percent of the men preferred a nonworking wife, primarily so that they would *not* have to do household chores.[57]

How does the work of employed housewives get done in less time? As noted before, it is not clear whether convenience foods and other efficiencies are responsible for whether the women lower their standards. In some cases, these working women may have older children who need less care and are able to help, or they have hired help. However, Vanek postulates that it is mostly a matter of efficiency, and that women who are at home expand their work so that they will feel useful.[58]

The amount of time spent on housework has apparently not decreased since 1920 in spite of labor-saving devices. Instead, standards of cleanliness and performance seem to have changed so that the same number of hours are spent working. A woman may now be worried about being a gourmet cook, and the media have assured that she will be concerned about the cleanliness of her kitchen floor. She is also more likely to spend time chauffering children and participating in community affairs.[59]

As Unger points out, however, it is very difficult for a woman to escape the housewife role. Although the roles of wife and mother may be relatively freely chosen, the choice of being married and not doing housework is very limited. Few women have resources equal to those of their husbands and are able to exert power to get help with the housework. They may also be reluctant to exert the power they do have for all the cultural reasons mentioned above. In the final analysis, Unger has succinctly stated that the "attractive alternative" to housework for many women is virtually nonexistent: employed wives know that their husbands may already be threatened by the fact that they are not the sole breadwinners. The wives may even be afraid of losing their mates if they complain and demand equality. Maribel Morgan's theme from *The Total Woman*—that you must stay home to care for your man or you will lose him—is sounding in their ears.[60] As Unger points out, employed or not, the housewife is in a bind. "Divorce will increase the woman's responsibility for the children and decrease her social status without necessarily increasing her career opportunities. It is not surprising that she is reluctant to provoke a confrontation with her husband over housework."[61] Many working wives may also feel a personal responsibility for doing the housework. In a national survey, Mason and Bumpass found that although a woman was employed, her attitudes about division of housework might still be traditional.[62]

The other alternative of quitting work may be equally distasteful to many women. Many wives continue to carry the burden of outside work and housework because they enjoy the stimulation of outside work or they need the money in these harder economic times. However, the burden is a great one, and the double load may stir resentments that may hurt their marriages in other areas.

Why Change?

If people are comfortable in traditional roles, with the wife staying home and the husband earning the income, you might ask, "Why should they change?" "I can see why working wives need more help with the housework," you might say, "but why should those who are in traditional marriages consider changing?" The answer to that question has many parts. First of all, not everyone does need to change. There are many people who can keep traditional roles and be perfectly satisfied with them. However, economic change is *forcing* a great deal of social change. In 1975, 52 percent of all married women living with their husbands and school-aged children were in the labor force. Thirty-three percent of those with pre-school children were in the labor force, as well, and this group was rapidly growing.[63]

In the future, it is likely that even more young women will want or have to combine careers and marriage. They may not all be able to hold down the two full-time jobs of housework and outside employment. Research also seems to bear out that satisfaction is greater in marriages with more nearly equal division of roles.[64]

In addition, not everyone *is* happy with the traditional roles when they exist. A noted sociologist, Jessie Bernard, has pointed out that the rates of depression and the indices of poor mental health among housewives are so strikingly high that if such rates were attributed to any other group of workers in the country, they would be considered a national social disaster.[65]

The "His" and the "Her" Marriage

Bernard's analysis of how men and women view marriage points up some of the difficulties in the structure of marriage today and how these difficulties relate to sex roles. In her classic book, *The Future of Marriage*, she shows that men and women perceive marriage differently. When a couple is asked questions about marital problems, decisions, or even specific mathematical counts of how much sexual activity they have had in the last month, the man and the woman answer differently. They answer so differently that Bernard has termed their marriages the "his" marriage and the "her" marriage. In general, the differences show that men seem to be happier in marriage than women and that marriage is actually better for them.[66]

The "His" Marriage

You may be surprised by that last sentence. Our culture has generally believed that a woman is "better dead than unwed" and that she therefore chases a man until she catches him. Conversely, we believe that bachelors are lucky, happy men who avoid marriage at all cost until they are trapped into it. Contrary to these societal beliefs, however, it is the man who seems to be the happiest in marriage and to benefit the most from it. Insurance companies have known for years that married men are better risks than single men: they live longer, they are healthier, they have fewer accidents, they are much less likely to commit suicide, they have better mental health, they are less likely to commit crimes, they make higher incomes, and they report themselves as happier than any other group. They are twice as likely as their wives to say they would marry the same person again, and when widowed or divorced, they remarry quickly.[67]

In contrast, our lively, happy bachelor has a terrible record. "In general the 3,320,000 male single workers hardly earned enough to feed themselves and buy *Playboy*, let alone follow its philosophy."[68] In 1970, their median income was $5,800. They have poorer physical health than married men, poorer mental health, are more likely to be in mental or penal institutions, and are much more likely to commit suicide. They commit suicide four times as often as married men and four times as often as single women; they try five times as often as married women. They seem to have a difficult time building and keeping friendship networks, at least in comparison to single women.[69] By comparison, the married man is in much better shape and seems to prefer to be married.[70]

Bernard does show there are costs to men for getting married, and these are the giving up of sexual freedom and the gaining of responsibility for taking care of a family. She believes, however, that these costs have been modified as both men and women have been allowed more sexual freedom outside of marriage these days and as many women begin to help their husbands provide for the family.[71]

The costs of the provider role are also an extension of the male stereotype of being good, tough, and successful. It is no accident that married men make more money and advance in their careers more quickly than single men do. Not only do they have a support system helping them, but they feel a responsibility to move ahead and be successful. Many men work longer and harder hours at work than they would prefer because they "owe it to their families."

The husband-father role thus reinforces the masculine stereotype that one must succeed. As the two go hand in hand, it is difficult for a man to say that he does not want success and more money. This is the new arena for proving himself masculine. The days of sports competition and sexual chasing may be behind him, but the days of being tough and being good are not. He must be good, he must succeed. He must provide a nice house and car for his family and a good education for his children—not just out of the desire to have those things, but to show that he is a man. Thus, material possessions become symbols of success and manhood. A man who buys his wife a fur coat is really saying, "See how successful I am; see what a man I am to get this for my wife." Because manhood is really the issue, many men strive so hard for success that they have little time left for their families. They may also have little time left for themselves and many accumulate various health problems like hypertension and ulcers. In the tradition of being properly "tough and cool," many men do not complain about these medical problems until they become quite serious.[72] Yet they continue, and they report themselves as happy because they are fulfilling the masculine stereotype and doing what they feel they *should* do. Traditional marriage reinforces the masculine stereotype and may hurt the male in such a family. The husband may be healthier than when he was single, but he is still in a self-destructive role.

The "Her" Marriage

What about the married woman? She seems to start out with some advantages that marriage reverses. Women, both single and married, have much better physical health than men and they live longer. However, in comparison to her single sisters, married women have much poorer mental health. Married women report much higher rates of anxiety, phobia, and depression than any other group except single men. Marriage does not protect them as much from suicide as it does their husbands. They do not make incomes that are as good as their single counterparts, they have fewer friends than single women, and they report themselves as much less happy. When a husband and wife are interviewed about their marriage, the wife is likely to say that the problems in it are more numerous, are started sooner, and are more severe. Wives are also only half as likely as husbands to say that they would marry the same person again. Indeed, only half of the married wives say they would marry the same person again.[73]

Why are married women so much less happy than their husbands or even than their single sisters? If it were a matter of gender alone, we would certainly expect single women who are not only female but stigmatized as being unwanted and unchosen to be less happy. Yet single women seem to cope better than married women. Conversely, married women seem to fare more poorly in marriage than their husbands. What kinds of constraints does the institution of marriage impose that seem to change the happiness of women but not that of men?

Jessie Bernard has pointed out that women who become wives in our culture frequently lose legal and personal identities and become dependent. This dependency may lead to depression. In fact, Bernard asserts that housewives are among the most depressed group in the country. As we have noted, they exhibit much higher rates of such dysfunctional mental symptoms as anxiety, paranoia, and phobias than do either married men or single women.[74] Walter Gove, in a national study of mental health, corroborates Bernard's findings and hypothesizes that the structure of the marital role is what leads to women's depression. In particular, he mentions five points that we will examine in more detail below:

1. Expectations for women's role are unclear; this ambiguity creates anxiety and frustration for many women.

2. A housewife has only one structural base for her role, the family, while a man has two. If something goes wrong on his job, the man can turn to his family, and vice versa. A housewife does not have this option.

3. Many women find their major job of housekeeping extremely frustrating.

4. Housewives have little structure to their time and it is possible to put things off; a woman may not have to "get herself together." In addition, mental symptoms or alcohol and drug use may not be readily visible to others.

5. Even when a married woman works, she is not in as good a position in terms of salary and status as the working male.[75]

The "Shock Theory" of Marriage

Bernard takes Gove's hypothesis and elaborates it even further in what she calls the "shock theory" of marriage. In this theory, she describes some of the legal, social, and personal changes that occur in women's lives when they become wives. In most instances the changes can be divided into three main categories of problems: (1) changes that create dependency in women, (2) changes that affect women's success of self-esteem, and (3) the nature of the housewife role. We see in these problems an elaboration of Nielsen's thesis (in chapter 1) that the structure of society's institutions creates sex-role behaviors.

Changes That Create Dependency: Becoming a Legal Nonentity. Many of the changes that create dependency in women are legal in nature. When a woman marries, she gives up a good portion of her legal identity as an individual. As one lawyer succcinctly put it, "the wife and husband are assumed to be one and that one is the husband." A more elaborate version of that phrase states:

> Whatever may be the reason of the law, the rule is maintained, that the legal existence of the wife is merged in that of the husband, so that, in law, the husband and wife are one person.
>
> The husband's dominion over the person and property of the wife is fully recognized. She is utterly incompetent to contract in her own name. He is entitled to her society and her service; to her obedience and her property. . . .
>
> In consideration of his marital rights the husband is bound to furnish the wife a home and suitable support.[76]

Specifically, what does this mean? First of all, it means that the husband is the legal head of the family in most states. He has the legal authority to determine the family's standard of living, such as allowance for the wife and kind of house lived in, child-rearing method, and household management. He must support his wife, but it is he who decides what the level of support should be. The courts have refused to intervene even when husbands with plentiful resources let wives be undernourished and underclothed. Second, the wife must provide services as a companion and housekeeper without compensation. In return she is *not entitled* to any share of the family assets: not a share in the property nor even an allowance. Further, the courts presume all household goods to be the husband's even if the wife has, through her service, enabled him to buy them. Until the late 1800s, wives could not sue in court, could not enter into contracts, and could not own or control their own property. Some states still limit women's rights in that regard, although the Married Women's Property Act in the late 1800s gave women the right to own and control their own property, including their earnings from outside employment.[77] There has been little a woman could do to change this situation. Even marital contracts entered into by the couple have not been enforced by the courts. A wife has little way of enforcing the provision that her husband support her, since it is he, as head of the household, who determines the level of support. As the Citizen's Advisory Council on the Status of Women summed up the case, "a married woman living with her husband can, in practice, get only what he chooses to give her."[78] Even community property laws do not help because the husband has control of the use and disposal of the community property funds.[79] The homemaker's dependency is even further increased by other legal considerations that make women dependent on their husband's health insurance, pension funds, and social security.[80]

Our tax laws also push women into dependency. Let us suppose that a woman wants to go to work and that she will earn $15,000 at her new job while her husband is already earning $15,000. Because the family's income is treated as a whole, every dollar she earns is treated as though she has already earned $15,000. If her husband pays 25 percent taxes on his $15,000, then she will have to begin paying in the 25 percent range and move upward from there with every dollar she earns. (In contrast, if the couple were singles living together, the tax bracket would begin at zero for her $15,000 just as it had for his.) This has been called the "marriage penalty," because the effect of the tax law is to make the married couple pay more taxes than two single people. (The Reagan administration responded to heavy pressure and cut the marriage penalty about in half for most couples. However, the penalty is still substantial for many couples.) The tax law may also make it unprofitable for a woman to take paid employment. If she raises the couple's taxes and incurs other expenses as well, she may decide to stay home and thus remain dependent.[81] While one could postulate that it would be the husband who stayed home, this is seldom the case because of norms about male "breadwinners."

Dependency has insidious effects. A person who is dependent on another for "daily handouts," or in the larger sense for decisions about general welfare, loses a sense of control over her life and experiences anxiety, depression, frustration, and stress. Even in cases where a devoted husband gives a wife everything she wants, she is still taking handouts and has no assurance they will continue and no sense of management of her own life. She is even more helpless because getting out of the marriage may further reduce her income. According to the International Women's Year Commission Poll of 1975, only 14 percent of divorced women get even temporary alimony, and only 44 percent of divorced mothers are awarded child support, and only about half of those collect it regularly.[82]

There are other legal and social losses of identity for a wife. She may find (if she is not working) that credit cards are in her husband's name alone and that she has no credit history of her own. Wives who have their own income may have credit reported separately, but many do not know this and end up without a credit rating if they divorce.[83] The mortgage on the family home may read "John Doe and Wf. [wife]." She is legally and socially refered to by her husband's name, Mrs. John Doe, rather than the name, Mary Smith, with which she has identified herself previously.

Changes That Affect Self-Esteem. In social interaction, a married woman may also find that her status has changed. Vendors of appliances, cars, and sporting goods, who previously paid attention to her, may defer to her husband as though she did not exist. At social events, her husband's opinion may be solicited about politics or economics. Although she may have been a bright political science major, she is asked, "What does John think about the election?" If she is not working outside the home, she may find no social confirmation of her skills or intelligence.

A wife may also find that her husband is the primary one to determine the interests and friends of the family. He may keep up his baseball games and bowling, but she is likely to give up her skiing if he doesn't ski. Studies show that wives adjust their patterns of behavior to those of their husbands. In a similar fashion, she may see her friends for lunch, but it is his friends they entertain for dinner. Married women consistently report fewer friends than their single counterparts.[84] If the couple moves frequently, her only friends may be wives of her husband's office colleagues—and she will lose these friends if she loses her husband.

Finally, another factor enters into the whole picture: that of the *sources* of self-esteem for women. Jessie Bernard suggests that most young women are used to receiving a good proportion of their self-esteem from the admiration and approval of others—particularly men. When they marry, they are not likely to send out "available" kinds of vibrations. They may also mute their sexuality and wear their necklines higher and shorts longer as society (and her husband) believes befits a wife and mother. As this happens, the attention they get from other men is likely to diminish. They often do not realize why this has happened and feel they are "getting fat" or need some new clothes. As women are trained to find their self-esteem in the approval of others, this lack of others' approval may be a substantial element in a new wife's discomfort.[85]

The Nature of the Housewife Role.   Thus far we have looked at legal changes in the status of women and changes in the sources of their self-esteem. Married women who do not work may also be unhappy and frustrated because of the nature of the houswife role. One clue that leads us to this conclusion is the finding that compared to housewives, married women who work outside the home report themselves as more satisfied and happier.

Working wives report themselves as happier even when their days are long and arduous because they are doing a job outside the home as well as housework.[86] Thus, it would seem that something about the nature of the housewife's *role* might make women unhappy.[87] If we look at the role, we can certainly see elements that might cause distress. The young woman with small children may well be isolated in her home. She may not have a car at her disposal; she may not have funds to pay a baby-sitter; and she may have little chance to get out, to be with adults, and to do things. Solitary confinement is considered a punishment in all prisons. We forget that confinement with small children may be punishing as well. Her isolation may also mean that she depends excessively on her husband for companionship and emotional support. His approval and his interaction with her may be tremendously important to her, and she may become depressed if they are not forthcoming.

The housewife's *work* is also a source of distress: it is low status, it is not paid, it is never really done but just done enough to be done over. It has also been pointed out that the housewife's work is interrupted by the demands of her schedule so that she often has to go from activity to activity without finishing any of them. People who are unable to finish activities are left without a sense of completion or fulfillment.[88] As we have seen, labor-saving devices have not decreased the number of hours spent doing household chores.[89] The phrase "just a housewife" may also describe her feelings about what she does. Her work is noticed only if it is not done, and it is seldom valued when it is done. She must go way beyond the boundaries of the ordinary to achieve recognition as a "gourmet cook," "marvelous seamstress," or "wonderful hostess." Even here, there is little possibility for growth or advancement. It is certainly true as

For Better or For Worse   by Lynn Johnson

© 1981 Universal Press Syndicate. Reprinted by permission.

well that society gives housework little status. In Britain, for example, housework is legally *not* defined as work because no wages or salary are received for it.[90] Oakley, in her well-known study of housewives, points out also that housework is the most disliked aspect of the housewife role. In her study, women reported the job as monotonous, fragmented, and isolating, although they appreciated the ability to regulate their own time.[91]

Of course, we have painted the bleakest possible picture. Not all young housewives live far from others and suffer from lack of companionship. Many enjoy at least some of the tasks associated with the housewife role. Others escape housework by hiring outside help. If these women do not work outside the home, however, they must still suffer the personal and legal consequences of being dependent.

As we have shown above, their sisters who combine outside jobs and housework may escape much of the housewives' dependency, but they usually end up doing the better part of two full-time jobs. In a questionnaire answered by 205 housewives, 46 percent got no help from their husbands in preparing meals, and only 10 percent received regular help. An additional 47 to 49 percent of the husbands never helped with other tasks such as cleaning or laundry either.[92]

Are Wives Employed Outside the Home Actually Happier?

Wives who work outside the home report themselves as happier than housewives, even though the demands on them are actually greater. Why the self-report of happiness? The main reasons seem to be the enhanced self-esteem of working wives and their greater ability to have social contact with others. They are also doing work that is valued; no matter what kind of work it is, it is paid, whereas housework is not. They have control over some resources of their own; they are not dependent. Wives who work outside the home also get more decision-making power, specifically the ability to make large, far-reaching decisions.[93] Working wives seem to gain power relative to their husbands. They report themselves as more satisfied with their marriages and as having more agreement with their spouses,[94] and they report better mental and physical health than housewives do.[95] Some studies show that they are also more sexually active and satisfied, although *less* likely to be ready to engage in extramarital relationships.[96]

What Is the Solution to Problems in the "Her" Marriage?

What is the significance of all of this? Is the structure of marriage so bad for women that they should avoid it? Obviously, this is not a possible or desired solution. While the trend seems to be that women are staying single longer, and possibly more women are staying single permanently, most still want to get married. They still want to have legitimate children, and they want the level of intimate emotional involvement symbolized by marriage. They also want companionship and more control over social interaction in this "couples society" than they can get as single women.[97]

Is the solution then that every woman should work outside the home and have her own funds so that she will not be dependent? This may be a solution for many women, but it is unrealistic for others. Some women really like housework and the associated tasks of the housewife's role, and others want to stay home with their children—especially when they are young.

In addition, it may be difficult for women in traditional marriages to begin to work outside the home. As the provider role is an extension of "masculinity," many men express discomfort when that role is threatened. Few men are delighted at the prospect of sharing household duties with a working wife. Some husbands of wives who work outside the home express more dissatisfaction with their marriages, their health, and even their jobs. Even though they actually communicate more with their wives and are in general agreement with them, they do not perceive themselves to be as happy as husbands of women who stay home.[98]

This reported dissatisfaction should not be regarded as a factor that should dissuade women from working, however. Unger points out that many of these men may have been more dissatisfied with their jobs and themselves to start with.[99] Men whose wives work outside the home may make less money than those whose wives do not, and they may already feel somewhat inadequate. They may also be less traditional than men whose wives do not work and more willing to admit marital and job problems. More recent studies also show that benefits accruing to couples where the wife is in the labor force outweigh any disadvantages.[100] Men report a feeling of relief that they are not solely responsible for the support of the family. They also report that their working wives are more interesting people and more fun to be with,[101] and the family has greater resources and flexibility.

The message in terms of sex roles is clear. People who participate in work that is valued and fulfilling are happier. (They are particularly happy if they have a support system to do other things for them.) Those who are forced into dependent positions and made to live vicariously through the accomplishments of others will have little self-esteem and are likely to be unhappy. This lack of happiness is not a matter of gender. When roles are reversed and men do the jobs that many housewives do, they too are unhappy.[102]

Thus, the solution is not in reversing roles. Nor is the problem of overly demanding or frustrating marriage roles solved simply by sharing the traditional kinds of labor between both sexes. Both sexes sharing the burdens of providing and the frustrations of housework sounds ideal, but it may be unrealistic for some couples, given the way the economic world is now structured. (Later on we will see how dual-career couples manage.)

Yet, this shared solution is probably the one most likely to be tried in the near future, as it is the one over which individual couples have the most control. Many women may insist on shared work before they will even consider marriage. As their monetary contribution to the household is more and more needed, they will have the power to enforce change in the direction they wish. Men may also be more willing to share the housework when they find themselves relieved of some of the stresses and strains of producing enough income for a family.

The amount of sharing and exchange will probably be negotiated, however, and there is still a great deal of ambivalence about modified roles. While many men may be relieved to reduce the emphasis on work, others may lose some of their definition of masculinity and feelings of self-esteem if they modify their achievement orientation. Women may enjoy their more valued labor force participation, but some may feel a loss of femininity if they are not caring for children or doing other household tasks that they have been socialized to believe women should do.

Changing the Values Implied in Different Kinds of Work

Perhaps the best way to encourage change in the definitions of what is masculine and what is feminine work and to encourage both sexes to enjoy all kinds of endeavor is to change the value placed upon that work and the opportunities to do it. As "masculine-style" labor force participation is already valued, it seems that the way to achieve a more equitable valuation is to increase the value placed upon housework. The Swedes have partially solved the dilemma by recognizing that housework is a valuable contribution to the economy. Sweden pays its housewives or househusbands and gives them two weeks' paid vacation a year. The government also arranges for couples to have rotating work shifts so that husbands and wives can share household and child-care duties. Either parent can take maternity/paternity leave or take time off from work for sick children. While any change that challenges general cultural norms is difficult to implement, and the Swedes do not claim to have all the answers, their approach seems to be one logical solution to changing the values regarding housework.[103]

Oakley points out the potential for similar change in this country. Housewives as a group are dissatisfied with their tasks and working conditions. There even seems to be some degree of class consciousness, such as that manifested by the current International Wages for Housework Movement (IWHM). Those in this movement demand that the government pay housewives for the work they are doing and award back pay for years of past labor. Adherents of IWHM argue that housework is really an aggregation of services, such as cooking, waitressing, chauffeuring, and janitorial work, that are paid work when done outside the marriage tie, and they reject the idea that housework should be an unpaid service or an extension of the love of a woman for her family.[104] Judith Laws points out that the Displaced Homemaker Movement also addresses the problem of unpaid household labor when it demands support for divorced women who have devoted unpaid labor to their families for years and are left after divorce without a source of self-support.[105] Alice Cook has proposed legislation that would compensate women for the advantages given up during their child-raising years.[106]

There is much to be said for paying for housework. It would not only reduce the dependence of the "housespouse" upon the provider but would also raise the status and self-esteem of those engaged in the work. It is likely that the work could then be more equally shared between the genders. Housewives would not necessarily be isolated in an all-female world. A happy spin-off from the entry of more men into housework is that its esteem would probably be further increased. If studies show that college students downgrade the esteem of an occupation when the proportion of women in it increase, it is likely that an occupation's prestige will increase as men participate more fully.[107] Of course, there are the questions of how housework should be valued (by the job? by hours of labor? at what rate?) and who should pay the housewife (her husband? the government?). Both are difficult to answer.

Another possibility for change is to modify the concept that masculinity is achieved to a great extent by hard work and success in a career.

While this may seem the hardest concept to change, forces are at work to modify it. Many young men are expressing increasing ambivalence about the demands of the traditional career world. We saw that many fear success as much as they wish to succeed.[108] The ethic of hard work also seems to have been modified. People are enjoying their leisure now and not feeling guilty about it. They are not willing to work and slave for an undefined future. This is not true of the majority of young men, and the work ethic may return with hard economic times, but some modification of the desire to work hard and achieve seems to have been made. In addition, as more and more women enter occupations, paid work may not be defined as "masculine." Work may come to be seen as something that all adults do to support themselves and to find fulfillment. If success and achievement can be both feminine and masculine, then perhaps care of a house and children can be both feminine and masculine too. We will see later that many men are entering more actively into a fathering role or even taking complete care of a family as custodial fathers in single-parent homes.

Thus, changing the definitions about what is masculine work and what is feminine work and changing the values placed on that work, by pay or other means, may be our best sources of modifying traditional family roles. These roles are being modified whether we like it or not by the economic situation and by women's increasing awareness of their opportunities. They are also being modified by men's awareness of the physical and emotional burdens they have carried.

The Transition to Parenthood

For many couples, the transition to parenthood is likely to mean a move toward more traditional sex roles in the family.[109] It is also likely to mean variations in marital satisfaction. Alice Rossi has written a classic essay in which she discusses the process and difficulties of this transition. She and other sociologists show that its timing and nature have a profound effect on the couple's interaction.

Nonparenthood

Parenthood is not always the option chosen by young couples today. More couples are opting for childlessness, and many more are delaying the time when they have their first child or they are having fewer children than before. From 1860 to the 1930s, the birthrate in this country steadily declined and stayed low until the end of World War II. Then there was a rush of marriages that had been deferred during the depression of the 1930s and the war, and the birthrate rose again. In the late

1940s, the 1950s, and the 1960s, women who were asked how many children they wanted chose between two and four. Those who wanted four were the largest group among those choosing all alternatives.[110]

For the "me" generation of the 1970s, however, children cut into the time, energy, and money for other things, including careers for women. More certain methods of birth control meant that parenthood could more assuredly be postponed or avoided. Couples actively used contraception to avoid pregnancy. According to a national fertility study done in 1975, at any one time about 80 percent of all married couples used contraception. Of couples married five to nine years, only 2.1 percent had not used contraception at some time.[111] The motivation to use contraception was demonstrated by the lower birthrate and by the fact that women had babies later after they were married.

The January 1973 Supreme Court ruling that the decision about abortion should be left to a woman and her physician also made it easier for women to use this method as a backup when contraception failed.[112] Couples began to make sure they actually achieved their desired family size. However, because this right to abortion is now being threatened by groups on the political right, abortion may not be so available in the future.

In the past it was difficult for couples to avoid parenthood completely. Childless couples were accused of being selfish or immature and were pressured by relatives to become parents. For women especially it may be still difficult to forego the role of mother. Motherhood is tied up with definitions of femininity and may even be considered a life's work. While fatherhood is also part of the definition of masculinity, general sexual prowess will substitute for the man; not so for the woman. In addition, some couples end up having children because they are not careful about contraception. However, with the new emphasis on careers, pleasure, and small families, more couples have resisted society's pressure and have opted to stay childless.[113]

Parenthood

Even for those couples who want only one or two children or who delay those children a number of years after marriage, the transition to parenthood is difficult. Rossi points out that one of the things that makes the transition to parenthood so difficult is its abrupt nature: one day you are childless and the next day you are a parent.[114] Even the long months of pregnancy and preparing a nursery cannot prepare a couple for the responsibility and time and energy demands that will suddenly be made upon them. The demands are made more difficult by the fact that there is little preparation for parenthood in our culture. We live in small, nuclear families where we may never take care of little babies.[115]

Parenthood has been romanticized in our culture, and the practicalities and difficulties of caring for a new infant are seldom discussed. Yet most young couples experience some disruption of marital roles and some feeling of slight-to-moderate crisis when a first baby arrives. Studies vary in the amount of crisis that the couples report, but several studies have found that over 80 percent of their respondents report at least a slight crisis.[116]

The parenthood crisis includes disrupted marital roles and communication as well as the physical demands made upon the parents.[117] Marital satisfaction is reported by some researchers to be disrupted.[118] Feldman and others believe that the birth of the first child marks a decided drop in marital satisfaction that is the beginning of a long decline over the life of the marriage.[119] On the other hand, although marital satisfaction may decline, parental satisfaction may increase. There may be an upsurge of pride, family feelings, and shared interest in a child.

The transition to parenthood has specific implications for sex roles. Rossi points out that when child bearing is postponed for a while after marriage, the couple has a chance to establish more equalitarian roles. It is expected that women will work after marriage while the couple establishes a home and gets started in a career (careers). While the wife is contributing resources, it is likely that the couple will share decision making and divide much of the household labor. In some cases, the wife will be supporting the husband through advanced training, and this will strengthen her power position in the family.

Parenthood makes it difficult to maintain this equality. Most businesses give maternity leave but not paternity leave, nor are men as likely to take such a leave even when offered. Thus, it becomes more feasible for a woman to stay home with a newborn infant than it does for a man. Once she is at home without income or social status, her power drops drastically. Because she is at home and the father is working, it is also "logical" that she be the one to do the housework and to get up with the children at night. It is difficult for the couple to do things together, so they may separate their chores and some recreation. He baby-sits while she "goes out with the girls," for example. The young wife who is isolated with a baby may be without funds for sitters or without a car. Her friends may be working or far away. She must regulate her schedule according to the needs of the baby, and she is left with the housework. She is also left with no income and status of her own.[120] We have looked before at the pressure this puts on the housewife. Rossi says that "for many women the personal outcome of experience in the parent role is not a higher level of maturation but the negative outcome of a depressed sense of self-worth, if not actual personality deterioration."[121]

Thus, parenthood has a tendency to initiate or perpetuate more traditional sex roles.[122] Even when the wife returns to work, she is usually the partner held responsible for the greatest part of child care and housework. Cultural expectations perpetuate this belief even when the couple would rather do otherwise. Businesses expect a mother to take time off to be with a sick child, but they tend to look askance at a man who sacrifices business hours to spend time with his child.[123] Thus, the mother must usually combine the demands of two work roles. Frequently, this leaves her little time or energy to pursue her career vigorously. She may also have lost ground in her career by taking time off to have and be with children. The couple who started out on a more nearly equal basis may become quite traditional in allocation of work roles.

On the other hand, fathers are taking a greater role in parenting. There are changing norms that specify that men *should* spend more time with their children and interact in emotional and nurturing ways with them. The changing norms make it easier for fathers to fight the constraints of the corporation and to spend time with their children if they really wish to do so.[124]

The Middle-Aged Family

A Changing Orientation to Masculine and Feminine Behavior

The parenting of teenagers and the gradual departure of children from the home may coincide with other changes in the parents' lives. Middle age appears to be the time of stock taking for many people. Men are at a crucial point in their careers and are either actively moving up the job ladder or are aware that they are unlikely to ever have the occupational success they may have once dreamed about. Women who are mothers recognize that their role will be different as children leave home. For women who have been primarily mothers and homemakers, the loss of the mothering role may be a significant change in their lives.

Neugarten points out that middle age is not so much a specific time of life at it is a perception of age. Men may become aware of their advancing years when they see colleagues twenty years younger moving up the career ladder. They may alternatively come to a recognition of their age the first time their son beats them at tennis or when a contemporary friend has a heart attack. While the time of the perception of middle age varies, it often comes in the late thirties and the first few years of the forties for most men.[125]

Levinson and other researchers believe that the awareness of middle age and the evaluation of personal goals and one's total life that takes place at this time represent a midlife crisis. As the masculine striving for career success may be stymied by outside forces, the pause in the man's move up the career ladder may give him time to think of other things he is missing.

Levinson describes four concerns of the men going through this evaluation.[126] The first concern is with mortality. Men (and women) feel the vulnerability of their aging bodies and have a much stronger sense that time is passing and they will die. Neugarten talks about the change in measuring time as "time left to life" rather than in terms of "time from birth." The person is concerned that he or she must do things now, because there is so little time left in the future. The feeling is based somewhat on the belief that sudden death might occur, but more on a sense that the vigor of youth may not hold out long enough to accomplish things.

The second concern of this period is trying to make an appropriate transition from being young to becoming older. For some, this transition is not easy and is marked with a desperate attempt to stay young. Such men may work frantically at being physically fit, try younger styles of dress, take up dangerous sports, or look for young sexual partners.

The third and fourth concerns of the transition relate more directly to sex roles: there is an attempt to deal with real feelings and relationships with others, something young men may have done only at a superficial level, and also an attempt to get in touch with the more feminine parts of the self. This fourth concern may involve "feelings" but may, in addition, mean more involvement with one's family, more desire to try artistic and cultural things, and less emphasis on achievement and ambition. The physical, competitive world cannot usually be dealt with at the same pace in any case, and the integration of the "masculine" and "feminine" parts of his nature (Levinson's terms) may give a man more depth and satisfaction.[127]

For the man who is able to make the integration, work may take on new meaning. He may mentor or help protégés and perhaps become more satisfied with a present job situation rather than continually strive to get ahead. For some men, it is a period of rethinking and restarting rather than integration. Old job choices and old marriages may give way under the stress of the period, and new ways of working and living may be found.[128]

Women may experience many of the same concerns, particularly the vulnerability of the body and the sense of passing time. Faced with the realization that their mothering roles may not be as important as before, women may also begin assessing what they want to do with the rest of their lives.[129] Some women who formed their identity and sense of self entirely around the finding of a suitable mate and around motherhood may find themselves "bankrupt" at this time (whether they have actually married or not). If they feel less needed by husands whose interests are taken up with careers or by children who are grown, they may suffer a real identity crisis and even depression and may need to reevaluate their lives.[130] Deutscher believes that the wife probably has more problems adjusting during the postparental years, in particular, than does the husband, who may be occupied with his career for all his stock taking.[131] Hill hypothesizes that the husband's power will rise during this period in the family where the wife has been primarily a homemaker and mother. He believes that for emotional exchange the wife will depend more on her husband, who does not have the same needs. At the same time, health concerns surface, and the wife may be aware of losing her husband and of what that loss will mean to her.[132] As the health of middle-aged women is better than that of men, the man does not suffer similar concerns about his wife. Hill also believes that role conventionality increases: wives are more likely to do tasks stereotyped for females, and men are more likely to do tasks stereotyped for males.[133]

However, Neugarten reports that the most common feeling of women in this period from the thirties through the fifties is one of freedom. They have time and energy for the self, and they feel a satisfying change in their self-concept.[134] This improvement in self-concept seems to come in spite of factors that would seem to militate against it. Both Bell and Sontag have described the "double standard of aging," where men are described as getting "character lines" and distinguished grey hair, while women are seen as become old and wrinkled.[135] Yet women do not seem to suffer from poor body image. Parlee and Neugarten also report that menopause (perhaps starting in these years) is not a factor that affects many women adversely. While some suffer from physical discomforts, most see it as a period to be gotten through and as a relatively unimportant factor in their lives.[136] As one woman wryly put it, "If it's not the pause that refreshes, it at least is not the pause that depresses."[137] Many women raised in the days before "sure" contraception actually seem to find refreshment after menopause in renewed enjoyment of sex without fear of pregnancy. Parenthetically, the sexual enjoyment of middle-aged and older couples who have always enjoyed their sex life does not seem to decrease.[138]

The degree of difficulty that women seem to have in getting through the midlife crisis and assuming new identities may actually be based more on exterior than on interior causes. There is still discrimination against older women in the labor force, and it may be difficult for women who have never worked, or with rusty skills, to find a job. Family reactions to a woman's decreased availability to her husband and children may be relatively hostile.[139] As men may also be going through simultaneous midlife changes, some instability in the family may occur as a result of envy or dissonance in roles. One professor expressed his feelings this way:

> I'm afraid I'm a bit envious of my wife. She went to work a few years ago when our children no longer needed her attention, and a whole new world has opened to her. But myself? I just look forward to writing another volume, and then another volume. . . .[140]

Even for the woman who has continually combined a work identity with home roles, the midlife transition may not be easy. While work can have an important integrative function when women are losing a motherhood role, women can suffer the same concerns about their careers that men do.[141]

Perhaps as a result of these life assessments, the personalities of men and women change during these years. The changes seem to be the reverse of traditionally stereotyped personality traits for each sex. "Men seem to become more receptive to affiliative and nurturant promptings"; they cope with the environment in more contemplative and abstract ways. Women, in contrast, seem to become more aggressive and self-assured. They are less guilty about egocentric impulses,[142] although they also continue to cope in their accustomed affective and expressive manner. David Gutmann's cross-cultural work substantiates the fact that this is a tendency in many societies. He says that "older men are more diffusely sensual, more sensitive to the incidental pleasures and pains, less aggressive, more affiliative, more interested in love than conquest or power, more present than future oriented. At the same time, women are aging in the reverse direction: becoming more aggressive, less sentimental, and more domineering."[143]

What is the effect of these changes on the marital satisfaction of the middle-aged couple? When we look at marital satisfaction, we must remember, of course, that families that have survived to the empty-nest stage may well be happier to start with. A great deal of happiness in the postparental stage may also depend on the type of relationship the couple has maintained. For couples who have had traditional marriages, the postparental stage may mean that marriage becomes something of an empty shell.[144] For couples who have shared activities and communication all along, the postparental years may become more meaningful.

Most studies of marital satisfaction in the postparental years show an increase in satisfaction as the children leave home.[145] In spite of the problems of midlife transition and the difficulty in finding new directions, family tension probably decreases and companionship increases during this period. While the increase in companionship is small (some researchers have noted that it is lower during this period than during the first fifteen years of marriage and probably does not really increase significantly until after the retirement of the husband),[146] it seems enough to offset any negative effects of this period. Data from six national surveys show that women, in particular, are happier in the postparental period and get more enjoyment out of life than women of similar ages who still have a child at home.[147] The more recent studies seem to show even greater satisfaction, probably because of the changing role of women. More and more middle-aged women are reentering the labor force, and they see freedom from child care as an opportunity to pursue their own neglected interests.

The Postretirement Family

Changes in the personality traits and interests of men and women continue and are accelerated in the postretirement family. The changes in roles do not seem to affect marital satisfaction adversely.[148] In fact, there is evidence that many older persons consider their marriage relationships to be as satisfactory as they were in previous years, if not more so.[149] However, those perceived as satisfactory in the later years were usually satisfactory from the beginning.[150] (Satisfaction also seems to decrease somewhat in the advancing years, probably because of health and economic problems.)

Companionship and being able to express true feelings to one another were considered the two most rewarding aspects of the marriage relationship by respondents of one study of 400 older husbands and wives.[151] In contrast, having different values and lack of mutual interests were seen as the most troublesome aspects of marriage.[152] Marital satisfaction related to a high degree of morale and positive feelings.[153] The relationship of marital satisfaction to morale was higher for women than for men, even in the older years.[154] However, the loss of a spouse through death has a greater negative impact on the psychological well-being of men than of women, presumably because older women have established stronger kin and friendship networks to sustain them.[155]

The effect of retirement on morale may differ for men and women as well. Some studies have shown that retirement from one's own career does not seem to hold the significance for women that it does for men.[156] It has been speculated that this is true because the work role is not as primary a role for women[157] and because women have more opportunity to practice role transitions—as with the transition from mother to wife in the empty-nest years.[158] Other research has shown, however, that women for whom the work role is important may actually suffer more than men from retirement.[159] Women who had made social and economic plans for retirement seemed to suffer the least;[160] of course, the same is true for men. Couples who were used to experiencing leisure-time activities together were the most satisfied.[161]

Thus, we see that sex roles may undergo dramatic change in the oider iamily. The change is one of a reorientation of personality rather than a changing orientation toward tasks. While older women become more assertive and older men more passive, they are unlikely to greatly modify their provider and housekeeper roles. The sex-role orientation that is changed is manifested, in general, across all activities rather than in particular sex-stereotyped activities. The reasons for the different personality traits have not been fully explored. It is generally assumed that this change in roles is associated with the freedom of women from their motherhood responsibilities and the contemplation induced in men by midlife stock taking of their career achievements. Why the changes in sex-role orientation take the direction they do is not completely clear. Why is it that men become aware of the emotional relationships they have missed and do not take the path of denying those emotional needs even more firmly so that they can concentrate on the career success that has so far eluded them? Why is it that women do not seek further expressive and affiliative bonds but instead become more assertive? What is the relationship of these changes to physical strength or to cultural norms regarding age and status? It may be that the older family holds clues to many questions about sex-role norms and behavior in our society.

→ *Summary*

When we look at the "ideal family" of the American dream, we see that both men and women are less likely to chance such a dream and are staying single longer. For women, this postponement of marriage may be caused by greater educational and career opportunities and fewer people to marry, and for both sexes it may be caused by doubts about the institution of marriage itself. Even as changing sex roles aid the delay of marriage, the postponement of marriage affects sex roles. With the longer period of independence, women are more likely to be started in careers and to learn the kind of assertiveness that makes it difficult to revert to dependent relationships. Men may learn to take care of domestic chores and be more willing to share equalitarian marriage relationships. With more contraception available and fewer social taboos against cohabitation, marriage becomes more a symbol of commitment rather than a necessity. More men and women may be choosing not to make this kind of commitment and thus may not get married at all.

Although this period of changing sex roles may create ambiguous expectations and possible conflict between spouses, it seems that the change may actually increase marital satisfaction in the long run. As more and more wives join the labor force, more women will have their own resources, which will probably push marriages toward the equalitarian model. Because working wives report themselves happier than traditional ones, general marital satisfaction will probably increase. In addition, as women take on the provider role and men do more in the home, it is likely that each will better understand both sets of tasks, and they will have congruent expectations for husband-wife roles. As they have more in common, their communication and companionship are also likely to increase. Another factor that may well lead to greater marital satisfaction is the present limiting of the parental role with its attendant frustrations. Thus, the fact that the traditional marriage of the American dream has probably never existed in great numbers and does not widely occur today may actually be positive. We do not have to rely on a dream about a kind of marriage that never existed; we can explore the potential of the non-traditional alternatives that are developing.

Essay Questions

1. Discuss the reasons that men and women are staying single longer and the effect this has on sex roles.

2. Why has the traditional family of the American dream been a myth rather than a reality in our culture? Discuss contemporary reasons why the dream is likely to remain a dream.

3. According to Blood and Wolfe, power in marriage is determined by the resources one brings to the marriage. What resources do they have in mind for the husband and for the wife? How is their resource theory modified by the beliefs of the couple, the social class of the couple, and the cultural norms of the society in which they live?

4. Contrast the experience of married and single men. How is marriage good for men, although there have always been myths to the contrary? Why do you believe those myths existed (that is, what are the costs of marriage to men)?

5. Discuss the reasons a woman may be "shocked" when she enters marriage. Be sure to include legal, social, and personal reasons for her shock and possible loss of self-esteem. Are men "shocked" too?

6. Discuss the "her" marriage as described by Jessie Bernard. Why does she say about housewives, "if their symptoms belonged to any other group in American society, their condition would be considered a social disaster of the worst magnitude"?

7. Why are married women who work outside the home apparently happier than housewives, although they may have longer hours and more work to do? What conditions of housework itself contribute to the unhappiness of the woman who stays at home? Be very specific in your answer and quote studies where possible. What suggestions do you have for change in this situation?

8. When wives work outside the home, there is usually a realignment of power to some degree because the wife is contributing resources. Why does decision-making power change faster than the division of labor? How much help can a working wife usually expect with household chores?

9. When couples become parents, there is often a reversion to traditional sex roles. Why does this happen, and what could you suggest to prevent it?

10. How are some of the component tensions and rewards that make up a level of marital satisfaction related to sex roles? Do you see changes in these tensions and rewards for better or for worse?

11. Discuss the changing orientation toward sex roles in the postparental family. How does this change relate to the departure of children from the home and to men's career interests at this time? How does the change affect power and marital satisfaction?

12. Discuss why you think changes in sex-role orientation in the older family take the direction they do. Why don't the spouses cling to their traditional roles in a time of change?

Exercises

1. To understand how you learned assumptions about marriage roles, list below how you saw the interaction in your own family:

   My mother typically made decisions about _____

   My father typically made decisions about _____

   They both made decisions about _____

   My mother typically did these kinds of household or outside-the-house work (yard work, and the like) _____

   My father typically did these kinds of household or outside-the-house work _____

   Both typically did these kinds of work _____

2. Have both men and women in the class answer the following questions and compare answers: Did your mother work outside the home when you were a child? How did you feel about this? How did your father feel about it?

3. What are your feelings about the following words:

Housewives	Single parents
Women managers	Househusbands
Working mothers	Men managers
Divorced women	Unemployed men

4. According to what you learned in childhood, what do "responsible" men do? What do "responsible" women do? Do you believe the same things now? If not, why not?

5. Have the men and women in the class answer the following questions and compare their answers:

    a. In my marriage, I have to _____

                I need to _____

                I want to _____

    b. I may not want to get married because _____

    c. Do you believe that both men and women are "shocked" to enter marriage? If so, how are they "shocked"?

6. You are a husband in a white middle-class family where the last child has just graduated from college. Your wife, who has never worked, is talking about finishing her college education and getting a job. You have just been passed over for promotion at work and you pulled a muscle in your leg while playing tennis last weekend. How do you feel about your age, your life, and your marital relationship?

Notes

1. Eleanor D. Macklin, "Nontraditional Family Forms: A Decade of Research," *Journal of Marriage and the Family* 12 (1980):905–922.

2. U.S. Bureau of the Census, "Marital Status and Living Arrangements: March 1979," *Current Population Reports,* series, P–20, no. 349 (Washington, D.C. Government Printing Office, 1980).

3. Peter Stein, "The Never Marrieds," in Peter Stein, ed., *Unmarried Adults in Social Context* (New York: St. Martins Press, 1981).

4. Christine Doudna and Fern McBride, "Where are the Men for the Women at the Top?" in Peter Stein, *op. cit.,* p. 14.

5. *Ibid.,* p. 22.

6. Doudna and McBride, *op cit.,* p. 23.

7. *Ibid.*

8. Paul Secord, *Too Many Women: Demography, Sex and Family,* quoted in Doudna and McBride, *op. cit.,* p. 29.

9. *Ibid.,* p. 29.

10. Paul C. Glick and Graham B. Spanier, "Cohabitation in the United States," in Stein, ed., *op. cit.,* p. 198.

11. E.D. Macklin, "Nonmarital Heterosexual Cohabitation," in Arlene Skolnick and Jerome Skolnick, eds., *The Family in Transition* (Boston: Little-Brown, 1980), p. 285–306.

12. Glick and Spanier, *op. cit.*, p. 208.

13. R. Stafford, E. Backman and P. diBoni, "The Division of Labor Among Cohabiting and Married Couples," *Journal of Marriage and the Family* 39 (1977):43–57.

14. Mirra Komarovsky, "Cultural Contradictions and Sex Roles: The Masculine Case," in Skolnick and Skolnick, eds., *op. cit.*, pp. 205–216.

15. S.S. Angrist and E.M. Almquist, *Career and Contingencies: How College Women Juggle with Gender* (New York: Dunnellen Press, 1975).

16. Ira Reiss, "Sociological Perspective on Love," in Ira Reiss, ed., *Family Systems in America*, 3rd ed. (New York: Holt, Rinehart and Winston, 1980) pp. 133–40; William Goode, "The Theoretical Importance of Love," *American Sociological Review* 24 (1959):38–47.

17. John Cuber and Peggy Harroff, *The Significant Americans* (New York: Penguin, 1965).

18. David Heer, "The Measurement and Bases of Family Power: An Overview," *Journal of Marriage and the Family* 25 (1963):134; Robert Blood and Donald M. Wolfe, *Husbands & Wives: The Dynamics of Married Living* (New York: Macmillan, 1960).

19. Blood and Wolfe, *op. cit.*

20. *Ibid.*

21. Constantina Safilios-Rothschild, "The Study of Family Power Structures: A Review, 1960–1969," *Journal of Marriage and the Family* 32 (1970):539–52.

22. Richard Centers, Bertram H. Raven, and Arnoldo Rodriguez, "Conjugal Power Structure: A Re-examination," *The American Sociological Review* 36 (1971):264–78.

23. *Ibid.*

24. *Ibid.;* P.B. Johnson, "Social-Power and Sex-Role Stereotypes" (Ph.D. diss., UCLA, 1974).

25. Blood and Wolfe, *op. cit.*

26. Dair L. Gillespie, "Who Has the Power? The Marital Struggle," *Journal of Marriage and the Family* 33 (1971):445–58.

27. *Ibid.*

28. Blood and Wolfe, *op. cit.*

29. Heer, *op. cit.*

30. *Ibid.*

31. *Ibid.*

32. Michael Young and Peter Willmott, *The Symmetrical Family* (New York: Pantheon, 1963).

33. Hyman Rodman, "Marital Power and the Theory of Resources in Cultural Context," *Journal of Comparative Family Studies* 3 (1972):50–69.

34. Centers, Raven, and Rodriguez, *op. cit.*

35. Lois W. Hoffman and Ivan F. Nye, *Working Mothers* (San Francisco: Jossey-Bass, 1974).

36. Leland J. Axelson, "The Marital Adjustment and Marital Role Definitions of Husbands of Working and Nonworking Wives," *Marriage and Family Living* 25 (1963):189–95.

37. Robert K. Leik, "Instrumentality and Emotionality in Family Interaction," *Sociometry* 26 (1963):131–45.

38. Blood and Wolfe, *op. cit.*

39. Marie L. Richmond, "Immigrant Adaptation and Family Structure among Cuban Exiles in Miami, Florida" (Ph.D. diss., Florida State University, 1973).

40. *Ibid.*

41. Blood and Wolfe, *op. cit.*

42. John Scanzoni and Greer Litton Fox, "Sex Roles, Family, and Society: The Seventies and Beyond," *Journal of Marriage and the Family* 42 (1980):743–58.

43. R. Berk, S. Berk, and C. Bersheide, "Housework, the Labor of Love," in A.E. Fisher, ed., *Women's Worlds: NIMH Supported Research on Women* (Washington, D.C.: U.S. Government Printing Office, 1976); B. Duncan and O.D. Duncan, *Sex Typing and Social Roles: A Research Report* (New York: Academic Press, 1978); K.O. Mason, J. Czajka, and S. Arber, "Change in Women's Sex-Role Attitudes, 1964–1975," *American Sociological Review* 41 (1976):573–96; L. Hauerstein, "Married Women: Work and Family," *Families Today* 1 (1979):365–86; L.W. Hoffman, "Maternal Employment: 1979," *American Psychologist* 34 (1979):859–65.

44. Judith Long Laws, *The Second X: Sex Role and Social Role* (New York: Elsevier, 1979), p. 89.

45. Susan Hesselbart, "Does Charity Begin at Home? Attitudes toward Women, Household Tasks, and Household Decision Making" (Paper presented at the American Sociological Association meeting in New York, August 1976); S.M. Miller, "The Making of a Confused Middle-Aged Husband," *Social Policy* 2 (1971):33–39; Warren Farrell, *The Liberated Man* (New York: Bantam, 1975).

46. Walter L. Slocum and F. Ivan Nye, "Provider and Housekeeper Roles," in Ivan Nye, ed., *Role Structure and Analysis of the Family* (Beverly Hills, Calif.: Sage, 1976), p. 33; Nona Glazer-Malbin, "Housework," *Signs* 1 (1976):905–22; Mike McGrady, *The Kitchen Sink Papers: My Life as a Househusband* (New York: Signet, 1976).

47. Scanzoni and Fox, *op. cit.*, quoting Berk *et al.*, *op. cit.*; Hauerstein, *op. cit.*; S.L. Hofferth and K. A. Moore, "Women's Employment and Marriage," in R.E. Smith, ed., *The Subtle Revolution: Women at Work* (Washington, D.C.: The Urban Institute, 1979), pp. 99–124.

48. Joann Vanek, "Keeping Busy: Time Spent in Housework, U.S. 1920–1970" (Ph.D. diss., University of Michigan, 1973).

49. Anne Oakley, *The Sociology of Housework* (New York: Pantheon, 1974).

50. Blood and Wolfe, *op. cit.*; Young and Wilmott, *op. cit.*

51. Joseph H. Pleck, "Men's New Roles in the Family" (Rev. version of paper prepared by the Ford Foundation Merrill-Palmer Institute Conference on

the Family and Sex Roles, Detroit, Michigan, November 10–12, 1975); Joseph H. Pleck, "The Work-Family Role System," *Social Problems* 24 (1977):417–27.

52. Constantina Safilios-Rothschild, "A Macro- and Micro-Examination of Family Power and Love: An Exchange Model," *Journal of Marriage and the Family* 41 (1979):301–13.

53. Julia A. Ericksen, William Yancey, and Eugene P. Ericksen, "The Division of Family Roles," *Journal of Marriage and the Family* 41 (1979):301–13.

54. Vanek, *op. cit.*; Pleck, *op. cit.*, p. 8; Nadine Brozan, "Men and Housework: Do They or Don't They?" *New York Times*, November 1, 1980, p. 20Y.

55. *Detroit Free Press*, "A Bleak Picture of the Working Woman," June 5, 1979.

56. Vanek, *op. cit.*

57. *Ibid.*

58. *Ibid.*

59. *Ibid.*

60. Maribel Morgan, *The Total Woman* (New York: Simon and Schuster, 1973).

61. Rhoda Unger, *Female and Male: Psychological Perspectives* (New York: Harper & Row, 1979), p. 299.

62. Karen Mason and Larry Bumpass, "U.S. Women's Sex Role Ideology, 1970," *American Journal of Sociology* 80 (1973):1212–19.

63. U.S. Bureau of the Census, *Current Population Reports*, no. 8 (Washington, D.C.: Government Printing Office, 1976), pp. 23 and 31.

64. Philip Slater, "Parental Role Differentiation," *American Journal of Sociology* 67 (1961):296–311.

65. Bernard, *op. cit.*

66. *Ibid.*

67. *Ibid.*, pp. 16–28.

68. "The Single Man: He's in Bigger Trouble Than You'd Ever Guess," *Detroit Free Press*, November 10, 1974, p. 1D.

69. *Ibid.*

70. Bernard, *op. cit.*

71. *Ibid.*

72. Sidney Jourard, "Some Lethal Aspects of the Male Role," in J. Pleck and J. Sawyer, eds., *Men and Masculinity* (Englewood Cliffs, N.J.: Prentice-Hall, 1974), pp. 21–29.

73. Bernard, *op. cit.*

74. *Ibid.*

75. Walter Gove, "The Relationship Between Sex Roles, Marital Status, and Mental Illness," *Social Forces* 51 (1972):34–44; W.R. Gove and J. Tudor, "Adult Sex Roles and Mental Illness," *American Journal of Sociology* 78 (1973):812–35.

76. Joan M. Krauskoph, "Partnership Marriage: Legal Reforms Needed," in

Jake Chapman and Margaret Gates, eds., *Women into Wives: The Legal and Economic Impact of Marriage* (Beverly Hills, Calif.: Sage, 1977), p. 94.

77. *Ibid.*, p. 94.

78. *Ibid.*, p. 96.

79. *Ibid.*, pp. 98–99.

80. *Ibid.*, p. 101.

81. Susan Kinsley, "Women's Dependency and Federal Programs," in Chapman and Gates, *op. cit.*, pp. 79–91.

82. Margaret Gates, "Homemakers into Widows and Divorcees: Can the Law Provide Economic Protection?" in Chapman and Gates, *op. cit.*, p. 226, quoting the 1975 International Women's Year Commission Poll.

83. Krauskoph, *op. cit.*, p. 99.

84. Bernard, *op. cit.*, p. 43.

85. *Ibid.*

86. Bernard, *op. cit.*, pp. 41–42; also p. 345, table 27, quoting the National Center for Health Statistics, "Selected Symptoms of Psychological Distress" (Washington, D.C.: U.S. Department of Health, Education, and Welfare, 1970), table 17, pp. 30–31.

87. L.S. Radloff, "Sex Differences in Depression: The Effects of Occupation and Marital Status," *Sex Roles* 1 (1975):249–65.

88. Bernard, *op. cit.*, pp. 18–52.

89. Vanek, *op. cit.*

90. Helena Lopata, *Occupation Housewife* (New York: Oxford University Press, 1971).

91. Anne Oakley, *op. cit.*

92. Vanek, *op. cit.*; Oakley, *op. cit.*; Pleck, *op. cit.*

93. Safilios-Rothschild, "Family Power Structures."

94. Lois Hoffman, "Parental Power Relations and the Division of Household Tasks," *Marriage and Family Living* 22 (1960):27–35.

95. R.J. Burke and T. Weir, "Relationship of Wife's Employment Status to Husband, Wife, and Pair Satisfaction and Performance," *Journal of Marriage and the Family* 38 (1976):279–87.

96. M.P. Whiltey and S.B. Poulsen, "Assertiveness and Sexual Satisfaction in Employed Professional Women," *Journal of Marriage and the Family* 37 (1975):573–81; J.N. Edwards and A. Booth, "Sexual Behavior In and Out of Marriage: An Assessment of Correlates," *Journal of Marriage and the Family* 38 (1976):73–81.

97. Angrist and Almquist, *op. cit.*

98. Carl Ridley, "Exploring the Impact of Work Satisfaction and Involvement on Marital Interaction When Both Partners are Employed," *Journal of Marriage and the Family* 35 (1973):229–38; Burke and Weir, *op. cit.*

99. Unger, *op. cit.*, p. 292.

100. Alan Booth, "Wife's Employment and Husband Stress: A Predication and a Refutation," *Journal of Marriage and the Family* 39 (1977):645–50.

101. Miller, *op. cit.*; Farrell, *op. cit.*

102. McGrady, *op. cit.*

103. "Sweden: The Western Model," in Reiss, *Family Systems*, pp. 435–52; Ira L. Reiss, "Sexual Customs and Gender Roles in Sweden and America: An Analysis and Interpretation," in H. Lopata, ed., *Research on the Interweave of Social Roles: Women and Men* (Greenwich, Conn.: JAI Press, 1980).

104. S.S. Simister, "Out of One Kitchen into Another," in *Wages for Housework* (Toronto: Amazon Press, 1975), quoted on p. 158 of Laws, *op. cit.*

105. *Ibid.*

106. Alice Cook, "Working Mothers: Problems and Programs (Unpublished ms., School of Industrial Relations, Cornell University), quoted in Laws, *op. cit.*, p. 159.

107. John C. Touhey, "Effects of Additional Women Professionals on Rating of Occupational Prestige and Desirability," *Journal of Social Psychology* 29 (1974):86–89, quoted in Laws, *op. cit.*

108. Adeline Levine and Janice Crumrine, "Women and the Fear of Success: A Problem in Replication," (Paper presented at the American Sociological Association meeting, August 1973, New York); L.J. Hoffman, "Fear of Success in Males and Females: 1965 and 1972," *Journal of Consulting and Clinical Psychology* 42 (1974):353–58.

109. Alice Rossi, "Transition to Parenthood," in Peter Rose, ed., *Socialization and the Life Cycle* (New York: St. Martin's Press, 1979), pp. 132–45; M.E. Lamb, "Influence of the Child on Marital Quality and Family Interaction during the Prenatal, Natal, and Infancy Periods," in R. Lerrier and G. Spanier, eds., *Child Influences on Marital and Family Interaction* (New York: Academic Press, 1978), pp. 137–64.

110. Reiss, *op. cit.*, pp. 353–71.

111. Charles Westoff and Elsie Jones, "Contraception and Sterilization in the United States, 1965–1975," *Family Planning Perspectives* 9 (1977):153–157.

112. Reiss, *op. cit.*, p. 362.

113. *Ibid.*, pp. 201–205.

114. Rossi, *op. cit.*

115. *Ibid.*

116. Ersel E. LeMasters, "Parenthood as Crisis," *Marriage and Family Living* 19 (1957):352–55; Daniel F. Hobbs, "Parenthood as Crisis: A Third Study," *Journal of Marriage and the Family* 27 (1965):367–72; Daniel F. Hobbs and Sue Peck Cole, "Transition to Parenthood: A Decade Replication," *Journal of Marriage and the Family* 38 (1976):723–31; Candyce S. Russell, "Transition to Parenthood: Problems and Gratifications," *Journal of Marriage and the Family* 36 (1974):294–302; Everett D. Dyer, "Parenthood as Crisis: A Restudy," *Marriage and Family Living* 25 (1963):196–201.

117. Dyer, *op. cit.*; LeMasters, *op. cit.*

118. Harold Feldman, "Development of the Husband-Wife Relationship" (Unpublished research report, Cornell University), pp. 151–53.

119. Boyd C. Rollins and Harold Feldman, "Marital Satisfaction over the Family Life Cycle," *Journal of Marriage and the Family* 32 (1970):20–28; table on p. 69 of Bernard, *op. cit.*; Wesley R. Burr, "Satisfaction with Various Aspects of Marriage over the Life Cycle: A Random Middle-Class Sample," *Journal of Marriage and the Family* 32 (1970):36.

120. Candyce S. Russell, "Transition to Parenthood: Problems and Gratifications," *Journal of Marriage and the Family* 36 (1974):294–302.

121. Rossi, *op. cit.*, pp. 137–38.

122. *Ibid.*, p. 141.

123. See the movie released in 1980 depicting a divorced father with custody, "Kramer vs. Kramer."

124. Robert A. Fern, "Men and Young Children," in Pleck and Sawyer, *op. cit.*, pp. 54–61; Mark Fasteau, "Men as Parents," in David and Brannon, *op. cit.*, pp. 60–66; David B. Lynn, *The Father: His Role in Child Development* (Belmont, Calif.: Wadsworth, 1974).

125. Bernice L. Neugarten, "Adult Personality: Toward a Psychology of the Life Cycle," in Bernice Neugarten, ed., *Middle Age and Aging* (Chicago: University of Chicago Press, 1968), p. 144.

126. Daniel Levinson with Charlotte Darrow, Marie Levinson, Edward Klein, and Braxton Mckee, *The Seasons of a Man's Life* (New York: Ballentine Books, 1978).

127. *Ibid.*

128. *Ibid.*

129. Ellen Goodman, *Turning Points* (New York: Fawcett-Columbine, 1979).

130. Kathleen M. Mogul, "Women in Midlife: Decisions, Rewards, and Conflicts Related to Work and Careers," *American Journal of Psychiatry* 136 (1979):1139–43.

131. Irwin Deutscher, "The Quality of Postparental Life: Definitions of the Situation," *Journal of Marriage and the Family* 26 (1964):52–59.

132. Reuben Hill, *Family Development in Three Generations* (Cambridge, Mass.: Schenkman, 1970), p. 48.

133. *Ibid.*

134. Neugarten, *op. cit.*

135. Inge Powell Bell, "The Double Standard," in Beth B. Hess, *Growing Old in America* (New Brunswick, N.H.: Transaction Books, 1976), pp. 150–62; Susan Sontag, "The Double Standard of Aging," *Saturday Review of the Society* 50 (1972):29–38.

136. Neugarten, *op. cit.*, p. 200; M.B. Parlee, "Psychological Aspects of Menstruation, Childbirth, and Menopause: An Overview with Suggestions for Further Research," in J. Sherman and F.L. Denmark, eds., *Psychology of Women: Future Directions of Research* (New York: Psychological Dimensions, 1978).

137. Bernice Neugarten, Vivian Wood, Ruth Kraines, and Barbara Loomis, "Women's Attitude toward the Menopause," in Neugarten, *op. cit.*, pp. 195–201.

138. William Masters and Virginia Johnson, "Human Sexual Response: The Aging Female and the Aging Male," in Neugarten *op. cit.*, pp. 269–80.

139. Mogul, *op. cit.*, p. 1140.

140. B. Neugarten, "The Awareness of Middle Age," in Neugarten, *op. cit.*, p. 97.

141. Mogul, *op. cit.*

142. Neugarten, *op. cit.*, p. 96.

143. David Guttman, "The Country of Old Men: Cross-Cultural Studies in the Psychology of Later Life," quoted in Orville G. Brim, Jr., "Male Mid-Life Crisis: A Comparative Analysis," in Hess, *op. cit.*

144. Jessie Bernard, *The Future of Marriage* (New York: Bantam Books, 1972).

145. Wesley Burr, "Satisfaction with Various Aspects of Marriage over the Life Cycle," *Journal of Marriage and the Family* 32 (1970):29–37.

146. Boyd C. Rollins and Harold Feldman, "Marital Satisfaction over the Life Cycle," *Journal of Marriage and the Family* 32 (1970):20–28; Rollins and Feldman, "Marital Satisfaction over the Life Cycle; A Reevaluation," *Journal of Marriage and the Family* 36 (1974):271–82; Graham Spanier, Robert Lewis, and Charles Cole, "Marital Satisfaction over the Family Life Cycle: The Issue of Curvilinearity," *Journal of Marriage and the Family* 37 (1975):263–75.

147. Norval Glenn, "Psychological Well-being in the Postparental Stage," *Journal of Marriage and the Family* 37 (1975):105–10.

148. Rollins and Feldman, "A Reevaluation."

149. Edrita G. Freid and Karl Stern, "The Situation of the Aged within the Family," *American Journal of Orthopsychiatry* 18 (1948):31–54; Aaron Lipman, "Role Conceptions and Morale of Couples in Retirement," *Journal of Gerontology* 16 (1961):267–71.

150. Freid and Stern, *op. cit.*

151. Nick Stinnett, Linda Carter, and James Montgomery, "Older Persons' Perceptions of Their Marriages," *Journal of Marriage and the Family* 34, no. 4 (1972):665–70.

152. *Ibid.*, p. 667.

153. Bernice Neugarten, Robert Havinghurst, and Sheldon Tobin, "The Measurement of Life Satisfaction," *Journal of Gerontology* 16 (1961):134–43.

154. Gary Lee, "Marriage and Morale in Later Life," *Journal of Marriage and the Family* 40, no. 1 (1978):131–39.

155. *Ibid.*; Greg Arling, "The Elderly Widow and Her Family, Neighbors, and Friends," *Journal of Marriage and the Family* 32 (1970):428–34.

156. M.F. Lowenthal, C. Thurnher, and D. Chiriboga, *Four States of Life: A Comparative Study of Women and Men Facing Transitions* (San Francisco: Jossey-Bass, 1975).

157. E.B. Palmore, "Differences in the Retirement Patterns of Men and Women," *The Gerontologist* 5 (1965):4–8.

158. C. Kline, "The Socialization Process of Women: Implications for a Theory of Successful Aging," *The Gerontologist* 15 (1975):486–92.

159. M.W. Laurence, "Sources of Satisfaction in the Lives of Working Women," *Journal of Gerontology* 16 (1961):163–67.

160. Carolyn Johnson and Sharon Price-Bonham, "Women and Retirement: A Study and Implications," *Family Relations* 29, no. 3 (1980):380–85.

161. Dennis K. Orthner, "Leisure Activity Patterns and Marital Satisfaction over the Marital Career," *Journal of Marriage and the Family* 37 (1975):91–102.

Chapter Eight

The "Ideal Family" of the American Dream: Variations

We have seen that even in the white middle class, the "ideal family" of the American dream is far from reality. The reality varies even more greatly as we look at other social classes and groups. Recently, the numbers of those experiencing important variations in family structure and behavior have also increased. More people are opting for childless marriages and dual-career marriages; single-parent families are becoming more prevalent; and remarriage is occurring more often. Let us look at some of these variations on the ideal family of the American dream.

Childless Marriages

Married couples' desire for children has usually been taken for granted; however, a small percentage of married couples have always opted for voluntary childlessness, and another small percentage have not been able to have children and have not wished to adopt. By the 1960s, as contraceptive use had improved and more and more women entered the labor force, the option of not having any children was more openly discussed. While in the past childless couples had been accused of selfishness and immaturity, they now received support from sociological findings in which surviving childless marriages reported higher marital happiness than marriages with children.[1]

In 1967, 3 percent of all married couples said they expected to be childless; by the late 1970s, 5 percent said they expected to have no children. However, over 15 percent of the women in such surveys do not answer the question, so there is room for variation in the number expect-

ing to be childless. In addition, many who expect to have children postpone having them and end up childless.[2] It is clear that the birthrate in
the United States has consistently dropped since the baby-boom years of
the 1950s. We now have the lowest birthrate in our history. Childless
couples differ from the traditional family of the American dream in
spousal interaction and satisfaction, as well as in the obvious fact that
they have no children. Looking at childless marriages is particularly interesting because of the possible interaction of childlessness with the
wife's career plans and the possible greater equality of sex roles between
spouses.

Most studies of couples who are considering or have opted for
childlessness have been done on relatively small samples. Nevertheless,
the results of these studies are very similar. Frequently the wives are the
ones likely to make the decision not to have children and to be firm in
sticking to it. In one study, approximately one-third of the wives had
reached the decision to remain childless and had chosen partners with
that decision in mind. The other two-thirds had, with their husbands,
reached the decision to remain childless after a series of postponements
of parenthood.[3]

Most of the couples stressed the importance of marital interaction
and the opportunity to work, travel, and enjoy leisure as their primary
reasons for not wanting children.[4] Some studies show that those who did
not intend to have children were equalitarian in sex-role attitudes,[5] although to get any real measure one would have to compare their attitudes with those of couples who do have children. Most of the studies
that have compared childless marriages and marriages of the same dura-
tion with children have found that childless marriages are happier in all
stages of the life cycle.[6] Their greater happiness is largely due to the companionship and marital interaction that they are able to maintain.[7]

Highly educated women are more likely to remain childless than are
women with less education. Between 7.3 and 14.3 percent of college-
educated women in one study expected no children, while 4.9 percent of
the high-school educated expected none. This relationship held up at all
age levels, so it did not just represent postponement of having children.[8]
The highly educated wives tended to be more successful at their jobs
than most wives in the paid labor force, and they also had higher-status,
better-paying occupations.[9] Thus, women who are highly educated and
more likely to have careers are less likely to want children because of perceived conflict with their work roles. Even though the percentage of families without children is growing, it is predicted to remain under 10 percent of all marriages at least through the 1980s.[10] There is even a chance
that the number of childless marriages may not rise dramatically. What is
not clear is whether this low birthrate simply represents a delay in having

the first child as couples marry later and establish their careers or represents the decision of many couples not to have any children.[11]

Dual-Career Families

As educational and occupational opportunities for women expand, more and more women establish a career, in contrast to simply holding a job. Hence in many marriages two spouses are committed to demanding and time-consuming work. Just how they reconcile this work with family demands and other aspects of their lives is a frequent topic of current research. Most of this research concentrates on how a woman's career line differs from a man's and how the paths of both spouses' careers interact.

Almost all who have examined the dual-career family point out that women and men do not handle the conflict between work and family demands in the same way. Being married and having a family is much more likely to affect the woman's career than the man's. There is conflicting research as to whether or not staying single makes women more productive. While some researchers say that single women do produce more and rise higher in their chosen career patterns,[12] others find that married women are as productive as those who stay single.[13] They do agree, however, that children affect women's professional development. Almost all the professional women with children who have been studied cut back on their professional involvement during child-rearing years. Some cut their workload back to part-time work; almost all cut out the extras like professionally related travel, speaking engagements, and some research and publication.

Researchers also agree that a woman's career line is different from a man's in most cases.[14] Paloma *et al.* distinguish various types of careers. The *regular career* is one in which a person pursues professional training just after graduating from college, and after completing that training, begins work and continues full-time work without long interruptions. An *interrupted career* begins as a regular career but is interrupted, usually for child rearing. *Second careers* are those that begin after a divorce or after the children are grown, and a *modified second career* is one in which professional training and a career take place after the last of the children is old enough not to need full-time mothering, usually at the beginning of school or nursery school.[15] Obviously, women are more likely to have one of the last three career lines. Paloma and her colleagues found that only 38 percent of the professional women interviewed in their sample had "regular" careers. These women had had to make extensive compromises, although they had maintained a full-time uninterrupted work schedule. Usually the compromises included eliminating the "extras" of evening work, travel, and annual meetings. Sometimes the compromise was on the family side: having no or few children and spending minimal time with them. Thirty-six percent of the Paloma sample had "interrupted" career lines, having frequently substituted part-time work for full-time involvement while the children were young; 27 percent of their sample had "second" careers or "modified second" careers.[16]

Most of the women in dual-career families were not willing to give up having children altogether. They compromised by limiting the number of children and frequently by postponing children for a long time after marriage. They also compromised in other ways. One woman typified the sort of compromise made when she said, "I turned down a chance for an administrative, eleven-month, time-consuming job to keep the flexibility of a normal academic year for my spouse and children."[17] Although this particular respondent regretted her decision, most of the women interviewed accepted compromise as a necessary part of combining career and marriage. They did point out, however, that they envied their husbands who did not have to make similar compromises.

Special Problems

In spite of the possibility of compromise, the demands of two careers mean that all dual-career couples have certain stresses and problems. Two major problems seem to involve decisions about *where the couple should work* at their different careers and *how to allocate time* between career and family demands. In spite of the seriousness of the problem, one study found that only half the career wives had discussed the issue of geographic location with their prospective husbands before marriage.[18] When the decision was made after marriage, it was primarily influenced by where the husband could best work. The husband took account of his wife's interests, but usually in a secondary way. For example, he would take a position in a large metropolitan area because his wife would be more likely to find work there; however, she was the one to take the risk of finding another job.[19] At the same time, the husband's employment was more contingent upon his wife's career than many couples realized. The career interests of the wife might threaten the husband's employment in certain jobs where the employer was afraid the husband would move if his wife could not find work.[20] Particularly if the wife were in a high-status occupation, her career interests restricted his geographic mobility.[21] If the dual-career couple opted to remain where they were for family reasons, both spouses might share the professional costs of limited geographic mobility.[22]

Another major stress for dual-career families is the allotment of time between work and family roles. Time-consuming professional careers frequently conflict with family responsibility.[23] For women, this overlap is particularly disturbing because work demands usually give way to those of family. Joseph Pleck points out that:

> For women, the demands of the family role are permitted to intrude into the work role. . . . For husbands, the work-family boundary is likewise asymmetrically permeable, but in other directions. Many husbands literally "take work home."[24]

Thus, many women find their lives subject to the overlapping demands of home and work. To cope, these career women say it is necessary to be very well organized and to have a great deal of physical vitality. They often mention feeling physically fatigued, however, and they say they have to give up leisure and even seeing their friends to pursue their careers.[25] Many dual-career wives felt that their careers suffered because of family demands. If they spent fewer hours in the office or took time off from their careers, they felt isolated, especially from access to new ideas and social support from the professional group.[26] Even for couples that shared household roles more equally, demands on the woman's time were greater than those on the man's.[27]

When it comes to dividing time between work and family, each couple has its own particular way of allocating labor. Usually, couples try to spend money to save time: they buy appliances and hire out some of the tasks like housecleaning. The wife is likely to do more of the cooking and grocery shopping, and the husband more of the outside tasks. Some couples allocate specific tasks according to preference or convenience (the spouse who works near the dry cleaners picks up the dry cleaning); but they pinch-hit if the spouse who is responsible is too busy to do what is needed. All the couples agree that they save household labor by lowering standards to some extent and by increasing efficiency as much as possible.[28] Child care is handled in a similar fashion. Couples hire help when they can or informally modify their work schedules while working full time. Some couples have arranged their schedules so that one or the other is home at all times with young children, which makes it unnecessary to hire child care. In such cases, the dual-career arrangement affects the husband's career as well as the wife's. In most instances, however, it is the wife who is primarily responsible for the child-care arrangements.[29] In almost all cases, women do more of the household work and child care than men. Husbands contribute the most to housework when they are married to equal-earning wives, but few wives are in that category.[30]

Coping with Conflict Between Family and Career Roles

Bailyn has identified two basic styles for dealing with the conflict between family and career demands on time: *accommodation* and *equal sharing*.[31] In accommodation, one spouse has the primary responsibility for work and less responsibility for the family, while the other has the reverse. As one can imagine, it is usually the woman who has the primary responsibility for the family sphere. An unfortunate variation of this coping style is the "adversaries," in which both are involved in careers and only minimally involved at home, yet they want a well-ordered home and family. There is a continuing question as to who will accommodate and do the home work role.

In the *equal-sharing* option, both spouses are involved in home and career. In one form of equal sharing, the spouses try to balance both work and home demands; they are the "acrobats." They want to have a well-ordered home, provide real and emotional support for each other, pursue successful careers, be good parents, and still have time for their relationship. Needless to say, they need to be supermen and superwomen to accomplish this task. In a less stressful version of equal sharing, dual-career couples become "allies" by emphasizing just one of the roles—career or family—and reducing emphasis on the other. They may do this by lowering their aspirations and stepping off the fast-career track, thus reducing the career role; or they may do it by having no children or only one child, thus reducing the domestic role.[32] Another possibility is "recycling" either career or peak family commitments. Usually, the most demanding years of family and career coincide, but couples can decide to have children later or to have careers that peak later so that peak demands of the roles do not occur the same time.[33] Finally, one pattern of accommodation that seems to fit into many dual-career couples' lives is "segmentation," or compartmentalizing each area so that the couple is not dealing with family and work demands during the same hours or days. Sometimes segmentation means geographic separation or commuting, where the couple works in separate locations during the work week and gets together on weekends. Alternatively, it may mean that certain time at home is allocated for the family and nothing else is allowed to interfere.[34] These are all, of course, "ideal" types, and many couples combine styles.

If the spouses both want total career commitment, then it is probably essential that one or both careers be very flexible, with flexible hours or work that can be done at home. It may also be easier if the spouses are at two different phases in their careers. If one is settled and secure, that person can take over more of the home role while the other one is moving up.[35]

Sometimes the styles of accommodating work and family roles change. At times, the accommodating partner becomes nonaccommodating, and vice versa. In other cases, the cycle of life may change roles. Deutscher has pointed out that couples in later years may be happier because of the reduced demands of family, the reduced demands of work, or both.[36]

Benefits and Burdens of Dual-Career Marriages

While some researchers have emphasized the stress upon the dual-career family during the peak years of child rearing, findings from a national sample show that the extra income from the working wife is particularly beneficial during the parental stage of the family.[37] This study also points out that extrafamily work role seems to keep wives from narrowing their focus to interests too exclusively concerned with children.[38] Simpson and England have introduced the theory of *role homophily,* in which they postulate that very similar marital roles (such as both spouses equally combining work and family commitments) build marital solidarity. They have tested their theory on traditional families, in which the greatest marital satisfaction occurs before child bearing and after children are launched,[39] and thus the greatest satisfaction coincides with the period of least sex-role differentiation. They believe that the small sex-role differentiation in the dual-career marriage is similarly likely to promote marital solidarity.[40]

Other variables that affect marital satisfaction of the dual-career couple are the attitudes of the spouses toward each other's work. Most dual-career couples have reported that the husband's attitude toward the wife's work is generally supportive, even when her work means travel and time away from home.[41] The wives emphasized that the husband's attitude was extremely important in freeing them to advance their careers.[42] Most dual-career couples said that they did not feel directly competitive in their work because they were in different fields or because they made it a point to cooperate. Those who did feel competitive were competitive in many areas, like general status and hours worked, as well as in actual professional accomplishments.

In the final analysis, there was no real equality of the sexes in terms of role sharing when one compared the obligations of the women in dual-career couples to those of the men. The men had much more freedom and opportunity to pursue their careers than the women did. Some researchers suggest that the future holds the promise of greater development of equality in dual-career marriages.[43] Young people are starting out their married lives more committed to an equal relationship; the concern about occupational equality for women is pushing many employers into policies that more readily accommodate family roles; and men seem to have lessened their work involvement, as the health hazards of excessive involvement have now been documented, and thus they have more time for family roles.[44] The woman may also gain equality because she has more leverage and is appreciated and needed. In addition, the married wage earner does not have to live with fears that she will not survive without the marriage; she has an attractive alternative. The Rapoports and Paloma have suggested that the dual-career family of the 1980s may develop very differently from the pattern found in the 1960s and 1970s and include considerably more equality.[45]

Single-Parent Families

The single-parent family is the fastest growing family form in America. Since 1960, the proportion of single-parent families has doubled and is presently growing at two and one-half times the rate of husband-wife families.[46] The divorce rate doubled between 1965 and 1975, and the number of children involved in divorce has tripled since 1953.[47] About 55 percent of all divorces now involve children. In fact, 20 to 30 percent of the children growing up in the 1980s will find their parents divorced. An additional 3 to 5 percent will be affected by a long-term separation, and about 9 percent will lose a parent by death. Two percent will have a never-married mother. Thus, between 34 and 46 percent of all children will spend some time in a single-parent family. In 1974, the number of children living in single-parent homes was about 14.4 percent of all children. So at any one time, approximately one-seventh of all children are living in a single-parent home, and over the period of their childhood approximately one-third to one-half of all children will spend some time in a single-parent family.

Fathers who have custody of their children have become increasingly more common. Single-parent families headed by fathers are now about 10 percent of all single-parent families and amount to 14.5 million fathers rearing 3.5 million children.[48]

How does divorce and single-parent-family status affect the sex-role attitudes and behavior of single parents and their children? We have more information about families headed by women than we do about those headed by men. Brown and her colleagues tell us that women who have less traditional sex-role attitudes adjust more easily to divorce and single-parent status. They are less likely to have invested their identity in the housework role, and they are more likely to be working or to take a job to support themselves and their children.[49]

Special Problems

Single-parent males with custody seldom suffer a debilitating loss of income, but for single custodial mothers, the biggest family burden is usually an economic one. Many single-parent mothers have never worked, have outdated skills from work in the past, or are now working at jobs that have relatively low average incomes. They are subject to all the problems of low income, few fringe benefits, occupational segregation, and discrimination that face all working women. In 1974 the mean family income of male-headed families was $13,788, and of female-headed families, $6,413.[50] Fifty-one and a half percent of children under eighteen years of age in female-headed families and 63 percent of children under six fell below the poverty level. These statistics are particularly high because of the prevalence of divorce and death among poor families, low and irregular levels of alimony and child support, little public assistance, and fewer opportunities for female heads of families to work at all.[51] If these women are not able to make provisions for their children to be cared for by family or friends, they must often pay exorbitant rates for day care.

A recently completed study by Mavis Hetherington and colleagues found that another major problem for both single-parent mothers and fathers is role overload. This is particularly a problem for the single-parent mother, as she is often not able to buy replacement services, like housecleaning help, as most of the fathers are able to do. Custodial mothers have to deal with the tasks normally performed by two parents: earning an income, taking care of a house, having time for children, and doing all the extra errands and maintenance chores that are needed. They are concerned about areas that may be new to them, like insurance, mortgages, taxes, wills, and judging the appropriateness of charges by service people.[52]

In contrast, single-parent fathers with custody found that their major problem was adjusting to household routines and combining the demands of home and work roles. However, most of the fathers had mastered this combination by a year or so after the divorce and felt comfortable in their new roles. They were also more likely than mothers to get household and child-care help from paid employees or from female relatives and friends.[53] A continuing problem for many of the custodial fathers is the problems and needs of adolescent daughters, particularly in the realm of sex education and general sexuality.[54] In general, girls in father-custodial families tend to be less well adjusted than those in mother-custodial families; boys are less well adjusted than girls in mother-custodial families.[55]

The single-parent mother also has to deal with stigma and loneliness. Many of the women found that, while their married friends were supportive for a time, they were later excluded from couples' gatherings. At times they were even viewed with suspicion and fear as a threat to existing marriages. The single-parent mother usually found that she made new friends among other single and divorced people who acted as more of a support system. In most cases, it was difficult for her to get into social situations where she could meet men without intimating that she was encouraging sexual advances; it was often difficult for her to get and to pay baby-sitters so that she could leave for entertainment. Many of these women also felt the loss of identity connected with the ex-husband's status and her status as a wife. Many felt unattractive and rejected.[56]

Fathers without custody reported themselves feeling lost and isolated after divorce, with especially feeling of loss over their children.[57] In the first year after the divorce, many suffered from self-doubt and depression and tried to overcome these problems with frantic dating and social activities. Many tried various forms of self-improvement, such as going on diets or taking courses. Single-parent custodial fathers, though, seemed to suffer less from isolation. The single man with custody is viewed with approval by the community and also has more chance for an active social life. Hetherington describes single-parent fathers as going through a "hip, hirsute, and honda" syndrome, where they put a great emphasis on clothes, often grew beards or long hair, and bought motorcycles and sports cars. These fathers were more likely to keep a support system of married friends because they wished to have companions to do things with when the children visited. Even fathers without custody saw more of their children than they did before the divorce and reported that their relationship with their children had improved.[58] However, poor parenting practices included extreme indulgence with an "every day is Christmas" type of approach to the children. Contact with the children gradually became less frequent among most fathers, although fathers continued to see sons more than daughters.[59] These fathers also seemed less concerned with their adolescent children than with their preadolescents.[60]

In spite of the problems, most single parents of both sexes seemed to feel that they were coping well. In one study, mothers reported themselves as deriving "considerable satisfaction from their successful negotiation of the progression of problems that confronted them as they went about the business of earning a living, caring for their children, and attempting to meet their needs for intimacy and adult interaction."[61] Many mentioned their increased autonomy and independence. There was also a feeling of individual achievement and self-fulfillment on the part of many women.[62]

While some wished to remarry to regularize their positions, others seemed to deemphasize remarriage in their new-found independence. This willingness to stay single seemed to be reinforced by bonds with other single parents. The leveling off of the remarriage rate, especially for women in the higher economic, occupational, and social strata, reflects this new-found autonomy.[63]

Similarly, in many studies single-parent fathers with custody report relative confidence and satisfaction.[64] Levine found these fathers reevaluating their roles in the world; they were independent, self-assured, open-minded, flexible, and supportive of the women's movement.[65] How men are affected by parenting is very important. Travis reports that many men feel the trait of "being able to love" is not highly characteristic of themselves.[66] Yet Keshet and Rosenthal find that men caring for their children often made this caring a major focus in reorganizing their lives.[67] In general, studies report that single parents seem to be forced into less stereotyped behavior. Many of the mothers were forced to assume certain parts of a male parent's role: they had to work at paid employment, be authority figures to their children, and cope with bills, insurance, and household repairs. In a similar way, fathers had to do nurturing, maternal tasks, and household chores.

Sex-Role Attitudes

I wanted to test whether the sex-role attitudes of single parents went along with the more androgynous behavior they were forced into by their single-parent status. The psychological theory of "cognitive consistency" tells us that people come to hold values that support the behavior that they must, of necessity, perform. If this theory is applied to single parents who are doing both masculine- and feminine-stereotyped tasks, it would seem likely that the parent would modify traditional sex roles in a more liberal direction. The process might even become self-reinforcing, my colleagues and I believed. More liberal sex-role attitudes would lead to even less stereotyped masculine and feminine behavior, or more "androgyny."*

We attempted to test whether or not single parents and their children actually did have more liberal sex-role attitudes and less stereotyped behavior. We mailed a sex-role attitudes questionnaire to a random sample of single-parent mothers who had been divorced in Washtenaw County, Michigan, between 1970 and 1976. The questionnaire assessed background information about the mothers' sex-role attitudes and behaviors. Any children in the family also answered a parallel children's questionnaire that had been developed by a child psychologist. We had 134 usable responses to our questionnaire survey, and we also matched fifteen of these mothers to a sample of fifteen custodial fathers and interviewed these thirty single parents in depth to get some idea of differences between male and female single parents.[68] The interview data, of course, are just explanatory and indicative, as the sample size is very small, but the variations we found are provocative.

While both male and female single parents were more liberal than you would expect in the population as a whole, we found that the custodial fathers were generally more conservative than the mothers (they had an average sex-role attitude score of 35.9 compared to the mothers' more liberal score of 30.6). Girls of single-parent fathers were considerably more conservative in their attitudes than girls of single-parent mothers. Boys' scores did not differ markedly no matter who was the custodial parent, but boys were more conservative than girls. The correlations be-

---

*For our purposes here, we are defining *androgyny* as the ability of a person to operate by using both "masculine" and "feminine" stereotyped behavior.

tween the adults' and children's scores show that children do indeed have attitudes similar to those of their custodial parent, and that this similarity is greatly increased when child and parent are of the same sex.[69]

There were some interesting variations between mothers and fathers in the variables that seemed to correlate with more liberal attitudes. Highly educated mothers had the most liberal sex-role attitudes, but income, age, and occupation did not affect attitude. Many of the women who were well educated were unemployed or working at menial occupations.

Fathers with more education had more liberal sex-role attitudes than less educated fathers, although as with the single-parent mothers, occupational status and income level did not seem to affect values. This contradiction may occur with the fathers because the high-ranking occupations among the custodial fathers (those that demanded more education) were split between those that would attract liberal and those that would attract conservative people.

Neither fathers nor mothers were good about translating their attitudes into behavior with their children. Mothers declared themselves as wanting to see nonstereotyped characteristics in their children. They would say that they hoped their boys would be thoughtful and their girls would be independent. (Independence, being her own woman, and self-confidence were characteristics often desired by mothers for their girls.) Fathers desired cross-sex traits in their girls, but seldom were willing to ask for them in their sons.

When it came to putting their desires into concrete action, however, both mothers and fathers were more traditional. They gave their children neutral or traditional toys most (90 percent) of the time. While girls got sports equipment such as ice skates and skis, they did not get footballs, baseball bats, or basketballs. There was only one instance of a boy getting a doll, although some younger boys got stuffed animals. Similarly, parents often gave their children chores that were stereotyped for their sex: boys were more likely to carry out the garbage while girls vacuumed. Although chores tended to be switched around when more than one child was present in a family, older girls often did more housework than older boys.[70] Both boys and girls of custodial mothers and fathers were likely to engage in sports and take lessons of a type usually deemed appropriate for their own sex. (Almost 60 percent of the more "liberal" girls wanted lessons in masculine-stereotyped areas in the future; however, boys wanted traditionally male-stereotyped activities only.)[71]

This study provides tentative reinforcement for our belief that it is easier for girls to engage in cross-sex activity than it is for boys. It also points out that fathers, in particular, are leery about boys departing from masculine stereotypes. In addition, the study indicates that even very liberal parents may not translate their liberal attitudes toward sex roles into action where their children are concerned. Although the single parents themselves may engage in more androgynous behavior and their children may see this as a model, the parents are not directly encouraging such behavior in their children. The single parents in this sample were unconscious of the fact that they were not living up to their own values. If this kind of behavior is true for a very liberal sample of parents, it may give us some indication of how very traditional the sex-role socialization of most children really is.[72]

Effect of Single-Parent Families on Children

What does the literature tell us about the general effect of single-parent families on children's gender identity, sex-role attitudes, and behavior? Drawing conclusions from the studies of single-parent families is very difficult because they vary so much in their definition of what is a single-parent family (separation, death of father or mother, absence of one parent by divorce) and in their methodology and samples.[73] Most of the research has studied custodial mothers and absent fathers. Yet it seems important to look at this research because of the growing number of single-parent families and the concern these parents have about the impact of the family structure on the children.

Basically few general differences seem to be found between children in single-parent and two-parent homes. When differences are found, father absence has usually occurred before the age of five,[74] and such differences are similar to those found in nuclear families with low father availability.[75] Differences that are found between single-parent and two-parent homes seem to be concentrated in certain areas of cognition, self-control, and some kinds of sex-typed behavior. In single-parent families with custodial female parents, both male and female children are likely to show the female pattern of higher verbal than quantitative scores.[76] Hetherington and others have suggested that this is because the children see the verbal skills modeled by women but do not have a similar, mathematically oriented male model to emulate. (One has to believe that males are mathematically oriented and females verbally oriented to accept this explanation.) They also suggest that the anxiety in single-parent homes may repress the problem-solving skills that math requires, and that poor parenting practices after divorce result in the development of less sustained attention.[77]

Studies report that boys in single-parent families headed by mothers show less self-control and more antisocial behavior[78] than boys in two-parent families, although this is not the case for girls.[79] Hetherington and her colleagues suggest that this difference may be accented because boys in two-parent families are less compliant than girls, and children are less compliant to mothers than to fathers. It may also reflect the boys' desire to separate from a feminine parental figure.[80] The divorced mother is also likely to "clamp down" in the period immediately following the divorce, and she is more likely to give her sons threatening commands than her daughters, as well as to give sons less affection and affiliation.[81] It is important to point out that the mother's attitude and behavior seem to be more important than the father's absence in affecting children's behavior.[82]

The effect of single-parent families has also been extensively studied with respect to sex-role preferences and sex-typed behavior of children. Many of these studies emphasize the importance of the father in developing certain sex-typed behaviors in both boys and girls. Some studies find that boys reared by warm, dominant, masculine fathers in nuclear families are more masculine than other boys.[83] Other studies find that girls who receive warmth and high evaluation of feminine behaviors from their fathers are more feminine.[84] In these instances, presence of the father may actually interfere with the development of more androgynous traits in these children.

In father-absent families, there is no difference in sex typing in girls at an early age, but early studies found more dependency in preschool boys from single-parent families than in boys from two-parent families.[85] Adolescent boys show no differences in sex-typed behavior or in sex-role preferences in most studies.[86] In a few, they may show a "compensatory masculinity," where they manifest excessively masculine, assertive forms of behavior at some times and at others show feminine behaviors such as dependency.[87] As a result of her comprehensive and thorough study, Hetherington argued that such compensatory masculinity "is a result of the father-absent boy's attempts to maintain a masculine identification when no masculine role model is present"[88]; yet others have suggested that this is an erroneous assumption, as fatherless boys are not so lacking in role models as is commonly assumed.[89] Adolescent girls from fatherless homes may show some discomfort and either aggression or shyness in sexual interaction with men in later years.[90]

Thus, the studies seem to conclude that early father absence may affect the behavior of young boys and later that of adolescent girls. However, some of the behavior differences seem to be due as much to the custodial mother's attitudes and the behavior occasioned by divorce as they are to father absence.[91] There is some evidence that single-parent mothers may be more restrictive and overprotective.[92] In a longitudinal study, however, Hetherington found that mothers who encouraged independent, mature behaviors and who were warm and nurturing had children who were highly androgynous.[93] Thus, most of the studies show little or no difference between children from single-parent families and from two-parent families. The differences that do occur seem to be due as much to the attitude of the parent(s) as to the structure of the home.

In conclusion, children do not seem to suffer from ill effects in single-parent homes, and most single parents seem to cope relatively well with their situation. Indeed, they may have developed some of the assets of the androgynous person: confidence and a more flexible repertoire of behaviors with which to face the problems of the world. If we can judge from the Michigan study, some single-parent families seem to hold more liberal sex-role attitudes than the population as a whole and model a greater variety of behaviors to their children, although they do not seem to be consciously training them to be more androgynous. Even with all their problems and difficulties, single-parent families may end up being among the vanguard in adopting more liberal sex-role attitudes—and possibly more liberal behavior.

Remarriage

Goode reminds us that the divorced status in our society is not a "regularized one; there are no specific rules and customs relating to divorced persons. They are set aside from the great majority of married couples and their role is not clearly defined."[94] For the single-parent mother, in particular, coping without a partner may be difficult. Thus, there is a push to remarriage: not only does the divorced person find a companion to share work and pleasure, but he or she becomes a member of the couples world again and has a "regularized" position. Therefore, the proportion of marriages that are remarriages has climbed steadily. Between 1969 and 1976 the number of marriages that were remarriages climbed from 23 percent to 31 percent for brides, and from 23 percent to 33 percent for grooms.[95] Approximately one out of five currently married persons has been married before.[96]

One-third of the women who remarry after divorce do so within one year, almost half remarry within two years, and approximately two-thirds remarry within five years. More men remarry, and they remarry a little faster.[97] Those with no or few children remarry faster.[98]

Serious adjustments often have to be made when one remarries. For our purposes here, we will concentrate on the divorced who remarry and on the changes that affect sex-role behavior. The reconstituted family has many problems. Finances are often problematic, with a remarried husband making child support payments to his former family and having less left for his new family. Former husbands may also stop sending child support payments when the wife remarries, and the new family may suffer a lower standard of living. Other problems are also evident. Each spouse comes to the marriage with patterns of behavior that may have been established in the first marriage. If the remarriage includes children, the partners are also faced with the adjustments of dealing with one another's children and frequently with ex-spouses as well. While these children are usually those of a custodial mother, many fathers also have their children present at least some of the time. More than half the fathers in one study had children from a former marriage living with them.[99]

What are the implications of remarriage for sex roles? Because of the financial situation of most remarried couples, it is likely that the wife in a remarriage will continue working. It is also likely that she has worked and supported her single-parent family before the remarriage, although this is not always the case. Her participation in the labor force is thus well established, and it is unlikely that she will be relegated to a domestic role. Her financial contribution means that she is more likely to gain power as the remarried pair makes decisions. Routines facilitating her employment have probably also been established; she is likely to have had some help with housework from children or paid employees, and she is likely to continue to expect to share the burdens of her domestic role. At least two studies have found that remarried men do more household chores than men in first marriages.[100] In the Weingarten study, remarried spouses of ten years or less who have primary responsibility for the housework are twice as likely as first marrieds to report that their spouses often help with the housework. The study suggests that the remarried are more likely than the first married to feel that the work they do in and around the house contributes a great deal to their "most important values"; at the same time men may be less involved with parenting—at least parenting someone else's children. Weingarten reports that remarried men are less likely to report satisfaction with the parenting role.

Children in remarriages have a tremendous effect on the interaction between the spouses, and this may also affect sex roles. Eighty-eight percent of the remarried families with children are raising some combination of natural children and stepchildren.[101] In the majority of remarried households where the children are those of the mother (90 percent), she probably has greater power. It is her routines that have been established, and she has the immediate support of her relatives.

Each parent has probably also become intensely involved with his or her own children during the single-parent phase, and it is difficult for the married pair to build as strong a bond as each parent has with his or her respective children. The old ties challenge the new relationship;[102] each parent and his or her children have a history and memories in which the other parent cannot participate.[103] The conflict is heightened when one partner is experiencing a first marriage and the other a remarriage. It has been said that "the latter tends to understand the limits of romance while the former still clings to certain ideals about love and marriage."

It seems likely, then, that the wife will have more power in the remarried family than in the first-married family. Of course, other factors may erode her bases of power. She may be extremely dependent on the financial contribution of her husband or on his help with her children. She may be placed in the role of stepmother herself, which is conceded to be more difficult than that of stepfather, and she may be an outsider to the unit of her husband and his children.

There has recently been a small decline in the remarriage rate, attributed by some to the greater likelihood that divorced people will cohabit and not remarry. Glick and Norton predict, however, that this decline will only reduce the proportion who remarry from 80 percent to perhaps 75 percent.[104] Remarriage, with its attendant opportunities and problems, will thus remain an important part of our family system.

Blue-Collar Families

The working class, which comprises at least two-fifths of American workers, has a lifestyle and sex-role interaction that differ in many ways from the middle-class norms for the "ideal family" of the American dream. Who are these working-class families? Miller and Reisman define them as "regular members of the nonagricultural labor force in manual occupations."[105] Eshleman refines the description by saying that the men in these families not only have manual skills, but they earn wages by the hour and are dependent on swings of the business cycle for their employment. Most have little formal education beyond high school, and many of their wives work.[106] The working class is distinguished from the lower class by the steadiness of their employment and their relatively stable family lives; they are distinguished from the lower middle class by the fact that the working class is largely comprised of skilled and semi-skilled manual workers, while the lower middle class includes lower white-collar workers such as clerical and sales workers.[107] However, there is some overlap between these two groups, and some working-class people move up into the lower middle class.

Some writers have suggested that a working-class lifestyle doesn't exist, as many of these families have good incomes that they spend on middle-class consumer goods like campers and boats.[108] Others argue that the affluent, happy working-class family is a myth. They point out that the working-class level of life includes an element of insecurity that is seldom found in the groups above. The central goal of life for people in this class is to create a secure place for self and family; ill health and unemployment frighten them, as they have little chance to move to other jobs.[109] The insecurity leads to an emphasis on traditional values that extends through the political scene into the sex roles in the home.

Let us look at the life cycle of these blue-collar men and women and see where their lives differ from those of the middle class. Several excellent books have been written describing the blue-collar way of life, including Rainwater, Coleman, and Handel's *Workingman's Wife*,[110] Komarovsky's *Blue-Collar Marriage*,[111] and Rubin's *Worlds of Pain*.[112] The title of Rubin's book seems to describe accurately the life of these working-class couples. Most marry young. Life in the parental home is hard, with poverty and often drunkenness and violence. Forty percent of those interviewed in Rubin's survey had at least one alcoholic parent.[113] Parents try to keep control by restricting the behavior of their growing daughters, and the daughters try to escape from that control. Marriage is seen as liberation,[114] as a way of getting out of the family home and having one's own home and family. For the male, it is seen as a confirmation of his adult status.[115]

Most couples marry sooner than they expect—usually because the girl is pregnant; in 44 percent of the couples studied by Rubin, the girl was pregnant before marriage.[116] Ninety-two percent of the men and 65 percent of the women had had premarital sex, and few had regularly used contraceptives, so the pregnancy rate is not surprising. In this group there is a definite split in views of the sexual nature of good girls and bad girls. Only "bad girls" plan to have a sexual life and use contraceptives; thus, many girls get pregnant. The prevailing norm for the men is that if you get a girl pregnant, you marry her. Almost no one considers not getting married or having an abortion.[117] They are not stopped by religious scruples, but they simply say that it is "not a choice," or "it never occurred to me."

Special Problems

The early years of marriage are particularly difficult for these young couples. The men, who are just out of high school or who may not have finished high school, have insecure jobs and little money.[118] In fact, they often move from job to job in the early years, trying to find work with meaning and dignity as well as good wages.[119] Many hold eight or ten jobs in six years. The women, who are still in their teens, frequently have several children in quick succession. Both feel the heavy duty and responsibility of providing for a family. Although they wanted to get married, they feel tied down and regret having lost the fun of the premarriage years. They are also faced with the problem of making very little income go a long way; the couple frequently have to live with in-laws because they cannot afford a place of their own.[120]

The problems they face are exaggerated by several factors. Both spouses are very close to their mothers and spend a great deal of time phoning and visiting them. The ties of the husbands to the mothers frequently hurt the marital relationship.[121] One wife tells of a stormy first year of marriage. No sooner did they marry, she says, than "he started going out with his four buddies every night, just as if he was still single. Sometimes if he drank too much he would go to his mother's house to sleep and not come home at all." [122]

The women are frustrated and angry that the men leave them alone to cope with the house and kids while they are out having fun with their friends. The men, who feel tied down, maintain their male status by going out with the boys and not being a henpecked husband. Thus, each spouse maintains close ties to his or her family of origin and to a same-sex friendship group. The woman has less freedom to do things with her girlfriends, but she often visits with them at length on the phone and in person. While Komarovsky says that the clique of friends is a group where the spouses can complain and thus drain off resentments about their mates, the clique also serves to draw the couple apart. [123] Although recent studies have found that women have been tolerating fewer absences by their husbands. [124]

Friendship and Sex

The couple expect separateness to some extent; they do not believe that marriage is for friendship. [125] The couple's families push them into conforming to traditional segregated roles. [126] They counsel the wife to have patience, that the husband will settle down; they counsel the husband to take more interest in his wife and children. In the meantime, the spouses do little together. Leisure hours are usually spent watching television, or the husband may be busy on do-it-yourself projects around the house or cooperating with his buddies in fixing up a car. Weekends are frequently spent visiting with one or the other's family, [127] where the men will watch a ball game and the women will talk. [128]

The following excerpts from Lillian Rubin's *Worlds of Pain* give an insight into the interaction between husband and wife.

> Frank comes home from work; now it's about five, because he's been working overtime every night. We eat right away, right after he comes home. Then, I don't know. The kids play a while before bed, watch TV, you know, stuff like that. Then, I don't know . . . maybe watch more TV or something like that. I don't know what else—nothing, I guess. We just sit, that's all.
>
> The husband: I come home at five and we supper right away. Then, I sit down with coffee and a beer and watch TV. After that, if I'm working on a project I do that for a little while. If not, I just watch TV. [129]

It is seldom that the couple go out together by themselves. They may take the children with them to the bowling alley on Friday night, or they may occasionally invite other couples over for cards and some beer, but nights out on the town or middle-class dinner parties are almost unknown. [130]

Sexual communication in the blue-collar family has usually been at a minimum. Traditional inhibitions have made sex interests and repertoire limited until recently. Spouses in the traditional blue-collar marriage have seldom discussed their feelings or desire:

> One wife says, "Experimental? Oh, he's much more experimental than I am. Once in a while I'll say, 'Okay, you get a treat; we'll do it with the lights on.' And I put the pillow over my head."[131]

Parenthetically, an interesting element of this quote is the way it suggests the degree to which sexuality can be used as a vehicle for power negotiations. Women who are not in the paid work force are often left with little other base of power. This kind of sexual negotiation can, of course, have long-term negative effects on marital communication and satisfaction.

With the recent emphasis on sex in the media and the proliferation of sexual manuals, there has been pressure on the blue-collar couple to change their ways. The men are interested in more variety in their sexual lives and press their wives to try new kinds of sexual behavior.[132] Yet the hangover from the good-girl/bad-girl tradition inhibits many wives from enjoying the new sexuality. Many wives particularly resist oral sex and are worried that their husbands will think they are cheap if they engage in such activities. One wife says:

> Sometimes I enjoy it, I guess. But most of the time I'm too worried thinking about whether I ought to be doing it and worrying what he's really thinking to get much pleasure.[133]

Some husbands reassure them, but others show their own ambivalence about the new sexual standards. One husband commented as follows when asked whether he and his wife practiced oral sex:

> No, Alice isn't that kind of girl. . . . She wasn't brought up to go for all that fancy stuff. . . . There's plenty of women out there to do that kind of stuff with. You can meet them in any bar any time you want to. You don't have to marry that kind.[134]

Yet in spite of this attitude, there is change, and greater mutuality in sex appears to occur between the more modern blue-collar spouses who are isolated from the traditional pressures of relatives.[135]

Women's Work and Men's Work

There is little disagreement in the blue-collar family about what is men's work and what is women's work. The women expect the men to provide a decent living for their families, and if the men are underemployed or unemployed, the women show their resentment.[136] Both men and women agree that a man's life is easier than a woman's, especially when the woman works.[137] This is because it is the "woman's job" to do everything in the house: cleaning, cooking, child care, and even bill paying. She also is likely to do a large portion of the yard work as well. The husband seldom gives regular assistance, although he will "help out" if asked by the wife. Men with high-school educations or better are more likely to help with some shopping and infant care.[138] For the most part, however, the home is considered the woman's job by both sexes. When one woman was asked if she would change places with her husband, she replied:

> I guess I wouldn't like to change places with him because I couldn't support the family like he does. . . . On the other hand, that's all men have to do. I don't mean it's easy, but it's all they do. We—women, I mean—have a lot more to do and worry about all the time. I guess what it boils down to is that the man does the harder physical work, but the woman does the harder emotional work.[139]

Another woman (mother of three, married seven years) said:

> The man's life is a lot easier; there's no doubt about it. He gets up in the morning; he gets dressed; he goes to work; he comes home in the evening; and he does what he wants after that.
> As for me, I get up in the morning; I get dressed; I fix everybody's breakfast; I clean up the kitchen; I get the children ready for school and the baby ready to go to his babysitter; I take him to the babysitter. Then I go to work. I work all day; I pick up the baby; I fix dinner; I do the dishes; I clean up; I get the kids ready for bed. After the kids are finally asleep, I get to worry about the money because I pay all the bills. . . .[140]

Komarovsky and Rubin point out that the working-class wife—especially the one who does not work outside the home—may not feel as much pressure as the middle-class wife. While she does not have money or time to pursue interests and leisure-time activities, there is also no pressure on her to be a gourmet cook, to have read the latest books, and to be a charming hostess or even an interesting companion in a wide range of activities.[141] The working-class wife is not a joiner of organizations. The PTA gets the biggest working-class membership. Few women or men belong to "fraternal" organizations or clubs, and few attend church regularly.[142]

By the middle years, the couples compromise more and show greater acceptance of their roles. The men settle down and like marriage[143] and do not go out with their male buddies as often. The wives have often accepted their lot with more or less resignation. They rationalize that they could have it worse and say about their husbands, "I guess I shouldn't complain; he's a steady worker, he doesn't drink, and he doesn't hit me."[144] However, these wives feel discontent with the emotional aspects of their marriage and with the constant workload.

They want more communication from their husbands,[145] but there is little about which these couples can communicate. Rubin says, "Despite the yearning for more, relations between husband and wife are benumbed, filled with silence; life seems empty and meaningless; laughter, humor, fun is not a part of the daily ration." She quotes a couple married seven years. The wife says:

> There's plenty of time [to talk], we just don't do it. He doesn't ever think there's anything to talk about. I'm the one who has to nag him to talk and then I get disgusted.

He says:

> I'm pretty tight-lipped about most things most of the time. . . . Sometimes I'm not even sure what she wants me to be telling her. And when she gets all upset and emotional, I don't know what to say or what to do.[146]

To provide the extras—and sometimes the necessities—many of the wives "help out" by working. In Rubin's study, 58 percent of the wives worked outside the home, most in part-time jobs.[147] This work outside the home gets mixed reactions from both husbands and wives. Of the women who stay at home, most are glad to do so. They believe that the jobs they could get would be dull, and they don't want the double load of housework and paid employment. On the other hand, those who do work like the sociability and feelings of competence that it gives them. One worker pointed out that a paycheck is "a way to tell how successful you are."[148] Myra Feree's study of 135 working-class wives whose last children were in school and who thus were free to work also showed that wives in the paid labor force were happier. Almost twice as many housewives as employed wives said they were dissatisfied with their lives.[149] Feree points out that satisfaction with the housewife role in particular may have deteriorated, as more and more working-class families move away from relatives and the women become isolated in the home. The housewives who had social support groups and who felt appreciated for their contribution (25 percent of the total) enjoyed their role. In contrast, the full-time workers had a hard time combining roles: 33 percent felt inadequate at handling both home and work roles.[150]

Blue-collar husbands vary in their attitude toward their wives' work. In most of the research, husbands complained that working wives were getting too independent and said that they weren't "feminine" enough.[151] As compensation, the husbands tended to assert their authority in very direct ways, and the wives complained that their husbands would not "let them do things."[152] The men also made most of the decisions. The women decided whether to buy the children shoes or what to have for dinner, but the men made the big decisions about cars, houses, and jobs.[153] Although some researchers have thought that blue-collar women have power in the family because they pay the bills, these women actually have little chance to make decisions; they simply do the bill-paying chores.[154] In evaluating the more obvious dominance of the husband in the blue-collar home, Rubin suggests that the working-class man needs to assert himself in obvious, direct ways because he does not have the indirect authority of the middle-class man that stems from higher education, job status, and income security.[155]

Changes in Blue-Collar Families

Some blue-collar families seem to be shifting away from highly segregated conjugal relations. About one-third of the families surveyed in the Rainwater, Coleman, and Handel study said that the husband participated more in the family, particularly in involvement with the children.[156] These couples are often ones who have moved away from relatives and are thrown on each other for social resources. There is also a new attitude toward the children in the working-class families. The parents want to spend more time with the children and to give them the good things that they never had.[157] Rainwater points out, however, that the parents are not really socializing their children to grow up differently; they are still stressing conformity to external standards, orderliness, neatness, and obedience, instead of the more white-collar emphasis on individuality, initiative, and creativity.[158]

The father is likely to teach the child physical toughness, aggression, and fear of him,[159] and while the wife is nominally more lenient, she actually does a lot of the disciplining.[160] Rubin reports that fathers heavily emphasize masculine roles for their boys and that during many interviews there were fathers who would ridicule sons and call them "sissy" if they cried. Male children, as a result, are very emotionally controlled at an early age.[161] The father is unlikely to change his behavior, she points out, and as there are few norms in this class that would push him to change, both younger and older males would still be looked upon as odd if they were expressive.[162]

Among working-class women there is little support for the women's movement. They believe in equal pay but do not believe that any woman should get a job if a man needs it. They see the movement as "putting down" housewives, and they feel alienated from most of its goals. While they would like to talk to other women about their discontent with their lives and their marriages, they are afraid to do so for fear they would be considered "women's libbers."[163] They know they are discontented with their lives, but they do not see the women's movement as articulating their discontent.

Thus in the middle class, the division between the sexes is rigidly defined, whether as parents, workers, or lovers. The roles are more rigid than we would usually find in the middle class. Yet there is pressure for change toward more liberal sex-role behavior in the blue-collar family as families move away from relatives and the media teach them to expect more companionship, affection, and sex. Any real modification of sex-role behavior, however, will probably depend on an extended period of prosperity and security for the working class.

Black Families

> The dynamics of black family life are not identical to those of the white family, but there are many similarities. The black family does not seem to operate in unique ways.[164]

Writing about "the black family" is very difficult because there is no one black family any more than there is one white family. The literature reflects this confusion. Some studies deal with the black middle class[165] and others deal with ghetto socialization.[166] Between these two extremes, however, there is a working-class family that can be described and compared to the white working-class family.

Even the description of the black working-class family is fraught with difficulty because of biases in the research about the black family. Some have viewed the unique dynamics of the black family as culturally deviant. In the well-known Moynihan report, *The Negro Family: The Case for National Action*, Moynihan argued that the black family "matriarchal structure" was so out of line with dominant family norms in America that it retarded the progress of blacks as a group.[167] Moynihan stated that the family "serves to perpetuate the cycle of poverty and deprivation,"[168] and Fraiser said that the disorganization of family life and the lack of stability affects the Negro child.[169] Bernard mentions crowding in black families as dysfunctional. All these authors tend to emphasize the problems of a "black matriarchy" and the resulting emasculation of the black male.[170]

Other researchers have suggested that black family characteristics come from a unique American heritage, that the black family is thus a cultural variant of the white American family,[171] and that the unique structures and styles of the black family have evolved to perform survival functions.[172] The implication of this last approach is that the special cultural adaptations of the black family, rather than being structures that cause disorganization and weaknesses, are positive, functional adaptations to a racist society. Among these strengths and adaptations are mentioned strong kinship bonds, a strong work and achievement orientation, a positive orientation toward religion, and the adaptability of family roles, all resulting in equalitarian roles rather than in matriarchy.[173] Many recent studies have adopted this positive perspective and have used quantitative analysis to illustrate that black families are stable, equalitarian, and functional units.[174] The studies have particularly attempted to refute earlier charges of a dysfunctional matriarchal structure.

Demographic Approaches to Black Families

With these perspectives in mind, let us look at some of the recent information about particular characteristics of the black family. Certain *demographic* characteristics of black families deserve note. In 1973, black family income was only 58 percent of white family income (a $7,269 median for black families compared to a $12,595 median for white families). Twenty-nine percent of black families, but only 7 percent of white families, were living below the poverty line of $4,275.[175] Black life expectancy was also shorter than that for whites. Black males could expect to live 6.1 years less than the 67.6-year life expectancy of white males, and black females had a life expectancy of 66.5 years compared to white female life expectancy of 74.2 years. Infant mortality rates were also twice as high among blacks. Black families are more likely to live in substandard housing and crowded urban areas where crime prevails. Thus, many black families start out with some specific disadvantages.[176]

Other demographic characteristics that are related include an older age at marriage, lower rates of marriage and remarriage, and larger family size.[177] While the majority of black families have both spouses present, there are more female-headed black families than female-headed white families. In 1975, 61 percent of the 5.5 million black families in the country had both spouses present, compared to 87 percent of the 49.4 million white families.[178] Thirty-four percent of black and 10 percent of white families had a female head. There was a sharp drop in husband-wife families among blacks, from 74 percent in 1960 to 61 percent in 1975, with the more difficult economic conditions of that time.[179]

Marriage is approached with ambivalence by many young blacks.[180] It is sometimes difficult for the young black woman to find a man to marry; there were only 87 black men for every 100 black women of marriageable age in 1975. Higher infant mortality rates among black male infants and higher accident rates and victims-of-crime rates among young black males account for much of this difference. Black males are also more likely than black females to marry outside their race.[181] Rainwater points out that for the woman in the lower-class family, marriage may mean giving up a familiar and comfortable home that places few restrictions on her behavior (in contrast to the white working-class home) to marry a man who may not be a good provider. The woman may be reluctant to be tied down by a man she feels is not worth the restrictions. He may be reluctant to take on the role of provider, particularly if he feels that he will not be able to fulfill it well.[182] We must remember that young black males have one of the highest unemployment rates of any group in the United States. Thus, many young blacks postpone marriage. When they do marry at a later age, it is often an impulsive decision and there may be only a tentative commitment to the marriage.[183]

Partially as a result of this ambivalence, illegitimacy rates have risen; in 1979 half of all black births occurred out of wedlock.[184] Heterosexual relationships tend to develop at an earlier age among black teenagers, and sexual expression is more acceptable in the black subculture.[185] The reaction to premarital pregnancy is seldom a resort to abortion or marriage. It is expensive for the young black woman to have an abortion, and federal funding is no longer available in most areas; she may also see little sense in marrying a young black male who has no job and little chance to support a family. Children are seen as a positive good, and having a child is a mark of adult female status.[186] Little real stigma is connected with illegitimacy, and the pregnant girl's mother and extended family system will probably help her care for her child.[187]

Some in the black community also believe that practicing any form of birth control is a form of genocide. In one study of 159 households in a medium-sized New England city, 20 percent of the black females and 47 percent of the black males under 30 agreed with the statement, "Encouraging blacks to use birth control is comparable to trying to eliminate this group from society."[188] While this point of view may seem extreme, Staples points out that government concern over the size of black families has (not so accidentally) coincided with the growing numbers of blacks in urban areas who upset the political balance.[189]

Fertility among young black women at every age level is higher than that of whites. In 1973, black women had 2.8 children per woman ever married, compared to 2.2 among white women. Fertility varies with social status, however; the more education a woman has and the higher social class she is in, the fewer children she is likely to have. College-educated black women have fewer children than college-educated white women.[190] In the black middle class, marriages with one or no children are very common. However, because of higher overall fertility, more blacks live in large families: 56 percent of urban nonwhites live in families of six or more, compared to 36 percent of urban whites.[191]

The Extended Family: Support System or Deterrent to Upward Mobility?

Although approximately 75 percent of black families are nuclear in form (including a single parent with children), approximately 25 percent can be classified as extended, or including relatives other than just husband, wife, and children living with the family.[192] The definition of "extended family" may be used rather loosely among some researchers; many seem to define an extended family as a kinship network, whether or not members of this network all live in the same household. Eugene Litwak coined the term "modified extended family" to represent patterns of networks that develop among nonkin nuclear families. If we use this latter definition, many extended families can be found in higher socioeconomic groups as well as in the lower class.[193]

The importance of this extended family system is one of the unique elements of the black family.[194] Researchers suggest that many in the black community could not survive without such helpful ties. Martin says:

> The economic interdependency of family members is a main element of the extended family structure. Many have no choice but to depend on relatives for economic assistance. Others maintain a stance of economic dependency out of habit or to ensure that aid will be available if they need it. The built-in mutual aid system in black extended families . . . is a major survival component. Without this mechanism, the extended family structure would be jeopardized.[195]

There is no doubt as to the prevalence of these extended-help networks in the black community. Scanzoni's 1971 study showed that although a large majority of working-class respondents were raised in a nuclear family, one-third had received task-oriented help and two-thirds had received expressive help from other relatives.[196] Staples states that 48 percent of elderly black women have related children living with them.[197] Stack found that such an extended kin network often operated through a core of women and that it offset family economic strains.[198] Several researchers have documented the existence of such cultural systems of help, even when finances are more secure.[199] The degree of mutual aid depends on the degree of kin relationship and the distance between members, but reciprocal obligations are always implied.[200]

While researchers agree that the extended family is a survival mechanism for poor blacks, they are divided on whether or not such ties hurt upward mobility.[201] McQueen and Stack seem to think that the extended kin network is such a drain on the resources of the upwardly mobile that they have to cut themselves off from great involvement in it to move upward.[202] Such isolation does not necessarily exclude casual visiting or joint holiday celebrations, support of aged parents, or occasional help, but it does mean separation from meeting the everyday needs of many relatives.[203] Heiss, however, believes that upwardly mobile families keep their kin ties even after gaining more secure status.[204] McAdoo says that the "extended family pattern is not just a structural coping tactic, but has evolved into a strong and valuable cultural pattern,"[205] although Heiss points out that middle-class families who are not close to kin do not seem to suffer for it.[206]

Black Men and Women in the Paid Labor Force

Staples has pointed out the irony for working-class black men of a culture that values high masculine achievement orientation and job success and an economic situation that allows them very little chance of success. It is difficult for them to fulfill the provider role in the family when they are subject to periodic unemployment and low wages even when they do have jobs. He points out that some of these men deal with the painful dilemma by abdicating the role and leaving home.[207] Both Staples and Cazenave assert that the fathers who are not beset by economic difficulties play viable, important roles in their families.[208] According to Staples, "the black father is not simply a shadowy figure who provides . . . [children] with money or metes out punishment. He is a frame of reference, the person in general most respected and admired, and the most likely to be emulated by the children."[209]

Cazenave also emphasizes that while employment may be problematical for many working-class black men, the provider role is still very important in their lives and in their concept of masculinity. He examined a sample of middle-income letter carriers in New Orleans and discovered that these men saw the provider role as their most important one (47 percent), with husband next important (28 percent), and father after that (22 percent). They also felt that the most important part of the *father* role was being the economic provider. Cazenave believes that for these men, the provider role was not emphasized in and of itself, as in the case of cultural norms for masculine job success. Rather the role was emphasized as a means to an end: a way to carry out father and husband roles. He hypothesized that as socioeconomic conditions improved in these families, the black men would put more emphasis on husband and father roles.[210] He confirmed these findings on a sample of black men who were in professional, white-collar jobs. Husband was chosen as the most important role by the married men in this sample (34.5 percent), the provider role was second with 31 percent, and the father role last with 19 percent.[211]

He points out, however, that black men in all social classes had certain traits in common that do not fit neatly into the cultural stereotype of masculinity. Black men put an emphasis on success and achievement, but they also are high on certain expressive dimensions like being warm and being gentle. In addition, they are likely to emphasize the value of certain other characteristics that are related to racial discrimination and prejudice, such as "stands up for beliefs" and "fights to protect family."[212]

Another characteristic of the black family is that the wife is more likely to be employed.[213] In 1970, 59 percent of black wives were employed and were likely to work even when the husband's income was good. Black middle-class wives are more likely to work than white middle-class wives, and some have suggested that their income is necessary to keep the black family in the middle class.[214] Both black wives and black husbands seem to assume that the wife will work. Black men seem to have a less stereotyped view of the female sex role than white males;[215] they believe their wives have the knowledge and competency to hold a job.[216] Being a good provider is seen as an essential part of the mother as well as the father role,[217] and black women believe they can combine employment and good relations with children.[218] Black women also believe that their men want them to work.[219]

This high degree of maternal employment has many implications for black families and their sex roles. Harrison and Minor quote a study in which black children report that they see both parents as fulfilling instrumental (provider) and expressive functions.[220] In a similar fashion, McAdoo reports shared child rearing and decision making by black husbands and wives when the wives are working.[221] Others, however, have declared that the employment of black women has led to a matriarchy.[222]

The Black Matriarchy: Myth or Reality?

In the 1950s, Blood and Wolfe reported that 19 percent of the black families in their survey of families in Detroit were husband dominated, 38 percent were equalitarian, and 43 percent were wife dominated.[223] Aldous and Centers, Raven, and Rodrigues also found more wife-dominant families among blacks than among whites, although the differences were small.[224] These studies, however, had methodological problems and are outdated. More recent studies have found equal percentages of wife-dominant relationships in black and white families.[225] Some show greater power for the black male in the majority of relationships.[226] The discrepancy seems to lie in the difference between working-class and middle-class families and in the definition of what is wife dominant or matriarchal. Authors have tended to lump female-headed households and female-dominated households together. It is impossible to get any real measure of the strength of male and female dominance if one includes families where a female is dominant by default because of the absence of a male. Dietrich has also pointed out the inadequacy of decision-making measures like Blood and Wolfe's questionnaire for lower-class families. Her research has found much more equal sharing of decision making in these families.[227]

Most researchers agree that employment of black women has been the reason for greater equalitarianism in black marriages. Scanzoni points out that because of economic constraints, black women could work where black men often could not. This resulted in an alteration of traditional division of labor over the decades: wife employment behavior has become more institutionalized in black society, and black families have "come to value its rewards and accept its costs. . . ."[228] Staples points out that black families have been characterized by role flexibility, as females have worked outside the home and males have assisted in household tasks and child rearing.[229] In a midwestern sample that included 25 percent blacks, black women saw themselves as more capable than white women saw themselves, and black men and women both saw themselves as more nurturant *and* more instrumental than white men and women saw themselves.[230]

The pattern of dominance may vary in black families according to social class and also possibly according to age, geographic region, and social context.[231] Rainwater emphasizes the matrifocality of the lower-class black family and says that the wife makes most of the decisions that keep the family going and has the greater sense of responsibility to the family.[232] This description agrees with Tenhouten's findings that both white and black lower-socioeconomic groups *believed* that the mother should dominate parental roles.[233] Yet even in this study, *ideology seems to contrast with actual observed behavior.* Tenhouten asked the two oldest children in the families to describe the power relationships that they saw. Two-thirds of the cases described neither the mother nor the father as having more power, but remembered them as negotiating their differences. In only 2 to 4 percent of the cases was the mother seen as dominant.[234] Staples also emphasizes that even in the lower class, wives are not dominant matriarchs but share family decision making with their husbands.[235] Others agree that the relationship between husband and wife in lower-class black families may be the most equalitarian of all. Middleton and Putney studied forty families: ten white middle class, ten black middle class, ten white working class, and ten black working class. The families were classified as patriarchal, matriarchal, or equalitarian according to the way they responded to a questionnaire asking how they made decisions.[236] Middleton and Putney found that middle-class blacks were far more equal in their decision-making processes than lower- or upper-class groups.[237]

The dominance of one or the other spouse is probably a function of the partners' resources.[238] In black working-class families, black women make a substantial contribution and gain power, which both they and their mates believe they should have. The Waller and Hill principle that the person with the least interest in the situation has the most power probably also operates here. These women have little to lose if their marriages break up: their husbands may not be good providers, and the women can return to the extended family nest.[239] Black women are also likely to have had educations that equal or exceed those of their husbands and so can probably get equal or better jobs. In the black middle class, the wife is likely to be working at a rewarding job and to have limited the number of children she has. Norms for equality in this class also support her position.

However, in spite of generally equalitarian husband-wife relationships, maternal control over most family matters is probably greater in all socioeconomic black groups than in similar white classes.[240] Heiss did a recent study that assessed who had control in the family by asking questions like, "When you did something wrong, who punished you?" "Who kept track of family money?" "Thinking back now, who do you think made the important decisions in the family when you were a child?" and found maternal dominance in all these areas in all blacks families.[241] However, he points out that this situation does not seem to have the detrimental effect on black males that some have assumed. Both families with maternal and those with paternal control produced males who achieved the same grades and the same years of schooling.[242]

Division of Labor

In a parallel to white families, division of labor in the black family is not as equalitarian as decision making. Findings differ on whether black husbands do more child care and housework than white husbands. Blood and Wolfe found that black men did slightly less housework than white husbands.[243] Another study in the late 1960s showed no difference in the participation of black and white husbands in housework,[244] and a third study in 1976 showed that black men did slightly more housework than white husbands, although neither did more housework just because their wives worked.[245] Although in other research black men were seen to be more expressive and more involved in child rearing than white men,[246] the 1976 study showed that they spent approximately fifteen minutes a day in child care, compared to nineteen minutes for white men.[247]

Another comparison of black and white families found very little difference in the interaction of black and white fathers with their children and in the goals they held for them. White fathers emphasized the importance of helping with homework; black fathers tended to emphasize the importance of providing their children with money and training them athletically. However, black fathers seemed to be somewhat more expressive in interacting with their children and seemed to enjoy them more.[248] As Cazenave points out, this expressiveness increases as the men have better incomes, can concentrate less on the provider role, and have more time for expressive parental activities. Even the low-income respondents, however, spent more time with their children and thought of themselves as closer to their families than their fathers had been. They reported that they played more with babies, were more involved in child care activities such as baby-sitting, and helped more with homework than their fathers had done.[249]

Companionship and the Black Marriage

The black family parallels the white working-class family in the degree of conjugal role segregation. In the lower class, the husband and wife tend to think of themselves as having very separate kinds of functioning in the family organization. As long as the husband fulfills his provider role, he does not expect to do much around the house; conversely, if he is unemployed, his wife may not do much for him. Separate incomes earned by wife and husband are treated as separate money, and both sexes seem to have an equal but separate right to peer group activity outside the home and are also likely to engage in separate activities.[250] Heiss states, "It appears that the norm of togetherness is not universally accepted in the black community and its absence does not cause much in the way of dissatisfaction."[251] Komarovsky similarly reports a dearth of joint activities inside or outside the family and suggests that it is not just a lack of enabling income that keeps these activities from taking place, but a real difference in values.[252] The values seem to support such segregation, whether or not the family is involved with a connected network of kin that may drain their resources away from one another.[253] There is also some tentative indication that little verbal communication takes place between black spouses.

Marital Satisfaction

Blacks frequently report dissatisfaction with their marriages. Whether this is a matter of lack of companionship and interaction or a matter of economic variables is an important question. Certainly satisfaction varies by sex and social class. Women and high-status men give more value to shared activities in their concept of a good marriage.[254] Scanzoni finds black men are more content than black women, and that lower-status black men in particular seem quite content with a system of very separate marital roles.[255] Still other literature traces marital satisfaction to economic variables and finds marital tensions among lower-class husbands and wives because of economic strain.[256] Seventy-five percent of one male sample said they never wanted to get married.[257] In his study of lower-class black males, Liebow found similar disenchantment with the institution,[258] and Blood and Wolfe found that 63 percent of their female sample would not marry if they had it to do over.[259]

In sum, we need to stress again the great class variation in black families. In most black families, however, although women contribute more income to the family and power is somewhat more equally shared between husband and wife than in white families, traditional division of labor is still evident. Women do almost all the housework and the great bulk of the child care. Their burden does not seem to be relieved by much companionship with or emotional support from their spouses. Men are still the main providers in most black families;[260] they believe that being providers and training their sons in athletic prowess (and perhaps in ghetto survival) are their most important functions.[261] Men may be more expressive toward their children, but this expressiveness does not seem to carry over into general adult roles.[262] While a matriarchy is not evident, the black woman has achieved a degree of equality by taking care of herself and claiming her social and sexual rights.

The Violent Family

The Epitome of Male Dominance: Wife Abuse

The first time Frank hit me, I was three months pregnant . . . that was the first indication of his tremendous jealousy.

There were times when I didn't dare go shopping for groceries; *I felt like a prisoner in my own home.* I was afraid of his accusations and abuse when I got back.

(These words were spoken by an abused wife, Martha, as she recalled the shoving, punching, kicking, and choking she had received from her husband.)[263]

Something that is never mentioned when we talk about the ideal family of the American dream is violence in the family; yet the statistical data on interspousal violence indicate that the problem has reached epidemic proportions in our nation. According to a study for the U.S. Civil Rights Commission in 1978, an estimated 1.8 million women are abused each year. Many estimate that the number is twice that, and other estimates say that 50 percent of all women will be battered at some time in their lives.[264] The statistics on husbands abused by their wives are more difficult to ascertain. Gelles reports that men were more likely to admit abuse than women but that they were seldom hurt by the abuse of wives.[265] They were also likely to be abused—or murdered—by wives who were defending themselves.[266] (Women are seven times more likely to murder in self-defense than men are.) While husband abuse may well occur more than is realized, we will confine ourselves here to talking about wife abuse because of its implications for sex roles.

Wife abuse may be the epitome of male power and female submissiveness. Because of a long cultural history of women being considered men's property and men having power over them, many men feel they have the "right" to abuse their wives and many women are socialized to submit to such abuse. Laws and the economic situation for women perpetuate the dominance of men and make it difficult for women to escape the abusing situation. Married women may have few economic resources and may be totally dependent on their husbands for support. Others contend that being a married woman makes women feel powerless; many women are taught that their effectiveness and creativity don't count—only their beauty and ability to appeal to men do. Such women may develop a "learned helplessness" as a result of their general dependency and low self-esteem.[267]

With that background, let us look at some of the myths about wife abuse. Contrary to popular belief, few who use violence in the family can be considered mentally ill.[268] Family violence also occurs in all social classes, although it is probably more prevalent in the working class. In one study of applicants for divorce, 23 percent of middle-class couples and 40 percent of working-class couples gave physical abuse as a major complaint.[269] Violence is not usually provoked by a major trauma; in a family with a cycle of violence, any minor incident can provoke it.[270] However, certain variables are connected with the use of violence. One in four women are hit when pregnant,[271] alcohol is connected with 50 percent of the batterings,[272] and it is likely that hard economic times with high unemployment provoke the use of violence.[273]

Abusers are often persons who were abused themselves as children and who use violence in other parts of their lives.[274] Many have suggested that when wives are abused, the husbands are sadistic and the women are masochistic—that is, they like being beaten; but this idea is not borne out by the facts. Martin points out that women may have to tolerate violence, but they don't enjoy it.[275] Other myths that protect the wife abuser are that the wife must have done something to deserve the violence and that arguments between husband and wife are a family matter and not to be interfered with by friends, neighbors, or the legal system. The fact that many women do not report their abuse or leave home after they are beaten makes many of these myths seem legitimate.

Legal, Economic, and Social Systems Ecouraging Abuse

Many times, women do not report abuse, or they escape from it, because the legal, social, and economic systems fail to support them when they do report it. Police hate to respond to domestic disturbance calls. Almost 25 percent of police fatalities occur in these situations, some when a wife—afraid of her husband's anger—turns on the policeman.[276] Yet a study in Kansas City shows how necessary police response is. Forty percent of the city's homicides were found to be cases of spouse killing spouse. In more than 85 percent of these homicides, the police had been summoned once before the murder, and in 50 percent of the cases the police had been called to quell disturbances five or more times within the two-year period before the homicide.[277]

Officers are usually directed by their superiors to avoid making arrests in domestic disputes except in cases where a person is severely injured. In many cases, they cannot make an arrest unless there is a witness to the abuse or unless the injuries are extremely obvious and severe. Even then, only one in about a hundred cases finally goes to court,[278] and women are often threatened by their husbands with injury or death if they prosecute. By the time any case does get to court, the wife's injuries have usually healed, there is no witness, and beliefs about family arguments being private matters prevail. If the wife has the knowledge and money to get a restraining order (they often cost $75 and are issued during nine-to-five office hours, not when the wife may need it), she is still not protected. If the husband violates the order and beats his estranged wife, he is usually only cited for contempt of court. To even get the order, the wife usually has to show that she has initiated divorce proceedings.[279]

The social and economic systems may also have failed women so that they cannot leave abusing husbands. They may have no job or economic resources of their own and no safe shelter to go to. They are often threatened with injury or death if they leave. The self-esteem of many of these women has eroded, and they have developed a sense of helplessness that tells them they cannot cope with the outside world. Frequently, marriage counselors or others tell them that they should stay with their husbands and try to work things out.[280]

In her book *The Battered Woman*, Walker describes the cycle of family violence that makes it difficult for the wife to leave home. There is usually a three-stage cycle of violence, she says. It starts with a tension-building stage in which the wife accepts the husband's criticisms (she *did* burn dinner) and unconsciously reinforces his aggressions. He fears his behavior will make her leave, so he becomes oppressive and jealous. It is usual to have verbal harangues and psychological humiliation during this phase. The second, or "explosion," phase follows, where the man batters his wife when he loses control. He wants to "teach his wife a lesson" and often does not realize the harm he has done. If the wife resists, she is often hurt more; arms raised in defense get broken. Phase three is calm and loving: the batterer tries to make up with his wife and may profusely apologize. He is afraid she will leave him and pleads that he needs her and promises reform. Such behavior makes it very difficult for the wife to leave, especially when she is ambivalent about such departure anyway.[281] Women who do leave may find themselves drawn back to their husbands because they can't cope on their own.[282] If they stay or return, they reinforce their husband's behavior so that it is likely to occur again and to escalate in level of violence. If she stays, the wife may eventually be killed or may kill her oppressor.[283]

Thus, it is vitally important that women be able to escape from an abusive situation; even if the escape is only a temporary one, the wife's negotiating from strength and refusal to go back shows the husband that his behavior will not be tolerated. The most urgent need is for shelters for these battered wives. A decade ago, when Erin Pizzey wrote *Scream Quietly or the Neighbors Will Hear*,[284] little attention was paid to the problem of wife-beating, and there were few places a wife could go in an emergency. But by the late 1970s there were 300 shelters nationwide, and even more crisis hotlines.[285] Each shelter was filled almost as soon as it was opened,[286] and hotlines were overloaded. Fort Worth, Texas, had to install a social worker to handle the wife-beating calls, which were coming in at a rate of over 400 a month. All but five states have enacted new legislation (minimal, however) to deal with wife abuse, and courts in thirty-four states can issue orders to restrain batterers.[287] Still this is not nearly enough: one-third of all the women seeking refuge are turned away because there is not enough room for them.[288] Neither do women have the economic resources to see them through a period of adjustment and job retraining. Yet the U.S. House of Representatives defeated the Domestic Violence Assistance Act in May of 1978, which would have provided $16 million in aid for shelters, counseling, and job training for battered women. As Gelles has pointed out, we spend billions in military defense and in fighting crime, but we will not spend $16 million to protect a large number of our citizens.[289]

Similarly, legal remedies are not effective if they are not enforced; the infrequent citations for violating restraining orders are not enough to stop men from abusing their wives and estranged wives. Yet if women cannot stop abuse or escape from it, they risk severe injury and even death as the violence escalates.[290] It is also likely that children in the home will be abused and that these children will grow up to be wife and child abusers.[291] Those who deal with wife abuse say it is imperative that there be immediate public and private funding to provide shelters and job retraining at a minimum. Beyond the immediate, however, they also point out that we must rethink some of our basic societal assumptions about the power relationship of women and men and about the toleration of all kinds of violence in this society.[292]

Summary

In this chapter we have seen that the variety of family forms and behavior is far greater than the homogeneity implied in most discussions of the American family. This variety is likely to increase as fertility continues to decline, as women enter the work force in greater numbers, and as the percentage of those divorcing and remarrying remains high. It is also likely that ethnic families will continue their greater fertility and increase their numbers by birth or through migration to the United States.

Many of these variations in family form or behavior (dual-career families and black families, to mention two) may be closer or moving closer to some of the ideals of the American dream than white middle-class families have actually been before. The companionship and sharing of the "symmetrical family" described by Young and Willmott[293] is more of a reality today in most homes than it has ever been. There are important implications for sex-role behavior as the spouses in these varied family forms share tasks and responsibilities. Husbands and wives not only learn to do work that was previously stereotyped for "the other sex," but they probably experience many of the emotions that go along with such behavior. Children are exposed to parental models of both sexes who are both instrumental and expressive. The varied family forms that have developed and grown seem to hold forth the promise of more androgynous behavior in the future.

Essay Questions

1. Do childless couples plan their childlessness before marriage or do they drift into it? How do childless marriages compare to marriages with children in terms of power, division of labor, and marital satisfaction?

2. How would you image power relationships in dual-career families would differ from those in which the wife was a homemaker or worked at a part-time job to which she was not committed? How do you suppose the various styles of interaction between the spouses (accommodation, equal sharing, and the like) would relate to power in the family?

3. How do sex-role attitudes in single-parent families seem to differ from those in two-parent families? Is the behavior of the single parent consistent with his or her attitude?

4. From the indications of the Michigan study, do custodial single-parent fathers have different sex-role attitudes and behavior than custodial single-parent mothers? How do the attitudes and behavior of girls and boys of custodial fathers and mothers vary?

5. How does remarriage affect the sex-role attitudes of the single-parent? How do you think power relationships would develop in a family where the mother was a single parent for six years, has teen-aged children, and has just remarried a man of moderate income who has no children of his own?

6. Why don't abused wives leave their husbands? (You should deal with both cultural beliefs and economic realities in your answer.) What happens when they stay with their husbands? What do you think would be the most urgent need in changing the cycle of violence?

7. Describe the interaction between couples in the blue-collar marriage. Why is it said that the working-class marriage is characterized by separateness of roles and lack of communication? What role do the families of the spouses play in sustaining their children's marriage?

8. Discuss whether or not you believe that the black extended family is a deterrent to upward mobility for its members. What evidence can you give to support the fact that it may or may not be such a deterrent?

9. Is "black matriarchy" a myth or a reality? Discuss the variation in power relationships in black families as they vary by social class. Does the division of labor in the black family reflect the fact that it is a "matriarchy"?

10. Compare the role of women in white working-class and black working-class families. How are their attitudes similar or how do they differ toward marriage, sex, work, interaction with parents, and child rearing?

Exercises

1. Discuss whether or not you want to have any children when you marry. If you are a woman, do you think that having children would affect your career success or your relationship with your husband? If you are a man, discuss the same issues. Compare the answers of men and women in the class and comment on any differences.

2. Assume you are a partner in a dual-career marriage. The wife in this marriage has an offer to move to a new job in another city a thousand miles away. The move will mean doubling her salary and a chance at increased upward mobility; she may never again get such an opportunity. If the husband moved with her, he would have to give up his present job as a university professor and try to find another one in a new city. (There are several universities there, but the job market for university professors is very tight.) Do you think that the couple should make the move? Should she move without him? How would you resolve the issue?

3. Assume you are a single parent who believes in more liberal sex roles. How would you organize your household and your behavior toward your children so that you would be teaching them liberal

sex-role attitudes and letting them practice nontraditional sex-role behavior? What would you do if the children wanted to do traditional
things or if their friends laughed at them for nontraditional behavior
and told them they were "odd"?

4.   Assume you are a single-parent mother who is remarrying a man
with a thirteen-year-old daughter and an eleven-year-old son. His
children live with his ex-wife, but your children, two girls who are
ten and twelve, live with you. What problems do you foresee in the
remarriage? In what ways might your sex-role attitudes and behavior
change and how might you transmit them to your children? (Hint:
little behaviors like letting the man drive the car when you are going
out may show children a great deal.)

5.   You know from talking to a woman in your class that she is being
abused by her husband. He is a middle-class business executive, and
she says he is really very nice and only hits her when he has been
drinking. One day she comes to class with a broken arm and very
bad bruises all over her body and tells you that her husband beat her
up the night before. What advice would you give her? (She has three
small children and no income of her own.)

6.   Imagine that you are a spouse in a white working-class marriage. Describe your feelings about marriage, work, talking to your spouse,
and raising your children. What are your plans for the evening and
for a vacation this year? (If you are male, describe feelings from the
husband's point of view; if you are female, describe feelings from the
wife's point of view.)

7.   One researcher has said, "The working class tends to cling to the
concepts of masculinity and femininity as a way of being more normal." The individual tends to perceive others as being more successful (proving masculinity or femininity), and this perception reinforces
the belief that the "system" is right and the individual is somehow
deficient. It is difficult for the individual—especially the working-
class man—to change perceptions because of the barriers of privacy,
especially when moving slightly up the social ladder. Therefore, rigid
definitions of traditional masculinity and femininity tend to get reinforced. Does this apply to every group? If not, why does it apply
more to the working class?

8.   Imagine that you are a black working-class wife who has two young
children. You work as a sales clerk while your mother takes care of
the children. Your husband, who is an electrician's apprentice, is unemployed because of the economic recession. He wants to move to
the sunbelt, where he can find work. What kind of interaction would
you have with your husband and your family in making the decision
about whether or not to go? Do you think you would decide to move?

Notes

1. Jessie Bernard, *The Future of Marriage* (New York: World, 1972); Eleanore B. Luckey and Joyce K. Bain, "Children, a Factor in Marital Satisfaction," *Journal of Marriage and the Family* 32 (1970):430–44; Robert G. Ryder, "Longitudinal Data Relating Marriage Satisfaction and Having a Child," *Journal of Marriage and the Family* 35 (1973):605–06.

2. Jean Veevers, "Voluntary Childless Wives: An Exploratory Study," *Sociology and Social Research* 57 (1973):356–66.

3. *Ibid.*

4. Veevers, *op. cit.*; Ellen M. Nason and Margaret M. Paloma, *Voluntary Childless Couples: The Emergence of a Variant Lifestyle* (Beverly Hills, Calif.: Sage, 1976).

5. Sharon K. Houseknecht, "Reference Group Support for Voluntary Childlessness: Evidence for Conformity," *Journal of Marriage and the Family* 38 (1977):285–92; Houseknecht, "Voluntary Childlessness," *Alternative Lifestyles* 1, no. 3 (1978):379–402.

6. Linda Silka and Sara Kiesler, "Couples Who Choose to Remain Childless," *Family Planning Perspectives* 9 (1977):16–25.

7. Sharon Houseknecht, "Childlessness and Marital Adjustment," *Journal of Marriage and the Family* 41 (1979):259–65.

8. Paul C. Glick, "Updating the Life Cycle of the Family," *Journal of Marriage and the Family* 39 (1977):5–13; Ira Reiss, *Family Systems in America*, 3rd ed. (New York: Holt, Rinehart, and Winston, 1980), p. 358.

9. Veevers, *op. cit.*; Judith Blake, "Is Zero Preferred? American Attitude Toward Childlessness in the 1970's," *Journal of Marriage and the Family* 41 (1979):245–57.

10. Blake, *op. cit.*

11. U.S. Bureau of the Census, "Crude Birth Rate of the White and Black Population: 10-Year Averages, 1860–1870, and 5-Year Averages to 1970–1974," no. 70–3 (Washington, D.C.: Government Printing Office, 1978), p. 23.

12. Margaret Paloma, Brian Pendleton, and T. Neal Garland, "Reconsidering the Dual-Career Marriage," *Journal of Family Issues* 2, no. 2 (1981):205–24.

13. T.W. Martin, B.J. Berry, and R.B. Jacobsen, "The Impact of Dual-Career Marriages on Female Careers: An Empirical Test of a Parsonian Hypothesis," *Journal of Marriage and the Family* 37 (1975):734–42; R.J. Simon, "The Woman Ph.D.: A Recent Profile," *Social Problems* 15 (1967):221–336.

14. Paloma, Pendleton, and Garland, *op. cit.*, pp. 214–15.

15. *Ibid.*

16. *Ibid.*, p. 217.

17. *Ibid.*, pp. 206–08.

18. Lynda Lytle Holstrum, *The Two-Career Family* (Cambridge, Mass.: Schenkman, 1972), p. 17.

19. *Ibid.*, pp. 33–35.

20. *Ibid.*, p. 40.
21. Bam Dee Sharda and Barry Nangle, "Marital Effects on Occupational Attainment," *Journal of Family Issues* 2, no. 2 (1981):148–63.
22. Paloma, Pendleton, and Garland, *op. cit.*
23. *Ibid.*, pp. 55–56.
24. Joseph Pleck, "The Work-Family Role System," *Social Problems* 24, no. 19 (1976):417–24.
25. Holstrum, *op. cit.*, pp. 88–89.
26. *Ibid.*, pp. 96–97.
27. Ida Simpson and Paula England, "Conjugal Work Roles and Marital Solidarity," *Journal of Family Issues* 2, no. 2 (1981):180–204.
28. *Ibid.*, pp. 68–71.
29. *Ibid.*, p. 74.
30. Suzanne Model, "Housework by Husbands," *Journal of Family Issues* 2, no. 2 (1981):225–37.
31. Lotte Bailyn, "Accommodation of Work to Family," in Arlene Skolnick and Jerome Skolnick, eds., *Family in Transition*, 3rd ed. (Boston: Little, Brown, 1980).
32. *Ibid.*
33. Paloma, Pendleton, and Garland, *op. cit.*
34. Bailyn, *op. cit.*, pp. 571–72.
35. Carol C. Nadelson and Theodore Nadelson, "Dual Career Marriages: Benefits and Costs," in Fran Pepitone-Rockewell, ed., *Dual Career Couples* (Beverly Hills, Calif.: Sage, 1980), pp. 91–110.
36. Bailyn, *op. cit.*, p. 577.
37. Rhona Rapoport and Robert Rapoport, "Three Generations of Dual-Career Family Research," in Pepitone-Rockewell, *op. cit.*, pp. 23–48.
38. *Ibid.*
39. Simpson and England, *op. cit.*
40. Simpson and England, *op. cit.*; Holstrum, *op. cit.*, p. 44.
41. *Ibid.*
42. *Ibid.*, p. 137.
43. *Ibid.*, pp. 105–06.
44. Nadelson and Nadelson, *op. cit.*, pp. 21–110; Holstrum, *op. cit.*, pp. 162–67; Bailyn, *op. cit.*, p. 568.
45. Rhona Rapoport and Robert Rapoport, *Dual-Career Families Re-examined* (New York: Martin Robertson/Harper & Row, 1976); Paloma, Pendleton, and Garland, *op. cit.*, p. 220.
46. Heather Ross and Isabel Sawhill, *Time of Transition: The Growth of Families Headed by Women* (Washington, D.C.: Urban Institute, 1975).
47. A.J. Norton and P.C. Glick, "Marital Instability: Past, Present, and Future," *Journal of Social Issues* 32 (1976):1.

48. U.S. Bureau of the Census, "Marital Status and Living Arrangements: March 1974," *Current Population Reports,* series P–20, no. 271 (Washington, D.C.: U.S. Government Printing Office, 1974), in Mary Jo Bane, "Marital Disruption and the Lives of Children," *Journal of Social Issues* 32, no. 1 (1976):105.

49. Prudence Brown, Lorraine Perry, and Ernest Harburg, "Sex Role Attitudes and Psychological Outcomes for Black and White Women Experiencing Marital Dissolution," *Journal of Marriage and the Family* 39, no. 3 (1977):549.

50. Bane, *op. cit.,* p. 111.

51. *Ibid.,* p. 112.

52. E. Mavis Hetherington, Martha Cox, and Roger Cox, "Stress and Coping in Divorce: A Focus on Women" (Paper presented at the Michigan Council on Family Relations meetings, October 1978).

53. *Ibid.;* Marie Richmond-Abbott, "Sex Role Norms and Behaviors in Single Parent Families" (Paper presented at the National Council on Family Relations Conference, Portland, Oregon, October 1980).

54. H.A. Mendes, "Single Fathers," *The Family Coordinator* 25 (1976):439–40; Dennis Orthner, Terry Brown, and Dennis Ferguson, "Single-Parent Fatherhood: An Emerging Life Style," *The Family Coordinator* 25 (1976):429–38.

55. E. Ferri, "Characteristics of Motherless Families," *British Journal of Social Work* 3 (1973):91–100; V. George and P. Wilding, *Motherless Families* (London: Routledge-Kegan Paul, 1979); G.B. Spanier and R.F. Castro, "Adjustment to Separation and Divorce: An Analysis of 50 Case Studies," *Journal of Divorce* 2 (1979):241 and 253.

56. Hetherington, Cox, and Cox, *op. cit.*

57. Mavis Hetherington, "Effects of Father Absence on Personality Development in Adolescent Daughters," *Developmental Psychology* 7 (1972):313–325.

58. *Ibid.,* p. 25.

59. R.D. Hess and R.A. Camara, "Post-Divorce Family Relations as Mediating Factors in the Consequences of Divorce for Children," *Journal of Social Issues* 35, no. 3 (1979):79–87.

60. Mendes, *op. cit.*

61. Ellen Lewin, Medical Anthropology Program, University of California, San Francisco, "Single Mothers and Their Families: A New Tradition of Matrifocality" (Paper presented at the AAA meeting, Cincinnati, Ohio, December 1979).

62. W.J. Goode, *Women in Divorce* (New York: Free Press, 1956).

63. Jean Lipman-Blumen, "The Implications for Family Structure of Changing Sex Roles," *Social Casework* 57 (1976):67–79.

64. Orthner, Brown, and Ferguson, *op. cit.*

65. D. Levine, "Redefining the Childcare 'Problems'; Men as Child Nurturers," *Childhood Education,* November/December 1977, pp. 55–61.

66. C. Travis, "Men and Women Report Their Views on Masculinity," *Psychology Today* 10 (1977):34–43.

67. Harry F. Keshet and K.M. Rosenthal, "Fathering after Marital Separation," *Social Work* 23 (1978):313–320.

68. Richmond-Abbott, *op. cit.*
69. *Ibid.*
70. *Ibid.*
71. *Ibid.*
72. *Ibid.*
73. Elizabeth Herzog and Cecelia E. Sudia, "Fatherless Homes: A Review of Research," *Children* 15, no. 5 (1968):73–81.
74. M. Deutsch and B. Brown, "Social Influences in Negro-White Intelligence Differences," *Journal of Social Issues* 20 (1964):24–35; A.H. Rees and F.H. Palmer, "Factors Related to Change in Mental Test Performance," *Developmental Psychology Monograph* 3 (1970):1–57.
75. E.M. Hetherington, M. Cox, and R. Cox, "The Impact of Divorce on Children: A Longitudinal Study" (Unpublished paper, 1978); R.W. Blanchard and H.B. Biller, "Father Availability and Academic Performance among Third Grade Boys," *Developmental Psychology* 4 (1971):301–05; Alexander Rosin and James Teague, "Case Studies," *Psychological Reports* 34 (1974):971–83.
76. L. Carlsmith, "Effect of Early Father Absence on Scholastic Aptitude," *Harvard Educational Review* 34 (1964):3–21; H.P. Oshman, "Some Effects of Father Absence upon the Psychological Development of Male and Female Late Adolescents: Theoretical and Empirical Considerations," (Ph.D. diss. University of Texas at Austin, 1975), *Dissertation Abstracts International* 36 (1975):919B–920B, University Microfilms, no. 75–16, 719.
77. Hetherington, Cox, and Cox, "Stress and Coping in Divorce" *op. cit.*, p. 13.
78. *Ibid.*, p. 25.
79. E.M. Hetherington, M. Cox, and R. Cox, "The Aftermath of Divorce," in J.H. Stevens, Jr., and Marilyn Matthews, eds., *Mother-Child, Father-Child Relations* (Washington, D.C.: NaEYC, 1977); M. Rutter, "Parent-Child Separation: Psychological Effects on the Children," *Journal of Child Psychology and Psychiatry* 12 (1971):233–60; J. Tuckman and R.A. Regan, "Intactness of the Home and Behavioral Problems in Children," *Journal of Child Psychology and Psychiatry* 7 (1966):225–33.
80. Hetherington, "Children and Divorce," p. 28 of draft presented at American Psychological Asso. Meeting, New York, Sept., 1979; later published in R. Henderson, ed., *Parent-Child Interaction: Theory, Research and Prospect* (New York: Academic Press, 1980).
81. *Ibid.*, p. 29.
82. *Ibid.*
83. H.B. Biller and L.J. Borstelmann, "Masculine Development: An Integrative Review," *Merrill-Palmer Quarterly* 13 (1967):253–94; E.M. Hetherington, "The Effects of Familial Variables on Sex-Typing, on Parent-Child Similarity, and on Imitation in Children," *Minnesota Symposium on Child Psychology* 1 (1967):82–107.
84. P.H. Mussen and E.E. Rutherford, "Parent-Child Relationships and Parental Personality in Relation to Young Children's Sex-Role Preferences," *Child Development* 34 (1963):589–607; R. Sears, L. Rau; and R. Alpert, *Iden-*

tification and Child Rearing (Stanford, Calif.: Stanford University Press, 1965).

85. J.W. Santrock, "Relation of Type and Onset of Father Absence to Cognitive Development," *Child Development* 43 (1972):455–69.

86. A.G. Barclay and D. Cusumano, "Father Absence, Cross-Sex Identity, and Field-Dependent Behavior in Male Adolescents," *Child Development* 38 (1967):243–50; Biller and R.N. Bahm, "Father-Absence, Perceived Maternal Behavior, and Masculinity of Self-Concept among Junior High School Boys," *Developmental Psychology* 4 (1971):178–81.

87. Hetherington, *op. cit.*, p. 16.

88. Hetherington, *op. cit.*, p. 16.

89. Herzog and Sudia, *op. cit.*, p. 181.

90. E. Mavis Hetherington, "Effects of Father Absence on Personality Development in Adolescent Daughters," *op. cit.*, p. 28.

91. Hetherington, 1972, *Ibid.*, pp. 24–25.

92. Hetherington, Cox and Cox, "The Aftermath of Divorce," *op. cit.*

93. E.M. Hetherington, R. Cox, and M. Cox, "The Development of Children in Mother-Headed Families" (Paper presented at Conference on Families in Contemporary America, George Washington University, June 11, 1977), p. 18.

94. William Goode, *After Divorce* (Glencoe, Ill.: Free Press, 1956).

95. Paul Glick, "Remarriage: Some Recent Change and Variations," *Journal of Family Issues* 1, no. 4 (1980):457.

96. Lucille Duberman, *Marriage and Its Alternatives* (New York: Praeger, 1977).

97. Paul H. Jacobson, *American Marriage and Divorce* (New York: Holt, Rinehart and Winston, 1959), pp. 69–70.

98. Glick, *op. cit.*, p. 468.

99. Leslie Westoff, *The Second Time Around* (New York: Viking, 1977), p. 73.

100. Weingarten, *op. cit.*

101. *Ibid.*, p. 552.

102. G.L. Schulman, "Myths That Intrude on the Adaptation of the Stepfamily," *Social Casework* 49 (1972):131–39.

103. M. McGoldrich and E. Carter, "Forming a Remarried Family," in E. Carter and M. McGoldrich, eds., *The Family Life Cycle: A Framework for Family Therapy* (New York: Gardner Press, 1980); Jamie Kesket, "From Separation to Stepfamily: A System Analysis," *Journal of Family Issues* 1, no. 4 (1980):517–32.

104. Paul C. Glick and Arthur J. Norton, "Marrying, Divorcing, and Living Together in the U.S. Today," *Population Bulletin* 32 (1977):1–39.

105. S.M. Miller and Frank Reisman, "The Working Class Subculture: A New View," in Arthur Skostak, ed., *Blue Collar World* (Englewood Cliffs, N.J.: Prentice-Hall, 1964).

106. J. Ross Eshleman, *The Family: An Introduction* (Boston: Allyn and Bacon, 1974).

107. Helen Hacker, "Class and Race Differences in Gender Roles," in L. Duberman, ed., *Gender and Sex in Society* (New York: Praeger, 1975), pp. 134–83.

108. Lee Rainwater, "Some Aspects of Lower-Class Sexual Behavior," *Journal of Social Issues* 22 (1966):98–108.

109. Lee Rainwater, Richard Coleman, and Gerald Handel, *Workingman's Wife* (New York: Oceana Publicationa, 1959).

110. *Ibid.*, p. 219.

111. Mirra Komarovsky, *Blue-Collar Marriage* (New York: Random House, 1964).

112. Lillian Rubin, *Worlds of Pain* (New York: Basic Books, 1976).

113. *Ibid.*, p. 38.

114. *Ibid.*, p. 26.

115. Komarovsky, *op. cit.*, p. 130.

116. Rubin, *op. cit.*, p. 60.

117. *Ibid.*, pp. 66–67.

118. *Ibid.*, pp. 76–77.

119. *Ibid.*, p. 155.

120. Komarovsky, *op. cit.*, p. 100.

121. Rubin, *op. cit.*, p. 17.

122. Komarovsky, *op. cit.*, p. 29.

123. *Ibid.*, p. 44.

124. Rubin, *op. cit.*, p. 196.

125. Komarovsky, *op. cit.*, p. 127.

126. *Ibid.*, p. 39.

127. Rainwater, Coleman, and Handel, *op. cit.*, p. 210.

128. Rubin, *op. cit.*, p. 186.

129. *Ibid.*, p. 124.

130. *Ibid.*

131. Lillian Rubin, "Blue-Collar Marriage and the Sexual Revolution," in Arlene Skolnick and Jerome Skolnick, eds., *The Family in Transition*, 3rd ed. (Boston: Little, Brown, 1980), p. 160.

132. *Ibid.*

133. *Ibid.*, p. 165.

134. *Ibid.*, p. 166.

135. Rainwater, Coleman, and Handel, *op. cit.*, pp. 72–73.

136. Rubin, *op. cit.*, p. 91.

137. *Ibid.*

138. Komarovsky, *op. cit.*, pp. 54–56.

139. Rubin, *op. cit.*, p. 106.

140. *Ibid.*, p. 101.

141. Komarovsky, *op. cit.*, p. 59.

142. Shostak, *op. cit.*, p. 46; Rubin, *op. cit.*, p. 201.

143. *Ibid.*, p. 95.

144. Rubin, *op. cit.*, p. 94.

145. *Ibid.*, p. 116.

146. *Ibid.*, p. 124.

147. *Ibid.*, p. 167.

148. *Ibid.*

149. Myra Marx Feree, "The Confused American Housewife," *Psychology Today*, September, 1976, pp. 87–93; M. Feree, "Working Class Jobs: Housework and Paid Work as Sources of Satisfaction," *Social Problems*, 23 (1975):431–41.

150. Feree, *op. cit.*, p. 89.

151. Rubin, *op. cit.*, p. 176.

152. *Ibid.*, p. 97.

153. *Ibid.*, p. 112.

154. Shostak, *op. cit.*, p. 104.

155. Rubin, *op. cit.*, p. 97.

156. Rainwater, Coleman, and Handel, *op. cit.*, p. 72.

157. *Ibid.*, p. 212.

158. Victor Gecas and Ivan Nye, "Sex and Class Differences in Parent-Child Interactions: A Test of Kohn's Hypothesis," *Journal of Marriage and the Family* 36, no. 4 (1974):742–49; Melvin Kohn, *Class and Conformity* (Homewood, Ill.: Dorsey Press, 1969).

159. Shostak, *op. cit.*, p. 110.

160. Komarovsky, *op. cit.*, p. 73.

161. Rubin, *op. cit.*, p. 126.

162. *Ibid.*; Rainwater, Coleman, and Handel, *op. cit.*, p. 221.

163. Rubin, *op. cit.*, p. 130.

164. Jerome Heiss, *The Case of the Black Family* (New York: Columbia University Press, 1975).

165. Franklin Fraiser, *The Negro Family in the U.S.* (New York: Dryden Press, 1966); Fraiser, "Black Bourgeoisie," in Robert Staples, ed., *The Black Family: Essays and Studies* (Belmont, Calif.: Wadsworth, 1971).

166. Lee Rainwater, "The Crucible of Identity: The Negro Lower-Class Family," *Daedalus* 95 (1966):172–216; David A. Schulz, *Coming Up Black* (Englewood Cliffs, N.J.: Prentice-Hall, 1969).

167. Daniel Moynihan, *The Negro Family: The Case for National Action* (Washington, D.C.: Office of Policy Planning and Research, U.S. Dept of Labor, 1965).

168. *Ibid.*, p. 30.

169. Fraiser, *The Negro in the United States* (New York: McMillan, 1957), p. 636.

170. Jessie Bernard, *Marriage and Family among Negroes* (Englewood Cliffs, N.J.: Prentice-Hall, 1968), p. 130.

171. Robert Staples and Alfredo Mirande, "Racial and Cultural Variations

among American Families: A Decennial Review of the Literature on Minority Families," *Journal of Marriage and the Family,* 42 (1980):887–901.

172. J. Allen Williams and Robert Stockton, "Black Families Structures and Functions: An Empirical Examination of Some Suggestions Made by Billingsly," *Journal of Marriage and the Family,* 35 (1973):39–57.

173. Albert McQueen, "Adaptations of Black Urban Families," quoting Robert Hill, "Strengths of Black Families," in David Reiss and Howard Hoffman, eds., *The American Family* (New York: Plenus Press, 1979), p. 84.

174. Heiss, *op. cit.;* John Scanzoni, *The Black Family* (Boston: Allyn and Bacon, 1971).

175. William Kerkel, *The Family in Perspective* (Santa Monica, Calif.: Goodyear, 1977), p. 369.

176. *Ibid.*

177. McQueen, *op. cit.,* p. 86.

178. U.S. Bureau of the Census, 1975, quoted in Diane Holland Painter, "Black Women and the Family," in Jane Chapman and Margaret Gates, eds., *Women into Wives,* (Beverly Hills, Calif.: Sage, 1977), p. 107.

179. McQueen, *op. cit.,* p. 87.

180. Staples and Mirande, *op. cit.,* p. 891.

181. Jacquelyne Jackson, "But Where Are All the Men?" in Robert Chrisman and Nathan Hare, eds., *Contemporary Black Thought* (Indianapolis: Bobbs-Merrill, 1973), pp. 158–76.

182. Lee Rainwater, "Husband-Wife Relations," in Robert Staples ed., *The Black Family: Essays and Studies* (Belmont, Calif.: Wadsworth, 1971), pp. 251–55.

183. *Ibid.*

184. Staples and Mirande, *op. cit.,* p. 891.

185. Staples, *Introduction to Black Sociology* (New York: McGraw Hill, 1976), pp. 128–133.

186. McQueen, *op. cit.,* p. 87.

187. Kerkel, *op. cit.,* p. 378.

188. Kerkel, *op. cit.,* p. 377; Elmer Martin and Joanne Martin, *The Black Extended Family* (Chicago: University of Chicago Press, 1978).

189. Fraiser in Staples, ed. *The Black Family: Essays & Studies, op. cit.,* p. 184.

190. U.S. Bureau of the Census, Population Reports (Washington, D.C. Government Printing Office, 1973). 1973, tables 17 and 18; as quoted in Heiss, *op. cit.,* p. 15.

191. Heiss, *op. cit.,* p. 16.

192. Eugene Litwak, "Occupational Mobility and Extended Family Cohesion," *American Sociological Review* 25 (1960):9–21.

193. Staples, *op. cit.,* pp. 125–36.

194. Heiss, *op. cit.,* p. 22.

195. Martin, *op. cit.,* p. 29.
196. Scanzoni study quoted in Harriette Pipes McAdoo, "Factors Relations to Stability in Upwardly Mobile Black Families," *Journal of Marriage and the Family* 4, no. 4 (1978):762.
197. Staples, *Introduction to Black Sociology* (New York: McGraw-Hill, 1976), pp. 125–36.
198. Carol Stack, *All Our Kin* (New York: Harper & Row, 1974).
199. H.G. Guttman, *The Black Family in Slavery and Freedom, 1750–1925* (New York: Pantheon Press, 1976).
200. B. Yorburg, *The Changing Family* (New York: Columbia University Press, 1973).
201. McAdoo, *op. cit.,* p. 763.
202. McQueen, *op. cit.;* Stack, *op. cit.*
203. McAdoo, *op. cit.,* p. 764.
204. Heiss, *op. cit.,* p. 122.
205. McAdoo, *op. cit.,* p. 775.
206. Heiss, *op. cit.,* p. 124.
207. Robert Staples, "Masculinity and Race: The Dual Dilemma of Black Men," *Journal of Social Issues* 34, no. 1 (1978):169–83.
208. *Ibid.;* Noel Cazenave, "Middle-Income Fathers: An Analysis of the Provider Role," *The Family Coordinator,* 28 (1979):583–93.
209. Staples, "Masculinity and Race . . ." *op. cit.,* p. 178.
210. Cazenave, *op. cit.*
211. Noel Cazenave, "Race, Socio-Economic Status and Age: The Social Context of Masculinity" (Paper presented at the National Institute of Child Health and Human Development Conference on Gender Role Research, Bethesda, Md., September 1981).
212. *Ibid.,* p. 12.
213. Algea Harrison and Joanne Minor, "Interrole Conflict, Coping Strategies, and Satisfaction among Black Working Wives," *Journal of Marriage and the Family,* 40 (1978):799–805.
214. Bart Landry and Margaret Jendrik, "The Employment of Wives in Middle-Class Black Families," *Journal of Marriage and the Family,* 40 (1978):787.
215. Virginia O'Leary and Algea O. Harrison, "Sex-Role Stereotypes as a Function of Race and Sex" (Paper presented at the 83rd Annual APA Meeting, Chicago, August 1975).
216. John Scanzoni, "Sex Roles, Economic Factors, and Marital Solidarity in Black and White Marriages," *Journal of Marriage and the Family* 37 (1975):130–44.
217. Lena Myers, "Black Women: Selectivity among Roles and Reference Groups in the Maintenance of Self-Esteem," *Journal of Social and Behavioral Sciences* 21 (1975):39–47.
218. Harrison and Minor, *op. cit.*
219. J. Leland Axelson, "The Working Wife: Differences in Perception among

Negro and White Males," *Journal of Marriage and the Family*, 36 (1970):457–64; Barbara F. Turner and JoAnne MacCaffrey, "Socialization and Career Orientation among Black and White College Women," *Journal of Vocational Behavior* 5 (1974):307–19.

220. Joyce Beckett, "Working Wives: A Racial Comparison," *Social Work* 21 (1976):463–71.

221. McAdoo, *op. cit.*, p. 775.

222. R. Blood and D. Wolfe, "Negro-White Differences in Blue Collar Marriages in a Northern Metropolis," *Social Forces* 48 (1969):59–64.

223. *Ibid.*

224. Joan Aldous, "Wives Employment Status and Lower-Class Men as Husbands-Fathers: Support for the Moynihan Thesis," *Journal of Marriage and the Family* 31 (1969):469–76; Richard Centers, Bertram Raven, and Aroido Rodrigues, "Conjugal Power Structure: A Re-examination," *The American Sociological Review* 36 (1971):264–78.

225. Delores Mack, "Where the Black Matriarchy Theorists Went Wrong," *Psychology Today* 4 (1971):24; Robert Blood and Donald Wolfe, "The Power Relationship in Black Families and White Families," in Robert Staples, ed., *The Black Family: Essays and Studies* (Belmont, Calif.: Wadsworth, 1978); Warren D. Tenhouten, "The Black Family: Myth and Reality," *Psychiatry* 23 (1970):145–73.

226. Earl Baughman, *Black Americans* (New York: Academic Press, 1971).

227. Katheryn T. Dietrich, "A Re-examination of the Myth of Black Matriarchy," *Journal of Marriage and the Family* 37 (1975):367–74.

228. John Scanzoni, "Sex Roles, Economic Factors, and Marital Solidarity in Black and White Marriages," *Journal of Marriage and the Family*, 37 (1975):130.

229. Staples, *Introduction to Black Sociology, op. cit.*, pp. 125–26.

230. Scanzoni, "Black and White Marriages," p. 135.

231. Charles Willie and Susan Greenblatt, "Four 'Classic' Studies of Power Relationships: A Review and Look to the Future," *Journal of Marriage and the Family* 40 (1978):691–96.

232. Lee Rainwater, "Husband-Wife Relations," in Staples, *The Black Family*, p. 165.

233. Tenhouten, *op. cit.*,

234. *Ibid.*

235. Staples, *Introduction to Black Sociology*, p. 126.

236. Charles V. Willie, *A New Look at Black Families* (Bayside, N.Y.: General Hall, 1976).

237. Russell Middleton and Snell Putney, "Dominance in Decisions in the Family: Race and Class Differences," in C.V. Willie, ed., *The Family Life of Black People* (Columbus, Ohio: Charles E. Merrill, 1970 pp. 16–22; Willie and Greenblatt, *op. cit.*

238. *Ibid.*, Willie.

239. Waller and Hill, as discussed in Heiss, *op. cit.*, p. 184.

240. Rainwater, in Staples, *The Black Family*, p. 165.

241. Heiss, *op. cit.*, p. 20.

242. *Ibid.*, p. 82.

243. Blood and Wolfe, *op. cit.*

244. J. Robinson, *How Americans Use Time: A Social Psychological Analysis* (New York: Praeger, 1977).

245. George Farkas, "Education, Wage Rates, and the Division of Labor Between Husband and Wife," *Journal of Marriage and the Family* 38 (1976):473–83.

246. Scanzoni, "Black and White Marriages," p. 141.

247. Farkas, *op. cit.*

248. Sharon Price-Bonham and Patsy Skeen, "A Comparison of Black and White Fathers with Implications for Parent Education," *The Family Coordinator*, 28 (1979):53–59.

249. Noel Cazenave, *op. cit.*

250. Rainwater, in Staples, "The Black Family," p. 164.

251. Heiss, *op. cit.*, p. 136.

252. *Ibid.*, p. 185, quoting Komarovsky's views on blue-collar marriage.

253. Elizabeth Bott, *Family and Social Network*, 2nd ed. (New York: Free Press, 1971).

254. *Ibid.*, p. 87.

255. Kerkel, *op. cit.*, p. 375; Scanzoni, "Black and White Marriages," p. 191.

256. Robert Staples, "Educating the Black Male for Marital Roles," in Staples, *The Black Family: Essays and Studies, op. cit.*, pp. 347–353.

257. Carlfred Broderick, "Socio-Sexual Development among Urban Negroes and Whites," *Journal of Marriage and the Family* 27 (1965):200–03.

258. E. Liebow, *Tally's Corner* (Boston: Little, Brown, 1966).

259. Blood and Wolfe, in Staples, *The Black Family: Essays and Studies, op. cit.*

260. McAdoo, *op. cit.*, p. 761.

261. Price-Bonham and Skeen, *op. cit.*

262. Balswick *et al.*, *op. cit.*

263. W. Walker, *The Battered Woman* (New York: Harper & Row, 1979).

264. Mary O'Reilley, Attorney, in *Catalyst*, no. 6, Winter, 1979; Joan Aldous, "Occupational Characteristics and Males' Role Performance in the Family," *Journal of Marriage and the Family* 31 (1969):707–12.

265. Richard Gelles, "The Myth of Battered Husbands," *Ms.*, October 1979, p. 18.

266. *Ibid.*

267. Lenore Walker, *The Battered Woman* (New York: Harper & Row, 1979).

268. Susan Steinmetz and Murray Strauss, "The Family as a Cradle of Violence," *Society* 10 (1973):55–56.

269. Work of George Levinger and John O'Brien, reported in Steinmetz and Strauss, *op. cit.*

270. Del Martin, "Battered Women: Society's Problem," in Jane Chapman and Margaret Gates, eds., *The Victimization of Women* (Beverly Hills, Calif.: Sage, 1978), p. 123.

271. Gelles, *op. cit.*, p. 18.

272. Walker, *op. cit.*

273. Steinmetz and Strauss, *op. cit.*, p. 53.

274. Martin, *op. cit.*

275. *Ibid.*, p. 123.

276. Steinmetz and Strauss, *op. cit.*

277. Martin, *op. cit.*, p. 115.

278. *Ibid.*, p. 118.

279. *Ibid.*

280. Martin, *op. cit.*, p. 124.

281. Walker, *op. cit.*

282. O'Reilley, *op. cit.*

283. Martin, *op. cit.*, p. 126.

284. Erin Pizzey, *Scream Quietly or the Neighbors Will Hear* (Baltimore: Harmondsworth, 1974).

285. Joseph Bell, "Rescuing the Battered Wife," *Human Behavior*, (1977), p. 167–9.

286. Martin, *op. cit.*, p. 137.

287. Bell, *op. cit.*

288. Martin, *op. cit.*

289. Gelles, *op. cit.*

290. Martin, *op. cit.*, p. 126.

291. *Ibid.*, pp. 127–32.

292. Martin, *op. cit.*; Gelles, *op. cit.*; Walker, *op. cit.*; Steinmetz and Strauss, *op. cit.*

293. Michael Young and Peter Willmott, *The Symmetrical Family* (New York: Pantheon, 1963).

Chapter Nine

The Marketplace: Men's and Women's Roles at Work

A Man's work gives him a secure place in a portion of reality, in the human community.[1]

A 1973 report by the American Management Association found that 40–52% of the middle and supervisory managers surveyed found their work, at best, unsatisfying.[2]

The grievances and discontent of the young worker cannot be ignored. They affect the very basis of the system—productivity.[3]

Most of us, like the assembly-line worker, have jobs that are too small for our spirit. Jobs are not big enough for people.[4]

These quotes show the importance of work in our capitalistic, profit-oriented society. A man's life is defined by his work, his occupation. The first question a man is usually asked is, "What do you do?" People shape their perception of him according to his answer. Yet the quotes also show an ambivalent attitude toward work in a changing society where achievement is equated with money rather than with making a creative product. While work is important, it may not be satisfying. Yet whether it is satisfying or not, a man is expected to work, to be achievement oriented, and to put other life goals, such as family interaction and fatherly care of children, in a secondary position. In the American culture, work is also important to a man because work and occupational success are associated with masculinity and thus with self-worth.

Men's Roles at Work: Occupational Success and Masculinity

To understand fully what we mean by the association between occupational success and masculinity in the American culture, we must take a look at the relationship between achievement, occupational success, money, status, and masculinity. We must remember, first of all, that American culture is a product of the *Protestant Work Ethic*. The Protestant Work Ethic is the belief that a man is shown whether he is "good" or "saved" (religiously) by the way he prospers in the world. It was believed that God would punish sinners with poverty and illness and reward moral persons with health and wealth. This ethic was gradually expanded to mean that if you achieved in the world, you were in fact "good" or worthy as a person.[5]

In the American culture, the next step in this logic was to equate achievement with economic success. Success in frontier society was equated with the physical, the practical, the powerful, the big, and the new. This country did not and does not now particularly value intellectual success (witness the salaries paid to college professors in contrast to business executives), nor have we traditionally valued the fine arts. While values are changing as the country ages and refines its tastes, the emphasis on physical prowess, youth, mobility, and tangible symbols of success (money) is still predominant.

Thus, economic success has not necessarily meant craftsmanship or producing goods of quality in the old sense of the word *achievement*. As Myron Brenton points out, "truly creative jobs, those in which the individual feels a sense of autonomy, call for his best efforts, provide a solid sense of accomplishment, a real recognition of his particular service, and a knowledge that what he's doing is truly a worthwhile contribution to the world, are relatively few in number."[6] Rather, occupational success is measured by the fruits of labor: pay, prestige, and status.

Myths About Men and Work

In the next step in belief, pay and status as measurements of occupational success become equated with worthiness as a man, with masculinity.[7] The adult male has had little alternative to this definition of success for proving his masculinity. Physical strength and sexual prowess are also symbols of masculinity, but the breadwinner role is primary if the adult male wishes to feel masculine. (We should note here that as women gain greater equality in the marketplace in their fight for sex equity, physical strength and sexual prowess may become more important ways to prove masculinity. For the moment, however, the man who is successful at work in terms of gaining money is successful in fulfilling the stereotyped masculine role of breadwinner for his family.) "Money comes to be valued not only for itself and the goods it will buy, but as symbolic evidence of success, and thereby, personal worth."[8]

It is also believed that occupational success is more readily achieved if one has certain traits that society has deemed masculine, such as aggressiveness, competitiveness, and unemotionality. Thus, to succeed confirms the fact that one had masculine traits to begin with. In the honoring of these "masculine" traits, we see again the extension of the boyhood prescriptions to be "tough," "cool," and "good."

Masculine stereotypes also limit job choice and may limit occupational satisfaction.[9] A man may say that his son is free to do anything he pleases, but the same man may get upset if his son decides to go into an occupation often designated for women, like nursing, ballet dancing, or even teaching. Homophobia is a control mechanism that keeps many men from seeking creative jobs they might enjoy. A man may also get upset if his son takes less than a professional job when a profession may more readily guarantee occupational success. Thus, masculine-feminine stereotypes or job-prestige stereotypes may limit job choice and ultimately occupational satisfaction.

In addition, occupational success usually carries with it all the burdens of the original masculine role prescription. It is wearing to always have to be competitive and tough. Having to be tough is worse when one cannot show any doubt, fear, or other emotion. One slip is enough to undo a career. The failure of Edmund Muskie to win the presidential nomination was attributed by many political observers to the fact that after a fatiguing and dirty campaign, tears came to his eyes at one point when his wife was criticized.

Occupational success may carry additional burdens. Most corporation hierarchies and blue-collar assembly lines today offer little in the way of concrete achievement or an immediately seen product of which a man can be proud. The corporation man's achievement may consist largely of personnel manipulation.[10] A promotion may also mean moving out of a job one enjoys to a job one dislikes, like from sales or teaching to administration. In addition, high occupational achievement usually allows little or no leisure. Men who are advancing through the corporation ranks must show commitment by working numerous overtime hours, and even blue-collar workers are often forced to work overtime or weekend shifts.

Having money is a precarious base on which to build a sense of self-worth. Money can be lost overnight (as in the stock market failures of the Great Depression), and many men have committed suicide after losing their money.[11] Basing self-worth on earning money may influence other areas of a man's life. For example, a man may feel anxiety if his wife decides to return to work and then makes a salary close to his, and his marriage may even be threatened because he is not the one providing all the money. Daniel Levinson describes one physician who wanted to do more research and to work less in the private practice that provided his income. When the doctor's wife went to work and became successful at her career, he could have pursued his research. However, he was so threatened by the money she earned that he ended up working more hours in his private practice so he could make more income than she did.[12]

Occupational success—even achieving youthful dreams—may also not bring with it a sense of satisfaction. In *Seasons of a Man's Life*, Daniel Levinson says most men believe that if they attain the "dream" (one's own idea of success), life will be good and they will be happy. In reality, however, attainment of their goal often leaves them feeling empty and dissatisfied.[13] A 1973 report by the American Management Association found that 40 to 52 percent of the middle and supervisory managers surveyed found their work "at best, unsatisfying."[14]

For most men, however, it is not attainment of the dream but failure to attain the dream that is the burden of the masculine role. In the blue-collar world, the satisfaction of doing quality work on a craft job has been largely eliminated by automation.[15] The fear that automation will soon eliminate *all* jobs is not far behind the loss of job satisfaction. The lyrics of Tom Lehrer's song "Automation" say it well: "They'll invent a little button that will push all the buttons and they won't need you and me."[16]

The changing nature of jobs and of job obsolescence affect all social classes and groups. Many successful engineers and scientists in the aerospace industry, for example, found themselves unemployed as the industry was cut back. There is only room for a few men at the top of the corporation pyramid. Most men cannot be dramatically successful in their occupations.

Job *alienation* is accelerated when men have fewer job choices. As the economy slows down, fewer new jobs are available and competition is intensified for the existing ones. Professors cannot find new academic situations easily as colleges contract. In a time of economic recession, businessmen may not be willing to risk job turnover and to give up stock benefits and pension funds. Blue-collar workers are similarly tied to the company by seniority and pension plans. These workers cannot complain or change jobs; if they do, they may lose their retirement benefits or may not find another job at all. Yet few are satisfied where they are. In a 1976 poll done by Harris on a national sample of almost 2,000 men, only 36 percent were very satisfied with their work, another 37 percent were somewhat satisfied, and 21 percent were somewhat dissatisfied.[17]

As success means continually moving upward—not staying in a job with which you are happy and comfortable—few really get what they want in life or feel successful. The Harris poll showed that men were not philosophical about their lack of success; rather than blaming the system or bad luck, they blamed themselves for any failure. Eighty-two percent of the men polled believed that if you try hard enough you can usually get what you want in life.[18] Thus, the great majority of men who did not succeed blamed themselves for not being "good enough." As a collorary to not being "good enough," they may not have felt masculine. These men often felt discouraged, beaten down, and alienated. However, they could not quit; they had families to support. They could not complain; complaining was not masculine. Yet they could not dismiss work; work was important to them even with its attendant dissatisfaction. Three out of four said they would work even if guaranteed a good income.[19]

The results of discouragement and alienation are clearly seen. Studs Terkel, in his book *Working,* has documented the disaffection of men and women from all working groups:

> A stockbroker says, "I can't say what I'm doing has any value. This doesn't make me too happy. Oh, I'd like some morning to wake up and to go to work that gave me joy."[20]

> The president of a UAW local says, "The almighty dollar is not the only thing in my estimation. There's more to it—like how I'm treated. . . ."[21]

The Blue-Collar Worker

While the middle-class worker may dislike his job, he may have power and privilege that make it palatable. He is sustaining the system and is closer to the rewards. However, the blue-collar worker has little hope for such power and privilege. He is forced to do monotonous jobs so his alienation is particularly intense. It is worst among the young workers, who are the last hired and the first fired. Lack of seniority means the worst shifts or split shifts.[22] For young and old, there may be also the incredible authoritarianism and petty discipline of the factory.[23] The blue-collar worker is particularly alienated because he has no place to go: it is unlikely that he will be promoted,[24] and the traditional way out of the factory—education—may not guarantee him a job anymore.[25] In addition, there is less and less respect for the man who works with his hands.

To understand this alienation we can look at another Terkel quote from an assembly worker:

> I don't like the pressure, the intimidation. How would you like to go up to someone and say, "I would like to go to the bathroom"? If the foreman doesn't like you, he'll make you hold it, just ignore you. Should I leave this job to go to the bathroom, I risk being fired. The line moves all the time. . . .
> You really begin to wonder. What price do they put on me? Look at

the price they put on the machine. If that machine breaks down, there's someone out there to fix it right away. If I break down, I'm just pushed over to the other side till another man takes my place. . . .

I don't eat lunch at work. I may grab a candy bar, that's enough. I wouldn't be able to hold it down. The tension your body is put under by the speed of the line. . . .[26]

The average working-class man is much closer to poverty than to affluence, in spite of the highly touted salaries of assembly line workers. The blue-collar worker must cope with frequent unemployment as well. Layoffs and unemployment have spread now to the skilled crafts, to the construction workers, and to the more highly skilled auto workers.[27]

On the factory line, the alienation of the blue-collar worker shows up in absenteeism, drug use, alcoholism, sabotage, and hostility toward other workers such as women and blacks. At home, his alienation may be taken out on his family, sometimes in wife and child abuse. As the probusiness government of the 1980s attempts to cut unemployment benefits and to reduce safety standards, the working-class man becomes more convinced that no one is going to help him; he becomes alienated from the total society and may become radicalized as a voter.[28]

The "Man in the Grey Flannel Suit"

Although the middle-class worker has more hope of gaining power through the system, he too is alienated. Some middle-class workers drop out: nearly 50 percent of the businessmen surveyed by the American Management Association had changed or considered changing occupational fields in the last five years.[29] Yet most cannot drop out, and most would not want to. Terkel believes that Freud's statement about work was correct, that a man's "work at least gives him a secure place in a portion of reality, in the human community."[30]

Yet it is clear that "most of us, like the assembly-line worker, have jobs that are too small for our spirit. Jobs are not big enough for people."[31] Even those at the very top of the occupational prestige and income pyramid find themselves alienated. They may be involved in monotonous paper shuffling or they may simply not be able to climb any higher because there is no more room at the top.

In *Men and Women of the Corporation*, Rosabeth Kanter has documented the alienation of even corporation executives who have reached the highest rung on the corporate ladder. She points out that those who cannot climb to the top and who are stuck in a job often become discouraged, dispirited, and cautious. They may turn their attention at work from achieving in occupational areas to achieving in social areas. Those who have been halted may also refuse to take risks and may develop a management style that is very controlling and conservative so that they can preserve what they have.[32] Brenton has pointed out that others opt for a reduced form of competition that involves making one's particular rung of the ladder as safe and plush and comfortable as possible.[33]

The Effect of Men's Work on Health and Leisure

In the climb up the career ladder or just in the attempt to get more money many men put the building of relationships with their wives and children second to their occupation. They may believe that they show their concern for their family by working long hours and bringing home a paycheck. They may seldom have chances to play with their children or to take vacations with their wives. They may also find it difficult to make the transition from the nonemotional, controlled world of the office or factory to a more expressive communication style at home. During this time of intense career involvement, families may grow apart, but a man may not be aware of the intimacy he is missing. (We will discuss the effect of work on marital satisfaction a little later in this chapter.)

Levinson, in his discussion of the midlife transition that many men go through, points out that the "masculine" striving for career success in the middle class may be stymied by outside forces in middle age. This possible pause in a man's move up the career ladder may give him time to think about the things he is missing. Mentoring or helping protégés may take the place of the desperate climb to the top. A man's family may become a new source of intimacy and satisfaction. He may even explore his relationships with other men and attempt to free some of the feelings of brotherhood stifled by homophobia.[34] However, in the period before such a transition, or if such a transition does not occur, a man may sacrifice many intimate relationships because of his obsession with occupational success.[35]

Health and Stress: Hazards of the Male Role

Thus, for some, alienation and occupational dissatisfaction may be reduced during the midlife transition. For others, the midlife transition may add additional stress. The competitive, achievement-oriented male work style, combined with the repression of emotions demanded by the workplace and the male role, makes men more prone to a variety of health disorders. We see this stress most clearly in the middle years. We hear of a man of forty who has had a heart attack and think, "He was so young." Ulcers may begin to manifest themselves at this time.[36]

Researchers point out that many more men than women have personality profiles that make them stress and illness prone; they are the hard-driving, competitive type "A's."[37] While many working and non-working women may experience the same type of stress as men, they are more likely to relieve the stress by unburdening their feelings to some-one.[38] Goldberg has pointed out that men seldom talk to other men about their problems because they don't want to seem vulnerable.[39] As a result, they may never become close to other men and suffer doubly from a lack of intimacy. They may also fear dependence on a woman, Goldberg says; but when men do unburden themselves, it is largely to women.[40]

In addition, men are trained to ignore minor aches and pains and slight physical discomfort. The fact that they do not often listen to their bodies until their bodies rebel means that many men miss the chance to avoid illness or to catch illness an an early stage.[41] In *The Hazards of Being Male*, Goldberg points out that a man is in a double bind if he does try to take care of himself. If he goes to bed when not feeling well or otherwise pampers himself, he is considered hypochondriac, self-indulgent, and perhaps not quite masculine. If he pushes himself until forced to stop, he may risk illness and early death.[42]

The problem of stress at work is widely recognized today, and both individuals and businesses are more aware of fitness than ever before. Jogging has become the national pastime; two running books and two diet books are currently on the national best-seller list (September 1981), and businesses encourage executives and other workers to stay fit by installing gyms and encouraging exercise. The emphasis on fitness does not really deal with the problem at its roots, however. Being physically fit is compatible with being masculine; but the competitive stress of the business environment and the repression of emotions accompanying that stress are also considered masculine, yet are not healthful.

Extension of the Work and Worth Ethic to Leisure

The rapid expansion of leisure and sports activities may point up another stressful element of the male role in America: the cultural—and particularly the male—emphasis on action. Europeans have commented for years that Americans never relax when they have free time from work, that they are always *doing* something, preferably something worthwhile. Thus, you will find a businessman practicing his golf putting, taking lessons on his tennis serve, waxing his car, fertilizing his lawn, or jogging to improve his health.[43] There is also the prescription that one should be "good" at his leisure pursuits, again adding to the stress of the male role. As a recent article, "Our Endless Pursuit of Happiness," has pointed out, the American male seldom has a real rest or change of pace. He carries the competitive stress of the work world into most of his leisure-time activities.[44]

Away from the Work Ethic?

Yet there is some indication that the heavy stress on the work ethic and success is abating. Earlier studies documented the fact that the desire to achieve had gone down for adolescents (see chapter 4), and we see the phenomenon of the middle-aged career dropout who wants to "get away from it all." Another new trend is that of corporation men who are not willing to sacrifice their families if promotions mean moves and family disruptions.[45]

In fact, men seem to put family values more and more at the top of their value structures. In the Harris poll, the top four things that men valued were health, love, peace of mind, and family life, with 84 percent and more mentioning them as being personally "very important." Work came in a distant fifth, with only 65 percent mentioning it as one of the most important things in their lives. Thirty-five percent also said they would like more leisure time, and define leisure as an opportunity to do things they enjoy with people who are close to them.[46]

It remains to be seen, of course, if this decreasing emphasis on work and increasing emphasis on hedonism will be sustained as economic times become more difficult. Some college professors have already noted that the casual student of the 1970s has given way to the dedicated business major of the 1980s who is depending on a college degree to get himself or herself a job.

In summary, we note some contradictory trends. The work ethic remains strong in American culture, and men are judged in terms of their occupational success. Yet few can really succeed, and many are alienated from and discouraged with their work. Their masculine self-image suffers as a result. They may retrench and emphasize other parts "of the masculine package," such as physical prowess and sexuality. On the other hand, they may be willing to try more varied routes to feelings of self-worth, such as greater emphasis on fatherhood.

Women Wage Earners

In the United States in this century, women have moved in ever larger numbers into the labor force. Between 1900 and 1980, female labor force participation grew from 18 percent to 50 percent. (The number of women who work for pay or who are trying to find a job almost doubled between 1950 and 1974 alone.) This movement into paid market activity has had profound consequences for women's lives and for the economics of our society. The reasons for the movement are varied and are closely connected with world events as well as with the economic scene in our own country.[47]

Historical Perspectives on Women's Work in This Country

The historical pattern of women's market work in the United States shows that women were heavily involved in economic production in our early history. In the agrarian society of early America, women had to plant and harvest crops, tend animals, and do other things that produced a money income, as well as work within the household to produce cloth, make clothes, make butter and cheese, preserve food, and the like. In addition, with the short life expectancy, many women became widows and ran businesses or farms; other women were midwives, nurses, teachers, printers, laundresses, and innkeepers. In the early 1830s and 1840s, women worked in textile mills and tobacco factories. By 1890, estimates are that at least 1 million women were employed in factories, with others working in agricultural and domestic service.[48] Many of the women who worked in the factories, however, were not from the "proper middle class." An 1887 Bureau of Labor study found that of 17,000 factory workers surveyed, 75 percent were of immigrant stock. Black women were also more likely to work, and in 1890 more than 1 million of 2.7 million black women were employed in agriculture or as domestics. Thus, the 1900 census showed that 41 percent of all nonwhite women worked outside the home, while only 17 percent of white women were employed, and many of these were immigrants. The great majority of white women did not work outside the home,[49] and their proper work was considered to be that of homemaker and mother.

In spite of the sentiments about women's "proper place," however, various things were happening that would enable women to move into the economic marketplace. Women's education was steadily increasing, and some of the first graduates of the women's colleges pioneered in business and professional careers. Almost 50 percent of the women graduating from college became doctors, social workers, business women, lawyers, and architects. They joined with women who worked at home to promote women's rights and to push for women's suffrage. Their reasons for wanting suffrage included a great concern for supporting child labor legislation and for improving factory conditions.

However, few women entered the paid labor force until the 1940s. Most of those who worked before that time were young, single, and poor. They were segregated into occupations that were defined as "work for women." Thirty percent were clerical workers, and many of the rest were in textile or food-processing factories. Three out of four female professionals worked in elementary-school teaching or in nursing. As one of the well-known historians of this era points out, there was a "woman's place" in the paid work force as well as at home.[50] Not only was certain work considered women's work, but it was presumed that women should not be paid as much as men and that women should never be placed in a position competitive with or superior to that of men. There was almost no support for the employment of middle-class homemakers.

As we have seen before, women's employment has usually increased when men are absent. It was World War II that marked the real turning point in women's employment in the United States. In 1940, 25.6 percent of all women worked; by 1945, that figure had risen to 36 percent, as 6 million women entered the job market to take the place of men who had been called into military service.[51] These women did not fit the stereotype of young, single, and poor. Women who entered the labor market at this time were married and over thirty-five. By the end of the war, it was just as likely for a wife over forty to be employed as for a single woman under twenty-five. At the end of the war, many of these women returned home, but the boom in the economy enabled some to keep their jobs. In spite of the "feminine mystique," which insisted that women should gain their greatest fulfillment as homemakers and mothers, many women—single and married—continued to work.[52] During the 1950s, the employment of women increased four times faster than that of men. By 1960, 37 percent of the women in the country were in the labor force, and 30 percent of these were married. By the mid-1970s, 45 percent of the female population was employed outside the home, more than two-fifths of these female workers were married, and many were from the middle class.[53]

Traditional attitudes about "women's place" persisted throughout this period, although they were in conflict with the actual economic behavior of women. Chafe has stated that this gap between traditional attitudes and actual behavior ironically facilitated expansion of the female labor force. As traditional values were given lip-service, women could enter the labor force "to help out" and were not perceived and resisted as crusaders who would change the status quo.[54]

Reasons Why Women Entered the Paid Labor Force

There are many reasons why women continued to enter the labor force after World War II, despite traditional values. Real wages rose and job opportunities expanded as the economy boomed. Women were also getting more education, which made the type of working opportunities available more attractive. There was a slow change in sex-role attitudes as well, and by the mid-1960s, the revival of feminism made it difficult to maintain the traditional view of women's place as being in the home. These changing attitudes influenced and combined with several demographic changes. Women began to marry later and were thus more likely to be in the labor force longer in their early single years. They also had fewer children, so that their last child was born sooner in their lives and they were freed from child care earlier to reenter the paid economy. As divorce rates rose, many more women had to rely on themselves as their only support base.[55]

Other demographic and technical changes also helped women enter the labor market. The move from rural areas to the cities made it easier for many women to find jobs. The development of many labor-saving devices (like self-cleaning ovens and frozen foods) also meant that they could spend less time in housework and food preparation. In addition, the 1970s were a period of economic inflation in the United States. Families had gotten used to a higher standard of living, frequently maintaining a large home and two cars, sending children to college, and enjoying expensive leisure-time activities. It was difficult to maintain this standard of living with inflation and, as a result, there was more pressure for married women to enter the work force.

One of the striking trends of female employment during the 1960s and 1970s was the increasing number of mothers who were working. The fastest rise of all took place in the employment of mothers with preschool children. From 1959 to 1974, the employment rate for mothers with children under three more than doubled, from 15 to 31 percent.[56] While some of this rise was due to the need for greater family income, these young women also had more education and thus had greater job opportunities and changing sex-role attitudes to support their employment. By 1979, 51 percent of the women in this country were in the paid labor force (making up 48 percent of that labor force). Three-fourths of these women were working full time.[57] In 1980, 69 percent of single women, 80 percent of married women, and 56 percent of widowed, divorced, or separated women were employed full or part time outside the home.[58]

The Present Picture: Problems of Working Women

As a 1979 headline in the *Detroit Free Press* proclaimed, "[It Is] a Bleak Portrait of Working Women."[59] Women make only 59 percent of the salary of men (if you compare their salaries to those of white men alone, they make only 55 percent of a male's salary); both black and white women who are college graduates have lower mean earnings than white men with eighth-grade educations.[60] Using 1979 figures, The *New York Times* pointed out that the median income for college graduates is $12,028 for women, as compared to $19,433 for men.[61] To put it another way, women account for 65 percent of the full-time workers earning less than $7,000 a year,[62] and only 8 percent of all working women but 42 percent of all working men have incomes of more than $12,000.[63] The difference in income between white men and "black and other" men who work full time all year has tended to decline over the past twenty years; about 40 percent of the difference in their wages has been eliminated. Black women now make approximately what white women do. In contrast, the difference in earnings between all women and white men has remained virtually the same.[64]

In addition to low pay, women suffer from other deficits. The National Commission on Working Women, a Washington-based arm of the National Manpower Institute, surveyed 150,000 women and discovered that although wages were a major difficulty for many, other problems were also severe. The women complained of differentials in fringe benefits, no chance to train for better jobs, increasing pay differentials as men got promoted, sex harassment on the job, inadequate child care facilities, the stress of the multiple roles of wife-worker-mother, and extremely limited leisure time. (Fifty-five percent of the professional women surveyed and 50 percent of the clerical, sales, and blue-collar workers said they had *no* leisure time!) These women wanted additional education but lacked the time and money to get it; they wanted job counseling but could not find it. Their husbands did not object to their jobs but were of almost no help with household chores. The women described themselves as frustrated, working in a dead-end job with no chance in sight for advancement or training. They felt underpaid, underutilized, and afforded little or no respect for the work contributed.[65]

Let us look at these problems one by one. The National Research Council of the Academy of Sciences recently completed an assessment of job discrimination for the Equal Employment Opportunity Commission. In this assessment, they tried to pinpoint the reasons for the differential between men's and women's wages. The factors they found that affect wage rates and other benefits basically divide into measurable parts: human capital inequalities and institutional barriers, with a third residual category of discrimination.[66]

Human Capital Inequalities. According to human capital theory, some differences in earnings are due to inequalities in *human capital,* or characteristics of workers that enable them to produce more for the firm. Such characteristics would include education, experience, training, and commitment to work. Believers in this theory say that men usually have more human capital than women do and thus command higher wages.

There are many basic difficulties with this theory, including the fact that productivity is almost impossible to measure in some jobs, that wages may not reflect the entire reward paid for a job, and that we do not have an open, competitive market for all jobs (remember the "old boy" network). Beyond the basic difficulties, however, the statistics show that even women who make certain kinds of investments in their own human capital get less return on it than men do. We saw that women with college educations get lower annual mean earnings than men who are high-school dropouts.[67]

The major difference in the amount of wages accounted for under human capital is attributed to differences in work experience: overall work experience, on-the-job training, and the like. Women are less likely to get on-the-job training than men are, as employers may believe that women are less committed workers and will not stay with the company. Women are also less likely to have continuous work experience. They may enter their careers after child bearing or interrupt them to raise children.[68] Women are the losers when they drop out of the market. One study that documents the gains from continuous work experience is the National Longitudinal Survey of the Work Experience of Mature Women, which interviewed a national representative sample of 5,000 women aged thirty to forty-four eight times in the ten-year period between 1967 and 1977. Women who worked continuously had real wage gains of about 20 percent, while those who entered and left employment were no better off in 1977 than they were on average in 1967.[69] Even the women with continuous experience, however, got less of a return on their experience than men did.[70]

Taking all these factors—education, on-the-job training, and continuous work experience—together, the National Research Council's report shows that only a relatively small percentage of the gap in salaries between men and women is explained by human capital factors. Other studies have shown a slightly larger percentage of the wage differential accounted for by human capital, but all current research believes that it accounts for less than half the gap in earnings between men and women. We must look elsewhere to find out why women earn so much less than men.

Occupational Segregation. Other factors such as institutional barriers and job segregation seem to be more important than work experience in explaining the wage gap. One of the major reasons that women's earnings tend to be so low is that women are clustered in a narrow range of jobs. One-third work in clerical occupations. Another quarter work in the fields of health care (not including physicians), education, domestic service, and food service. Many of these jobs require higher than average educational levels (teacher, social worker, nurse) but pay low median salaries. Few women have until very recently entered male-dominated professions, which are more highly paid. At present, women are only 1 percent of the engineers, 2 percent of the business executives, and 7 percent of the physicians.[71]

Job segregation by sex seems to be an important factor in wage differentials. If we look at the twelve major occupational categories, such as professional and technical, managerial, sales, clerical, and so on; we do not see much difference in male and female salaries, as the categories are so broad and job classifications differ markedly. When 479 job categories are used, however, studies show job segregation accounts for a substantial amount of the gap in earnings.[72] In one study that used both human capital and job segregation variables, every additional percentage of females in an occupation meant that workers in that job got an average of about $42 less in annual income.[73]

Wage differentials occur with job segregation because, by concentrating in only certain fields, women increase the supply of workers for these jobs and decrease their own wages. Economic theorists call this the *crowding theory.* In contrast, the short supply of engineers and physicians elevates wages in these male-dominated professions. Some of the jobs that have been designated for women are also contracting as a result of population trends and changes in our technology. Low-level clerks and secretaries may be replaced as word processing becomes more automatic. Elementary-school teachers are less needed as people have fewer children.[74] Yet women continue to enter the jobs traditionally designated as female. As these fields become crowded, wages go down.

If job segregation is one of the major reasons that women earn less than men, why do women choose these lower-paying jobs? Women are willing to take low pay and to enter occupations that may, in addition, have low occupational status because most of these jobs blend well with the stereotype of being "feminine." Many of the jobs with the highest percentage of female workers are nurturing in nature (teacher, social worker, nurse). In addition, some of these jobs have fairly flexible hours, which may aid a woman in combining them with domestic responsibilities. While many of the jobs may require a college degree, they do not require the commitment of many additional years of education. (Many women have not wanted to make the commitment of years of graduate education; they wish to remain flexible so that they can find a mate and adjust to his career needs.) The professions traditionally designated for men, such as engineering, business management, and medicine, may also require proficiency in mathematics or science, and women have been discouraged from taking courses in those areas. Thus, many women do not have the necessary prerequisites to enter those professions. Women may also choose jobs that do not penalize them if they take years off for child rearing. It is relatively easy to return to nursing or teaching, for example, even if one has been out of the profession for a number of years.[75]

Are women restricted to these jobs? Socialization, training, and custom have made it difficult for women to enter male-dominated fields, but more and more are doing so. Barriers still remain, however, and will be discussed below. In addition, many male-dominated jobs are less compatible with the dual roles of worker and homemaker. At least in the near future, women may be forced to forego some aspects of the roles of homemaker and mother if they do not want to be saddled with two full-time jobs.

While there are some indications of change (women entering law and medicine, for example), this occupational segregation by sex is likely to continue. It has hardly decreased at all among whites for several decades, although it has decreased substantially among minorities.[76] Women seldom have the full information or mobility needed to choose jobs.[77] Employers seldom have access to all the possible employees and are also constrained by other factors, such as union agreements and agreement to promote from within.

Discrimination: Sex as a Status Characteristic.   Human capital and job segregation explanations do not account for the discrepancy between women's and men's earnings. We must look further—at the whole idea of discrimination by sex.

Even in fields where men and women work together, men make more money than women do. It is not just the nature of the job, but the nature (sex) of the person that accounts for the difference in amount of pay. Thus, men who work in "women's" fields still earn $1,200 more annually than women do on the average, and in male-dominated occupations, men's salaries exceed those of women by an average of $2,400.[78]

Subcategories in integrated professions may also mean different pay scales. According to an American Medical Association survey, the average salary for all practicing physicians was almost $70,000, whereas women doctors as a category averaged only $45,000. This salary differential may reflect the fact that women are less likely to go into the high-paying specialities like cardiology or surgery. An interesting comparison between all health professionals can be seen when we realize that a nurse with ten years' experience averages only $20,000 annually. We see similar differences in other integrated professions. Male computer specialists get $3,714 more than their female counterparts. In retail sales, women and men are often in subcategories that pay differently. Men are more likely to sell the higher-priced goods like appliances or furniture, which consequently carry higher commissions.[79]

In addition, certain firms within the same occupational category are more likely to hire male workers, and others are more likely to hire a greater percentage of female workers. Without exception, the firms that are larger and more prestigious are more likely to hire men and to pay them more money. We see this in law firms, accounting firms, and even in restaurants, where the more prestigious restaurants (where bills and tips are larger) hire only male table servers. More segregation occurs in this fashion than by a random hiring process. This difference *among firms* is believed to account for more of the wage gap than is the difference *in any particular firm* in the jobs that men and women will take.[80]

However, within the same firm in an occupational category, men and women are still likely to have different jobs. Even if they do not start in different categories, promotions may soon serve to separate the sexes. One prime example of this situation occurred in an insurance company that was sued for sex discrimination. In this company, men were given "claims adjuster" jobs, and recruited women got jobs entitled "claims representatives." Each job required a college degree, yet not only were "claims adjusters" paid $2,500 more in wages than the "claims representatives" who did the same work, but only the adjusters could obtain promotions.[81]

Thus, a differential exists between men's and women's wages that cannot be accounted for by the human capital or job segregation explanation. Reasons for this gap probably comprise various factors that we can lump under the terms *stereotypes* and *discrimination*. The proportion of pay differential attributed to discrimination is estimated to be approximately one-third of the gap between female and male earnings.[82] When we talk about discrimination in this sense, we are not necessarily talking about an overt attempt to discriminate against women. We are also talking about the complex of customs, traditions, and understandings that lead to stereotyping and beliefs about who should do what work.

Myths That Justify Discimination.   Why would women in the labor force face such discrimination? To answer this question, we need to look at some of the stereotypes about women workers. One of the first stereotypes is that she is a *secondary worker*, that her income is a second income for the household, and that she does not really need the money. This myth persists in spite of facts that contradict it. The truth is that most of the women who work need the money badly. (While all people who work need money as a basis of independence, a large percentage of working women need the money they earn as basic self-support.) Twenty-three percent of them are single, and an additional 19 percent are widowed, divorced, or separated and are their family's main support. An additional 26 percent have husbands earning less than $10,000 a year. Only 32 percent of working women have husbands present who earn more than $10,000. Of course, whether or not women really need the money is not supposed to be an issue: if they do equal work, they should get equal pay. We do not usually ask whether a man needs the money when it is time to adjust his salary or to assess his promotion qualifications.[83]

Incidentally, single (never-married) women have earning profiles that are almost identical to those of married women, although their work experience is equal to that of men. After adjusting for all the differences in age, education, hours worked, and other factors, by being single, women increased their chance of getting higher wages by only 1 percent.

In this 1973 study, married women earned 56 percent of the average earnings of men, while single women earned 57 percent of men's average earnings.[84]

Women are also seen as workers who are not serious about their work and are less committed and reliable than men. Employers expect them to be absent more than men and are reluctant to invest in them because they may quit. There seems to be no time when a woman worker is freed from this stigma. When she is single, employers are afraid she will quit to get married. When she is married, they are afraid she will quit to have children or will follow her husband to a better job. If she already has had her children, employers are afraid she will be absent a great deal because of child care demands; and if she is older and her children have left home, she may be considered too old and unattractive for the job. The actual facts are that women are not absent from work any more than men (which is rather remarkable considering that many of them do have primary child care responsibilities). Women and men are both absent an average of five and a half days a year.[85] While the overall quit rates of women are higher than those of men, women do not quit more *from the same jobs.* The job attachment of anyone in a dead-end job is less than someone in a career that offers opportunity for advancement. Men who are bank tellers quit as often as women who are bank tellers; men who are physicians are no more or less committed to their work than women who are physicians.[86]

Most of the myths about women and work disappear when jobs are held constant and women are compared to men in the same job. Most studies show that women are as committed as men are and may actually work a little harder. A 1976 study of time use in the office showed working women, as contrasted to working men, taking fewer rest breaks, overstaying lunch hours less frequently, and chatting with fellow employees less often.[87]

Employers also say that they do not promote women because people don't want to work for a woman boss, that women don't want the top jobs, that they can't handle responsibility, and that they are too emotional to be in management. The first two statements are probably true in many cases. Traditional sex-role stereotypes have dictated that women be dominated by men and not vice versa. Many people are uncomfortable when these stereotypes are reversed. Even women workers may accept the stereotype and not wish to be supervised by another woman. In addition, women may not admit to wanting higher-echelon jobs because they know that the probability of their getting such a job is low and that to accept such a job may be to accept responsibility that may conflict with home and family responsibilities.

Rosabeth Kanter has pointed out in *Men and Women and the Corporation* that women managers may also be put in a position where it is difficult for them to supervise and to help their subordinates advance. Some women may not want supervisory positions or promotions that entail additional responsibility, but in most cases this is because such a promotion means that they do not have enough time to handle family responsibilities or they fear the difficulties that may come in exercising authority if co-workers resent them. The other two statements are stereotypes of women (emotional, unable to be responsible), and they are obviously individual characteristics that cannot be applied to all women.[88]

As we examine the facts about women workers, we begin to see that *sex is a status characteristic.* It is used as a category to discriminate at work and elsewhere in much the same way that other statuses such as race, religion, and age are used. It is the status of being a woman that influences a woman's career aspirations, hiring possibilities, promotion chances, and salary as much as the personal qualifications she possesses or gains through her education.

When we think of sex as status, we can see that some of the discrimination against women is a matter of the upper-status group (men) retaining power and privilege. As the work and abodes of men have always been more prestigious than those of women, men may consciously or unconsciously fear the dilution of their power and privilege if women join their ranks. The resistance of all-male clubs like The Harvard Club to opening their doors to women is a case in point. Thus, men may feel their status and their masculinity threatened when women advance to parallel or supervisory positions in the work force.[89]

In an interesting addition to this concept, one scholar has proposed that men may see the whole concept of masculinity as threatened by changing roles. As many have built their identities on a belief in the concept of masculinity, to feel the concept itself threatened is much more monumental than to have only the ability to prove oneself masculine temporarily threatened. After all, there are other outlets to prove masculinity, such as physical or sexual prowess, but if the whole concept of masculinity is questioned, then uncertainty and anxiety can be multiplied.[90]

Kanter has pointed out that men will close ranks against a woman newcomer and limit their talk to "masculine" subjects like the military or sports to underscore the woman's differences. She points out also that a great deal of the interchange in higher-echelon professional or business positions depends on common understandings and values. Men may fear that someone of a different status (race or sex) may not share their background or understanding. Such men are frequently used to dealing with women who have a formally lower status (like secretaries), so they have a difficult time adjusting to dealing with a woman on a parallel level.[91]

To get around this difficulty of status, organizations use various techniques (consciously or unconsciously) to keep women out of the mainstream of advancement and decision making. Women's jobs may be reclassified to a lower category or women may not be trained on the job as men are to be eligible for promotion. Women may also be shifted into fields that do not lead to higher positions, such as personnel jobs. Unions have blatantly discriminated against women. Women were formally barred from craft unions for many years, and even today requirements for membership may be difficult for women to meet. Union meetings may be held in halls or clubs where women feel uncomfortable going.[92] Harassment on blue-collar jobs may be overt and sexual; on white-collar jobs it may take the form of isolation, but the intent is the same: to show the woman that she should stay in her place.

In a more radical perspective on the relationship between job segregation and discrimination, Hartmann suggests that as industrial society developed, men could no longer maintain the personal control over women's work that they had in the more personal preindustrial economic system. She postulates that such control was continued by segregating industrial jobs by sex, with women making less money or possibly unable to get any work at all. Because of this segregation, women were and are partially or totally dependent on men for support, and as a result they perform domestic chores for their husbands. Thus men maintain control and get higher wages as well as services at home. Working at home weakens women's position in the labor market, and so patriarchy and capitalism are intertwined. Hartmann concludes that one cannot change women's position in the economic system without changing their household roles and cannot change household roles without changing job segregation in the economic system. As it is not to the benefit of those in power to change the system, it is unlikely that the system will be changed without conflict.[93]

Hartmann's inference that segregation of jobs by sex and discrimination against women are deliberate devices to enforce women's dependency may not be accepted by everyone. Yet at the same time it is quite clear that occupational segregation by sex as well as conscious and unconscious discrimination accounts for a great deal of the discrepancy in women's and men's wages and does perpetuate women's secondary status as workers.

Issues of Equality for Men and Women Workers

Legislation

The revival of the feminist movement and the increased numbers of working women have interacted to generate concern about the differential between women's and men's wages and about sex discrimination in the marketplace. A spate of laws and court interpretations has resulted from women's agitating for legal protection.

There are four basic federal measures that prohibit discrimination on the basis of sex. The *Equal Pay Act of 1963* (Section 6d of the Fair Labor Standards Act of 1938, as amended) requires that employees receive equal wages for "equal work on jobs the performance of which requires equal skill, effort, and responsibility and which are performed under similar working conditions."[94] This act does not prohibit discrimination in hiring or promotions, however. It was designed to aid women who were doing work equal to that done by men but were being paid less. In 1974, the Supreme Court interpreted this act to mean equal pay in all remuneration from the employer, including fringe benefits such as medical insurance and pension plans. However, *bona fide* (proved to be legitimate) seniority and merit systems were exempted from the act.[95]

Title VII of the Civil Rights Act of 1964 prohibits discrimination by race, color, religion, sex, or national origin in hiring, firing, promotions, training, seniority, retirement, and all other aspects of employment. The act also prohibits classification of employees in a way that will deprive an individual of employment opportunities. It applies to employment agencies and unions as well as to business. Feminists lobbied strongly for inclusion of sex as one of the categories against which one could not discriminate. Ironically, those opposed to the bill allowed sex to be included as a discrimination category because they believed this would defeat the entire bill. However, Title VII passed, and for the first time women were given a legal basis for insisting that they be allowed to compete with men for jobs and promotions. Even then, the Equal Employment Opportunity Commission (EEOC) refused for some time to enforce the sex provision and allowed employers to advertise "male jobs" and "female jobs."[96]

By 1966, pressure from feminist groups resulted in stricter enforcement of sex discrimination rules, and a 1972 amendment to Title VII (Title IX) expanded the law to include educational institutions and state and local governments, as well as employers with fifteen or more employees. Since 1972, the EEOC can bring suits against all those (except government agencies) who violate the act. Two executive orders in 1965 and 1969 prohibited discrimination by federal contractors and by the federal government itself.[97]

One other important piece of legislation was the *Age Discrimination Employment Act of 1967*, which prohibited government, private employers, employment agencies, and unions from discriminating against persons between forty and sixty-five years of age. For women in traditionally female occupations, this was an important protection because they could not often establish a case of sex discrimination.[98]

There have been major tests of all these laws, and some limitations have resulted. There is a limitation in Title VII that sex can be used to discriminate in jobs when sex is "a *bona fide* occupational qualification reasonably necessary to the normal operation of that particular business or enterprise." The courts have narrowly interpreted this provision, however, and in most cases the courts have held that being a certain sex was not a "*bona fide* occupational requirement" for hiring.

Pregnancy insurance and pension benefits have been other areas legally tested under the EEOC laws. For a time, the courts ruled that pregnancy and childbirth disabilities should be covered by health insurance, but recently they have ruled that pregnancy is not covered. The issue of pension benefits has never been legally resolved. Since women live longer than men on the average, insurance companies have regularly given them smaller monthly retirement sums than men—contending that the total sum paid would equal out over the long run. Women have contested these payments but have not yet won their suits.

A final area of concern has been the problem of seniority. The last-hired and first-fired policies that operate under seniority mean that those usually laid off would disproportionately be minorities and women. Despite disagreement in the court system, an appellate court ruled that "if present hiring practices were nondiscriminatory, an employer's use of a long-established seniority system to establish the order of layoff and recall of employees was not a violation of Title VII."[99]

Impact of Equal Employment Opportunity Laws

It is difficult to estimate the impact of the equal employment opportunity legislation on women. In a 1973 report done for the EEOC, two social scientists analyzed data from over 40,000 business establishments and noted that the occupational distribution of white women had changed very little in the years between 1966 and 1970.[100] In cases of sex discrimination, the Court held that sex discrimination was not a "suspect classification" under the equal protection clause of the Fourteenth Amendment. This ruling means that the Court does not automatically have an interest in reviewing cases dealing with the rights of the "suspect" group.[101]

One can see, however, that there has been an evolution from discriminatory "protective" laws to the principle of equal employment opportunity and finally to enabling such opportunity through some affirmative action. In 1971, the burden of proof of nondiscrimination was shifted to employers. If women are paid less than men or if men receive other disproportionate benefits, employers must show that women's lower status results from less education, less prior experience, or other relevant factors. If women are underrepresented in management and administration, employers must develop an affirmative action plan and show a "good faith" attempt to recruit and hire more women and minorities.[102]

Under the Reagan administration, however, the burden of proof of discrimination has been shifted back to the employee. This change will make it much more difficult for individuals to win discrimination suits. The administration has also made it clear that it has no intention of aggressively enforcing affirmative action laws. In addition, the federal government has modified the provisions of Title IX so that schools are no longer constrained to provide equal sports facilities for women.

Other Government Laws

Other government laws also affect those in the labor force, especially women. Tax and social security laws may make it less rewarding for a woman to work, and veterans' benefits may mean that it is more difficult for a woman to get some jobs or that she may not get the same benefits as a man would.

Income Tax Laws. Working women are most affected by income tax laws when they are married women who work in the paid labor market. When the federal personal income tax was first introduced in 1913, individuals were taxed only on their own incomes, whether or not they were married. Thus, everyone with the same income and deductions paid the same tax. As the income tax was progressive—that is, those with higher incomes were taxed at higher *rates*—it soon occurred to married couples of community property states that they could reduce their total tax payment by claiming that each spouse was responsible for only half the income tax paid. The Supreme Court agreed in 1930 that this interpretation of the tax laws was constitutional.

However, married couples with two earners were hit by a "marriage penalty." They not only paid more than a couple who could split one income, but they even paid more than two single people who each made $15,000 and could file separately.[103] This *marriage penalty* was the steepest when income was split approximately 50–50 between the partners. The marriage penalty rose sharply as tax rates rose, and in families where the spouses earned combined incomes of $50,000 to $75,000, the marriage penalty could amount to over $3,000. As more and more wives entered the labor force, more and more families were subject to this penalty.

In 1976, 8.5 million couples (23 percent of all tax-paying couples) paid such a penalty, and the number of dual-earner couples continued to increase. In recognition of this fact, some relief was given to dual-earner married couples by the tax cut bill enacted by Congress in 1981. This bill provides progressive relief from the marriage penalty in the years 1981 to 1984, until in 1984 dual-earner families will pay half the marriage penalty they had been paying.

Other possibilities that would provide more relief would be to allow dual-earner couples to file separately or even to mandate individual filing for everyone. In either case, the burdens of dual-earner families would be decreased. (Optional individual filing would be the more moderate course that would adjust tax burdens less drastically.) Under the present system, however, dual-earner families will continue to pay a marriage penalty even after 1984. The effect of this penalty and the increased tax bracket in which the wife's income places the couple may be enough to discourage some women from working.[104]

The Social Security System.   The social security system was instituted as a retirement benefit system financed by payroll taxes paid equally by employers and employees. By 1981, the combined tax rate for both contributions was 13.30 percent on a maximum of $29,700. By 1990, it is scheduled to rise to 14.30 percent of an individual's income. Benefits, however, have gone up even faster than taxes. When the system was first conceived, only individual workers were supposed to receive retirement benefits. In just a few years, though, benefits were expanded to include dependents and survivors. At the present time, an aged spouse can get benefits of either 50 percent of the other spouse's income or his or her own benefits, whichever is larger. Since 1979, divorced wives who were married at least ten years get the same benefits as a present spouse, as long as they do not remarry.

Under the present social security system, dual-earner couples pay more payroll taxes than single-earner families but may get only the same retirement benefits if the wife's earned benefits are not more than half her husband's. Dual-earner families pay in 26 percent of their incomes (including their employers' contribution), while single-earner families pay in 13 percent, and the wife who is not working in the paid labor force gets half the benefits of the working spouse without paying into the system.[105] Thus, one-earner couples and spouses or divorced spouses without sufficient pay-in records of their own are drawing more out of the system than they are putting into it. They are subsidized by two-earner couples who must choose between the benefits they draw out. As the number of older persons in this country increases, the system becomes more and more financially unsound.

Several possible changes in the present system have been suggested. Some have suggested a two-tier system much like Sweden's, where there is a basic minimum income for all and any earned retirement benefits are on top of the minimum income. Still others have suggested "earnings sharing," where during the time a couple is married all income is totaled and split between the spouses for retirement credit. Another suggestion is to give tax credits for homemaking. In this instance, there is the question of who pays for these credits: the couple themselves or society at large. The various packages of possibilities are endless.[106] With ever-increasing numbers of older people supported by fewer younger workers, the present financial difficulties of the system make it seem likely that benefits will be curtailed in some fashion. In the meantime, however, the wife who works outside the home is presently contributing more than she takes out of the pot.

Veterans' Benefits. Women workers may also suffer from the edge men get in veterans' benefits. While women do not have to serve in the military, they also do not often have the opportunity to do so and to acquire the resultant benefits. Thus, men frequently get veteran's points on civil service exams that enable them to score more highly than women applicants when they apply for civil service jobs. They have the benefit of the G.I. bill when they want to continue their education, and they can also take advantage of such things as Veteran's Administration loans for mortgages and veterans' hospitals.

In summary, we see that women in the job market suffer lower wages and lower job status than men for a number of reasons. They may not make the investment in their human capital that gives them access to the more prestigious and well-paying jobs. They are likely to enter jobs that are segregated for women only, which pay less and many of which may be glutted in the near future. They are also discriminated against for a variety of reasons, which include myths and the weight of cultural tradition. As unequal pay *per se* is illegal, the means for this discrimination is usually to place women in different jobs of secondary status. Government laws and policies add to the secondary status of women workers. Thus, institutional discrimination against women (conscious or unconscious) means that they retain their status as secondary workers with unequal wages and job status.

Special Situations

Women in Male-Dominated Professions: An Example from Medicine

It is difficult for women to enter the professions because professions by their definition are organized occupations that limit entry into their ranks and control the competency of their members. Patterson and Engleberg have proposed that professions establish "models" of their practitioners and that for many high-prestige professions in the United States, the normative model is male. Therefore, it is harder for women to get into and remain in many of the male-dominated professions. The medical profession has historically been male dominated in this country. The first woman was not admitted to an American medical school until 1847; women could not join the American Medical Association until 1915; and Harvard excluded women from their medical school until 1945. Some other medical colleges excluded women as late as 1960.[107]

More than half the physicians surveyed in a 1973 study (50 percent of the men and 62 percent of the women) believed that women were discriminated against in admission to medical school. Testimony at 1970 hearings before the Special Subcommittee on Education of the House Committee on Education and Labor showed that this belief was accurate. Many medical schools have separated women and men into separate pools of applicants and then rejected the same proportion of each. However, because the female pool consisted of the brightest women who had completed the premedical college program, many of the women who were rejected were as qualified as or better qualified than the men who were admitted. Nevertheless, more and more women are applying and being admitted to medical school. In 1965, only 7.7 percent of all American medical school students were women; by 1976 this proportion had risen to 20.5 percent. However, while women students perform as well as male students, their attrition rate is double that of the men—over 16 percent. It has been suggested that medical schools do not provide a welcoming or supportive atmosphere for the women they admit. Many of the women who complete school come from families of doctors and so can get support at home.[108]

As we noted before, female physicians are likely to choose medical specialties that have been traditionally stereotyped for women, such as pediatrics (one-fifth of women doctors), obstetrics, gynecology, psychiatry, public health, or anesthesiology. Ironically, the two most popular specialties with women—pediatrics and obstetrics—not only pay poorly but are two specialties where the time and hour demands are most likely to cause conflict with family roles.[109] Many more women than men are also likely to choose a salaried job over private practice: again, a reduction in risk. Thus, even when making it into a highly prestigious profession, women are paid less than men and are still concentrated in lower-status specialties.

Women in Blue-Collar Jobs

Women manual laborers who are employed in blue-collar industrial and service occupations comprise 38 percent of all employed women, or some 12.5 million women in all. Most of these women are white, but three out of five black women work in blue-collar jobs.[110]

Women entered the blue-collar labor force in this country in large numbers shortly after the first power looms and mills opened in Massa-chusetts in 1814. From the beginning, the conditions of work were poor: fourteen-hour days, extremely low pay, and unsafe working conditions. All-male unions did not admit women workers, but blue-collar women made valiant, if futile, attempts to organize and help themselves during this period.[111] In the late 1800s, women were admitted to national trade unions, although they were frequently still discriminated against on the local level. By the 1900s, women comprised more than half of all union members in five industries: women's clothing, gloves, hat and cap, shirt-waist and laundry, and tobacco. However, women's wages were only a little more than half of men's.[112]

As jobs expanded during World War II, women moved into manual areas where they had not worked before. While some returned to the home at the end of the war and others were forced to take lower-category employment, the number of women working in blue-collar jobs contin-ued to expand. Most of the women entering these jobs were from the working class and had few other job choices because of limited education and skills. A little-recognized fact is that the great majority of American women have only a high-school education. In 1973, 80 percent of all American women over age twenty-five had no more than a high-school education, and three out of five black women had not completed high school.[113]

Occupational Segregation in Blue-Collar Jobs. As in the white-collar organizations, blue-collar jobs are sex segregated. Certain industries have traditionally hired women: garment industries, laundry establishments, assemblers of small electric equipment, operators in communications in-dustries, beauticians, waitresses, hospital aides, and household domes-tics. When both sexes are employed in the same industry, men hold the more prestigious and higher-paying jobs. In the apparel industry, for ex-ample, men are the skilled cutters, pressers, and tailors, while women are the mass-production sewing machine operators.[114]

The usual consequence of this segregation is lower pay for women. The women in industrial and service jobs earn about 60 percent of a man's salary. In addition, many of the industries in which they work have poor fringe benefits, unstable employment, and exploitative part-time work.

Women have not recently rushed to labor unions to relieve their problems. Part of the reason is that certain women's jobs, like those in the textile mills, have not yet been unionized. Whereas three out of ten male workers in the United States are unionized, only one out of seven female workers is.[115] The overall percentage of working women who were active union members was only 12.6 percent in 1972. Blue-collar unions have not traditionally supported wage equality for their female employees, and most unions have few women in leadership positions. In the present period of high unemployment, seniority demands and the desire to keep men on the job have also taken precedence over any union demands for affirmative action. Yet union membership among women workers is increasing. Women have recognized that ultimately in most—but not all—cases, unionization improves their wages.

Union women have become more aware of the fact that they must push their unions to work for benefits for female members. In 1974, 3,500 women formed the Coalition of Labor Union Women (CLUW) to attempt to put more women into union leadership roles and to work for affirmative action and legislation for women. One of the major thrusts of their action is an attempt to reclassify women's jobs so that they can get into apprenticeship programs and also receive higher wages. Many women's jobs are now erroneously classified at such lower skill levels that they not only pay poverty wages, but their classification keeps women from getting training to move into better-paid employment.[116]

Women in labor unions are also eager to improve conditions on the job, although many of these conditions seem to be the result of fear and stereotypes, and changes are hard to legislate. Women often face male co-workers' hostility and undesired sexual advances. The men seldom help them learn their jobs (although they readily help another man); yet it is estimated that as much as 80 percent of some kinds of work is learned informally from others on the job. Manual jobs may also mean changing shifts and forced overtime, which wreak havoc with a working mother's child care arrangements and family obligations.[117]

Changing Values: A Source of Conflict in Blue-Collar Women. In the light of all the above, it may seem surprising that working-class women are not more oriented to unions, politics, and the feminist movement. Yet as we have seen in the section on blue-collar families, many of these women were raised in religious or ethnic backgrounds that may emphasize values conflicting with those of the feminist movement on issues like abortion, birth control, or even the general status of women. These women marry early and are unlikely to obtain higher education or to plan to be in the work force for any length of time. Their socialization emphasizes the role of the husband as "breadwinner" and the wife as "homemaker"; they feel guilt and fear the alienation of their husbands if they depart from these values and become committed to paid employment. They would like better pay, better working conditions, and more child care but are afraid to engage in conflict or to take on leadership roles to obtain them. They may need to work, but as they are ambivalent about doing so, they do not make the investment to better their working life.

Nevertheless, working-class women are becoming more aware of their needs and their rights. Fertility trends, divorce rates, and the feminist movement have affected them. Union membership is growing and probably will continue to grow as the number of women manual workers stays constant and service workers expand.[118] It will be particularly important for women workers to push for better jobs and wages in this period of high unemployment or they are likely to lose ground.

Black Women in the Labor Force

Black women have the second-highest labor force participation of any female labor group. Fifty-one percent of all black women work, and they have traditionally been in the labor force in large numbers. Only Asian-American women have more paid workers than blacks, although as white women have entered the labor force in greater and greater numbers, their percentage approaches that of black females.

Striking changes have occurred in the jobs and earnings of black women in the last two decades. Traditionally, the median income among employed black women was very low, with a large proportion of them working in domestic service and the less-skilled manual trades. The early textile jobs were usually closed to black women, as were clerical and secretarial positions. During the 1960s, however, nearly one-fourth of black women changed jobs and shifted into clerical occupations and the female-dominated professions.[119] The shift in occupation represented a marked improvement in their occupational prestige and in their earnings as they became nurses, teachers, and librarians, among other occupations.

Black women thus increased their earnings, and by 1977 they made 98 percent of what white men were making. They work harder and longer for the same pay, however.[120] Black women have traditionally completed fewer years of schooling than white women (11.9 years compared to 12.6 for the white median), and many are still in jobs with lower occupational prestige and wages. They compensate by working longer hours and remaining in the labor force rather than interrupting employment for long periods while children are small.[121]

Of course, there are many variations among black women workers. This fact is particularly clear in differences between age groups, where older black females are more likely to be in domestic and other service and the younger ones are more likely to be in the professions. Black women workers are also more likely to be single heads of families or to have husbands who earn lower incomes; they are therefore in the work force from necessity.

Differences also exist between black women and black men workers. By 1974, black women still had slightly higher educational attainment than black men, yet black women were earning only 62 percent of a black man's annual salary.[122] Sex segregation in occupations again tells the story. Black women are segregated into the overcrowded female occupations. Black men are more likely to be crafts workers, business executives, or high-status professionals. Black women are 79 percent of the black librarians, 97 percent of the black nurses, and 78 percent of the noncollege teachers. They are also 46 percent of the black professionals but only 7 percent of the engineers, 14 percent of the lawyers, and 24 percent of the physicians and dentists of their race.[123] (Even at that, note that their percentages relative to their population group are higher in these professions than they are for white women.)

It is sex discrimination rather than racial discrimination that now seems to be the basic problem for black women workers. They approximate white women in labor force participation, occupational prestige, education, and earnings. In one 1970 study, education, occupation, and region were held constant, and the wages lost because of discrimination were estimated. Black males lost $1,772 in comparison to white males, but black women lost nothing compared to white women.[124]

The Effect of Work on the Lives of Men and Women

Self-Concept of the Wage Earner

The intertwining of the breadwinner role with the concept of masculinity make a man's occupation (and particularly his occupational success in terms of money) an important source of a positive self-concept for most men. Yet, as we have pointed out above, it is difficult for men to really feel successful. They seldom produce a concrete product that they can point to with pride, their salaries may not seem adequate in more difficult economic times, and they may have little real chance to move up from their present position. As success is equated with upward mobility, many men are permanently doomed to feeling at least partial failures. While it may be necessary for most men to work to feel good about themselves at all, the nature of their work does not enhance their self-concept.

For women, the relationship of paid employment to self-concept can be examined in two directions. First, a woman who has a relatively high self-concept may be more likely to work. She is less likely to fear success and may have high educational and career aspirations that cause her to plan early for a rewarding occupation. Conversely, paid work seems to increase a woman's self-concept. One study on the meaning of work to the mothers of preschool children showed that a major reason that these women worked was the feeling of exerting control and mastery over the environment and a feeling of accomplishment that was more clear-cut than the feeling they got from housework.[125] Another major satisfaction found in working was the social contact that the mother had outside the home. These women felt stimulated, more interesting, and less dependent on their husbands for social interaction.

Marriage: Fertility, Power, and Division of Labor

In a similar fashion, work careers may have many indirect effects on marriages. A woman who is well educated and working at a career is less likely to get married; if she does marry, she is more likely to do so at a later age. She is also likely to have fewer children if she has any at all. This may not be a preplanned decision but an evolution as her work career progresses. A man who is preparing for and starting a career may also postpone marriage and desire children at a later time.

Marriages where both spouses work are likely to be more equalitarian, at least in decision making. A woman who has worked before marriage and continues to work is likely to come to the marriage with more resources for power (see chapter 7). She is likely to be older and to have had the experience of being independent and making her own decisions. She is not as likely to have children who tie her down and detract from her resources. She also has the obvious resources of a working wife: money, status, a sense of competence and self-worth, and less dependence on her husband for meeting her affiliative needs. As attitudes have changed to greater approval of working women, she is likely to get more cultural support for her role and to grasp the power that she gains through her resources. She is most likely to gain power if she has a high education relative to her husband and a good job that gives her status and income. Her power will be augmented if her husband is low in income and occupational status himself, provided that there is no ethnic or class ideology that detracts from her gaining power.[126] Power has many dimensions, however, and the working wife is likely to gain authority in decisions relating to external affairs but to lose authority in household matters.

Sharing of power in families where both spouses work has changed much more rapidly than sharing of household labor. We saw in chapter 7 that while some wives may get paid household help, most working wives get little additional household help from husbands or children. Husbands, who have demanding jobs of their own, are not usually pleased about sharing household work and child care. They are most likely to help if the wife simply cannot get things done herself and if there are no counterclaims on the husband's time.[127] Thus, wives in the paid labor force may suffer from a role conflict based on the incompatible demands for time and energy from home and work roles. Husbands who split household chores may suffer similar incompatible demands of time and energy.

Role Conflict

Yet, Rose Coser and Gerald Rabkoff have made an important observation about the role conflict of the working couple. The conflict is primarily one for women. It is a conflict of values and allegiances as well as one of time and energy. There is a normative expectation that women will allot the family certain resources of time, energy, and emotion. This expectation does not operate as fully for men. Men may be engaged in their occupations without fearing that they are not committed to their families. In fact, the commitment to their occupation (and the income and status it provides) may be seen as proof of their commitment to their families. The reverse is true for women. Time given to an occupation is seen as time taken from their families.[128]

Thus, it is still extremely difficult for married women to combine careers and marriage comfortably, particularly when there are children. As we have seen, this may lead to some women dropping out of the labor force or taking less demanding jobs. It may also lead to "superwoman" efforts on the part of these women to do the best in both worlds.

Effect of Parental Employment on Children

We can see that the norm for women taking care of the family still exists when we look at the literature on effects of parental employment on children. Very few studies assess the effects of the father's work or absence from the home on children; the overwhelming majority deal with the mother's employment. This emphasis is ironic, as cultural beliefs about men's commitment to work may mean that the employed father is away from children more hours than an employed mother. The studies of the effect of maternal employment on children are varied in aim, sample size, and rigidity. The general consensus is that there is no adverse effect of maternal employment on young children. No difference in school records or personality characteristics have been found between the children of working or nonworking mothers.[129] There is also no observable effect at later ages and no differences in the affection reported by adolescents toward their mothers. There is some indication that maternal employment may have a more positive effect on girls than on boys, however. Adolescent daughters of working mothers are more assertive and have more positive career plans of their own. There is some tendency for younger boys of working mothers to be passive and somewhat withdrawn; but older boys show few effects of maternal employment, except where the mother *has* to work. Then the son may not admire the father.

Part-time employment by a mother seems to have a favorable effect on adolescent children. Daughters of these mothers are very active in all ways and have close relations with their parents, but they are also independent. Mothers who work part-time seem to feel less harassed and to have more time to spend with their families.[130]

The mother's attitude toward employment is also very important in its effects on her children. The mother who wishes to work full time may compensate out of guilt; she may be too warm and giving and may not encourage independence in her children. The mother who is dissatisfied about working, however, is more likely to burden them with chores and to have hostile and aggressive children.[131]

In general, however, few if any significant differences have been found between the children of mothers who are employed outside the home and those who are not. The small effects that have been found vary by the sex of the child, by whether or not the mother chooses to work, and by whether her work is full or part time.

Marital Satisfaction

In terms of general marital satisfaction, the balance of tension and reward created by the couple's work is what ends up being important. The costs to men of being the sole provider are many and are of course intertwined with the masculine prescription to be good, tough, and successful. Men may work longer and harder hours than they would prefer because they feel they must provide a certain standard of living for their families. To provide a good standard of living also shows to some degree that they are "successful" and have fulfilled one of the prescriptions for being "masculine." (We have seen that black fathers, in particular, see the breadwinner role as an essential part of being a father and husband.) Of course, the irony is that many men strive so hard for success that they have very little time left for their families or themselves. Wives may also feel inferior when their husbands achieve and they are not enjoying comparable success.

If the wife is in the paid labor force, the attitude of both husband and wife toward the wife's work is one of the most important factors in determining marital satisfaction. A 1976 study done by Burke and Weir found that husbands of employed women were less content with their marriages,[132] but other subsequent studies found no difference in the husband's attitude toward his marriage whether or not his wife worked outside the home.[133] We should not be surprised by this discrepancy. Obviously, a working wife can provide less of a support system at home, and the husband may be expected to aid in household work and child care (although, as we have seen, few do very much of this). In addition, husbands may perceive a wife who earns income as a threat to their breadwinner role. Indeed, one-third of all working wives earn as much as or more than their husbands.[134] On the other hand, the wife's income may be very much needed by the family; some men report a feeling of relief that they are not solely responsible for providing for the family. Husbands may also find a working wife a more satisfied and interesting marital companion.[135] There is also evidence to indicate that men adjust their attitudes about women's employment to a more favorable view when their wives work.[136]

The wife's attitude toward work is also very important in determining whether she will work at all and if she does, how she will feel about it. In the National Longitudinal Survey of the Work Experience of Mature Women, attitudes toward women working changed markedly between 1967 and 1977. Remember, these are women who had reached twenty years of age during the 1950s. In 1967, 90 percent of the women thought it was all right for a woman with school-aged children to work if it was necessary to make ends meet, but there was almost no support for her working if she wanted to and her husband disagreed. By 1977, nearly 33 percent thought that a woman should work if she wished to, whatever her husband's opinion.[137] Studies have shown that women who approve of women working are more likely to desire employment themselves[138] and to actually be working.[139] The employment situation seems to reinforce attitudes about working. Wives with more work experience come to approve of women working even more than they originally did.[140]

Whether working wives are more satisfied than homemakers is a question that receives mixed answers from the research literature, as we saw in chapter 7. Some of the discrepancy in the results of the studies occurred because they were done on different social classes or at different times. An early study by Blood and Wolfe found that blue-collar wives in the paid labor force reported more satisfaction than homemakers, presumably because their income was needed and they gained power from their contribution. Most later studies, however, show blue-collar wives as gaining little power from the additional resources they contribute because of the patriarchal norms of this group. Blue-collar wives may also suffer more stress because they get almost no help with household chores.[141] In contrast, research seems to show middle-class wives who are in the labor force to be more satisfied than middle-class homemakers.[142] The studies point out that these women are probably working more from choice than necessity, that they are more likely to have higher educational levels and interesting jobs, and that the financial contribution they make probably enables the family to enjoy luxuries that they could not otherwise have. It has been pointed out that when both spouses work in this class, the carryover from traditional sex-role views depicts a husband's money as being used for necessities; the wife's contribution, for luxuries. While this view perpetuates traditional attitudes about women being secondary workers, it may also enable their husbands to retain the belief that males are the basic family providers. Thus the husbands may feel less threatened by their wives' employment. There is also some indication that these wives enjoy more shared interests and greater companionship with their husbands.[143] In either social class, the working wife with fewer home demands and more time to fulfill them is the most satisfied. The wife with older children who works part time or has flexible hours, therefore, is the most satisfied.

Thus, because of the number of factors involved, it is almost impossible to say whether women in the paid work force in general are more satisfied with their lives than homemakers or whether women wage earners in the middle class are definitely more satisfied than working wives who have blue-collar jcbs. One examination of six national samples between 1971 and 1976 found no meaningful differences in overall marital and other life satisfaction between employed and nonemployed wives.[144]

There was also evidence in the same national longitudinal sample that *some* of the husbands of women who were employed modified their own work patterns. Their employment decreased as their wife's employment increased. They worked less overtime, took longer vacations, and even took leaves of absence to go back to school. When they were less fully employed, they were more likely to help with the housework and child care. These husbands were mainly the spouses of wives with nontraditional attitudes.[145] Of course, the number of couples engaging in these more flexible patterns is very small, but the partial diminishing of the work ethic and changing attitudes toward traditional division of tasks may start a small trend in the direction of more flexible roles.

The Future: Women, Men, and Work

Gail Lapidus sums up the problems for the future as follows:

A political culture which treats freedom, equality, and achievement as supreme and universal norms collides with pervasive cultural assumptions about the need for a sexual division of labor, for differentiation and complementarity between male and female roles. Instrumental roles in the political and economic life are regarded as appropriately the domain of men, while expressive roles are treated as preeminently the sphere of women. The primacy assigned to the homemaking and maternal roles of women encourages the treatment of their participation in the labor force as secondary and residual.

These cultural norms are reinforced by patterns of socialization which receive formal expression in educational institutions. Differential expectations for boys and girls are embedded in educational curricula . . . and, of course, differential expectations elicit differences in behavior: boys are encouraged to be assertive and achievement-oriented while girls are rewarded for nurturing and compliance.

Finally, these values are mirrored and reinforced by public policy . . . ranging from taxation measures to the provision of social services. . . .[146]

This excellent summary of the condition of work in this country itemizes clearly the points that we have tried to emphasize in our discussion of the marketplace. First, in spite of an equalitarian political ideology, there are cultural assumptions about a sexual division of labor, so that men and women are expected to do different jobs. Preferably, women are expected to remain and work at home while men engage in paid labor outside the home; but if this cannot be accomplished, then women should be considered "secondary workers" in the paid labor force and go into appropriate occupations designated as feminine. We have seen that these attitudes toward women doing paid work are changing, but that the basic cultural assumptions about women as secondary workers remain strong and mean that women are segregated into certain fields that are low status and low paying. The second point made by Lapidus is that these cultural assumptions are enforced by our cultural institutions, from the curricula of educational institutions to the kind of job advertising that employers do. Finally, we see that these institutional policies and cultural assumptions are mirrored and reinforced again by public policy: tax laws, credit laws, and the like. If we accept Hartmann's thesis that the perpetuation of job segregation is a deliberate controlling of women so that they will be dependent on men and be willing to perform domestic chores for them, then we will be pessimistic about change in the future.[147] Even if we are not willing to accept this radical a view, we may also be pessimistic because males who have traditionally held positions of privilege and power may be reluctant to relinquish them.

Yet there are also important forces for change. It is likely that women will keep working in greater and greater numbers, pushed into the work force by the demands of inflationary prices and pulled by their own educational attainment, need for self-support, and need for personal satisfaction. By 1976, only 3 percent of the working women in one survey preferred to return to housework.[148] Women are also entering jobs that have traditionally been held by men and have been increasingly socialized to value these higher-paying jobs and to train for them. While men may be threatened by the movement of women into their traditional strongholds, they may not be able to stem the tide. The necessity of having two providers in a family may also provide a rationale that will allow men to accept more readily women's participation in the paid work force. While there may be some transfer of the "masculine mystique" to areas of physical and sexual prowess as a result, men may actually welcome some relief from the burdens of the sole-provider role. With the increasing emphasis on the health problems of achievement-oriented men and the greater stress on the need for positive fathering, men may be more willing to relinquish one of the measures of masculinity in return for other satisfactions. Thus, both men and women may be willing to change their orientation toward work and family roles. How much they are willing to do so may depend on many other contingencies, such as the nature of the economic and the political system in this country. The demands of a profit-oriented capitalistic system push us back into old molds (unless women are willing to substitute woman-hours for man-hours), and recessionary economic times may make it difficult for women to get jobs or for men to leave them. We will look at these and other contingencies in our next chapter.

Essay Questions

1. How is occupational success defined in the American culture? How does a man show this success, and how is such success related to masculinity?

2. How does the average middle-aged man in the American culture feel about his occupational success? If he has achieved prominence in his line of work and is happy with what he does, is this enough for him to be comfortable? If not, why not?

3. Why is the blue-collar worker particularly alienated? How is his consumption of leisure goods like boats and campers related to this alienation?

4. Discuss the reasons why women have been entering the labor force in greater and greater numbers since World War II. (You should include in your answer demographic and technological changes, as well as changes in values.)

5. What is the present situation of women workers in terms of how their salary and fringe benefits compare to those of men? What specific problems do women workers cite when asked about their occupations?

6. Discuss why or why not the "human capital" theory explains the difference between women's and men's wages.

7. How does occupational segregation contribute to wage differentials between men and women? Discuss segregation within occupational fields as well as between types of occupations. Why do women go into certain types of jobs, and why are these jobs paid less?

8. How do the income tax and social security laws discriminate against working wives? What changes might be made in each system to make things more equitable?

9. What part have labor unions played in helping women achieve better wages? How are unions handling the conflict between affirmative action and seniority?

10. How does the employment of a wife affect power and division of labor in the family? Is marital satisfaction likely to go up or down with a working wife?

11. Discuss the effect of maternal employment on children. How do variables such as mother's attitude toward work, father's attitude toward her work, hours worked, and supervision of children bear on the effect of such employment?

12. How will an economic recession, or an economy that is not growing, affect women's chances to improve their employment situation?

Exercises

1. Have you ever worked in a factory or on an assembly line? If so, discuss how you felt about your work. If you have never done that type of work, how do you imagine you would feel? Have you ever heard blue-collar workers talk about their jobs?

2. Pretend that you are a woman being interviewed for a beginning-management position. (Have a student play the role of the woman and another student play the role of the personnel interviewer.) The company does not really want to hire a woman but is being forced to interview women to comply with affirmative action requirements. What kinds of questions might be asked? How could a woman reply to "loaded" questions without giving in to sexism?

3. Assume you are a husband whose wife has just decided to go back to work full time. You are not pleased about losing your support system at home or having your breadwinner role challenged. What kinds of things might you say to your wife that would convince her that a job outside the home would not be in the family's best interest?

4. Pretend you are the president of an auto workers union. You are being asked by women members of your union to press for affirmative action, but you are really concerned with keeping jobs for all your union members. What would you tell the women members, and what would you do?

5. If you are a woman, pretend you are a man and discuss why it is important for you to succeed at your chosen occupation. If you are a man, discuss your own feelings about this subject.

Notes

1. Calvin Hall, *A Primer of Freudian Psychology* (New York: World Publishing Co., 1954).
2. Robert Gould, "Measuring Masculinity by the Size of a Paycheck," in Deborah David and Robert Brannon, eds., *The Forty-Nine Percent Majority: The Male Sex Role* (Reading, Mass.: Addison-Wesley, 1976), pp. 113–18.
3. Andrew Levinson, "The Rebellion of Blue-Collar Youth," *The Progressive,* (October 1972):87–101.
4. Studs Terkel, *Working* (New York: Avon, 1972), pp. 446–47.
5. Michael McGiffert, ed., *The Character of Americans* (Homewood, Ill.: Dorsey Press, 1964), chapters 5 and 6.
6. Myron Brenton, "The Breadwinner," in David and Brannon, *op. cit.,* p. 94.
7. Gould, *op. cit.*
8. Robert M. Williams, "Achievement and Success," in David and Brannon, *op. cit.,* pp. 107–10.
9. Brenton, *op. cit.,* p. 95.
10. *Ibid.;* Robert Blauner, *Alienation and Freedom* (Chicago: University of Chicago Press, 1964), chapter 2.
11. Gould, *op. cit.,* p. 115.
12. *Ibid.,* p. 116.
13. Daniel Levinson with Charlotte Darrow, Edward Klein, Marcia Levinson and Braxton McKee, *The Seasons of a Man's Life* (New York: Ballantine Books, 1978), pp. 247–48.
14. Betty Roberts, *Middle-Aged Career Dropouts* (Cambridge: Schenkman, 1980), p. 1.
15. Brenton, *op. cit.,* p. 96.
16. Tom Lehrer, "Automation," in *That Was the Year That Was* (Album R6179 from Reprise Records, July 1965).
17. Louis Harris and Associates, "The Playboy Report on American Men: A Study of the Values, Attitudes, and Goals of U.S. Males 18–49 Years Old," (Survey conducted by Playboy Enterprises, 1979).
18. *Ibid.,* p. 39.
19. *Ibid.*
20. Terkel, *op. cit.,* pp. 446–47.
21. *Ibid.,* pp. 256–65.
22. Harris, *op. cit.,* pp. 35–36 and 38.
23. Andrew Levinson, *op. cit.*

24. *Ibid.*

25. U.S. Department of Health, Education, and Welfare, "Blue Collar Blues," in J. Williamson, Jerry Boren, and Linda Evans, *Social Problems: The Contemporary Debates*, 2nd ed. (Toronto: Little, Brown, 1977).

26. Terkel, *op. cit.*, pp. 223ff.

27. A. Levinson, *op. cit.*

28. *Ibid.*

29. Roberts, *op. cit.*, p. 7.

30. Terkel, *op. cit.*, p. xx.

31. *Ibid.*, p. xxix.

32. Rosabeth Kanter, *Men and Women of the Corporation* (New York: Basic Books, 1977), pp. 129–205.

33. Brenton, *op. cit.*, p. 96.

34. D. Levinson *et al.*, *op. cit.*, pp. 197–244.

35. *Ibid.*

36. Herbert Goldberg, *The Hazards of Being Male* (New York: New American Library, 1976), pp. 103–09.

37. D. Mechanic and E.H. Volkart, "Stress, Illness Behavior, and the Sick Role," *American Sociological Review* 26 (1961):51–58.

38. S.M. Jourard and P. Richman, "Disclosure Output and Input in College Students," *Merrill-Palmer Quarterly Behavior Development* 9 (1963):141–48.

39. Goldberg, *op. cit.*, p. 126.

40. *Ibid.*, p. 105.

41. Sidney Jouard, "Some Lethal Aspects of the Male Role," in David and Brannon, *op. cit.*, pp. 24–25.

42. Goldberg, *op. cit.*, p. 95.

43. Williams, *op. cit.*, p. 112.

44. "Our Endless Pursuit of Happiness," *U.S. News and World Report*, August 10, 1981, p. 35.

45. Lotte Bailyn, "Accommodation of Work to Career," in Skolnick and Skolnick, eds., Family in Transition, 3rd ed. (Boston: Little, Brown) *op. cit.*, p. 568.

46. Harris, *op. cit.*

47. Ralph Smith, "The Movement of Women into the Labor Force," in Ralph Smith, ed., *The Subtle Revolution: Women at Work* (Washington, D.C.: The Urban Institute, 1979), p. 3.

48. William H. Chafe, "Looking Backward in Order to Look Forward," in Juanita Kreps, ed., *Women and the American Economy* (Englewood Cliffs, N.J.: Prentice-Hall, 1976), p. 9.

49. *Ibid.*

50. *Ibid.*, pp. 15–16.

51. Smith, *op. cit.*, p. 4.

52. Chafe, *op. cit.*, pp. 15–16.
53. Francine Blau, "The Data on Women Workers, Past, Present and Future," in Ann Stromberg and Shirley Harkness, eds., *Women Working: Theories and Facts in Perspective* (Palo Alto, Calif.: Mayfield, 1978), pp. 29–62.
54. *Ibid.*, p. 19.
55. Smith, *op. cit.*, p. 8.
56. Chafe, *op. cit.*, p. 25.
57. *Ibid.*
58. U.S. Dept. of Labor, Bureau of Labor Statistics, 1980 Census, Employment and Earnings, 27 (Washington, D.C.: U.S. Dept. of Labor, 1980).
59. "A Bleak Portrait of Working Women," *Detroit Free Press*, June 3, 1979, p. C-1.
60. Nancy S. Barret, *op. cit.*, p. 32. "Women in the Job Market: Occupations, Earnings and Career Opportunities," pp. 31–62 in Ralph Smith, ed., *op. cit.*, p. 32.
61. "Census Bureau, Current Population Survey," *New York Times*, February 26, 1979, p. D3.
62. Mike Duffy, "Women's Wages Lag Far Behind Men's," *Detroit Free Press*, November 26, 1978, p. C-1.
63. Census Bureau, *op. cit.*
64. Elizabeth Almquist and Juanita Wehrle-Einhorn, "The Doubly Disadvantaged: Minority Women in the Labor Force," in Stromberg and Harkness, *op. cit.*, pp. 63–88.
65. "A Bleak Portrait of Working Women," *op. cit.*
66. National Research Council, "Women, Work, and Wages: Equal Pay for Jobs of Equal Value" (Washington, D.C.: National Academy Press, 1981).
67. Barret, *op. cit.*, p. 32.
68. Francine Blau, *op. cit.*, p. 29.
69. Lois B. Shaw and Theresa O. Baker, "Work and Well-Being: A Decade of Changes in the Lives of Mature Women," Center for Human Resource Research, Ohio State University, Columbus (Paper presented at the annual meeting of the Sociologists for Women in Society, New York, August 1980), p. 19.
70. *Ibid.*
71. Francine D. Blau, "Women in the Labor Force: An Overview," in Jo Freeman, ed., *Women: A Feminist Perspective*, 2nd ed. (Palo Alto, Calif.: Mayfield, 1979), pp. 277–80.
72. National Research Council, *op. cit.*, p. 33.
73. *Ibid.*, pp. 54–56.
74. Mary Huff Stevenson, "Wage Differences Between Men and Women: Economic Theories," in Stromberg and Harkness, *op. cit.*, pp. 96–101.
75. Francine Blau, in Freeman, ed., *op. cit.*; Smith, *op. cit.*
76. National Research Council, *op. cit.*, p. 27.

77. *Ibid.*, p. 45.

78. *Ibid.*, pp. 56–58; Francine Blau, in Freeman, ed., *op. cit.*, p. 281.

79. U.S. Department of Labor, Women's Bureau, "Why Women Work," chart reproduced on p. 302; Kay Scholzman, "Women and Unemployment: Assessing the Biggest Myths," in Freeman, *op. cit.*, pp. 290–312.

80. Francine D. Blau, *Equal Pay in the Office* (Lexington, Mass.: Lexington Books, 1977), quoted on p. 39 of NRC report.

81. Smith, *op. cit.*, p. 39.

82. Isabel Sawhill, "The Economics of Discrimination Against Women: Some New Findings," *Journal of Human Resources* 8 (Summer 1973):383–395.

83. U.S. Department of Labor, Women's Bureau, "Why Women Work," Scholzman, in Freeman, *op. cit.*, pp. 290–312.

84. Sawhill, *op. cit.*

85. Janet Z. Giele, *Woman and the Future* (New York: Free Press, 1978), p. 105.

86. Mary F. McCarthy, "Women's Economic Roles, Problems, and Opportunities," in M. Richmond-Abbott, ed., *The American Woman* (New York: Holt, Rinehart and Winston, 1978), p. 198.

87. *Ibid.*

88. Kanter, *op. cit.*, chapters 6 and 7.

89. Goldberg, *op. cit.*; Kristin Moore and Isabel Sawhill, "Implications of Women's Employment for Home and Family Life," in Stromberg and Harkness, *op. cit.*, pp. 201–25.

90. Robert Stein, Professor, University of Colorado, personal communication.

91. Kantor, *op. cit.*; Stevenson, *op. cit.*, p. 99.

92. Sally H. Baker, "Women in Blue-Collar and Service Occupations," in Stromberg and Harkness, *op. cit.*, pp. 352–55.

93. Hartmann, Heidi, "Capitalism, Patriarchy and Job Segregation by Sex," *Signs* 1, pt. 2 (1976):137–69.

94. Mary Eastwood, "Legal Protection Against Sex Discrimination," in Stromberg and Harkness, *op. cit.*, p. 109.

95. *Ibid.*; Phyllis A. Wallace, "Impact of Equal Opportunity Laws," in Kreps, *op. cit.*, p. 125.

96. Wallace, *op. cit.*; Eastwood, *op. cit.*, pp. 109–12.

97. Eastwood, *op. cit.*

98. *Ibid.*, p. 111.

99. Wallace, *op. cit.*, p. 135.

100. *Ibid.*, p. 144.

101. J.K. Footlick, "The Landmark Bakke Ruling with Excerpts from the Supreme Court Opinion." *Newsweek*, July 10, 1978, pp. 18–24.

102. Nancy S. Barrett, "Women in the Job Market: Occupations, Earnings, and Career Opportunities," in Smith, *op. cit.*, p. 57.

103. Nancy M. Gordon, "Institutional Responses: The Federal Income Tax System," in Smith, *op. cit.*, pp. 201–21.

104. *Ibid.*, pp. 213–21.

105. Gordon, "Institutional Responses: The Social Security System," in Smith, *op. cit.*, pp. 223–55.

106. *Ibid.*, pp. 231–54; Giele, *op. cit.*, pp. 123–31.

107. Michelle Patterson and Laurie Engelberg, "Women in Male-Dominated Professions," in Stromberg and Harkness, *op. cit.*, p. 270.

108. *Ibid.*, p. 272.

109. *Ibid.*, p. 275.

110. Baker, *op. cit.*, p. 339.

111. Barbara Wertheimer, "Union Is Power: Sketches from Women's Labor History," in Freeman, *op. cit.*, p. 339.

112. *Ibid.*, p. 349.

113. Baker, *op. cit.*, p. 345.

114. *Ibid.*, p. 348.

115. *Ibid.*, p. 351.

116. Wertheimer, *op. cit.*, p. 354.

117. Baker, *op. cit.*, p. 368.

118. *Ibid.*

119. Almquist and Wehrle-Einhorn, *op. cit.*, p. 70.

120. *Ibid.*, p. 70.

121. Elizabeth Almquist, "Black Women and the Pursuit of Equality," in Freeman, *op. cit.*, pp. 440–41.

122. James Sweet, "Black-White Differences in Wives' Earnings and Contribution to Family Income," in *Women in the Labor Force,* Janet Sweet, ed. (New York: Seminar Press, 1973), pp. 168–98.

123. Almquist, *op. cit.*, p. 444.

124. Elizabeth Almquist, "Untangling the Effects of Race and Sex: The Disadvantaged Status of Black Women," *Social Science Quarterly* 56 (1975):116–28; Reynolds Farley, "Trends in Racial Inequalities: Have the Gains of the 1960's Disappeared in the 1970's?" *American Sociological Review* 42 (1977):422–30, as adapted in Almquist, *op. cit.*, p. 443.

125. Marcia W. Plunkett, "Meanings of Work for Mothers" (Paper presented at Women's Life Cycle and Public Policy Conference, University of Michigan, Ann Arbor, November 7, 1979).

126. Marie Richmond-Abbott, *Immigrant Adaptation and the Family Structure of Cubans in the U.S.* (New York: Arno Press, 1980).

127. Ivan Nye and Lois Hoffman, *The Employed Mother in America* (Chicago: Rand McNally, 1963), p. 286.

128. Rose Coser and Gerald Rabkoff, "Women in the Occupational World: Social Disruption and Conflict," in Rose Coser, ed. *The Family: Its Structure and Functions* (New York: St. Martin's Press, 1974).

129. Lee Burchenal, "Personality Characteristics of Children," in Nye and Hoffman, *op. cit.*, p. 118.

130. Elizabeth Douvan, "Employment and the Adolescent," in Nye and Hoffman, *op. cit.,* pp. 146–48; Ivan Nye, "The Adjustment of Adolescent Children," in Nye and Hoffman, 1963, *op. cit.,* pp. 133–41.

131. Nye and Hoffman, *op. cit.,* p. 204.

132. Ronald J. Burke and Tamara Weir, "Relationship of Wives' Employment Status to Husband, Wife, and Pair Satisfaction and Performance," *Journal of Marriage and the Family* 38 (1976):278–87.

133. Alan Booth, "Wife's Employment and Husband Stress: A Replication and Refutation," *Journal of Marriage and the Family* 39 (1977):645–50.

134. U.S. Census Bureau, 1978, Series P–23, no. 77–33.

135. Booth, *op. cit.*

136. Leland J. Axelson, "The Marital Adjustment and Marital Role Definitions of Husbands of Working and Nonworking Wives," *Marriage and Family Living* 25 (1963):189–95.

137. Patricia Rhoton and Anne S. Macke, "The Family Role Attitudes of Husbands and Wives: A Decade of Changes and Their Implications," Center for Human Resource Research, Ohio State University (Paper presented at the annual meeting of Sociologists for Women in Society, New York, August 1980).

138. Linda J. Waite and Ross Stolzenberg, "Intended Childbearing and Labor Force Participation of Young Women: Insights from Recursive Models," *American Sociological Review* 41 (1976):235–52.

139. Karen Mason and Larry Bumpass, "U.S. Women's Sex-Role Ideology, 1970," *American Journal of Sociology* 80 (1975):1212–19.

140. Karen Mason, G.R. Czajka, and Sara Arker, "Change in U.S. Women's Sex-Role Attitudes, 1964–1974," *American Sociological Review* 41 (1976):574–96.

141. Robert Blood, "The Husband-Wife Relationship," in Nye and Hoffman, eds., *op. cit.,* pp. 282–305.

142. John Scanzoni, *Sex Roles, Work, and Fertility* (New York: Free Press, 1977); Myra Marx Feree, "Causal Models of Stability and Change in Women's Work-Relevant Attitudes and Employment" (Final report for grant from the Employment and Training Administration, U.S. Dept. of Labor, Storrs, Connecticut, 1979); Mason, Czajka, and Arker, *op. cit.;* Ann Parelius, "Emerging Sex-Role Attitudes, Expectations, and Strains among College Women," *Journal of Marriage and the Family* 37 (1975):146–53.

143. Robert Blood and Donald Wolfe, *Husbands and Wives: The Dynamics of Married Living* (New York: Free Press, 1960), p. 246.

144. James D. Wright, "Are Working Women Really More Satisfied? Evidence from Several National Surveys," *Journal of Marriage and the Family* 40 (1978):301–13.

145. Rhoton and Macke, *op. cit.,* p. 17.

146. Gail Lapidus, "Occupational Segregation and Public Policy: A Comparative Analysis of American and Soviet Patterns," in Martha Blaxall and Barbara

Regan, eds., *Women and the Workplace* (Chicago: University of Chicago Press, 1976), p. 121.

147. Hartmann, *op. cit.*

148. Alfreda P. Inglehart, *Married Women and Work* (Lexington, Mass.: Lexington Books, 1976).

Chapter Ten

The Polling Place:
Law, Politics, and
the Women's Movement

The legal and political institutions of this country have been fortresses of tradition. Because laws are made by politicians and few women have been able to exercise political power, political and legal systems have historically resisted changes that would give women more rights. The laws of the land have usually discriminated against women. Only recently have women gained legal protection guaranteeing them such things as credit and equal employment opportunity. Even so, these new laws are only as good as their enforcement.

The women's movement has attempted to change the position of women by making people aware of the treatment of women as second-class citizens and by aiming for a wide variety of social change based on changes in values. Those people in the movement have also attempted through various kinds of political action to initiate legal change. Yet women still have not joined political elites in large numbers and are still divided on the issues of concern to them and the solutions to their problems.

We will examine in this chapter the position of men and women under the law, the history and present status of the women's movement, and the role of men and women in the political process.

Women, Men, and the Law

We attempt here to summarize briefly the recent laws that relate to work experience and other sex-role behavior. We have already described in some detail several of these laws in our discussion of the family and in the previous chapter on work. However, we believe it is important to get a single, comprehensive picture of all the relevant laws. Here we deliberately deal more with women and the law, as the laws limiting or affecting sex-role behavior have usually been those that limit the sex-role behavior of women. However, when unequal treatment under the law seems to exist or when men's behavior seems to be affected, we will try to point that out too. This summary is not meant to be an exhaustive treatment, but simply a description of the existing laws.

The Double Standard of the Law

Many laws that apply differentially to men and women seem to relate to the image of women as frail and theoretically sexually pure. Thus, many states have laws that prohibit using obscene language in the presence of women, and two states have laws that make it a crime to impugn the chastity of a woman.[1] Many states require only the man to get a venereal disease test before they issue a marriage license.[2] Statutory rape laws make it a crime for an adult male to have sexual intercourse with a female under a certain age; however, no such law applies to an adult female and an underage male.

Laws against rape are designed to protect the female, but only if she is proved to be "good" or "pure." Many laws assume that a woman who is sexually active cannot really be raped. Many also stipulate (or at least make an unstated assumption) that the victim should have resisted at whatever cost to herself. If she did not, it is frequently assumed that she really wanted to be raped and encouraged the rapist. The assumption that women really want to be raped or make false rape charges is seen in the fact that the burden of proof is placed upon the victim. (Rape is probably the only crime for which this is true.) The assumption that a "bad girl" deserves what she gets is often encouraged by reference to the victim's occupation (for example, cocktail waitress) or previous sexual history. Many lawyers have believed that the rape laws are really property laws designed to protect the property (wives and daughters) of men. If the victim of rape is living with her parents or under the protection of a husband, her claim of being raped is more likely to be believed and her assailant is more likely to be prosecuted. In 1974, California, Florida, Iowa, and Michigan passed laws that prohibited using the victim's past sexual conduct in the case; but victims are frequently grilled at length about their conduct before, during, and after the crime, in spite of these laws.[3] Susan Brownmiller details the history of rape and the beliefs about women and men that have shaped rape laws in her excellent book *Against Our Wills.* She shows that prevailing beliefs about women as good or bad and about men as creatures with irrepressible sex urges still dominate our rape laws.[4]

Divorce laws also show the double standard. In some states, discovery that a wife has had sexual intercourse with another man before marriage was grounds for divorce, while a husband's premarital intercourse was not. A single act of adultery by the wife is still grounds for divorce in one state (Kentucky), while such adultery by the husband is not considered grounds.[5]

Many believe that the opposition to abortion on demand is also largely based on the good/bad female dichotomy. The fact that state laws prohibiting abortion on demand have often been linked to state laws prohibiting information about contraception seems to show a punitive element rather than just a concern for possible life in the fetus: "Be good, or else. . . ."[*] Between 1967 and 1970, many states passed laws allowing abortion on restricted grounds, and in 1970, Hawaii, Alaska, and New York passed liberal laws that amounted to abortion on demand. In early 1973, the Supreme Court upheld a woman's constitutional right to abortion during the first three months of pregnancy.[6] Since that time, however, there has been an attempt to deny poor women abortion funding under Medicaid and to limit the right to abortion.

The swing toward right-wing philosophy in the early 1980s has reawakened antiabortion sentiments. Conservative right-wing groups are eager to amend the constitution so that abortion would be prohibited. However, because of the political difficulty in doing so, the first thrust of their efforts to limit abortion has been to attempt to pass antiabortion legislation in the U.S. Congress. The issue has become an explosive one, and liberal politicians who supported abortion and/or the Equal Rights Amendment have found themselves targeted for attempted removal from Congress by right-wing groups. Many have actually lost their seats because of the strong conservative effort against them. When the first woman Supreme Court justice, Sandra O'Connor, was nominated in 1981, right-wing groups also questioned whether or not she should be confirmed because they believed she might hold liberal views on abortion.

Women as Second-Class Citizens

The other category of laws affecting women comprises those that assume women are not the equals of men for citizenship purposes such as owning property, voting, or other participation in political and civil processes. Only after a long feminist struggle did women receive the vote by means of the Nineteenth Amendment in 1920. They are still considered second-class citizens in many states in terms of their fitness to sit on juries, in spite of the fact that this may mean a jury is unrepresentative of women's opinions. Women are especially considered second-class citizens when they get married, and specific legislation has had to be enacted to ensure that they have reasonable control over their own property, wages, and children. Despite the Married Women's Property acts, special restrictions on women's rights continue to exist in many states. A number of states restrict women's rights to make contracts and to engage in business on their own. Some states will not let women lease, mortgage, or own property unless their husbands are involved in the transactions. Other states keep women from serving as trustees. In five states, a wife must go to court to get approval to start a business, and if she is applying for a liquor license in New York State, she must submit a personal vita from her husband or another male relative.[7] A married woman must take as her legal domicile that of her husband (important in property and tuition cases). Although she does not have to take her husband's name (except in Hawaii), many state laws are based on the presumption that she will; and if, for example, she wishes to have a driver's license in her maiden name, she may have to go through a legal name change.

The support laws that supposedly protect married women actually mean little if the level of support can be determined by the husband. The assumption that the husband is the primary breadwinner may also hurt women's rights in some cases, such as where employee benefits extended to men are often not extended to women. The assumption of a male primary breadwinner hurts women under the social security laws.[8]

Credit Laws

The Equal Credit Opportunity Act passed in 1974 has been of great significance to women. It outlaws discrimination on the basis of sex or marital status in any aspect of a credit transaction. Under this act, single or married women are able to establish their own credit histories and to get loans. However, knowledge about the protection under this act is limited, and many women still suffer from credit discrimination. For example, a woman may not be aware that creditors are required to record credit histories of both spouses only if requested, and she may fail to make that request.

Another important act is the State and Local Fiscal Assistance Act of 1972 (revenue sharing), which prohibits exclusion from benefits or programs provided by the act by virtue of race, color, national origin, or sex.[9]

Equal Employment Opportunity (EEO) Laws

We reviewed the equal employment opportunity laws and executive orders in some detail in the previous chapter and refer the reader to that discussion. We should point out, however, that in spite of EEO laws, many states have laws that bar women "protectively" from certain occupations, such as mining, wrestling, and bartending. In some instances, the differences between similar but sex-differentiated occupations mean a considerable difference in pay (as between bartending and waitressing), and some have suggested that such protective laws are not completely chivalrous in nature. Most states have some type of protective labor laws that apply to women only and concern hours worked, weights lifted, or rest periods.[10] Congresswoman Martha Griffiths has stated that the result of the "so-called protective legislation has really been to protect men's rights in better-paying jobs."[11]

More recently, judicial decisions have weakened some of the equal employment opportunity laws. Decisions about pregnancy-related fringe benefits have gone against women in spite of the fact that EEOC guidelines say that pregnancy must be treated like any other temporary disability.[12] More serious still is the attempt by the Reagan administration to do away with many of the protections of Title IX and Title VII. Under a recent judicial decision, women's sports may not continue to receive the same funding as men's sports. As most women's sports are just beginning to come into their own and desperately need this kind of funding, this is a crucial decision.

One landmark case in discrimination was the celebrated Bakke case, in which Allan Bakke, a thirty-eight-year-old white engineer, sued the University of California's medical school at Davis, charging reverse discrimination and saying that less-well-qualified minority persons were admitted as students when he was not. The Supreme Court decision in that case was assumed to have great significance, as it would be the first time the Court had attempted to define the limits of affirmative action. The actual decision was somewhat ambiguous. The Court held that "quotas" (setting aside places for a certain number of minorities) were unacceptable, but found, in a 5-to-4 vote, that race may be considered as one factor in a university's admission policy. Bakke was granted admission to the medical school. Minorities and women were pleased with the decision that it is illegal to use quotas in the process of admission as these quotas are often used to limit rather than encourage admission. However, the other parts of the decision did not seem as favorable to affirmative action. The fact that the decision was based on Title VI of the Civil Rights Act of 1964 rather than on the U.S. Constitution was also seen to dilute the decision, and the Court was careful to make its decision applicable only to universities and not to businesses. Future cases will decide the real impact of the Bakke decision and whether or not the Court's rather tenuous commitment to affirmative action will extend to sex discrimination and to business.[13]

The Proposed Equal Rights Amendment

While we get ahead of our story to some degree by discussing the Equal Rights Amendment before talking about the women's movement itself, it is important to see the Equal Rights Amendment in the context of the other legislation that has been passed.

Many states have adopted equal rights laws, but because of the remaining inequalities, the various discrepancies in state laws, and the very real possibility of existing legislation being reversed, women have pushed for an Equal Rights Amendment to the Constitution that will guarantee them their rights. The proposed Equal Rights Amendment reads, "Equality of rights under the law shall not be denied or abridged by the United States or any State on account of sex."[14]

Although the Equal Rights Amendment was introduced in Congress in 1923, it did not pass both houses of Congress until March 22, 1972. After that it faced the long fight to be ratified in the necessary three-fifths of the states. Polls in 1975 showed the majority of men and women in favor of the amendment, and ratification looked relatively assured in 1978 when all but three of the states needed had ratified. The amendment's ratification had failed by only two to three votes in several states, and it was hoped that the amendment would pass in the next session of their legislatures. However, opponents of the ERA lobbied heavily against it and took advantage of the legislative process to bottle it up in committee in several states.[15]

Prospects for the passage of the ERA grew dim as the political climate of the country changed with the election of 1980, the resurgence of far-right groups, and the election of Ronald Reagan as president. Reagan ran on a conservative platform that disavowed support for the ERA and promised support for profamily legislation and antiabortion laws. In the election, many liberal members of Congress lost their seats as well. Most feminists felt that there was little chance of getting the ERA ratified, even after the time limit for such ratification was extended to June 1982. The National Organization for Women (NOW) continued to concentrate its efforts on passing the amendment, however, and held a "Last March for the ERA" in Washington in the fall of 1981 in a last-ditch effort to get it passed before the deadline. Although the mood of the country was conservative and the amendment was given little chance to be ratified within the time limit, the irony was that a June 1981 *Time* magazine poll reported 61 percent of the population in favor of it. A Washington-ABC poll about the same time confirmed that finding.[16]

Why Is the ERA Needed and What Would It Do If Passed?

The ERA has been needed all along to equalize laws throughout the country and to put the rights of women in constitutional form. In 1979, for example, there were still eight states where a woman did not have clear title to property in her name.[17] The push for repeal of prochoice legislation and affirmative-action laws in the conservative 1980s climate showed even more clearly how fragile the legislation protecting women was and how much women needed a constitutional amendment to ensure their rights.

The far-right groups have taken advantage of the confusion about the amendment to claim that it would destroy the family, would encourage homosexuality (no discrimination by "sex"), would cause women to be drafted, and would give rise to co-ed bathrooms. All these claims are totally false or greatly exaggerated. The right to privacy protects separate male and female bathrooms and dressing facilities; women can be drafted now if the president so chooses; homosexuality has nothing to do with equal protection under the law by gender. It is true that married women would lose some special privileges, such as automatic preference in child custody and support cases, but they would gain other benefits in the sense that their contribution to the marriage as homemakers would be recognized in any divorce settlement. Men would also gain, as protective laws that really *do* protect would be extended to men. Of course, this amendment would apply only to state and federal situations. Nothing in the private realm would be affected.[18] The real effect of the law would be to codify existing legislation and to remove inequalities between the states; any impact it had would be subject to the way it was enforced.

The Women's Movement

The real beginning of the feminist movement probably coincided with the growing emphasis on individual rights and democratic philosophy in the seventeenth century. While women were not specifically included in the ideal of human rights for men (read males), the whole principle of individual dignity and freedom encouraged women's desire to free themselves from the laws that made them little more than property and subject to men's control:

> Whether they fought for a reform of the marriage laws on the ground that no one should have property rights over other persons, whether they fought for equal educational facilities, or whether they emphasized the importance of suffrage as a means and the expression of their equality, the trend of thought behind all shades of feminist opinion was the democratic ideology.[19]

The general social reform movement of the early 1800s led women to fight for more education. In 1833, Oberlin College was the first college in the United States to admit both men and women; others followed suit, and all-women's colleges were also founded. The abolition movement of the 1830s was the real birthplace of the political part of the women's movement. Women such as the Grimkes and Lucy Stone, who fought for abolition, found that they were attacked for the very fact of speaking in public and were excluded from many men's abolitionist groups. As the abolitionist movement expanded, it included women like Lucretia Mott and Elizabeth Cady Stanton, who were delegates to a world antislavery convention held in London in 1840. Their exclusion from any real participation in that convention convinced these women that it was important to achieve women's rights as well as black rights.

They continued to work for women's property and family rights after returning from London, and in 1848 they advertised that a Woman's Rights Convention would be held in Seneca, New York. The turnout at this first meeting far exceeded their expectations, as some 300 women and men attended. The conference developed a list of twelve resolutions that were very similar in some parts to the Declaration of Independence and included a resolution that women should secure to themselves "their sacred right to the elective franchise." Most of the delegates were more interested in gaining rights to control their own property and wages, to get custody of their children when they divorced, and the like. After 1848 until the beginning of the Civil War, Women's Rights conventions were held every year.

When the Civil War began, women's rights supporters were urged to give up their struggle, support the war effort, and continue to push for abolition. They did so, assuming that they would be included in the Fourteenth and Fifteenth amendments, which secured the rights, privileges, and immunities of citizens to black males. However, many of the businessmen who wanted the black vote because they believed it would ensure Republican victories in the South saw no gain in giving women the vote. In fact, they were afraid that adding women's rights to the Constitution would jeopardize the whole bill. Thus, as the Fourteenth and Fifteenth amendments to the Constitution were interpreted, they guaranteed only the civil rights of males.

Women were disappointed and disillusioned, but in 1869 they formed the Women's American Suffrage Association, which attempted to push for women's right to vote. This association eschewed other women's issues in an attempt to make its activities respectable. At approximately the same time, Susan B. Anthony and Elizabeth Cady Stanton organized the National Women's Suffrage Association, which pushed for all kinds of women's rights and saw the vote only as a means for achieving those rights. During this same period, the temperance movement also attracted large numbers of women, including suffragists, who believed that restricting alcohol would improve their status *vis-à-vis* drunken or deserting husbands. Although the two suffrage organizations and the temperance movement coexisted for twenty years, the American Suffrage Association, with its limited aim of working only for women's suffrage, began to attract the majority of persons. Finally, in 1890 the two suffrage organizations merged to form the National American Women's Suffrage Association (NAWSA) with the single aim of achieving the vote for women.

Around 1900, a new generation of suffragists became the leaders of the organization, including Carrie Chapman Catt, who succeeded Susan Anthony as president of NAWSA. Gradual progress was made as a few western states gave the vote to women, but the major impetus to the campaign for suffrage came when Alice Paul, a young militant, formed the Congressional Union, a small, radical group, to work on a campaign for federal women's suffrage. This group organized parades and hunger strikes to call attention to their cause, and many of their members were vilified and even jailed for their efforts.[20] The women committed to suffrage had to make a tremendous effort to achieve their ends.

> Before women got the vote in 1920, they had organized 56 referendum campaigns, 480 campaigns to get state legislatures to allow suffrage referenda, 47 campaigns at state constitutional conventions for suffrage, 277 campaigns to include suffrage in state party programs, 30 campaigns to get women's suffrage in national party programs, and 19 campaigns to get the 19th Amendment through Congress.[21]

The 19th Amendment or Women's Suffrage Amendment (known as the "Anthony Amendment") was introduced into every session of Congress from 1878 on and was finally ratified on August 26, 1920.

Unfortunately, so much energy had gone into achieving the vote that the women's movement had little energy left for other issues. During the 1920s, the country was involved in enjoying itself as the war came to an end; in the 1930s, the country was occupied with getting out of the Great Depression; by the 1940s, the country was involved in another war.

In addition, few women took advantage of the franchise. In the 1920 election, it was estimated that only 43 percent of the eligible women voted; by 1940, only 49 percent were voting, compared to 68 percent of the eligible men. A women's bloc vote never really came about. Voters divided on the issues more by education, occupation, and region than by sex. As a result of their work-time experience during World War II, women briefly renewed the fight for equal rights during the Progressive party campaign of 1948, but they were overcome by the conservative advocates of "return to normalcy."[22] Women were urged to return to the home and hearth and to let families and the country get back to normal. The *feminine mystique* of the 1950s, however, coexisted with more and more women returning to the workplace. By 1960, 36 percent of all women were in the work force and concerned about their wages and treatment. It took the civil rights movements of the early 1960s to show them that they, as well as blacks, needed to fight for their rights. Many women gained political experience in the civil rights movement and the antiwar movement that followed in the mid-1960s and were thus better equipped to advance the feminist cause. Women began to vote in greater numbers from the 1960s onward, and they voted at roughly the same rates as men by 1976. The voting record of black women in particular was almost equal to that of black men in the presidential elections of 1964, 1968, and 1972.[23]

In 1961, President John Kennedy established a Presidential Commission on the Status of Women, partly as a way to repay women who had worked in his campaign and partly as a way, some believe, to get out of working for the Equal Rights Amendment. As a result of the commission's report, equal pay bills followed.[24]

In 1963, Betty Friedan published *The Feminine Mystique*, which was an indictment of the "happy homemaker" role. By 1965 to 1966, it was clear that there would be little change in that role if women depended on enforcement of the Equal Employment Opportunity legislation.[25] Betty Friedan, Martha Griffiths, and others organized the National Organization for Women (NOW) in 1966. The early organizers of NOW tended to be older, white, middle-class, college-educated women. While NOW was seen as radical, its style was actually somewhat conservative and stressed working through established legislative channels to achieve rights for women. Other women's groups also formed that emphasized working through the establishment to achieve change. Groups such as the National Women's Political Caucus, the Women's Equity Action League, Federally Employed Women, and many different organizations of professional women were active. All these groups also used formal organizations with elected officers.[26]

At the same time, another branch of the women's movement was forming among younger women. As early as 1964, Ruby Robinson presented to a Student Non-Violent Coordinating Committee's (SNCC) conference a paper in which she protested the inferior status accorded women within the organization. These younger, more radical women had become politicized in the civil rights and antiwar movements and in student demonstrations. In all these New Left movements, women's liberation ideas had taken hold, and women objected to being used only as envelope stuffers and sexual partners for the men of the movement while the men made major decisions and dominated meetings. Stokely Carmichael added fuel to their discontent with his now infamous statement, "The only position for women in SNCC is prone."[27]

The women in the New Left attempted to incorporate feminist ideas into the programs of their various organizations, but their task was not easy. Women who demanded at the 1966 Students for a Democratic Society (SDS) national convention that the organization adopt a plank supporting a women's rights were pelted with tomatoes and expelled from the convention. In other New Left organizations, women were manipulated into giving up their stand for women's rights.[28]

Eventually, women in the New Left splintered into two major factions: *politicos,* who believed that the political issues of their group should come before women's rights, and *feminists,* who favored an independent women's movement.[29] The feminists grew more and more discontented with the position of the New Left on women's issues, and the antagonism between the two groups reached a head in January 1969 at the counterinaugural demonstration in Washington organized by Mobilization for Peace. Men in the audience responded to a very mild feminist speech by booing the speaker and yelling such remarks as, "Take her off the stage and fuck her." The women in the audience were outraged, and many who had been hesitating about their political affiliation were convinced that they needed an independent women's movement.[30] Although the New Left males repented enough to include some women's rights issues in future platforms, many of the feminist women left the male-dominated movement to form their own loosely structured independent women's groups. These groups were different in nature and intent from the older, strictly organized National Organization for Women. Their membership was not only younger but generally espoused a much more radical philosophy.

"Liberal" versus "Radical" Feminism

The earlier feminists concentrated in NOW and similar organizations perceived sexism as "based on a 'society' or 'system' which created 'sex role stereotypes' which oppressed both men and women equally."[31] The *radical feminists* disliked this approach to explaining sexism because they believed that it had three major weaknesses: (1) it did not stress the fact the men were the true political enemy; (2) it made it look as though women were brainwashed ("socialized") into an inferior position rather than forced into it by the superior power—that is, it stressed the stereotypes created by the institutions rather than the domination of men; and (3) it was *ethnocentric* and applied mainly to middle- and upper-class women.

The radical feminists believed, in addition, that women's issues were part of a general revolutionary struggle, that you could not change the system within the established economic and political system and its institutions, and that women must exclude men from their movement, because they gained nothing by cooperation with their oppressors. Unfortunately, other than the programs of the various New Left organizations, they did not have a specific program for changing society. They believed that they could effect radical change on an individual grass roots basis by forming small, personal "rap groups" for "consciousness raising." Women would be drawn into these groups on the basis of their own experiences with sexism and would transform their personal experiences into a political awareness of sexism. "The revolutionary transformation of society would follow as more and more women had their consciousness raised and rejected the ideological and institutional bases of sexism."[32] The radical feminists used other techniques as well: street theatre, new-language, demonstrations (the famous "bra burnings," where uncomfortable clothes were rejected and thrown into trash cans before the Miss America pageant of 1968), and an emphasis on political lesbianism.[33]

However, this younger branch of the movement had tough going. At first the media ridiculed it, and then some of its issues were incorporated into the more mainstream liberal feminist philosophy. David Bouchier suggests that more moderate feminist publications like *Ms.* magazine played a big part in the co-optation of the radicals. They became the voice of the women's liberation movement to the outside world. As liberal feminists like Steinem and Abzug captured the leadership of the National Women's Political Caucus in the early 1970s, the leaders of the moderate organizations and certain sympathetic women politicians in state and national legislatures increasingly became the only spokeswomen heard within the movement.[34] The radicals were drowned out and seen as espousing different ideas that would be difficult to translate into action. Bouchier claims that in a sense the women's liberation movement had become a professional social movement with a large resource base and could not afford to step very far outside the dominant ideology.

The New Left further isolated the radical feminists by excluding them (or they excluded themselves) from the general leftist movement or attempted to use the radical feminist groups for its own ends. At one point, the Young Socialist Alliance tried to infiltrate the radical feminist movement with the idea of making socialist converts. While they were expelled after bitter conflict, the confrontation further weakened the radical feminists.[35]

Another major crisis occurred over the role of lesbians in the movement. Lesbians within the movement attempted to espouse the idea that lesbianism was the feminist ideal. They believed that lesbian women typified the independence needed by all women, as they were their own support, took care of their own affairs, and were not dependent on men in any way. The extreme of this view was that you were not really a feminist unless you were a lesbian. At the same time, straight women were not eager to be identified with lesbianism and felt that the lesbian rhetoric added a difficult and unacceptable value system to the women's rights philosophy. Many of the straight women dropped out of these radical groups, and many joined NOW or rejoined the New Left. Eventually, gay women predominated in the rap groups by about 4 to 1, and the focus of the groups changed from recruiting new members to building a women's culture for those who remained.[36]

In the meantime, the movement of many of these radical women into NOW and the pressure from the rap groups caused NOW to move in a more radical direction in the mid-1970s. Although NOW had also been troubled owing to factions and splits that developed because it had attracted so many different kinds of people, its wide appeal meant that it had grown tremendously since its inception. During this time, it went through a phase of decentralization and had three national offices with different functions.[37] In 1974, a hotly contested presidential election nearly split NOW into two groups. The winners recentralized the NOW political structure in Washington and established a paid staff and a hierarchy of state organizations.

Eventually the ideology of NOW also centralized and focused on a single issue: the passage of the proposed Equal Rights Amendment. As rightist groups rose that fought abortion, busing, and gay rights along with the ERA, the amendment became symbolic of the continuation of the movement for equal rights for women. When the potential amendment still lacked three states necessary for ratification one year from the March 22, 1979, deadline, NOW decided it would concentrate its primary efforts on the passage of the ERA. Freeman and Carden have pointed out that with this decision NOW became really an interest group rather than a social movement. It had developed a single-issue focus similar to the early suffrage movement that would make it difficult to consider other issues in the future.[38]

The 1970s

We need to return to the middle 1970s, however, and pick up the general story of the women's movement. The United Nations had condemned sex discrimination worldwide and had called 1975 the International Women's Year (IWY). One hundred thirty-three countries sent a total of 1,300 delegates to the IWY conference held in Mexico City. The aim was to develop a ten-year reform plan of action to begin a movement toward a total reform of society's laws, attitudes to enable women to become equal with men.

It was clear from the beginning of the IWY conference that the delegates were not going to listen to the dictates and platform of the white, affluent nations. In a confrontation between Chicanas, blacks, and Betty Friedan, it was made clear that while delegates from other nations respected the older leaders of the feminist movement, they wanted to speak for themselves. In spite of many disagreements, a ten-year plan was developed, and the delegates recommended another conference in five years to check on its progress.[39] In the United States, a National Commission on the Observance of Women's Year, with thirty-five private and four congressional members as well as dozens of committees on state levels, developed proposals to implement the plan in this country. Two of the major accomplishments of this commission were (1) an amendment to foreign aid bills by Charles Percy, which required that the impact on women be considered when instituting training programs in overseas countries, and (2) an agreement by the Census Bureau that it would target women who had been divorced five years or more to ask about problems in alimony and child support. The commission also worked toward the convening of a national conference in the following year.[40]

The National Women's Conference was convened at Houston in November 1977. The conference and its proposed program for women's rights was under heavy attack from rightist groups, spearheaded by Phyllis Schafly and 15,000 antiabortion demonstrators. Although these rightist groups were unable to disrupt the actual feminist gathering as they had hoped, the feminists had their own problems. There was an increasing concern about the need to deal with the problems of black and working-class women, particularly with such issues as day care and conditions of employment. It was also necessary to deal with the explosive and essentially disruptive issue of lesbian rights. Dealing with these issues was particularly difficult at this time because incorporating the demands of blacks and gays into the platform of the feminist movement added fuel to the attack from the right. However, after pain and agitation, the conference adopted a platform endorsing lesbian rights and a commitment to press for day care and improved conditions of employment, among other concerns of black and working-class women.[41]

It is appropriate here to digress from the chronological format to say something about the role of black women in the women's liberation movement.

Black Feminism and the Women's Movement

Black women have not been in the forefront of the current women's movement. A number of reasons have been advanced to explain their lack of interest and participation in the women's liberation movement as it developed. The women's movement arose at the same time that civil rights and the black power movement were also gaining prominence.

Many black intellectuals and spokesmen believed that sexism would be a racially divisive issue and were concerned about keeping the focus on the liberation of black males. In particular, because black women were often able to find jobs when black men could not and because the myth of black matriarchy was so prevalent, many black leaders believed that any further push toward liberation by the black woman would further emasculate the black man.[42]

One editorial in *Ebony* paid tribute to the black woman's accomplishments in the past but reminded readers that the "past is behind us, the immediate goal of the Negro woman today should be the establishment of a strong family unit in which the father is the dominant person," and the Negro woman should follow the example of the Jewish mother, "who pushed her husband to success, educated her male children first, and engineered good marriages for her daughters."[43] Many divisions of the black power movement, like the Black Muslims, particularly emphasized the submission of black women, and the black church stressed biblical injunctions about the importance of patriarchy.[44]

Racism among white women was also an issue. Many black women saw all whites—men and women—as sharing the same values and were reluctant to identify with anything affecting the white female.[45] In addition, the early women's liberation movement did not concern itself with many of the issues that were of greatest concern to black women: unemployment and underemployment, poor education in the schools, child care, minimum wage for service wage, and increased wages at all levels. Willa Mae Hemmons also points out that while white women were attempting to enter the labor force in greater numbers, many black women would have been happy to give up their necessary labor force participation if only they could have counted on the economic support of a black man.[46]

The women's liberation movement itself made little attempt to recruit blacks until very recent years. After the International Women's Year meeting in Mexico City in 1975, the issues of concern to nonwhite women (in this country or in the third world) were more clearly seen, and many of the issues like child care and a minimum wage for domestic service were made priorities at the Houston National Women's Conference. However, NOW's more recent absorption with the passage of the ERA has meant that many of those issues have been at least temporarily sidelined.[47]

At the same time, black women are coming to see that any women's power movement is important to them. Various female black intellectuals have pointed out the necessity for combatting sexism as well as racism. Michelle Wallace urged other black women to stop being superwoman and to push for their own aspirations in her 1979 book, *Black Macho and the Myth of the Superwoman.*[48] Shirley Chisholm has described how she has suffered more discrimination from being a woman than from being a black.[49] Pauline Stone has summed up many of the reasons that black women should be involved in eradicating sexism:

1. It would enable black women and men to attain a more accurate and deeper level of understanding. . . . Such problems as the black male unemployment rate, the absence of the black male in the family, the large representation of black women on welfare, and the high black illegitimacy rate are just a few of the many social problems afflicting blacks that are, in part at least, attributable to the operation of sexism in our society.
2. Elimination of sexism on the interpersonal level within black culture would result in . . . increasing the general pool of black abilities.
3. A feminist consciousness in ridding black males and females of their socially conditioned anxieties concerning masculinity and femininity would foster greater psychological well-being. . . .[50]

Whether black women will actually become more involved in the organized women's liberation movement will, however, depend a great deal on the direction that the movement takes in the future and on whether or not it addresses concerns of the black community.

Present Status of the Women's Liberation Movement

There is an irony in the present women's movement: the radical groups have become concerned with reform, such as establishing clinics for women, and the more conservative, structured organizations like NOW have become more radical. At the moment, the movement is fighting a defensive action. NOW attempted last-ditch measures to try to get the ERA passed before the extended deadline ran out on June 30, 1982. NOW organized a "Last March for the ERA" in Washington in late 1981 and then continued to lobby for its passage. However, most politicians agreed even then that there was little chance of the amendment being passed by the deadline. Indeed, no further states ratified the proposed amendment during the extended time limit, and several that had previously ratified it attempted to rescind their votes. In spite of desperate last attempts to gain ratification in three more states, which included sit-ins and fasting by movement members while the Illinois legislature was debating the proposed amendment, June 30, 1982 saw the expiration of the time limit without ratification. The irony in the defeat was that over 52 percent of the American public still approved the amendment and only 34 percent were actually opposed to it.[51]

People in the various branches of the women's movement vowed their determination to reintroduce the amendment in Congress and to again work for ratification. They asserted their belief that what they have learned about politics in the long struggle would enable them to succeed in getting the amendment ratified the next time.

Women are also concerned about keeping on the books the important legislation for which the movement was largely responsible. This legislation has come under attack by a number of conservative groups. Groups such as the National Association for Abortion Rights Legislation (NAARL) are determined to keep fighting to keep the right to choose abortion that was guaranteed by the Supreme Court in 1973. Planned Parenthood got ready to battle a Reagan administration proposal to require clinics to notify parents if minors obtain contraceptives (a proposal that would probably keep many minors from seeking contraception). Other groups continue fighting to maintain gay rights, to keep the focus on affirmative action, to keep the federal government from cutting day care and other similar issues. The difficulty of their task was pointed out in remarks by Phyllis Shafly, spokesperson of the conservatives, who vowed that she and her followers would fight against sex education, non-sexist textbooks and even the nuclear freeze.[52]

The movement is fighting not only well-organized and well-financed far-right groups but the implicit consent of the federal administration for these conservative actions. The Reagan administration has refused to support the Equal Rights Amendment or abortion rights and has made it clear by its pronouncements on Title VII and Title IX that it does not intend to enforce affirmative action laws. (It also attempted to allow colleges that discriminate to once again receive tax-exempt status, although this decision was revoked after a huge public outcry.)

In this fight, the women's movement has been able to count on few allies. Liberal senators were targeted for defeat and indeed were defeated in recent elections. Unions have been preoccupied with keeping jobs for their members rather than with affirmative action. The poorer groups associated with the women's movement have been occupied with survival in a recessionary economy. The media have given the womens' movement little publicity. There is also dissension among different factions of the movement itself and disagreement as to what goals to emphasize. In this climate, it seems important to examine the possibility that women may be able to exercise power through political elites or by mobilizing as a voting bloc.

Women and Men in Political Elites

Women have seldom been found in large numbers in political elites. Politics has always been seen as the dirty and smoke-filled arena reserved for men. Women have been few in numbers in the occupations that have led to political office. More than half the members of Congress have always been lawyers, and men have traditionally dominated the political parties. Another difficulty for women seeking political office is the inability to raise funds. Women are not likely to have the business connections and credit that men have; nor are they likely to be considered "winning candidates" and thus to be financed. Most of the early women in Congress were widows of congressmen.

There is evidence, however, that the outlook is changing slightly. As more and more women enter law school, they are gaining the requisite qualifications to run for office. Women are also participating more actively in politics and are being rewarded for their participation. (Black women, in particular, have used their experience in the civil rights movement to assertively enter the halls of Congress.)[53]

Women have probably been making the biggest advances in state legislatures. In 1963, there were 351 women legislators; in 1976, this total had increased to 685. However, this figure is only 9.1 percent of the total number of legislators. Until 1974, only three women had been elected state governors, and they came to office largely in their capacity as wives. However, in 1974 Ella Grasso was elected the Democratic governor of Connecticut; and Dixie Lee Ray, governor of the state of Washington. The number of women members of the House and Senate has grown very slowly, rising to only nineteen in the 1977–78 Congress. The two women in the Senate were Muriel Humphrey and Marion Allen, who were appointed to succeed their late husbands. In 1980, the totals were

Table 1. *Percentages of Men and Women in Political Elites*

	Women	Men
U.S. Population	51.3%	48.7%
U.S. Senators	1	99
U.S. Representatives	4	96
Governors*	4	96
Lt. Governors	12	88
State Senators	5	95
State Representatives	11	89
County Officials	5	95
Mayors and Councilors	9	91

*Ella Grasso has since died.
Source: National Women's Education Fund and the Center for American Women in Politics, printed handout, 1980.

17 women and 585 men.[54] In 1980, the statistics on women in politics still reflected how little they had joined the political elites (Table 1.).[55]

Even when elected to Congress, women have difficulty obtaining power. As power is based on seniority and committee assignments, influence comes from winning reelection enough times to gain prestigious assignments. Few women are reelected enough times to do this. Only eighteen congresswomen have served five or more terms between 1918 and 1978.[56] Women's records in attaining high administrative or appointive posts have been very limited. There have only been five female cabinet members. Two of these were Carter appointees: Secretary of Commerce Juanita M. Kreps and Patricia Robert Harris at HUD. President Reagan has also appointed only a small number of women and almost none to administrative policy making positions; however, he mollified women with the appointment of a conservative woman juror, Sandra O'Connor, as the first woman on the U.S. Supreme Court.[57]

Possibilities for the Future—A Bloc Vote?

Although women did not vote in great numbers right after they achieved the franchise, their political participation began to improve at about the time of the New Deal administration. Tables 2 and 3 show that year by year the voting turnout for women has increased; their voting activity now is almost parallel to that of men and is equal in the younger age groups.

Lansing suggests that in the late 1940s and the 1950s women voted less than men because they had little sense that they could influence anything by their vote. Recent changes in the level of women voting are closely associated with their increasing level of education and with their participation in the work force.[58] Younger women, who are among the best educated, participate most fully in the political process.

Table 2. *Percentages of Men and Women Voting in Elections, 1948–1976*

	1948	1952	1956	1960	1964	1968	1972	1976
Men	69	72	80	80	73	69	64	54
Women	59	62	69	69	70	66	62	53

Sources: Center for Political Studies, University of Michigan, 1972; data were obtained from U.S. Department of Commerce, Bureau of the Census, *Current Population Reports, Population Characteristics,* "Voting Participation in November 1972," ser. P-20, no. 244, December 1972; "Voting and Registration in the Election of November, 1976," ser P-20, no. 322, March 1978; in Marjorie Lansing, "Women in American Politics" in Richmond-Abbott, ed., *The American Woman* (New York: Holt, Rinehart, and Winston, 1979), p. 231.

Table 3. *Sex Differences in Presidential Voting by Age Group, 1964, 1968, and 1972*

Age Group	1964 Male	1964 Female	1968 Male	1968 Female	1972 Male	1972 Female
18–24					48	49
21–24	53	52	53	53	50	52
25–29	66	65	63	63	58	58
30–34					66	67
35–44	75	72	74	72	66	67
45–54	79	75	78	76	72	70
55–64	80	74	79	74	72	69
65–74	78	67	79	69	73	64
75 and older	67	50	68	51	67	49

Source: John Stucker, "Women as Voters," in Githens and Prestage, *op. cit.* (Adapted from Table 15.4, Lansing, *The American Woman.*

What is the relationship of feminism to women's participation in the political process? One recent study published in March 1981 shows that strength of general personal attitudes (liberal or conservative) is probably more likely than feminism specifically to influence greater political participation by women. Feminist attitudes are related to political participation, but this is only noticeably true for minority women, who, without such values, normally participate less than white women in campaign activity, voting, local political participation, and protest participation.[59] Feelings of efficacy or control were also important for women to have if they were to participate in the political process. In her study, Fulkenwilder points out that after the high point of the passage of the ERA through Congress with overwhelming votes in 1972, women's sense of political efficacy has declined. She notes that by 1976 a strong opposition to the ERA was evident in right-wing groups, the pay gap between men and women had actually widened, and most other feminist demands like day care and homemaker rights were being evaded by politicians. By 1976, more feminists than other women were likely to say that they did not feel they could influence or control government. Minority women were particularly likely to say that they did not feel they had control of government, as they saw the dismantling of many of the antipoverty programs and benefits.[60]

When women do vote, their stand on issues like abortion and the ERA is not very different from that of men.[61] In fact, early voting data described women as more conservative than men, but in the last three out of four elections, women have voted more heavily for Democratic presidential candidates. Recent polls conducted by Louis Harris and Gallup show that women do vote differently on some issues. They are less likely to seek military solutions to international problems, for example.[62]

While there is little hard data to support this opinion, pollsters and politicians estimate that women will begin to differentiate even more between candidates by their position on women's issues. Women political delegates already vote more liberally than men on women's issues.[63] At the same time, there is unlikely to be a women's bloc vote per se on such issues as abortion or the ERA, as a sizable minority of women disavow the women's movement stance in these areas.[64] Lansing suggests that if such a bloc vote does occur, college-educated women will be the most likely to organize as a women's bloc vote and to seek positions among the political elites.

The political process is an important part of any change. We can see in these changing times that the laws and protections that have enabled change to occur can easily be eliminated. The extent to which women participate in the political process may determine the future course of legal changes that affect sex roles. If they wish to exercise leverage on candidates to support women's issues, it is necessary that women consolidate their votes. If they wish to elect women candidates, they must be active in fund raising and political organizing. Although the present political climate is not promising in terms of action to affirm women's rights, women are more likely to have the means to enter the political arena and to gain political power as woman's socialization and occupational roles change. As a result, they are more likely to be able to influence and enact legislation that will help them in the future.

Essay Questions

1. Describe the "double standard of the law" as it applies to men and women. Be sure to include laws dealing with sexual attitudes and behavior, economics, and employment in your answer.
2. What is the text of the Equal Rights Amendment as proposed? Why have feminists pushed for its passage, and what would it actually do (in terms of alleged changes like co-ed bathrooms) if passed?
3. Discuss the statement, "Although women have had the vote for only sixty years, they are not participating equally in politics with men, both in voting behavior and participation in political elites." How accurate is this statement?
4. Discuss the possibilities of women developing a bloc vote in the future according to the information you have gained about their his-

torical participation in politics. Do you believe that feminism will influence and accelerate the development of such a bloc vote?

Exercises

1. Discuss your feelings about laws that protect women (such as laws putting weight limits on what they can lift at work, laws that keep them from taking "unsavory" work, and the like). Do you feel that such laws should be continued?
2. Do you believe that the situation of women and minorities has been improved with the equal opportunity employment laws? Why or why not?
3. How do you feel about the proposed Equal Rights Amendment and the possibility that women will lose certain privileges like preference in child custody cases? How do you feel about women being drafted to serve in the army? What do you feel should be the relationship between rights and responsibilities as the law changes? Discuss these issues.
4. If women had access to public sources of funding for campaign funds, do you believe that they would be better represented in political elites? Discuss why you think so or not.
5. Pretend you are a woman who would like to run for president of the United States. What particular issues would you emphasize in your campaign to appeal to a "women's vote"?
6. Do you believe that a woman would make as good a president of the United States as a man would? Discuss your feelings about this issue. Do the women differ from the men in the class in their views?

Notes

1. Barbara Deckhard, *The Women's Movement* (New York: Harper & Row, 1979), p. 157.
2. *Ibid.*, p. 151.
3. *Ibid.*, pp. 152–55.
4. Susan Brownmiller, *Against Our Will: Men, Women, and Rape* (New York: Simon and Schuster, 1975).
5. Deckhard, *op. cit.*, p. 155.
6. *Ibid.*, p. 156.
7. *Ibid.*, p. 165.
8. *Ibid.*, p. 169; Mary Eastwood, "Feminism and the Law," in J. Freeman, ed., *Women: A Feminist Perspective,* 2nd ed., (Palo Alto, Calif.: Mayfield, 1979), p. 391.

9. Deckhard, *op. cit.*, p. 171.

10. *Ibid.*, pp. 175–77.

11. Martha Griffiths, quoted in Deckhard, *op. cit.*, p. 177.

12. *Ibid.*, p. 183; Eastwood, *op. cit.*, pp. 396–400.

13. Jerrold K. Footlick with Diane Camper and Lucy Howard, "The Landmark Bakke Ruling," *Newsweek*, July 10, 1978, reprinted in *Annual Editions, Social Problems, 1979–1980* (Guilford, Conn.: Duskin Press, 1979).

14. Majorie Lansing, "Women in American Politics," in Marie Richmond-Abbott, ed., *The American Woman* (New York: Holt, Rinehart and Winston, 1978), p. 239.

15. *Ibid.*, pp. 239–41; Deckhard, *op. cit.*, pp. 85–89.

16. "Twilight of the ERA." *Time Magazine*, July 13, 1981, p. 17; M. Beck and others, "Last Hurrah for the ERA?" *Newsweek*, June 13, 1981, p. 24.

17. Deckhard, *op. cit.*, pp. 185–89.

18. *Ibid.*, pp. 280–300; Lansing, *op. cit.*, pp. 228–29.

19. Viola Klein, "Feminism: The Historical Background," in Jo Freeman, ed., *op. cit.*

20. Judith Hole and Ellen Levine, "The First Feminists," in Freeman, *op. cit.*, pp. 543–56.

21. Carrie Chapman Catt and Nettie Rogers Shuler, *Woman Suffrage and Politics* (New York, 1923), p. 107, quoted in Hole and Levine, *op. cit.*, p. 554.

22. Deckhard, *op. cit.*, pp. 342–43; Judith Hole and Ellen Levine, *Rebirth of Feminism* (New York: Quadrangle, 1971), p. 18.

23. Marjorie Lansing, "Voting Patterns of the American Black Woman," in Marianne Githens and Jewel Prestage, eds., *A Portrait of Marginality* (New York: McKay, 1977), p. 391; John Stucker, "Women as Voters," in Githens and Prestage, *op. cit.*, p. 276.

24. Deckhard, *op. cit.*, pp. 346–49.

25. Maren Lockwood Carden, *The New Feminist Movement* (New York: Russell Sage Foundation, 1974), pp. 59–70.

26. Hole and Levine, in Freeman, *op. cit.*

27. *Ibid.*

28. Carden, *op. cit.*, p. 60.

29. Jo Freeman, "The Women's Liberation Movement: Its Origins, Organizations, Activities, and Ideas," in Freeman, *op. cit.*, pp. 557–74.

30. Carden, *op. cit.*, p. 62.

31. David Bouchier, "The Deradicalization of Feminism: Ideology and Utopia in Action," *Sociology* 13 (1979):387–402.

32. *Ibid.*, p. 389.

33. Carden, *op. cit.*, p. 63.

34. Bouchier, *op. cit.*, p. 394.

35. Carden, *op. cit.*, pp. 63–65.

36. Freeman, *op. cit.*, p. 567.

37. *Ibid.*, p. 564.

38. *Ibid.*

39. P. Simpson, "The Impact of Mexico City," *Civil Rights Digest* 8 (1975):10–17.

40. *Ibid.*

41. M. Sheils, and others, "A Women's Agenda: National Women's Conference in Houston" *Newsweek*, November 28, 1977, pp. 57–58; A.T. Fleming, "That Week in Houston: National Women's Conference," *New York Times Magazine*, Dec. 25, 1977, p. 10–13.

42. Pauline Terrelonge Stone, "Feminist Consciousness and Black Women," in Freeman, *op. cit.*, pp. 575–88.

43. Quoted on p. 92 of Pauli Murray, "The Liberation of Black Women," in Mary Lou Thompson, ed., *Voices of the New Feminism* (Boston: Beacon Press, 1971).

44. Stone, *op. cit.*, p. 575.

45. *Ibid.*, p. 583.

46. Willa Mae Hennons, "The Women's Liberation Movement: Understanding Black Women's Attitudes," in La Frances Rodgers-Rose, ed., *The Black Woman* (Beverly Hills, Calif.: Sage, 1980).

47. Freeman, *op. cit.*

48. Michelle Wallace, *Black Macho and the Myth of the Superwoman* (New York: Dial, 1978).

49. Shirley Chisholm, "Women Must Rebel," in Thompson, *op. cit.*, pp. 207–16.

50. Stone, *op. cit.*, p. 583.

51. Adam Clymer, "Time Runs Out for the Proposed Equal Rights Amendment," *New York Times*, July 1, 1982, A-12.

52. M. Beck, "Tell tale Birth Control," *Newsweek*, April 5, 1982, p. 33; Lynn Rosellini, "Victory is Bittersweet for Architect of Amendment's Downfall," *New York Times*, July 1, 1982, A–12.

53. Lansing, in Richmond-Abbott, *op. cit.*, p. 236.

54. Naomi B. Lynn, "American Women and the Political Process," in Freeman, *op. cit.*, pp. 418–21.

55. Figures compiled by the National Women's Education Fund and the Center for American Women in Politics, printed handout, 1980.

56. Lynn, *op. cit.*, p. 422.

57. *Ibid.*, p. 424; Lansing, in Richmond-Abbott, *op. cit.*, pp. 236–37. Robert Kittle and Patricia Avery, "Appointments Issue," *U.S. News and World Report*, May 31, 1982, 51.

58. Lansing, in Richmond-Abbott, *op. cit.*, pp. 232–34.

59. Claire Knoche Fulkenwider, "Feminist Ideology and the Political Attitudes and Participation of White and Minority Women," *Western Political Quarterly* 34 (1981):25.

60. *Ibid.*, p. 23.

61. 1976 data from the University of Michigan.
62. Lansing, in Richmond-Abbott, *op. cit.*, p. 230; John Soule and Wilma McGraths, "A Comparative Study of Male-Female Political Attitudes at Citizen and Elite Levels," in Githens and Prestage, *op. cit.*, p. 185.
63. Soule, *op. cit.*, p. 181.
64. Lansing, in Richmond-Abbott, *op. cit.*, p. 241.

Chapter Eleven

Sex Roles Over the Life Cycle: Summary and Discussion of Future Possibilities

We have come full circle from our discussion of gender, status, and sex roles in the Preface. We have seen that male-dominated institutions initiate and perpetuate the differential status of many women, although there is little or no scientific evidence supporting differential treatment on the grounds that behavior is functionally related to biological differences. We have seen how gender thus limits one's socialization and assignment to social roles. Yet, socialization and cultural assignment of social roles are the major elements affecting the development of individual traits and such behaviors as occupational choice, political participation, and family role.

We also realize just how much sex or gender is a stimulus variable. We have seen that our culture believes that the sexes have different behavior patterns that are appropriate for each sex and that people react differently to the same behavior from a man or a woman because of expectations about what is appropriate behavior. These behavioral expectations are not only different for each sex, but they have status rankings; masculine traits and behaviors are preferred in the great majority of situations by most people. Thus, one's gender becomes a status that limits one's behavior and affects one's chances for success in the world in the same way that race and age might be statuses that constrain behavior in certain situations. The limits on behavior are carefully taught through sex-role socialization and are kept in practice by institutional arrange-

385

ments. Let us review for just a moment some of the socialization and institutional arrangements that operate over the life cycle.

Socialization into sex roles in our culture varies over the life cycle and also with such things as the social class or ethnic group to which one belongs. For the great majority of people, socialization into what is expected and appropriate gender behavior begins at a very young age. Although the young child imitates the behavior of both sexes, the child learns gradually to reproduce behavior stereotyped as appropriate for his or her own sex through maturational processes, a desire to do what is appropriate, and cultural rewards. The cultural messages that tell the child what kind of behavior is appropriate and that reinforce the proper action are very strong messages indeed. From the unspoken expectations and modeling of parents to the heavy-handed depictions on television and in school books, cultural messages about appropriate behavior are omnipresent and impossible to escape. Once the child reaches school age and leaves the parental home for hours each day, control over sex-stereotyped messages may be impossible even for parents who are most determined to raise their children in nonstereotyped ways. The norms of the peer group become particularly important in adolescence, and it is difficult for young men and women to deviate from prescriptions for traditional sex-role behavior. It is hard enough for the adolescent to develop a firm identity within the confines of traditional sex-role behavior, and few will risk the uncertainty of moving into uncharted territory. However, there are pressures for change in peer-group norms as more and more young women play sports or train for nontraditional occupations and as fewer young men are willing to sacrifice everything for achievement and success.

There are also pressures for change that stem from the years of singlehood that may follow school. As women get more education, make investments in careers, and stay single longer to pursue those careers, they are more likely to develop a resource base as well as nontraditional interests and behaviors. There is also evidence that marriages may become more nearly equal as women enter them with greater power and as the norms for equality become stronger. Women are older when they marry and are more likely to have an education that approximates their husband's than they were previously. Far greater numbers of married women are working and are gaining power by contributing resources to the marriage, and many fewer lose power by being tied down by large numbers of children. However, women still have primary responsibility for domestic chores and child care responsibilities. Because these domestic areas of their lives are devalued by society, wives are unlikely to really equal the power of their husbands. Where norms allow a woman to grasp more easily the power she gains (as in the black family), there is more change toward equality in decision making if not in sharing of domestic chores; where norms hold a woman back from using earned power (as in the blue-collar white family), traditional family relationships are likely to continue. Single-parent families are less likely to be traditional, as parents must take on the behaviors of both sexes. Even in remarriages, the legacy of this nontraditional behavior combines with other unique facets of the reconstituted family so that these families usually have less traditional roles.

As the years pass, the sex-role behavior of men and women may change. Many women today are through with their child-rearing years by their early forties, and they reenter the job market or more actively pursue exciting careers. These women develop assertive, achievement-oriented, and competent behaviors that they may not have been able to develop in earlier years. In contrast, a man's career may have peaked by his middle forties, and with the stimulus of a midlife crisis, he may reevaluate what he wants to do with the rest of his life. He may turn away from achievement-oriented behavior and toward more nurturant and generative types of activities, either with his own children or with protégés at work. He is also more likely to be aware of the stress engendered by inexpressiveness and to want to get in touch with his feelings during this period. Thus, in the middle years women develop more of the behaviors traditionally stereotyped as masculine, and men develop more of the behaviors traditionally stereotyped as feminine. As they age further, both sexes continue this cross-typed development. Family power relationships may realign as the woman without children and with a career gains power and the man who is close to retirement or retired loses the provider role. The later years probably reflect for both sexes more behaviors, activities, and interests in common and more of the same kinds of androgynous behavior that we find in early childhood.

Thus, there is a curvilinear development of sex roles over the life cycle, from relatively undifferentiated roles in early childhood, through the strictly polarized roles of adolescence and early adulthood, to the more undifferentiated roles of middle and old age. Some researchers have suggested that this curvilinear process of development could be accelerated and accentuated.[1] Others have pointed to the possibility that roles may become more polarized in a time when our culture seems to be experiencing a general turn toward greater conservatism.[2]

At this point we need to look at possibilities and probabilities in our immediate cultural future. Let us begin with a discussion of the limits of traditional sex roles as they are now learned. We strongly believe that these culturally prescribed limits on appropriate behavior are dysfunctional for both sexes. Sex stereotypes have negative effects on the health, happiness, and potential of both men and women. After looking at the present, we will examine some of the possibilities for moving beyond sex-stereotyped behavior.

The Present Situation

Limits of Sex-Typed Behavior

The differential expectations of the behavior of each sex, or "sex roles" that are learned and assigned, seem to limit personal and psychological adaptation to life as well as occupational choice and other institutional roles.

Women who are identified as high in femininity are likely to show high anxiety, low self-esteem, and low social acceptance.[3] These women are unwilling to engage in cross-sex behaviors even when such behaviors are rewarded and situationally appropriate, and they report discomfort when required to perform such atypical behaviors. These women also yield to group pressure for conformity and seem unable even to perform typical nurturant "feminine" behaviors with ease in some situations. In Bem's experiments, high-feminine-typed women did not initiate play with a kitten and were not particularly nurturant with a human infant. Bem suggests that high femininity without compensatory high masculinity may inhibit any behavior at all in situations where "appropriate feminine behavior" is ambiguous.[4]

Clinical psychologists have all described the "healthy" male personality as representing socially valued behaviors such as independence, assertiveness, and achievement orientation.[5] In contrast, the "healthy" female personality is supposed to contain such traits as submissiveness, dependency, noncompetitiveness, and lack of aggression.[6] Rychlak and Legerski have said that the model male should be ascendant-dominant; and the model female, retiring-passive. They state that "individuals who depart from these sexual role expectancies . . . will be more prone to personal maladjustment than those who fulfill them."[7]

Yet tests of such theories show that the personality traits of dependency, submissiveness, and passivity that are supposed to be internalized by a female are actually identified with poor mental health. Juanita Williams used the California Personality Inventory to measure the personality functioning of fifty-nine Caucasian, middle-class girls. She found that the girls who were ascendant-dominant were the healthiest with respect to current personality functioning.[8] Gurin, Veroff, and McEachern reported in 1960 that women are more likely to admit to and seek help for mental health disorders in areas including neurosis, psychosis, transient situational disorders, or attempted suicide.[9] The incidence of these disorders in women has also been increasing in the last few decades.[10] Attempts to explain this poor mental health in terms of biological or hormonal aspects of being female have failed;[11] nor can the higher rate of women seeking help for mental disorders be attributed to the greater willingness of women to admit problems and seek help.[12]

Most researchers attribute the poorer mental health of women to the roles that women are expected to play, the traits and behaviors elected by those roles, and the value placed upon them.[13] Gove details the dependency problems of the married woman who has only one social role while her husband has both work and family; the frustration, low prestige, and unstructured nature of the housewife role; the lack of clear expectations for the working woman; and the role conflict and frustrating discrimination that the working wife faces.[14] Bart discusses the loss of the important mother role in middle age and the effect of that loss on women's mental health.[15]

Thus, to be "feminine" does not seem to be psychologically healthy for women. At the very least, there is a conflict between what it means to be a "successful woman" and a success in terms of our cultural values. Choosing to be a successful woman may result in all the problems connected with the dependency and passivity demanded by that role.[16]

The distinction between mental health and masculine behavior is less clear. Males with pronounced feminine traits seem to have poor mental health.[17] High masculinity in males has been correlated with better adjustment during adolescence,[18] but high masculinity in adult males is correlated with high anxiety, high neuroticism, and low self-acceptance in some studies.[19] Masculine males seemed to have less nurturant capacity and sympathy for the problems of others and were less flexible and less willing to perform cross-sex tasks in one study.[20] However, in another study they were more confident and competent on numerous dimensions of personality and adjustment variables.[21] Other studies have detailed the danger of the male role for the physical rather than the mental health of men.[22] In 1900, life expectancy in the United States was 48.3 years for women and 46.3 years for men. In 1975, it was 76.5 years for women and 68.7 years for men. While some of the difference in life expectancy is attributed to biological factors such as prenatal disorders, vulnerability to recessive sex-linked disorders, and even a higher metabolism rate (which may result in greater energy expenditure and consequent failure to conserve resources), the largest part of the difference is thought to stem from the male role. This includes macho prescriptions to be daring and adventurous, resulting in a higher accident and death rate, and adult social responsibilities, including the stress of the provider role.[23] Boys who are struggling with the male role often develop "compensatory masculinity."[24] They are compelled to take risks, to smoke or drink to show their adult status, and later perhaps to use violence toward other men who do not conform.[25] The repression of emotions may also lead to stress and illness.[26]

Jouard has said that "all men are caught in a double bind. If a man fulfills the prescribed role requirements, his basic human needs go unmet; if these needs are met, he may be considered, or consider himself, unmanly."[27] If his needs are not met, he risks emotional disorder and physical illness. The pressure to be active and achieving is unremitting, although it can lead to tangible symbols of success that allow a man greater feelings of competency and self-esteem than a woman is likely to have. Other studies have shown that people who express their emotions are less likely to have physiological reactions to emotional stress.[28] Feminists and others have also warned that the male role is dysfunctional in that it predisposes those in power (males) to settle conflicts with power and war.[29]

Most researchers agree that behavior where both masculine and feminine traits come into play is more rewarding to both sexes. Boys and girls who are more highly sex typed are found to have lower overall intelligence, lower spatial ability, and lower creativity;[30] greater intellectual development has been correlated quite consistently with cross-sex typing: with masculinity in girls and femininity in boys.[31]

In Bem's studies, only the men with self-reported feminine and masculine qualities were high in both the instrumental and expressive domains; the "feminine" male was low in independence, while the "masculine" male was low in nurturance. In a similar fashion, only the women with self-reported feminine and masculine qualities were high in both independence and nurturance.[32] Helmreich, Spence, and Holahan found that both androgynous and masculine subjects had higher comfort ratings when doing different tasks, independent of the type of task.[33] Attitudes where both masculine and feminine traits come into play also seem to be correlated with relatively liberal general attitudes, with nonreligiosity, and with intelligence in women but not in men.[34]

Thus, we see that people with more undifferentiated or *androgynous* sex-role behavior seem to be able to operate more easily and more competently in more situations than those with sex-stereotyped behavior. We need to look further at what we mean by *androgyny* and at some further considerations about androgynous behavior and its relationship to masculinity, femininity, and mental health.

What Do We Mean By Androgyny?

"Androgyny is an ancient word taken from the Greek, andro (male) and gyn (female) and defines a condition under which the characteristics of the sexes and the human impulses expressed by men and women are not rigidly assigned," says Carolyn Heilbrun in her classic book, *Toward a Recognition of Androgyny*.[35] Androgyny has been recognized since the time of the Greek Pythagorian myth of creation, where people sought their other halves to reunite in mating and to find a sense of wholeness.[36] Almost all the religions of the world have beliefs about dualities that represent "masculine" and "feminine" characteristics as we define them in our culture and that must unite to form a whole person. The East has its myths of Siva and Sakti, Purusha and Prakriti, and Ysb and Yum. In some cultures the masculine principle is physical and powerful and the feminine principle is cerebral, nurturant, and peaceful. However, in other cultures the reverse is true. For example, Siva is the static mind power or masculine principle, and Sakti is the feminine force that is seen to be dynamic, embodying power and primordial energy.[37] Modern psychology expresses similar dualities in the work of Freud, Jung, and others.[38]

Originally, in studies of sex-role stereotypes in this culture, masculinity and femininity were thought of as two separate ends or poles of one long line. Thus, "perfect" masculinity was at one end of the line, and you could move along the line to "perfect" femininity at the other end. By this definition, if you were "perfectly masculine," you had no "feminine" traits, and if you were "perfectly feminine," you had no "masculine" traits.[39]

However, Jenkins and Vroegh and others argued that masculinity and femininity were not polar opposites but rather were independent measures, that attributes considered masculine are found in feminine girls, and that less masculine boys have more of some masculine attributes than more masculine boys do.[40] They believed that there were really two lines, one representing masculinity and one representing femininity, and that a person could be low on one, high on the other; low on both; or high on both.[41] Sandra Bem, who did some of the pioneering work in the measurement of androgyny, developed the Bem Sex Role Inventory, where a person's androgyny was measured by the difference between his or her masculinity and femininity scores. A large difference (high femininity, low masculinity or high masculinity, low femininity) meant that a person was sex typed. A small difference meant that a person was androgynous. Thus you could be androgynous by having low masculinity, low femininity scores or by having high scores on both measures. In one study, Bem found that 34 percent of the males and 27 percent of the females scored as androgynous.[42] However, she also found, and other experiments by Spence and Helmreich confirmed, that only those who were high in both femininity and masculinity had the kind of flexible responses to situations that really characterized the androgynous person.[43] Thus, androgyny came to be defined as being able to call forth elements of both masculinity and femininity and so being relatively high in measures of both.[44]

Unfortunately, the Bem Sex Role Inventory (BSRI) did not end the problems in measuring masculinity and femininity and their composite, androgyny. Laws points out that in the BSRI, only positively valued masculine and feminine items were used, and so there is likely to be a chance that people will rank themselves higher in both areas by giving socially desirable answers or saying that they have particularly desirable traits.[45] Spence, Helmreich, and Holahan believe that the BSRI, the Personal Attributes Questionnaire, and other measures of masculinity and femininity are really measures of instrumental and expressive personality traits rather than of sex roles, and that such instrumental and expressive traits may be only minimally related to sex-role behavior.[46] Other researchers discovered that some measures of personality and masculinity and femininity are correlated (agree) with each other, but other personality measures do not seem to be correlated. Thus, a person who took the Minnesota Multiphase Personality Inventory (MMPI) or Strong Personality Inventory would get approximately the same score on masculinity or femininity on either test, but if they took the Frank Personality Measure, they might get an entirely different score.[47] There is also the measurement problem of which dimensions of social and individual stereotypes are being tapped in the masculinity and femininity measures. Nichols found four subscales of masculinity and femininity: the obvious (true and agreed-upon characteristics), the subtle (true but not usually agreed-upon characteristics), the stereotyped (false but agreed-upon characteristics), and other (false and not agreed-upon).[48]

Thus, self-report by subjects on their own characteristics poses real problems. Laws points out that even subtle factors can affect this self-report. Female subjects interviewed in their homes by male researchers are more likely to give more feminine responses than when interviewed at their place of work.[49] Bileiauskas, Miranda, and Lansky discovered that subjects could easily fake even subtle masculinity-femininity tests. They asked their subjects to answer a questionnaire about masculine and feminine characteristics as they believed a member of the opposite sex would. Fake "males" and fake "females" were more masculine and feminine than real ones.[50]

When we speak of androgyny, then, we must realize that we are not speaking of a clear-cut measurable entity in terms of either personality traits or behavior in an individual. It is a loose, structural concept. Definitions of androgyny differ in the degree of masculine and feminine traits needed to consider someone as androgynous and in whether a person can be considered androgynous if these traits are theoretically possessed but not evidenced in any behavior. A pithy definition provided by Judith Laws asserts that androgyny is a "state in which feminine and masculine elements are present, accepted, and accessible within the individual."[51] Bem says, "It is possible for the person to be both instrumental and expressive, both agentic and communal depending upon the situation."[52] As Heilbrun so succinctly put it almost two decades ago:

> Androgyny suggests a spirit of reconciliation between the sexes; it suggests, further, a full range of experience open to individuals who may, as women be aggressive, as men, tender; it suggests a spectrum upon which human beings choose their places without regard to propriety or custom.[53]

Others have said that the "androgynous individual [is one] who identifies with both desirable masculine and desirable feminine characteristics and is freed from . . . sex-role limitations and is able to more comfortably engage in both 'masculine' and 'feminine' behaviors across a variety of social situations."[54] Further, "the concept of androgyny denotes a person who is flexible, socially competent, able to respond to shifting situational demands, and more complete and actualized in developing and maximizing personal potential."[55]

We will combine these definitions and use the term *androgyny* to mean *the possession of relatively high degrees of both masculinity and femininity—however these are defined—and the ability to call forth behavior using either masculine or feminine traits as situationally needed.*

One interesting sidelight of the studies on how to measure androgyny is that androgyny is probably valued by more people than is usually assumed. Ellis and Bentler found that descriptions of the "ideal male" and the "ideal female" are alike—that is, the ideal person is androgynous. Spence, Helmreich, and Holahan also found that descriptions of the "ideal self" by men and women were similar. Both sexes apparently saw the admirable person as androgynous. Measures of the "ideal self" as androgynous also correlate highly with the person who reports himself or herself as androgynous, having high social competence and high self-esteem.[56]

Relationship of Masculinity, Femininity, and Androgyny to Mental Health

If studies have shown that sex-typed behavior is dysfunctional for mental and physical health, one might expect that androgynous behavior would be more functional. While this largely seems to be the case, androgyny also seems to require a large percentage of the masculine qualities that are necessary for success in this culture if it is to correlate highly with good mental health. A study done by Jennifer Williams on a random sample of women hypothesized that there would be a low incidence of psychological disorders in androgynous women because of their greater ego strength and better ability to handle a variety of stressful situations. She discovered that high-masculine and high-feminine women differed little in their mental health and stress-handling scores. The low-androgynous group of women (who had low quantities of both masculine and feminine traits) had the highest number of visits to a health center, and the high-androgynous group (with high quantities of both masculine and feminine traits) had the best mental health, although they experienced the same vulnerability to life stresses. The high-masculine women seemed to have social skills that enabled them to manipulate their environments. Thus, high-masculine and high-feminine women had ways of coping with stress, although high-androgynous women had the best coping skills of all.

Another study attempted to measure neurosis level, locus of control, and self-esteem for male and female subjects with different degrees of sex typing.[57] The androgynous women were found to be less traditional, less inhibited, more open in marital and occupational choices, and more open in sexual behavior and attitudes. Masculine females and androgynous females had higher creativity scores and relied more on skill than on chance (higher internal locus of control). Androgyny was a help in being adaptive, but the more masculine females were even more feminist, politically aware, extroverted, popular with the opposite sex, and heterosexually involved. The more masculine in orientation, the more adaptive, competent, and secure the female subject was.[58] However, the less sextyped males reported more rather than fewer adjustment problems, including drinking, neurosis, poor self-image, and more external locus of control. The masculine males were more confident and competent in numerous dimensions.[59] Thus, the sex-typed males and masculine-typed females showed the most flexible and competent patterns of response.

When asked how they would ideally like to behave, both male and female subjects wanted to increase their male-typed traits: they wanted to become more masculine, assertive, decisive, and so on. Women wanted to keep their feminine traits; men did not want to increase theirs. The least masculine subjects wanted to increase their masculine traits the most of all.[60]

The pronounced valuation of masculine traits and behaviors in this study seems to be due to several factors. The study measured situations where "more masculine" traits would be useful in responding. The sample was also of younger people who tended to emphasize more achievement-oriented, active type of behaviors, as opposed to the contemplation of older men, for example.

At the same time, we should not underestimate the high value put on "masculine" traits in this culture. "Masculine" traits such as competitiveness and assertiveness are those deemed to lead to cultural success and are valued for that reason. They have also been traditionally equated with the mentally healthy adult in our culture.[61] Unger points out that "the extent to which sex-specific behaviors are mediated by social desirability has probably been underestimated."[62] Thus, given a society that rewards masculine attitudes and interests, we might suspect that androgyny is less rewarding to males and more correlated with good mental health among females. Streicker and Johnson found in one study that although students described themselves appropriately for their gender, achievement motivation and high self-esteem were much more highly correlated among females than among males. For males, maleness seemed enough to produce self-esteem without achievement.[63]

The male role has social value: women may be motivated to adopt it. In contrast, androgyny may result in a loss of status for males. It will mean for most men a move toward expressiveness and nurturance and away from control and dominance.[64] Men may not be willing to initiate changes that might mean they lose power; they may only be willing to initiate them in intimate areas of their lives or if their health is actually threatened.

Possibilities for the Future: Theoretical Considerations

A Theoretical Model of Possibilities for Sex Roles

In working on a model for *transcending sex roles,* Hefner and his colleagues developed a model of the various possibilities that exist for the relationship between the power positions of the sexes in our society. The model is an extension of one that suggests the possibilities of various relationships between the races. In pictorial form it would look like the following:

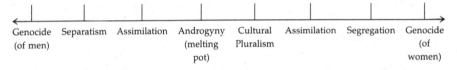

Genocide	Separatism	Assimilation	Androgyny	Cultural	Assimilation	Segregation	Genocide
(of men)			(melting	Pluralism			(of
			pot)				women)

On the far right, one has the extreme position of *genocide,* where men have life-and-death power over women. This situation actually existed in ancient Greece and Rome and possibly exists in various parts of the Islamic empire today. Under this situation, male values are supreme; women are seen as inferior and allowed to exist only for propagating the species.

The next alternative, *segregation,* is similar but less extreme. In this situation, men seldom have the power to actually kill women, but they have control over them. Men's sphere of influence (the public domain) is valued and separate from the domestic sphere of women, which is inferior.

The next alternative is *assimilation.* In this alternative, male values are still supreme and the male sphere of influence is still predominant, but women are allowed to enter the male arena (to have careers in business, for example) if they adopt the male system of values.

The next possibility for a relationship between the sexes is that of *cultural pluralism.* Under this system, masculine and feminine traits and behavior would be equally valued. Women and men would be distinct in their roles, but neither masculine nor feminine traits or pursuits would have greater acceptability.[65]

The middle ground of *androgyny,* or the melting pot style, has been discussed before. Under this system, there would be a blending of both traits and roles. Both men and women would have "masculine" and "feminine" traits of behavior and would perform similar roles.

Moving to the left side of androgyny, we see the possibility of *assimilation* again, but this time with feminine values being predominant. Under this system, such "feminine" values as nurturance and cooperation would be the norm for the society, and maternal kinds of roles would have great value. Men would attempt to adopt the values of women and would be allowed to partake in "feminine" roles to a limited degree. Margaret Mead's description of the Arapesh society in *Sex and Temperament* is probably as close as one can come to an existing example of this type of society.[66]

Moving still further left, we see the possibility of *separatism.* Under this system, the roles of men and would would again be separate as under segregation, but in this case the feminine role would have greater value. Women would choose to be separate from men and would not interact with them. Radical lesbian groups and others like SCUM (Society for the Cutting Up of Men) represent this point of view.

Finally, on the far left side is the possibility of *genocide,* this time with women having life-and-death power over men. In this extreme situation, men would be used as sperm banks but would have little role in society.

While this example depicts all the possible extremes, the actual possibilities for sex roles are probably going to be limited to the spectrum from assimilation on the right to androgyny on the left. The present cultural situation is probably one of an intermediate form of assimilation, with vestiges of segregation still occurring in some areas and possibilities of cultural pluralism and androgyny opening up in others.

However, Rebbecca, Hefner, and Oleshansky have suggested another possibility that in a sense represents an ultimate form of androgyny. They expand upon an earlier interpretation of androgyny made by Bem. Bem said about androgyny that:

> If there is a moral to the concept of psychological androgyny, it is that behavior should have no gender. . . . But there is an irony here, for the concept of androgyny contains an inner contradiction and hence the seeds of its own destruction. . . . The concept of androgyny necessarily presupposes that the concepts of masculinity and femininity themselves have distinct and substantive content. But *to the extent that the androgynous message is absorbed by the culture, the concepts of masculinity and femininity will cease to have such content, and the distinctions to which they refer will blur into invisibility.*[67] [italics added]

As Rebbecca, Hefner, and Oleshansky see it in "A Model of Sex-Role Transcendence," individuals go through three stages of sex-role development. Stage 1 is a stage of undifferentiated sex roles. A child is un-aware of culturally imposed restrictions on behavior according to biolog-ical sex. As the child grows older, he or she becomes aware of parental and societal values about sex roles and gradually moves into stage 2, which is a stage of polarized sex roles. In this stage, the child may be able to perform the behavior of both sexes but is aware of which behavior is appropriate for his or her gender and therefore adheres more or less strictly to the feminine or masculine role. Rebbecca, Hefner, and Ole-shansky see stage 3 as a moving back toward undifferentiated roles again. In the full development of stage 3, a person would have tran-scended sex roles. As they put it, "choice of behavioral and emotional expression is not determined by rigid adherence to 'appropriate' sex-re-lated characteristics. Individuals feel free to express their human qualities without fear of retribution for violating sex-role norms. This is a tran-scending of the stereotypes and a reorganization of the possibilities learned in stage 2 into a more personally relevant frame."

Therefore, under an ideal society, sex-role development would reach its full potential in stage 3—an undifferentiated stage where sex roles have been transcended—and, as Bem has said, masculinity and femininity have lost their meaning.[68] But Rebbecca, Hefner, and Oleshan-sky believe that individuals and institutions in our society are stuck at an intermediate and incomplete stage of sex-role development. It is difficult for an individual to move to stage 3 because there is no institutional or cultural value support for such a movement.

A Theoretical Model of Levels of Change

Two fairly recent analyses have been made of the attempt to liberalize sex roles within American society. Giele uses Smelser's theoretical model of how innovations will be selected and utilized in a society to suggest how sex roles may change in the American culture.[69] Polk's analysis can, with only a little distortion, be fitted into the same framework. Their combined analysis shows us how branches of the women's movement have concen-trated their efforts for sex-role change on certain levels of the society, but the analyses also point out that a combined thrust at every level is really necessary to effect any useful transition.

The first level of change that Smelser identified is that of individual personality and role characteristics of individuals. Giele and Polk point out that the earliest efforts at changing the relative status of the sexes were directed at the individual or personality level. This included the concept of sex-role socialization. Some of the major ideas of this level are that sex roles are systematically taught individuals from birth and rein-forced by cultural rewards. These sex roles are particularly difficult to un-learn because they are also connected with concepts of sexuality. Sex roles are basic roles and modify expectations for behavior in almost all other roles. The male role also has higher status, which is directly rewarding and provides males access to still further status and rewards.[70] The emphasis on this level implied that if individuals could be "resocialized" and if, in particular, women could learn behaviors that would give them access to the present system, the problem of sex discrimination would be solved without making further changes.[71]

Smelser sees the second level of change as that of organizing characteristics of such collectives as schools or places of work. These organizing characteristics are not only structural in nature but include definitions of appropriate masculine and feminine values and behavior. "Masculine" behavior includes competitiveness, aggressiveness, independence, and rationality. "Feminine" behavior includes cooperativeness, passivity, dependence, and emotionality.[72] Men usually learn only their own values and behavior, which are of higher status and lead to societal success; but women learn both behavior systems because they must survive as females and also in the culture. Women are, however, devalued if they use the alternative male values and behavior system (a woman at work is seen as pushy, not forceful, or rigid, not firm, for example). Although some feminists believe that masculine values have led to much of the destructive behavior in our society, it is difficult for women to enter work organizations where male values and behavior predominate because feminine values and behavior are not compatible with the organization as structured, and women are devalued when they use masculine ways of doing things.[73] In a similar fashion, men may have difficulty using "feminine" values or behavior in situations like interacting with their children or helping with housework, because these behaviors are defined as inappropriate for a man.[74]

The third level of change is that of change in the major societal complexes like the economic system and the government. This level of change is particularly important because changes in institutions must occur if individual and "cultural" or "value" (second-stage) change is to be achieved. If the government does not support nondiscrimination in education or does not support opportunities for the disadvantaged to enter the system, there is little possibility for ultimate change in spite of change on an individual level. Ideas about what is appropriately "masculine" or "feminine" are equally unlikely to change without the leading function of the law or without changing economic institutions.[75] Yet legal and economic institutions are controlled by men who gain power and privilege with that control. Polk states that at this level men "occupy and exclude women from positions of economic and political power; male roles have greater behavioral and economic options, including the option of oppressing women . . . and marriage is an institution of personal and sexual slavery for women."[76] It is unlikely that men are going to give up power and privilege at the institutional level unless forced to do so or convinced that it is in their best interest. Therefore, the third level of change may be slow in coming.

The fourth level of change that Smelser identifies is that of the institutional value system, which of course dominates all governmental policies as well as cultural norms that influence individual behavioral change. Our general values are those that support democracy and capitalism, though not necessarily in that order. Some feminists believe that to institute any sex-role change at all, we must institute basic changes in basic values and thus the economic and political systems. They believe that the oppression of women (and to some extent that of men in poorer classes) stems from the structure of capitalism. They reason that (1) the development of private property gave men resources with which to dominate women; (2) women were defined as property under capitalism because of their capacity to reproduce and give the society new workers; (3) because of the domestic labor of women, society gets two workers for the price of one—"surplus value" is produced and the worker gets no benefit; and (4) the existence of a reserve army of cheap female labor suppresses wages for all workers.[77]

Possibilities for the Future: Practical Considerations

We now have a theoretical model for various levels of possible change in traditional sex roles. We are also aware of demographic and other kinds of changes that have taken place in our society that may influence any move toward more liberalized roles. We need to assess the possibilities and probabilities of change in the immediate future. Let us first review what we already know.

Changes in the Individual and "Cultural Stereotype" Levels: What Does Biology Tell Us We Can Expect?

Researchers agree that similarities in personality and behavior traits between the sexes far outweigh minor differences stemming from biology. At the same time, there are certain things that biology can lead us to expect. It is likely that most men will continue to be larger and stronger than most women. This means that when physical power is important and there are no "equalizers," men are likely to dominate women. However, this strength advantage is likely to become less and less important as our society continues to refine its technology and to be more oriented toward services.

Women will continue to bear the children, but the burdens of pregnancy and child care will probably be lightened for them. Demography has shown us that more women are using contraceptives and planning smaller families. The future may even hold the possibility of surrogate mothers for women who do not want to take time out from occupations. Of course, infants will still remain in a state of prolonged helplessness and have to be raised by someone. If men do not participate more in child care or if institutional arrangements are not found for such care, it seems likely that many women may opt not to have children at all.

Certain slight visual, spatial, and cognitive differences in style between the sexes as well as possible differences in aggression will probably diminish or disappear completely as different kinds of experience and training are made available to both sexes. For example, as more and more women go into engineering, their training in math and use of spatial perception may overcome any slight deficiencies in those areas. Educators are already discussing ways of training boys in verbal abilities such as reading that will tap into their slightly different cognitive style.

Biology may also speed role change with the new emphasis on stress as a source of illness. Many men—and women—may be unwilling to risk high-stress occupations that will lead to heart attacks and death.[78] There also seems to be more recognition of the negative results of men limiting their emotional expression. Harrison has emphasized how denying emotional expression can lead to ill health.[79]

Changes in the Levels of "Culture" and Behavior

Recent research seems to show that we are modifying our definitions of appropriate masculine behavior to some degree. Williams and Bennet did a study in which they first found 60 to 75 percent agreement between judges on adjectives describing males and females. They then asked a clinical psychologist to take the adjectives describing each sex and to write a hypothetical portrait of the person they described. The portrait of the female was negative, as such portraits have been in the past. However, the portrait described by the masculine adjectives was equally negative. In part, the male was described as being:

> passive-aggressive, [having] false cockiness, bravado, [being] fearful, [and having] exaggerated defense of imagined slight to ego and potency, immature, depressed. . . . [having a] fascination with violence and brutality . . . most fearful of show of affection or relationships involving meeting human needs, compulsively cruel but in a fundamentally inept, weak, cowardly way.[80]

A recent article by Joseph Pleck has pointed out the pleasures of men being able to express their emotions and get close to other men, to women and to their children.[81] However, he points out that the work load has changed little even in androgynous families. His ideas are confirmed by a study of androgynous parents which showed that even in families that had split employment and child-care roles, the mother still did three-quarters of the household tasks.[82]

There may also be more resistance to certain kinds of androgynous behavior in women. Kahn found in one study that a male or female who cried or a male who became angry in a frustrating situation were seen sympathetically. However, women who got angry were not seen sympathetically, especially by men.[83] Other research shows that the woman who is seen as successfully adopting male roles is the one who retains an element of womanliness.[84]

Another study emphasized that the resistance to change in women's societal roles is particularly strong. Marie Osmond and Patricia Martin gave a questionnaire to approximately 500 male and female junior and senior college students in a stratified random sample at a large southern university. They found inconsistencies in the responses of the students, depending on what sex-role area was being tapped. Institutional roles for women was the area in which men and women disagreed the most. Men who were willing to change familial roles and who only moderately agreed with some of the sex-role stereotypes were unsupportive of women in leadership or supervisory positions.[85]

What Do Institutions Tell Us We Can Expect?

The Economic System. We begin our institutional analysis of possibilities for change with the economic system because the values of profit-oriented capitalism are a base that underlies the other values (competitiveness, aggressiveness, achievement orientation) and structures of our system. Socialist feminists say that the oppression of women (and other poorer groups) stems directly from the structure of capitalism; many of them would also say the oppression of women is only one aspect of the problems of an oppressive economic system.

What are the chances that the basic values of the economic system in this country will change? One writer suggests that the Republican dismantling of the welfare state in the 1980s may be enough to produce an electoral reaction that *could* produce a laborite or socialist alternative to the government, if the Democrats cannot get an attractive alternative together.[86] However, the political structure of the American government has given little chance to third parties; nor does it look as though there is any sort of mandate for overthrowing the government by force. In the near future, it looks as though we will live with the value system of profit-oriented capitalism although the system may be modified somewhat by certain forces that are at work.

American business has been built on a "bigger is better" foundation: on a belief that the growth of individual business as well as a growing economy is important. This tradition is strong, and institutions are slow to change even though the trend toward a steady-state economy without growth has been well established. If the economy does contract in the future, the switch to more conservation-minded, "small-is-beautiful" policies is probably inevitable.[87]

This change will hurt minorities and women at first. In a period of less than full employment, women (the last hired) will be the first ones laid off or unable to find work. In addition, their low wages will be suppressed even more by the oversupply of workers. If women are to find jobs, and jobs that pay them adequately, they will probably have to go into new fields (such as computers) or enter traditionally masculine fields. There is some indication that they are already doing this. Women will have to plan ahead to get appropriate training, be sure equal employment opportunity laws are enforced, and use union membership and old-girl networks as levers to help them get ahead in such a contracted economy.

As the economy contracts or stabilizes at a no-growth level and switches toward more service industries, other changes may take place. Fewer men will succeed, as there will be less room at the top, and they may have to look for alternative ways to demonstrate masculinity. There is also the possibility that couples will be less achievement oriented and have more leisure as the work is spread around. A steady-state economy and limited resources may also force business to seek alternatives to the exploitation of the environment.

At the moment, the values of economic exploitation are on the ascendancy. (James Watt, chairman of the Department of the Interior, who is anything but an environmentalist, has designed a new seal for his department. The traditional buffalo faces to the right instead of to the left in the revised seal. He has joked that this represents the new direction of his department, but the joke is in deadly earnest.) Strip mining is again being allowed, park lands are being sold to private enterprise, clean air and water statutes are not being enforced, car safety regulations are being rescinded. This kind of exploitation is not only injurious to the health of American citizens but perpetuates the big-business mentality that "what's good for Standard Oil is good for the country." With this type of mentality, it is extremely unlikely that business will make any effort to emphasize the good of minorities and women—or the good of its male employees—over its own profit. However, a period of steady-state economic growth could force business to rethink its policies of exploiting limited resources.

The present period is still one of heavy emphasis on the rights of business to make a profit at almost any cost. Pundits have dubbed the period one of *wealthfare* and have accused the government of "taking from the needy to give to the greedy." Indeed, the rich are getting richer while the poor are getting poorer, and there is little the poor (or women or those not so well off) have yet been able to do about it. One sees clearly in this contemporary time the influence of male-dominated economic institutions and the fact that those who have power and affluence will not willingly share it. Yet the changes in the economy may still modify the system.

The Family. Other institutions are heavily intertwined with the economy. Socialist feminists point out that women's domestic labor is an important source of value to the capitalistic system. The ability to draw women from the home into the paid labor force when they are needed and to shunt them back to the home when they are not needed is also important for the economic system. It is no coincidence that the contracting economy has given rise to calls from rightist groups in the society for the reestablishment of "family values." These family values imply that a woman's place is in the home and that she should not take a job from a man who needs it. The outcry against sex education, abortion, and contraception can also be seen in this perspective. Women who have no access to sex education or contraception are likely to have larger families and may need to stay home and take care of them.

If these conservative values predominate, family roles are likely to remain traditional. A woman without an income is dependent and not equal. A man who is the sole breadwinner is not likely to share tasks and child care. A woman with several children and no income is also unlikely to have the wherewithal to leave an unhappy marriage.

At the same time, we must remember that contraception is available and that women are opting to remain single longer, to have fewer or no children, and to pursue careers. The older age at marriage, fewer children, and their own incomes also mean that women have more leverage for equality in family roles. Thus, there are forces for and against change at the family level.

Religion. Also intertwined with family values is the position of religion. Conservatives buttress their arguments about women's place being in the home by reference to biblical passages and religious dogma. We noted before that religion was an important influence in black women's rejection of feminism. The fundamentalists claim that some religious values prohibit interference with bringing forth life and that contraception and abortion are sins. They also claim that any form of sexuality that does not result in procreation—such as homosexuality—is a sin. Yet some denominations are allowing women to be ordained as ministers and are attempting to get rid of sexist language in the prayer books and hymnals, at the same time that others are greatly helping conservative values gain ascendancy.

Education. The expansion of education in the past has helped role change. Highly educated men are more likely to at least give lip service to equality for the sexes; highly educated women are more likely to be employed, to have power, to have fewer children, and to insist on equality in their families. Expansion of education has also meant the creation of opportunities for women and minorities to get training and enter the system.

The present conservative "get the government out of education" mood means that these opportunities will be cut back. Fewer student loans mean that fewer minorities and women will go to school. Smaller universities and fewer opportunities for advanced training will probably mean the same thing as fewer students are admitted. Federal aid in the form of grants for research that support graduate students will also be cut back, as well as graduate assistantships by universities that have no federal money coming in. University teaching, which was a good field for women because of its relative autonomy and flexible hours, has already been restricted.

On the elementary- and high-school level, cutbacks in state aid mean that school systems will have to eliminate many of the counseling services and other extras that helped women, in particular. The unwillingness to enforce Title IX and Title VII may mean that it will be difficult for women to have the opportunities in sports and education that they have had. In the immediate future, then, it is unlikely that education will be as great a force for change as it was in the past.

The Legal and Political Systems. The last two decades have seen a tremendous improvement in women's legal status in this country. Among the legislation that has passed is (1) a Credit Bill, which prohibits discrimination in loan eligibility based on sex or marital status; (2) Title VII of the Civil Rights Act, which prohibits discrimination in employment based on sex; (3) Title IX of the Educational Amendments Act, which refuses federal aid to any educational institutional or program that discriminates by sex; (4) the legalization of abortion; (5) some revision of income tax laws; (6) the Displaced Homemaker Act; (7) some state equal rights amendments; and (8) provisions for abused wives.

Yet at the same time, much of this legislation is only as good as its enforcement, and a great deal of the legislation is under attack. The Reagan administration has been ambivalent about the implications of Title IX, and it looks as though women will again be discriminated against in sports funding and possibly in other areas; they must now prove intent of employer to discriminate if they sue under Title VII. The abortion decision is under attack, and right-to-life groups are trying to get an antiabortion amendment to the Constitution, or failing that, legislation prohibiting abortion passed by Congress. Federal aid to abortion for poor women has been eliminated. Sex education and contraceptive programs have been rolled back. Other past benefits of the welfare state have been reduced or dismantled. The CETA job retraining program has been practically eliminated, the number of those eligible for food stamps has been drastically reduced, unemployment benefits have been cut, and welfare eligibility has been tightened. Many of the gains of the last two decades have been reduced or eliminated. It is highly unlikely that further benefits will be installed in their place. A system of national health insurance seems to be only a dream and, in fact, benefits under Medicaid have already been cut back.[88]

What is the meaning of these changes? The poor who get sick will stay sick and be unable to enter the employment system, and there is likely to be more unwanted pregnancy. It will be difficult for those who do not already have a good education and a good job to get them. Blue-collar women, in particular, will probably have little chance for meaningful and well-paying work. It is ironic that rather than getting out of the welfare business, the government has probably instituted a system in which an even larger number of people—especially women—will need welfare.

Conservative values also meant opposition to the Equal Rights Amendment. Arguments against the amendment ran the gamut from saying that it was not needed to claims that its passage would mean unisex bathrooms and license for homosexuals. In reality, opposition to the Equal Rights Amendment came mostly from traditional women who did not want to give up special privileges (such as preference in child custody and divorce award cases) and from traditional men who did not want women to have equal pay or, more especially, equal privileges. Conservatives muddied the waters around the ERA to such a degree that it was unable to obtain ratification in the time allotted by the extended deadline. Ratification failed by narrow margins in the three additional states needed for passage.[89] Feminists, however, had gained political sophistication in the long fight to ratify the amendment and they vowed to put their new knowledge to use in a renewed attempt to have an ERA passed in the Congress and ratified by the states.

Thus, the legal and political systems at the moment do not favor change, whether this conservative role will continue will probably depend largely upon the federal administration in power.

Where We Stand

Thus, as we assess the situation in all four levels of change, the institutional and value picture is gloomy. Individual awareness of the limitations of sex-role stereotypes has taken place in many areas, and attempts are being made to change socialization and individual behavior. But many of these attempts are being stymied because the institutional structure perpetuates a different value system. It not only inhibits individual change, but the present value system and institutions are actively seeking to restrict change and to reverse that which has taken place.

Is There A Silver Lining? Another Side to Social Values

"The moral majority is neither," says a current bumper sticker. Whatever one's opinion about the morality of the conservative right wing, this group is certainly *not* the majority. New values persist in spite of the administration in Washington. Women have been delaying marriage, getting higher education, and entering nontraditional jobs. They have come to marriage with their own incomes and ideas of equality. They want fewer children and demand more power in their families. Women are participating more in the occupational world and in politics. While it will be difficult for poor women to follow this pattern, middle-class women who have established it are unlikely to give it up. Women have tried sports, education, and jobs and want more of them. Minorities are not likely to take a back seat again, either. The pendulum of social change may swing to the right, but it is likely to be forced back to the middle by popular demand. While there may be a period of retrenchment, there is also likely to be a move to the left again toward more liberal values. Liberal forces may unite under a peace-antinuclear movement again or may unite against world hunger or pollution. It is likely that women will be in the forefront of these liberal groups and that their roles will continue to change as they participate in confrontation and politics.

Summary

Although there is an awareness and acceptance of the need for liberalization of sex roles in many parts of the society, behavioral change has been slow to the present. While there may be "ideological acceptance" of change at higher levels, many are not willing to institute changes in their own lives. For some, a change away from traditional roles means a change toward scary, uncharted territory and ways of behaving. For others, a change in the status quo means a change in power relations that will put them at a disadvantage. On the other hand, conservative institutions may also limit individual change.

While those holding conservative values are probably not in a majority, the strong influence of a profit-oriented, capitalistic society limits individual attempts to resocialize, to restructure organizations, or generally to effect changes that will liberalize sex roles. The present conservative mood in the country has meant a slowing down of even the limited changes that have begun. Yet at the same time, some women are entering new occupations and gaining some access to positions of power. As they gain power, they may be able to influence the value structure if they themselves are not co-opted. While the constricting economy will restrict women's opportunities for a while, a steady-state economic system that takes into account the environmental limitations of the planet may be less competitive and less growth oriented and may allow previously "feminine" values to ascend (peace, conservation, and living in harmony with the environment). Women may move more easily into positions of power in a structure with this kind of political and economic orientation.

If we can optimistically postulate that after the step backward, we will again take two steps forward, what kind of changes should occur on each of the four levels if we wish to move toward each person realizing his or her own potential?

Possibilities for Change (One Person's Conception of a Better Future)

If sex-role change is to occur at the individual level, men and women would have to socialize their children in a different manner. They would have to be aware of their own expectations and of their behavior toward their children, and they would have to monitor the environment in which their children grow and play so that it is nonsexist. Both sexes would get all types of toys and equal chances to participate in sports and passive activities. Language, books, television, and school would change to reflect the different non-sex-typed options open to men and women. In the home environment provided for these children, men and women would share child care and employment responsibilities in whatever ratio they choose. This option contains great possibilities for more marital and family satisfaction if we can judge from the report of androgynous parents that their marital satisfaction stays high and does not follow the usual decline as time passes.[90]

On a more theoretical level, what kind of liberalized sex roles would we have if socialization changed in this fashion? Androgyny is only one possibility. It seems likely to this author that there would be a multistage transition with a different kind of liberalized sex role operating at each stage. Bernard has suggested various possible futures.[91] One possibility is a world not too different from the one we have now, except women would have more power. We suggest that this would be a first stage of transition to liberalized roles and that it might include two substages. In the first substage, women would be likely to assimilate the male value system. However, as they gained more power, they would insist upon an equal recognition of what have been known as "feminine" values, such as cooperation and nonviolence. Thus, the second substage of liberalized sex roles would be one of cultural pluralism, where both "masculine" and "feminine" values were given equal status.

As liberalized sex roles were more widely accepted, a second stage might develop that would be a unisex or melting pot type of system. This might occur in conjunction with a steady-state, technological, highly developed society. Finally, in the third stage, androgyny might come into being and ultimately sex roles would be transcended. As Bem said, "If androgyny comes to exist in the culture, the concepts of masculinity and femininity will cease to have such content and the distinction to which they refer will blur into invisibility."[92] Sex roles would be transcended, or to put it another way, "sex would simply no longer be a requisite characteristic for the occupancy of social positions or the performance of social roles."[93]

On the organization level, family roles would reflect in other ways the commitment to equality. Men, as well as women, would be free to choose not to work, and the definitions of work would include domestic chores.[94] More women and men might choose to stay single or not to have children. Fewer women or men who choose to work would have to be "supermoms" or "superdads" because institutional hours would be more flexible and day care would be available. Men and women would choose their occupations according to their unique talents and predispositions, not according to their gender. Education and periodic job retraining would be available to all. There would be national health care of some sort and probably a minimum wage so that all could live in a decent man-

AMY®   **By Jack Tippit**

"Roger, times have changed! What's wrong with
YOU taking care of the kids part of the time?"

Copyright 1980, The Register and Tribune Syndicate,
Inc. Reprinted by permission.

ner. Women would have the right to control their bodies by having access to contraception and abortion.

On the institutional or societal level, there would be a real commitment to liberalized roles. Women—and some men—would form a political bloc vote that could elect representatives charged with their interests who would institute new laws and speed the expansion of change. There would be changes in the income tax and social security laws so that they did not discriminate against the poor and women; there would be enforcement of equal-opportunity-for-employment legislation. The government would actively ensure that adequate income, health care, education, and occupational training were rights obtainable by all citizens. There would also be a link between these changes and the world situation of growing population and limited food and energy resources. In our best of all possible worlds, there would be commitment to limits to growth, population control, and living in harmony with the environment so that these other goals could be achieved.[95] It is possible, though not probable, given our political history, that a new form of government economy may arise that is not one of profit-oriented capitalism.

The values that institute all these possible changes and that would sustain them would have to be equalitarian and democratic (in the best sense of that word). Such values might even include "feminine" norms about not using violent solutions to problems.

Realism

Obviously, if we take off our rose-colored glasses, this "best of all possible worlds" is unlikely to come about totally and would be difficult to bring about even piecemeal. Even a move toward personal androgyny is threatened by "the stranglehold sex roles have on our thinking."[96] A real image of androgyny or transcendence of sex roles is hard to conceive because of our past stereotyped notions. Changed attitudes do not always lead to changed behavior, either. Spence and Helmreich have shown us that there is little relationship between an individual's score on an androgyny scale and that person's attitude about sex roles.[97]

Androgynous behavior will also be resisted. While women may desire to adopt some masculine-stereotyped behaviors and enter the circles of power that lead to societal success, such behavior will be fought against, as it threatens the power structure of the status quo. Stein has pointed out that this is particularly true because the whole status of "masculinity" as a concept will be threatened if men do not have the (almost?) exclusive right to the breadwinner role, occupational achievement, and success. There are other outlets to prove "masculinity" within the old definitions (sports success, domination of women physically, for example), but the breadwinner role is the buttress of the masculine concept, and men who have built their identities on that concept are going to feel very threatened when the *concept itself* is threatened. (A few women achieving power can be considered exceptions: they "act like men"—but a lot of women being successful?)[98] Goode has also pointed out that men believe they are burdened more than advantaged; as individuals, they do not feel they are part of a conspiracy to dominate women. They feel hurt that their "gifts of support" are being spurned by their wives and children, and they feel threatened. Goode believes, however, that they will adjust when they cannot dominate the system. He points out that many men now are not living up to the stereotypes and are getting away with it. He also emphasizes that there is a worldwide demand for equality (of which women's equality is only a part), and it is stronger and more persistent than it has been in any previous epoch. He believes men as a sex are different from a dominating class as they share few collective goals and women *can* enter the system. Yet he too believes that men will resist the change to different roles.[99] They are unlikely to give up behaviors that are esteemed and lead to cultural success. As Heilbrun succinctly puts it, "We tend to fear change, change which threatens our institutions and habits, threatens our individual security regardless of whether those institutions serve us individually well or ill."[100] Unger also warns us that it is important not to confuse personality change with social change. "Because people become more androgynous does not necessarily indicate that they will be more tolerant of the androgyny of others."[101]

Yet with all the inherent problems, women and men have a great stake in liberalizing sex roles so that they can reach their full human potential. They need not only to change on an individual level but to ensure that institutional changes give birth to a coherent program for social change that will enable them to realize the great variety of human options. To do this, they must probably begin to try to change in small, individual ways and then to work up to attacking the societal Goliath with their slingshots and arrows. They must, in Chessler's prescription for change, "withdraw energy and loyalty from interactions and institutions that are not supportive of . . . [their] best."[102] In this way, both women and men could realize their full potential, not as members of a particular gender, but as human beings.

Essay Questions

1. Discuss the ways in which traditional sex roles affect the physical and mental health of men and women and affect the flexibility of their behavior.

2. What is meant by the concept of androgyny? What are some of the problems in defining it?

3. Discuss possible patterns of interaction between the sexes and patterns of valuation of traits that societies can choose (for example, genocide, separatism, cultural pluralism, and so on). What groups are likely to support each of the patterns?
4. Discuss what biology and past socialization tell us we can expect in the way of change on an individual level in the future.
5. Discuss what the various institutions of society tell us we can expect in terms of future changes in individuals and institutions. (The institutions you should include are the economy, the family, religion, education, and the political system.)

Exercises

1. Imagine a particular situation and discuss how you would act in an androgynous fashion in that situation.
2. Imagine a society in which transcendence of sex roles has occurred. Describe what it would be like.
3. Discuss your conception of "the best of all possible worlds" in terms of sex roles. Do you think it can be achieved?
4. Discuss what you see as the particular barriers now present in the achievement of such a utopia.
5. Draw up a "five-year plan" for yourself in which you discuss changes you would like to make in your own social sex role. If you don't want to make any changes, discuss why not.

Notes

1. Meda Rebecca, Robert Hefner, and Barbara Oleshansky, "A Model of Sex-Role Transcendence," in Alexandra Kaplan and Joan Bean, eds., *Beyond Sex-Role Stereotypes: Readings toward a Psychology of Androgyny* (Boston: Little, Brown, 1976), pp. 89–97.
2. Janet Giele, *Women and the Future* (New York: Free Press, 1978), pp. 2–36; Judith Laws, *The Second X* (New York: Elsevier, 1979), pp. 304–350.
3. F. Consentino and A.B. Heilbrun, "Anxiety Correlates of Sex-Role Identity in College Students," *Psychological Reports* 14 (1964):729–30; M.D. Gall, "The Relationship Between Masculinity-Femininity and Manifest Anxiety," *Journal of Clinical Psychology* 25 (1969):294–95; R.R. Sears, "Relation of Early Socialization Experience to Self-Concepts and Gender Role in Middle Childhood," *Child Development* 41 (1970):267–89.
4. Sandra L. Bem, "Probing the Promise of Androgyny," in Kaplan and Bean, *op. cit.*, p. 59.
5. I.K. Broverman, D.M. Broverman, F.E. Clarkson, P.S. Rosenkrantz, and S.R. Vogel, "Sex Role Stereotypes and Clinical Judgments of Mental

Health," *Journal of Consulting and Clinical Psychology* 34 (1970):1–7; E.H. Erickson, *Childhood Society* (New York: Norton, 1961); S. Freud, *New Introductory Lectures on Psychoanalysis* (New York: Norton, 1965).

6. *Ibid.*, Broverman, *et. al.*

7. J.F. Rychlak and A.T. Legerski, "A Sociocultural Theory of Appropriate Sexual Role Identification and Level of Personal Adjustment," *Journal of Personality* 35 (1967):31–49; Broverman *et al., op. cit.*

8. Juanita Williams, "Sexual Role Identification and Personality Functioning in Girls: A Theory Revisited," *Journal of Personality* 41, no. 1 (1973):1–8.

9. Gerald Gurin, Joseph Veroff, and S. Feld, *Americans View Their Mental Health* (New York: Basic Books, 1960).

10. B. Landau, "Women and Mental Illness," *Ontario Psychologist* 5 (1973):51–57; W.R. Gove, "The Relationship Between Sex Roles, Marital Status, and Mental Illness," *Social Forces* 5, no. 1 (1972):34–44.

11. M.B. Parlee, "The Premenstrual Syndrome," *Psychological Bulletin* 80 (1973): 454–65; P.B. Bart, "Depression in Middle-Aged Women," in V. Gornick and K. Moran, eds., *Women in Sexist Society* (New York: Signet, 1971), pp. 163–86.

12. K. Clancey and P. Gove, "Sex Differences in Mental Illness: An Analysis of Response Bias in Self-Report," *American Journal of Sociology* 80 (1975):205–16.

13. Walter Gove and Jeannette Tudor, "Adult Sex Roles and Mental Illness," *American Journal of Sociology,* 78 (1973):812–35; E. Haavio-Mannila, "Sex Differences in Role Expectations and Performance," *Journal of Marriage and the Family* 29 (1967):368–78.

14. Gove, *op. cit.*

15. Bart, *op. cit.*

16. Jennifer Williams, "Psychological Androgyny and Mental Health," in Hartnett, Oonagh, Boden, and Fuller, eds., *Sex-Role Stereotyping* (London: Tavistock, 1979), pp. 200–14.

17. Sears, *op. cit.;* Williams, *op. cit.*

18. P.H. Mussen, "Long-Term Consequences of Masculinity of Interests in Adolescence," *Journal of Consulting Psychology* 26 (1962):435–40.

19. E. Harford, C.H. Willis, and H.L. Deabler, "Personality Correlates of Masculinity-Femininity," *Psychological Reports* 21 (1967):881–84; Mussen, *op. cit.*

20. Sandra Bem, "The Measurement of Psychological Androgyny," *Journal of Consulting and Clinical Psychology* 42 (1974):155–62; Bem, "Sex-Role Adaptability: One Consequence of Psychological Androgyny," *Journal of Personality and Social Psychology* 31 (1975):634–43.

21. Warren H. Jones, Mary Ellen Chernovetz, and Robert Hansson, "The Enigma of Androgyny: Differential Implications for Males and Females?" *Journal of Consulting and Clinical Psychology* 46, no. 2 (1978):310.

22. James Harrison, "Warning, the Male Sex Role May Be Dangerous to Your Health," *Journal of Social Issues* 34 (1978):65–87.

23. J.H. Pleck, "The Male Sex Role: Definitions, Problems, and Sources of Change," *Journal of Social Issues* 32 (1976):155–63; R.C. Brannon, "No 'Sissy

Stuff'," in D. David and R. Brannon, eds., *The Forty-Nine Percent Majority* (Reading, Mass.: Addison-Wesley, 1976).

24. P. Tiller, "Parental Role Division and the Child's Personality," in E. Dahlstrom, ed., *The Changing Roles of Men and Women* (Boston: Beacon Press, 1967).

25. W. Churchill, *Homosexuality in a Cross-Cultural Perspective* (Englewood Cliffs, N.J.: Prentice-Hall, 1967).

26. S.M. Jouard, *The Transparent Self* (New York: Van Nostrand, 1971).

27. *Ibid.*

28. Clifford Notarius and Robert Levinson, "Expressive Tenderness and Physiological Response to Stress," *Journal of Personality and Social Psychology* 37, no. 7 (1979):1204–10.

29. L. Komisar, "Violence and the Masculine Mystique," in David and Brannon, *op. cit.*; Marc Fasteau, *The Male Machine* (New York: McGraw-Hill, 1974).

30. Eleanor Maccoby, "Sex Differences in Intellectual Functioning," *The Development of Sex Differences* (Stanford, Calif.: Stanford University Press, 1966).

31. Bem, "Probing the Promise."

32. Sandra Bem, W. Martyna, and C. Watson, "Sex Typing and Androgyny: Further Explorations of the Expressive Domain," *Journal of Personality and Social Psychology* 34, no. 5 (1976):1016–23.

33. Robert Helmreich, Janet Spence, and Carole Holahan, "Psychological Androgyny and Sex-Role Flexibility: A Test of Two Hypotheses," *Journal of Personality and Social Psychology* 37, no. 10 (1979):1634.

34. Laws, *op. cit.*, p. 325.

35. Carolyn Heilbrun, *Toward a Recognition of Androgyny* (New York: Knopf, 1964).

36. Laws, *op. cit.*, p. 304.

37. June Singer, *Androgyny: Toward a New Theory of Sexuality* (New York: Anchor Press, 1976), p. 18.

38. C.G. Jung, "Anima and Animus," *Two Essays on Analytical Psychology: Collected Works of C.G. Jung*, vol. 7, (New York: Ballinger Foundation, 1953), pp. 186–209; Calvin Hall, *A Primer of Freudian Psychology*, (New York: World, 1954).

39. Laws, *op. cit.*, p. 313.

40. Noel Jenkins and Karen Vroegh, "Contemporary Concepts of Masculinity and Femininity," *Psychological Reports* 25 (1969):679–97.

41. Anne Constantinople, "Masculinity-Femininity: An Exception to a Famous Dictum," *Psychological Bulletin* 80, no. 5 (1973):389–407.

42. Bem, "Measurement of Androgyny."

43. Helmreich, Spence, and Holahan, *op. cit.*

44. Laws, *op. cit.*, p. 312.

45. *Ibid.*, pp. 319–20.

46. Spence, Helmreich, and Holahan, *op. cit.*

47. B.F. Shepler, "A Comparison of Masculinity-Femininity Measures," *Journal of Counseling Psychology* 15 (1951):484–86.

48. R.C. Nichols, "Subtle, Obvious, and Stereotype Measures of Masculinity-Femininity," *Education and Psychological Measurement* 22 (1962):449–61.

49. Laws, *op. cit.*, p. 318.

50. V.J. Bieliauskas, S.B. Miranda, and L. Lansky, "Obviousness of Two Masculinity-Femininity Tests," *Journal of Consulting and Clinical Psychology* 32 (1968):314–18.

51. Laws, *op. cit.*, p. 306.

52. Bem, "Probing the Promise," p. 48.

53. Heilbrun, *op. cit.*, p. x.

54. Warren Jones, Mary Ellen Chernovitz, and Robert Hansson, "The Enigma of Androgyny: Differential Implications for Males and Females," *Journal of Consulting and Clinical Psychology* 46, no. 2 (1978):298–313.

55. *Ibid.*, p. 298.

56. L.J. Ellis and P.M. Bentler, "Traditional Sex-Determined Role Standards and Sex Stereotypes," *Journal of Personal and Social Psychology* 25 (1973): 28–34; Spence, Helmreich, and Holahan, *op. cit.*

57. B.P. Dohrenwend, "Social Status and Stressful Life Events," *Journal of Personality and Social Psychology* 28 (1973):225–35.

58. Jones, Chernovitz, and Hansson, *op. cit.*, pp. 299–310.

59. *Ibid.*, pp. 304–10.

60. *Ibid.*, p. 308.

61. Broverman *et al.*, *op. cit.*

62. Rhoda Unger, *Female and Male Psychological Perspectives* (New York: Harper & Row, 1979), p. 470.

63. Anne B. Streicker and James E. Johnson, "Sex-Role Identification and Self-Esteem in College Students: Do Men and Women Differ?" *Sex Roles* 3, no. 1 (1977):19–26.

64. Laws, *op. cit.*, p. 358.

65. Robert Hefner, Meda Rebbecca, Barbara Oleshansky, and Virginia Norden, "Sex-Role Transcendence Study" (Final report under contract #NIE–C–74–0144 between the National Institute of Education and the University of Michigan, 1976).

66. Margaret Mead, *Sex and Temperament* (1935; reprint ed., New York: Morrow, 1963).

67. Bem, "Probing the Promise," p. 59.

68. Rebbecca, Hefner, and Oleshansky, *op. cit.*, p. 95; Hefner *et al.*, *op. cit.*

69. Harrison, *op. cit.*

70. Barbara Bounee Polk, "Male Power and the Woman's Movement," in Jo Freeman, ed., *Women: A Feminist Perspective* (Palo Alto, Calif.: Mayfield, 1979), pp. 589–606.

71. Giele, *op. cit.*, pp. 4–5.

72. Polk, *op. cit.*, p. 592.

73. *Ibid.*, pp. 592–93.

74. Giele, *op. cit.*, pp. 86ff.

75. *Ibid.*, p. 31.

76. Polk, *op. cit.*, p. 594.

77. *Ibid.*, p. 595.

78. Harrison, *op. cit.*, pp. 65–85.

79. *Ibid.*

80. John Williams and Susan Bennett, "The Definitions of Sex Stereotypes Via the Adjective Check List," *Sex Roles* 1, no. 4 (1975):327–37.

81. Pleck, *op. cit.*

82. John de Frain, "Androgynous Parents Tell Us Who They Are and What They Need," *Family Coordinator*, 28 (1979):237–42.

83. A. Kahn, "Latitudes of Emotional Expressions in Women and Men" (Paper presented at meeting of the American Psychological Association, New York City, September 1979, quoted in Unger, *op. cit.*, p. 433).

84. Jane Kristal, Deborah Sanders, Janet Spence, and Robert Helmreich, "Inferences about the Femininity of Competent Women and Their Implications for Likability," *Sex Roles* 1, no. 1 (1975):215–235.

85. Marie Osmond and Patricia Martin, "Sex and Sexism: A Comparison of Male and Female Sex-Role Attitudes," *Journal of Marriage and the Family* 37, no. 4 (1975):744–58.

86. Walter Dean Burnhan, "American Politics in the 1980's," *Sociological Focus*, 14 (1981):149–60.

87. Giele, *op. cit.*

88. "The Politics of Sickness," *Society*, 19 (1982):22–69.

89. Adam Clymer "Time Runs Out for the Proposed Equal Rights Amendment," *New York Times*, July 1, 1982, A–12; Lynn Rosellini, "Victory is Bittersweet for Architect of Amendment's Downfall." *New York Times*, July 1, 1982, A–12.

90. de Frain, *op. cit.*

91. Jessie Bernard, "Sex Differences: An Overview," in Kaplan and Bean, *op. cit.*, pp. 19–20.

92. Bem, "Probing the Promise."

93. Heilbrun, *op. cit.*, p. xi.

94. Kay Shaffer, *Sex Roles and Human Behavior* (Cambridge, Mass.: Winthrop, 1981).

95. Giele, *op. cit.*

96. Laws, *op. cit.*, p. 359; Spence and Helmreich, *op. cit.*

97. Spence and Helmreich, *op. cit.*

98. Robert Stein, Professor, University of Colorado, personal communication.

99. William Goode, "Why Men Resist," *Dissent* 27 (1980):181–93.

100. Heilbrun, *op. cit.*, p. xi.

101. Unger, *op. cit.*, p. 473.

102. Phyllis Chessler, "Psychotherapy and Women," (Paper presented at the American Psychological Association, 1970.) quoted in Laws, *op. cit.*, p. 375.

Glossary

Accommodation   A dual-career marriage style wherein one spouse has the primary work responsibility and lesser home responsibility, while the other has the reverse.

Achieved Status   Social position achieved through one's own efforts.

Alienation   The feeling of being isolated from and unable to influence a particular area of life, such as one's job or the political scene.

Androgyny   A person's ability to function by using both "masculine" and "feminine" stereotyped behavior.

Ascribed Status   Social position resulting from such inherited characteristics as family background, social class, race, and sex.

Assimilation   A stage of sex-role development in which the minority is incorporated partially or totally into the majority society on the dominant group's terms.

Attractive Alternative   An opportunity to do something as attractive as what you are now doing. (For example, a career may be an attractive alternative to marriage for some people.)

Biological Theories of Sex Roles   Theories assuming that behavioral differences between men and women are based on biologically inherited traits.

Clitoridectomy   The cutting out of the clitoris, or group of nerve endings that are the seat of a woman's sexual pleasure.

Cognitive Developmental Theory   A theory, developed by Kohlberg and others, holding that children progress at individual rates through mental stages, develop a belief that they are of a particular gender, and then want to do the behaviors that are appropriate for that gender.

Cohabitation   Situation wherein two or more unmarried people of different sexes live together.

Conjugal   Pertaining to the nuclear family, as in relationship between husband and wife.

Couvade   A custom whereby the father takes to his bed when his child is born, pretends to have labor pains, and simulates fatigue after "giving birth."

Crowding Theory   The economic premise that an excess supply of workers in an occupation causes wages to fall, as employers have many workers to choose from.

Cultural Context   The social culture in which an action or situation occurs. (The culture in which resources are gained may determine whether or not having resources leads to having power.)

Cultural Pluralism   A state in which many points of view, value systems, or orientations coexist and are equally valued in a culture.

Demographics   The study of population trends, including rates of mobility, fertility, death, and illness.

Equal Sharing   A form of division of labor tried by dual-career couples in which both husband and wife share work and family roles even though both may emphasize work roles more than family roles, or vice versa.

Ethnocentrism   The belief that ones own culture is the foremost and best of all cultures. (Thus one views other cultures through one's own cultural lens.)

Fear of Success   Women's fear of being successful in a masculine area arising from perceived negative consequences of success such as isolation, stigma, and possibly losing a chance to marry.

Feminine Mystique   The concept, identified by Betty Friedan and prevalent in the 1950s, that women are ultimately feminine if they stay home and raise numerous children.

Feminists   Branch of the early women's movement that favored independence from any political organization. Informally used to refer to women who are in favor of equal rights for women.

Field Independence   Ability to distinguish a figure from a background, such as "finding the lion in the trees."

Formal Power   Power exercised through specific offices, institutions, or any legitimate authority like "head of household" or "leader."

Freudian Theory   Freud's theory of the development of sexual identity, which includes the child's progression through successive physical stages (oral, anal, phallic, latency, and adolescence), attraction to a parent of the opposite sex, and resolution of this attraction/conflict by identification with the parent of the same sex.

Gender Identity   (also sex identity) The sex (gender) one believes oneself to be.

Genocide   The killing or attempted killing of all members of a particular group.

Homophobia   Excessive fear of homosexuality.

Human Capital   The investment in education, job training, and work experience that workers bring to a job.

Ideology   A set of beliefs that incorporates the norms and values of a particular culture.

Informal Power   Power exercised in nonofficial ways, perhaps by manipulation.

Latency   In Freudian theory, the period from about five years of age to the onset of puberty.

Lateralization   The ability of the brain to transfer information from one side to the other.

Marriage Gradient   Jesse Bernard's depiction of men's tendency to marry down to wives with lower social status and education.

Marriage Penalty   The extra taxes a married couple pays when both spouses work. (Their combined tax is greater than that of two single people making the same wages.)

Marriage Squeeze   Condition caused by the baby boom of the 1950s, when more women were born than men were born in the 1940s: if women marry older men, there will not be enough men for all the women to marry.

Matriarchy   Dominance by the women in a cultural system.

Menarche   The first menstrual period or beginning of puberty.

Modeling   Demonstrating a particular behavior or serving as a model for someone to imitate. (For example, a father models masculine behavior for his son.)

Nineteenth Amendment   Amendment to the U.S. Constitution, passed in 1920, that gives female citizens the right to vote.

Norms   The values and rules by which a society operates. They may be formally stated (as in laws) or unspoken but commonly understood.

Occupational Segregation Theory   A theory stating that the segregation of the sexes in different occupations or groups within occupations leads to a salary differential between men and women.

Politicos   A group of women who, in the early years of the women's movement, felt that their allegiance was primarily to political groups like the Socialist party and only secondarily to women's interests.

Power   Ability to influence the actions of others so that they behave in ways that one desires.

Preference and Process   The idea that the process of achieving a certain behavior may lag behind the preference for that behavior, and vice versa.

Private Sphere   The household or domestic arena, which is set aside from the public arena of paid work.

Protestant Work Ethic   The belief that work and related success demonstrate one's moral worth (based on the early Protestant idea that God would show the faithful that they were "saved" by allowing them to be successful).

Public Sphere   Social, economic, and political interaction outside the household or domestic arena.

Radical Feminists   A group in the women's movement that believes women's issues are part of a general revolutionary struggle.

Resource Theory   The theory, developed by Blood and Wolfe, that those who bring resources to the family will gain power in the family.

Rites of Passage   Various rituals or special occasions that mark the transition from one status in life to another, as from child to adult.

Role Homophily   The theory, proposed by Simpson and England, postulating that similar marital roles (such as both spouses combining work and family commitments) build marital solidarity.

Secondary Workers   Workers (mostly women) who are not considered primary, full-time workers and who are often shunted out of the market when there are not enough jobs to go around.

Segregation   Separation of groups by race, sex, or class in one or many areas like housing and occupations.

Separatism   The stage in a model of possible sex roles in which the sexes are segregated but feminine values dominate in the culture.

Sex as Status   The idea that sex is a status, like race or class, that determines one's occupational choices and life opportunities.

Sex Role   Behavior, "masculine" or "feminine," prescribed by the culture for a particular sex in addition to the personality traits expected of that sex.

Sexual Scripts   Behavior that society deems appropriate for each sex, including occupational choice, parenting, and the like.

Social Learning Theory   A theory of sexual identity formation, developed by Mischel, Bandura, and others, according to which a child learns sex-role behavior by imitation and later identification with same-sex models.

Social Position   Position or status in society that results from one's sex and can determine one's social role and opportunities.

Social Role   The behavior that goes along with certain social positions in society. (For example, the social role of husband encompasses certain behaviors like being a breadwinner.)

Sociobiological Theories   Theories that link human social behavior to the biological development of early humankind.

Stages of Development   The stages a country or culture goes through as it evolves from a hunting-and-gathering or other type of subsistence economy to an industrial economy.

Stratification   Ranking of various social positions, occupations, and the like, according to their status.

Subsistence   The minimum food or shelter necessary to support life. A subsistence economy is one in which only a bare minimum of food is available.

Suspect Group   A group that the legal system assumes may be discriminated against and whose cases are therefore automatically reviewed.

Transcendence of Sex Roles   Moving beyond stereotyped sex-role behavior so that the concepts of "masculine" and "feminine" lose their meaning.

Name Index